HERMANN HESSE: LIFE AND ART

Hermann Hesse

Hermann Hesse
LIFE AND ART

JOSEPH MILECK

UNIVERSITY OF CALIFORNIA PRESS

Berkeley / Los Angeles / London

The photographs (many by Grete Widmann and
Martin Hesse) came from the Hermann Hesse-
Nachlass and the Marbach-Hesse-Collection in
Marbach am Neckar. They were included with the
kind permission of the Hermann Hesse-Stiftung
and Dr. Bernhard Zeller, the director of the
Schiller-Nationalmuseum, Marbach am Neckar,
Germany.

University of California Press
Berkeley and Los Angeles, California

University of California Press, Ltd.
London, England

First Paperback Printing 1980
ISBN 0-520-04152-6
Library of Congress Catalog Card Number: 76-48020
Printed in the United States of America

The paper used in this publication meets the minimum
requirements of ANSI/NISO Z39.48-1992 (R 1997)
(*Permanence of Paper*). ∞

Contents

Preface

In reply (January 9, 1956) to a young correspondent anxious to have Kafka explained to him, Hesse reiterated what he had always pointedly insisted upon:

> He who is capable of really reading a writer . . . will have his every question answered by the works themselves. . . . He [Kafka] depicts the dreams and visions of his lonely, difficult life . . . and it is these dreams and visions alone that should preoccupy us, and not the interpretations that sharp-witted interpreters can give these writings. This "interpreting" is an intellectual sport . . . one that is good for clever people . . . who can read and write books about Black sculpture or twelve-tone music but who never get to the heart of a work of art because they stand at the gate fumbling with their hundred keys, blind to the fact that the gate is really not locked.[1]

Hesse was obviously far more touched by a sensitive reader's open-hearted and open-minded response to literature than impressed by a critic's cerebrations, ingenious though they might be. The actual experiencing of literature was its absorption by readers and not its dissection by critics. A work of art was essentially its own explanation, it needed no elucidation. Hesse was clearly less than enchanted by those who wrote about literature.

Since I concur with this sentiment, though not fully and am somewhat taken aback by its hyperbolic statement, I feel obliged to account for my transgression. This book was not written in the belief that Hesse's readers required such "interpretations" to grasp his "dreams and visions," or that his literary spokesmen had to be improved upon. It was not this altruistic concern or conceit, nor the

---

1 *Briefe* (Frankfurt a. M.: Suhrkamp, 1964), pp. 458–459.

seduction of "intellectual sport," but psychological necessity that provided the major impetus: my longtime ready absorption of Hesse's writings simply had to be balanced by organized afterthought. I had not only to take in but also to understand both Hesse and his work in order better to understand myself and literature. If perhaps I have not also remained standing before the open gate like Hesse's censured critics with their hundred unavailing keys, it is probably due to this combination of ready absorption and necessary reflection. But whether or not I have succeeded in entering the inner sanctum, the book has already served my own immediate purpose, and will in some measure also serve its own purpose in the community of scholars, of those "who can read and write about books about Black sculpture or twelve-tone music." It will exceed my expectations, though not my hope, should my book also manage to serve Hesse's wider community of readers, should it manage to extend and to deepen the Hesse-experience for the lay reader.

In my undertaking I was primarily intent upon revealing Hesse the person and his world of ideas, characterizing his writings in both their substance and form, and drawing attention to the intimate relationship between his life and his art. My object was to see Hesse as he was and not to imagine what he was, to try to understand his works as he himself understood them and not as I might prefer to understand them, and to shed some light on his creative process. To avoid literary myth and to make possible the literary study I had in mind, biography had to be corrected and expanded and previous critical coverage of both Hesse's writings and his sundry literary involvements considerably extended.

Apart from correcting and adding lesser biographical details and dates, I have given more than the usual attention to Hesse's marriages and his children, his analyst J. B. Lang, his circle of patrons, and to the many painters, composers, and writers among his friends; to his early familiarity with English, Scandinavian, Russian, and Italian literature, his immediate attraction to romanticism and rejection of naturalism, and his particular interest in Tolstoy and Dostoevsky, and in St. Francis of Assisi and Boccaccio; to his preoccupation with Nietzsche, Schopenhauer, and Jacob Burckhardt, and with Catholicism, the Middle Ages, and the Orient; to Pietism's impact upon Hesse's life, and childhood's imprint on his art; and to his watercolors and his privately marketed self-illustrated manuscript collections of poems. I have detailed Hesse's general attitude to politics, his own political views, and his sporadic sociopolitical involvements; his quarrel both with the militarists and pacifists during the First World War, his vilification by both the Nazis and refugee German Jews during the thirties, and his altercation with an American army officer in the autumn of 1945 with the resultant banning of his books by the German press in the American sector. I have focused upon Hesse's almost unreserved embrace of Freud and more hesitant acclaim of Jung, and upon their influence on his art; upon the role Hesse believed psychoanalysis could play in literature and should not play in literary criticism, and upon his reaction to the association of art and disease, and of genius and insanity. And I have also traced the repeated ebb and flow of Hesse's literary popularity both in Germany and abroad.

I have extended coverage of Hesse's literary activities as much as his biography, and my interest in his evolving life and a surmised closely corresponding evolution in both the substance and form of his art determined my chronological approach. I have drawn brief attention to generally unknown literary beginnings and first publications, have accorded each of Hesse's major tales individual treatment more or less commensurate in length with its significance, and have, albeit collectively more often than individually, accounted for many of his shorter narratives—the legends, Italianate tales, Swabian short stories, and fairy tales—works that have to date been all but ignored. I have characterized Hesse's poetry, scanned his sociopolitical essays, and studied his extensive work as a reviewer and editor. I have also drawn attention to Hesse's numerous travel reports and nature sketches, recollections and reflections, literary studies and congratulatory and memorial articles, autobiographical snippets and letters, and even to his comparatively few diary fragments and translations. Nor have I ignored Hesse's considerable corpus of unpublished material: tales, dramas, librettos, poems, fragments, literary plans, essays, letters, and diaries.

At the extremes of storytelling there are those writers who spin their yarns and those who document their lives. Hesse belongs to the latter. He had to write and he had to write about himself and there is little of the much he wrote that is not confessional in form and therapeutic in function. With rare exception, each of Hesse's major tales begins where the immediately preceding tale breaks off, scrutinizes and finds wanting its predecessor's concluding promise of better possibility, and then itself terminates abruptly on its own upbeat of new hope. These were Hesse's own serial appraisals of the self and assessments of life, milestones along his own erratic course of self-realization, and the different theories of art and various philosophies argued in these works mirror Hesse's efforts to lend approbation to his own different adjustments to himself and to life and to make existence more bearable. But autobiography is not just confined to narrative substance, it permeates the very narrative fabric of Hesse's art, no less in his minor than in his major works. Hesse's protagonists are self-projections not only in their concerns, thoughts, and feelings, but even in their persons and experiences and, with rare exception, in the worlds in which they live and the circles in which they move. It is upon this autobiographical core that my study focuses. Concentration upon evolving self-realization, the foremost of Hesse's concerns, and upon life and art, the real and the ideal, erotic and social love, sensuality and spirituality, time and timelessness, multiplicity and oneness, aestheticism and social commitment, and middle-class Western culture—related and accompanying themes that evolve similarly from tale to tale—will, I hope, silhouette Hesse's variegated world of thought more sharply and make possible a better understanding of his works, singly and as an unbroken continuum; disclosure of the unusually personal texture of these works should provide a revealing glimpse into Hesse's workshop; and together these two foci may add something to our still limited understanding of the artistic personality and of the creative process.

But Hesse's tales are clearly not just a raw annotation of the self. Autobiography is only matrix and not product. Life transfigured—fantasized, poeticized, dramatized, and symbolized—becomes art with universal implications, and the art of Hesse's writings, like their concerns, evolved with his own evolving life in an upward and outward spiral. I have paid as much attention to this evolution of narrative manner as to evolving narrative matter. A young aesthete given to his dream world and purple prose becomes an "artist-burgher" intent upon adjustment and traditional poetic realism, and then a rebel-seeker determined to come to grips and to terms with himself and life at large and to push back the horizons of literary possibility. In my delineation of this progression, apart from genesis, biography, and substance, I have examined each of the major tales in terms of structure, mode of narration, description, and characterization; vocabulary, syntax, flow, and rhythm of sentences; symbolism, names, double self-projections, and various other of Hesse's literary devices and special features of form. I have accorded the earlier, more traditional, and less involved works much less attention than the novel and more demanding literary ventures beginning with *Demian*, and have treated *Das Glasperlenspiel* in a manner commensurate with its length, complexity, and significance. From all this I hope there emerges a telling portrait of Hesse the man and the artist, an informative characterization of his work, and a revealing exposure of the life and art relationship at its most intimate.

Since the number of Hesse enthusiasts and Hesse scholars to whom I am indebted in one way or another for this study is legion, I shall have to express my thanks without the usual mention of names. Besides these persons, I am particularly obliged to Hesse's sons Bruno and Heiner for biographical information, to Dr. Bernard Zeller for giving me free access to the Hesse-Nachlass in the Schiller-Nationalmuseum, and to the American Philosophical Society for a travel grant.

Berkeley, California   JOSEPH MILECK
Spring 1976

Note

Such references in the footnotes as Books and Pamphlets II:37; Prose IV:478; Poetry V-C:2; Reviews VI-A:21; Hesse as an Editor VIII-A:20; Letters VIII-C:32; and Manuscripts X:429, refer to Joseph Mileck, *Hermann Hesse: Biography and Bibliography* (Berkeley and Los Angeles: University of California Press, 1977).

Unless otherwise indicated, parenthetical dates of Hesse's collected works are those of first publication, and parenthetical dates of his individual works are those of completion.

The English translations of quoted passages of German are my own. To preclude doubt or confusion I have also chosen to refer to Hesse's works by their German titles. English equivalents are added parenthetically in the Index of Hesse's Works.

☙1
Background,
Childhood,
and Youth

CALW/BASEL 1877–1895

FAMILY

Hermann Hesse was born on July 2, 1877, in the little town of Calw on the Nagold River at the edge of the Black Forest. His family background was unusually varied. Johannes Hesse (1847–1916), his father, was born a Russian citizen in Weissenstein, Estonia. Here his grandfather, Karl Hermann Hesse (1802–1896), had established a flourishing medical practice after leaving his native Dorpat in Livonia. His great-grandfather, Barthold Joachim Hesse (1762–1819), a musician and enterprising businessman, had left Lübeck for Reval, then for Dorpat, while still a young man. Hesse's mother, Marie Gundert (1842–1902), was born in Talatscheri, India, the daughter of the Pietist missionary and Indologist, Hermann Gundert (1814–1893), whose family had its roots in Stuttgart. To this North and South German family stock Hesse's maternal grandmother, Julie Dubois (1809–1885), added a French-Swiss element, and his paternal grandmother, Jenny Agnes Lass (1807–1851), a Slavic strain.

This ancestry was as spirited and versatile as it was diversified. Karl Hermann Hesse, district doctor, state councillor, and beloved patriarch of pioneer Weissenstein, was a jolly Pietist who was still

Johannes Hesse (1847–1916).

HERMANN HESSE'S PARENTS.

Marie Hesse (1842–1902).

fond of skating at fifty and continued to tend to his garden at eighty.[1] Johannes Hesse, although a more sensitive and retiring person than his father, dedicated himself to the practical service of Christ at the age of eighteen, and, following his studies at the Basel Mission Society (*Basler Missionsanstalt*) and his ordination in Heilbronn (August 1869), served almost four years as a missionary in Malabar, India (1869–1873). Brought back to Europe by ill-health, he settled in Calw to assist Hermann Gundert, then director of the Calw Publishing House of the Basel Mission Society (*Calwer Verlagsverein*). Here he met and a year later married Gundert's daughter Marie. From 1881 to 1886 he edited the Mission's periodical in Basel and also taught language and literature at the Mission House. On his return to Calw he continued to assist his father-in-law until he assumed the latter's position in 1893. Staunch Pietist though he was, severe in his demands upon himself and upon others, Johannes Hesse was no avid, limited sectarian.[2] A cultivated literary taste and intellectual curiosity had taken him far afield. His thought and religion evidenced the broadening and tempering effect of Latin literature, Greek philosophies, and Oriental religions.[3]

Hermann Gundert was perhaps the most colorful of Hesse's immediate forebears. After more than twenty years as a pioneer missionary in India (1836–1859), he returned to Europe and was assigned by the Basel Mission Society to assist the director of its publishing house in Calw. He assumed the directorship in 1862 and continued in this capacity until his death in 1893. Like Johannes Hesse, Gundert was no ordinary Pietist missionary. Not only was he completely at home in English, German, French, and Italian, but just as capable of preaching in Hindustani, Malajalam, and Bengali. He was almost as fluent in Kannada, Telugu, and Tamil, and had some competence in at least ten other languages. A scholar at heart, Gundert's world in Calw soon became one of books. Much of his time was devoted to Indological studies, to a Malajalam translation of the Bible, a Malajalam grammar, and the completion of his Malajalam lexicon. His home was

---

1 For more information about Dr. Karl Hermann Hesse, see Monika Hunnius, *Mein Onkel Hermann: Erinnerungen an Alt-Estland* (Heilbronn: Eugen Salzer, 1921), 126 pp.

2 His broader interests are evidenced by such of his many books as: *Guter Rat für Leidende aus dem altisraelitischen Psalter* (Basler Missionsbuchhandlung, 1909), 128 pp.; *Lao-tzse, ein vorchristlicher Wahrheitszeuge* (Basler Missions-Studien, 1914), 64 pp.

3 For more information about Johannes Hesse, see: Hermann und Adele Hesse, *Zum Gedächtnis unseres Vaters* (Tübingen: Wunderlich, 1930), 85 pp.; Ida Frohnmeyer, "In Erinnerung," *Die Ernte* (Basel, 1941), pp. 65–72.

Marie Hesse
at the age of nineteen.

Hermann Hesse
at the age of three.

long a meeting place for scholars, theologians, and exotic visitors from the Orient.[4]

Marie Gundert Hesse was just as exceptional as her husband. She was born in Malabar and educated in Switzerland and Germany. Until 1870 she continually shuttled between Europe and India. Although the mother of nine children, of whom six survived her, she found time not only to assist her father and her husband in the publishing house, but also managed, despite her many daily tasks and endless prayer meetings, to master four or five languages, to dash off verse, and to write biographies of Bishop James Hannington and David Livingstone.[5]

The heart of Calw, with its narrow cobblestone streets, its closely set houses with their pointed gables and little gardens, is still much as it must have been in Hesse's childhood. The house in which Hesse was born still stands inconspicuously in the marketplace opposite the old city hall, marked by only a modest plaque. In Bischofstrasse across the river, the once imposing Calw Publishing House (*Haus des Calwer Verlagsvereins*) is now a textile shop. It was to this house that Hermann Gundert brought his family in 1860, and in which he remained until his death. And it was into this house that the Hesse family moved in 1886, after five years in Basel, and where, but for a brief period in Ledergasse (1889–1893), the family remained until shortly after Marie Hesse's death in 1902. Down Bischofstrasse a little way, the Perrot machine shop, in which Hesse worked from June 1894 to September 1895, is still in operation. A small stone fountain commemorates his apprenticeship.

SCHOOLING

A hypersensitive, lively, and extremely headstrong child, Hesse proved to be a constant source of annoyance and despair to his parents and teachers. As early as 1881, Marie Hesse sensed that her son would have no ordinary future:

[Johannes] pray with me for little Hermann, and pray that I find enough strength to bring him up. It appears to me that physical

4 For more information about Dr. Hermann Gundert, see Johannes Hesse, *Aus Dr. Gunderts Leben* (Calw und Stuttgart: Vereinsbuchhandlung, 1894), 368 pp.

5 *Jakob Hannington: Ein Märtyrer für Uganda* (Calwer Familienbibliothek, 1891), 272 pp.; *David Livingstone, der Freund Afrikas* (Calwer Familienbibliothek, 1892), 248 pp. For more information about Marie Hesse, see Adele Gundert, *Marie Hesse: Ein Lebensbild in Briefen und Tagebüchern* (Stuttgart: Gundert, 1934), 283 pp.

Calw, Hermann Hesse's birthplace.

The Gothic chapel of St. Nicholas on the old bridge over the Nagold River.

strength is not enough. The little fellow is unusually lively, extremely strong, very willful, and really astonishingly bright for a four-year-old. . . . This inner struggling against his tyrannical spirit, ranting and raging, leaves me quite limp. . . . God must take this proud spirit in hand; something noble and splendid will then come of it. But I shudder to think of what could become of this passionate human if subjected to a wrong or weak upbringing.[6]

By 1883, Johannes Hesse was seriously wondering whether it might not be better to farm out his intractable, precocious child:

Humiliating though it would be to us, I am nevertheless seriously wondering if we should not put him into an institution or farm him out to strangers. We are too nervous and too weak for him. . . . He seems to have a gift for everything: he observes the moon and the clouds, improvises on the harmonium, makes quite amazing pencil and pen drawings, sings very ably when he has a mind to, and he is never at a loss for rhymes.[7]

By 1886, however, when his family returned to Calw from Basel, Hesse had become quite manageable. Although school held little attraction for him, and his teachers even less, he was able with almost no effort to stand near the top of his class. It began to appear likely that he would follow in the footsteps of his father and his Gundert grandfather. From February 1890 to July 1891, Hesse attended Rector Otto Bauer's Latin School in Göppingen in preparation for the notorious Swabian state examination, which he had to pass for admission into one of the four exclusive protestant church schools of Württemberg.[8] Hesse passed the required entrance examination in the middle of July, and on September 15 began his studies in Maulbronn.

Hesse's stay was unexpectedly brief and ended most unhappily. His correspondence with his parents suggests that all began auspiciously in Maulbronn. He was impressed by the school, interested in his studies, and generally pleased with both his teachers and his fellow students. His French leave of March 7, 1892, was therefore a distinct surprise to family and school. Following this twenty-three-hour impulsive escapade, Hesse began to suffer from headaches and insomnia. He became progressively more listless and his behavior more

---

6 Adele Gundert, *Marie Hesse* (1934), p. 208.
7 Adele Gundert, *Marie Hesse* (1934), p. 231.
8 Together with his parents, Hesse had become a citizen of Basel in 1882. He became a subject of Württemberg in November or December of 1890.

The Hesse family in the year 1889.
Left to right: Hermann, his father,
Marulla, his mother,
Adele, and Hans.

The house in
which Hermann
Hesse was born.

Elementary school in Calw in 1886. Hermann Hesse, third from the right in the back row.

Secondary school in Bad Cannstatt in 1893. Hermann Hesse, in the middle of the back row.

erratic. On May 7, much to the relief of the school authorities who had begun to doubt his sanity, he was withdrawn from Maulbronn by his parents and taken directly to Pastor Christoph Blumhardt of Bad Boll for a cure. Although he continued to suffer from severe headaches and insomnia, the patient was actually content in his new surroundings until his unrequited love for Eugenie Kolb, seven years his senior, threw him into deep depression. He borrowed money, bought a revolver, and on June 20 disappeared, leaving a suicide note. He reappeared that same day, morose and defiant. Two days later, since Blumhardt was anxious to rid himself of his unpredictable ward, Hesse was placed in the care of Pastor Gottlob Schall of nearby Stetten. Because of his exemplary behavior in Schall's school for mentally retarded and emotionally disturbed children, Hesse was allowed to return to Calw on August 5. At home he quickly became agitated and unmanageable again and had to be sent back to Stetten on August 22. His long pent-up resentment and anger now erupted. Infuriated and deeply hurt by what to him was unmistakable parental rejection, fifteen-year-old Hesse began to inveigh against the establishment, his father, adult authority, and religion in the same vitriolic manner in which, thirty-three years later, an equally distraught Steppenwolf was to rail against sham Western culture and its establishment. Letters to his parents, albeit hyperbolic, signed "H. Hesse Nihilist (haha!)," "H. Hesse, Exsulans" (In exile), and "H. Hesse, Gefangener im Zuchthaus zu Stetten" (Prisoner in the penitentiary in Stetten), attest to the intensity of his agitation:

> There is probably little chance that I can be sent elsewhere. In any case, you are rid of me. . . . If you write and tell me that I am insane or weak-minded, I'll believe it just to please you, and laugh doubly hard. (August 30)

> What I would not give for death. . . . A miserable 1892! It began dismally in the seminary, a few blissful weeks in Boll, then disappointed love, and a sudden end! And now—I have lost everything: home, parents, love, belief, hope, and myself. . . . Stetten is hell for me. . . . I am going to be cold, ice-cold to everyone, everyone! . . . Farewell, farewell, I want to be alone. . . . Let me, the mad dog, die here, or be my parents! (September 1)

> The Inspector took Turgenev's *Smoke* away from me. . . . I want to have something more than the trite, even if only in my reading material. Of course you would like to put me off with Pietism. . . . Here I am lectured to: "Turn to God, to Christ, etc. etc.!" But to me God is simply an insanity, and Christ only a man, hundred times though you may curse me for the thought. (September 4)

The church school in
Maulbronn, once a
Cistercian monastery.

The fountain in the cloister.

I was forcibly put on the train, brought here to Stetten. Here I am, no longer any trouble to the world. . . . I do not deserve this. I love myself, just as everyone loves himself, but it is not for that reason that I cannot live here, rather because I need a different atmosphere to be able and to want to fulfill myself as a human being. . . . What good does it do me when papa goes on repeating: "Do believe that we have your good at heart." This remark is not worth a damn. . . . Here there is no hope and belief, no one loves or is loved here; the place is quite void of any ideal, of anything beautiful, anything aesthetic; there is no art here, no feeling . . . no spirit. . . . I am a human being and before nature I insist earnestly and solemnly upon the universal right of man. . . . I also learned something in Stetten: to curse. . . . I can curse myself and particularly Stetten, then my relatives, and then the odious dream and insanity that happiness and unhappiness are. If you want to write to me, please do not mention your Christ. Enough fuss is made about him here. "Christ and love, God and bliss" etc., etc., can be read absolutely everywhere, and in the midst of all this, hatred and hostility prevail. I think that if the ghost of Christ could see what he has caused, he would weep. I am a human being, no less than Jesus; I see the difference between the ideal and actuality as well as he did, but I, I am not as tough as the Jew! (September 11)[9]

When the storm abated, Hesse, at his own request, was sent to Pastor Jakob Pfisterer in Basel on October 5. By November 7, a contrite though despondent young rebel was ready to resume his studies, now at a secondary school in Cannstatt. That he would be no more successful here than in Maulbronn quickly became obvious. His nerves were still frayed, his headaches continued, and his studies soon became a meaningless torture. On January 20, 1893, overwhelmed by painful memories and by his hopeless situation, Hesse rushed off to Stuttgart, sold some of his books, again managed to buy a revolver, and again flirted with suicide. The Bad Boll-Stetten syndrome repeated itself. Things gradually went from bad to worse. Complaints about sundry physical ailments became more insistent and contrition yielded to truculence. In his resentful self-assertion, Hesse now began to frequent taverns, to consort with questionable characters, to smoke heavily, and to incur debts. His depression increased correspondingly. Acceding to his pleas, Hesse's parents finally permitted him to return to Calw on October 18, 1893. His for-

9 *Kindheit und Jugend vor Neunzehnhundert: Hermann Hesse in Briefen und Lebenszeugnissen 1887–1895* (Frankfurt a.M.: Suhrkamp, 1966), pp. 250, 251, 252, 261–266.

mal education ended with his withdrawal from the school in Cannstatt.

A subsequent apprenticeship in a bookshop in Esslingen terminated abruptly on October 30, 1893, only four days after it had begun. Truant Hesse was located in Stuttgart by his father on November 2, was promptly taken for a mental examination to a Dr. Zeller of Winnenden, and then brought back to Calw on November 3. Here he spent the next six months gardening, assisting his father in the Calw Publishing House, and reading avidly in his grandfather's library. In early June 1894, after his father had denied him permission to leave home to independently prepare himself for a literary career, Hesse became an apprentice machinist in the Perrot tower-clock factory in Calw. This was a trade that would afford him a livelihood, that he could some day ply abroad, in the United States, Russia, or Brazil, and that would permit him ample time for his literary interests. Fifteen months of grimy manual labor were enough to disabuse the young dreamer of his romantic notions. He left Perrot's in the middle of September, and on October 17, 1895, he began a more appropriate apprenticeship in the Heckenhauer bookshop in Tübingen. The storm had finally subsided.

LITERARY BEGINNINGS

According to his mother's letters and diaries, Hesse began to compose ditties before he was able to wield a pencil.[10] Of the many poems he wrote before his determined decision, at the age of thirteen, to become a poet or nothing at all, only three have survived the years: a simple quatrain, probably written in March 1882; a three-sentence prose poem, dated November 17, 1884; and an untitled poem of May and June 1886.[11] Of the considerably more poetry Hesse wrote after his decision and before his departure for Tübingen in the autumn of 1895, at least ninety-eight poems have been preserved; none of these has ever been published and all are now housed in the Schiller-Nationalmuseum in Marbach am Neckar.[12]

10 E.g.: "Hermann writes poetry all day long, often quite good, often pellmell. He is very quick at putting together whatever rhymes" (in a letter of May 15, 1882). Adele Gundert, *Marie Hesse* (1934), pp. 219–220.

11 The first of these poems ("Das Vöglein im Wald") was published in Adele Gundert, *Marie Hesse* (1934), p. 217. Autographs of the other two poems (*Das wilde Meer*; "Dürfen wir denn an den Ort") are in the Hesse-Nachlass, Marbach am Neckar.

12 These poems are listed in Joseph Mileck, *Hermann Hesse: Biography and Bibliography* (Berkeley and Los Angeles: University of California Press, 1977). See Poetry V-D-III.

In late April or early May 1892, just before his withdrawal from Maulbronn, Hesse sent two untitled poems ("Ich kannte ein Blümlein am frischen Quell" and "O Vöglein, kannst du mir sagen") to *Quellwasser* (Leipzig) and another, recalling his punishment following his truancy and with the appropriate title, *Der Karzer*, to *Fliegende Blätter* (Munich). These were his first attempts to appear in print. The three poems were promptly returned with polite rejection slips.[13]

For Christmas 1950, Hesse received a little story from a ten-year-old grandson. It reminded him of a tale that he had written for his sister Marulla in November 1887, when he, too, was only ten years old. After a good deal of searching, he found the tale in question, and on January 6 *Die beiden Brüder* appeared in the *Neue Zürcher Zeitung*. This was one of Hesse's earliest attempts, if not his first, at prose fiction. *Spielmannsfahrt zum Rhein*, the oldest of his extant unpublished tales, was probably written in the spring or summer of 1893, while he was still in Cannstatt.[14] On March 4, 1895, Hesse mentioned to Theodor Rümelin that a *Novelle* he was writing was progressing very favorably. In May, he informed his mentor, Dr. E. Kapff, of plans for a novel. A remark to Rümelin in a letter of July 1 implies that the *Novelle*, now titled *Barthy*, was finished.[15] The novel, however, probably remained a plan. In any case, neither work is extant, and *Die beiden Brüder* and *Spielmannsfahrt zum Rhein* remain our only samples of Hesse's earliest prose fiction.

---

13 Autographs of the three poems are in the Hesse-Nachlass, Marbach a.N.
14 This thirty-three-page autograph is the prose portion of *Erfrorener Frühling* II. Dez. 1893. In the Schiller-Nationalmuseum, Marbach a.N.
15 *Kindheit und Jugend vor Neunzehnhundert* (1966), pp. 439, 466, 499.

✌ 2
Apprentice Bookdealer

TÜBINGEN 1895–1899

A QUIET RETREAT

Hesse's four years at the Heckenhauer bookshop in Tübingen were relatively tranquil. Though he had his circle of student friends and upon occasion was not averse to carousing with them, he remained a lonely outsider, applying himself diligently to his job, and otherwise preoccupied with his writing and self-education. During his preceding two years in Calw he had steeped himself in German literature of the eighteenth and nineteenth centuries, and had become well acquainted with many of the major English, French, Scandinavian, and Russian authors of the same period. In Tübingen, he continued his prodigious reading but narrowed its scope drastically. For a time he devoted himself almost exclusively to Goethe. Then he fell under the spell of the German romantics and of Novalis in particular. As late as May 1895, Hesse had discounted romanticism in no uncertain terms: "Moreover one cannot long feel comfortable in the confined garden of the romantics, in this tinsel conjured forth from mold, this haze of incense." [1] Now, under the influence of this same romanticism and of late nineteenth-century aestheticism, he created his own confining incense-shrouded garden, a beauty-worshipping realm of the imagination, a retreat from and a substitute for the crass

---

1 *Kindheit und Jugend vor Neunzehnhundert* (1966), p. 472.

Julie Hellmann (1878–1972),
Lulu in *Hermann Lauscher*.

Hermann Hesse in Tübingen
at the age of twenty-one.

outer world in which he had become an unappreciated misfit. Hesse was tolerably content. He had found a niche and a way of life.

ROMANTISCHE LIEDER AND *EINE STUNDE HINTER MITTERNACHT*: REFUGE IN FANTASY

In Tübingen, Hesse proved to himself that he was indeed a writer. No longer in the shadow of home or school, he was finally able to pursue his literary interests more or less as he pleased. In late 1895, he wrote *Meine Kindheit*, eventually to become part of *Hinterlassene Schriften und Gedichte von Hermann Lauscher* (1901).[2] In 1896 or 1897, he submitted an essay to Christoph Schrempf, editor of the periodical, *Die Wahrheit* (Stuttgart). His exercise in ornate style was returned with copious corrections and red slashes. A presumptuous aspirant had looked forward to his first prose publication; a duly chastened novice sheepishly destroyed the work soon after its rejection.[3]

Hesse's early poetry found more ready reception than his early prose. *Madonna*, the first of his poems published, appeared in *Das deutsche Dichterheim* (Vienna) on March 1, 1896; seven others were published by the same periodical during the next two and a half years.[4] *Romantische Lieder* was submitted to a publisher in the autumn of 1898 and appeared at the beginning of 1899;[5] this was Hesse's first collection of poems to be published[6] and also his first published book. All but two of the fifty-six poems of *Romantische Lieder* were written from February 1897 to June 1898. Some sixty-six other poems written in Tübingen are still extant and have yet to be published.[7]

Most of this early poetry is heavy with pathos. Its atmosphere is scented, its sounds muted, its colors brilliant, and it abounds with exclamation marks and restive dashes. A lonely and aristocratic outsider indulges in melodramatic fantasies and melodic lament. He is morbidly preoccupied with love and death, strikes a suffering pose, and is fascinated by a romantic retreat of stormy seas and battlefields,

---

2 Unless otherwise indicated, parenthetical dates of collected works are those of first publication, and parenthetical dates of individual works are those of completion.

3 Hesse recalls this incident in "Nachruf auf Christoph Schrempf" (1944), *Gesammelte Schriften* (Frankfurt a.M.: Suhrkamp, 1957), Vol. 4, pp. 769–770.

4 See Poetry V-D: 753, 708, 4, 165, 784, 38, 39.

5 (Dresden: E. Pierson, 1899), 44 pp.

6 At least eight autograph collections of poetry (ranging from three to thirty-nine poems) predate *Romantische Lieder* (see Poetry V-C: 1a–1h).

7 See Poetry V-D-III.

18 / *Hermann Hesse*

temples and castles, and solitary kings and pale queens. Hesse could hardly have given his *Romantische Lieder* a more appropriate title.

In letters of November and December 1890, Hesse informed his parents enthusiastically and proudly of *Ein Weihnachtsabend. Trauerspiel in 1 Aufzug*, that he had just written.[8] By May 1895, he was prepared to concede to Dr. E. Kapff: "I do not feel that I have any talent for drama, but I hope some day to become a respectable writer of prose. . . ."[9] By March 1899 he had begun to doubt the merits of the theater: "As art it is second class, and furthermore its enormous apparatus that lays one's impressions open to hundreds of contingencies is against my taste."[10] This sentiment notwithstanding, Hesse was preoccupied with drama intermittently from 1900 to 1919. The resultant anaemic, romantic verse playlets, flimsy derivative librettos, and a one-act fragment in prose[11]—only two of these abortive efforts have been published—confirm what he himself had suspected in 1895. Drama was definitely not Hesse's medium, and the theater, but for opera, never held any real appeal for him.

Plauderabende, a fifty-page autograph medley of literary essays, vignettes, diary notes, and poems, was dedicated to his mother upon the occasion of her birthday, on October 18, 1897. *Zum 14. Juni 1898*, a similar fifty-page autograph medley of prose and poetry, was assembled for his father's birthday.[12] Neither of these collections was intended for publication. On April 14, 1899, Hesse informed his parents that he was writing a book-length study of German romanticism and that it was progressing very slowly.[13] A third potpourri, *Eine Stunde hinter Mitternacht*, comprising reveries, monologues, and vignettes written from 1897 to 1899 and sent to a publisher in February 1899, appeared in June; it was Hesse's first prose publication.[14]

8 *Kindheit und Jugend vor Neunzehnhundert* (1966), pp. 73–74.
9 *Kindheit und Jugend vor Neunzehnhundert* (1966), p. 466. Dr. Ernst Kapff (1864–1944) was the only instructor at the school in Cannstatt to impress Hesse favorably.
10 From an unpublished letter (March 8, 1899) to his parents. In the Hesse-Nachlass, Marbach a.N.
11 See Manuscripts X: 429.
12 Both of these autographs are in the Hesse-Nachlass, Marbach a.N. (see Manuscripts X: 2, 4).
13 Unpublished letter in the Hesse-Nachlass, Marbach a.N. *Deutsche Romantik* probably remained a fragment. "Novalis" (*Allgemeine Schweizer Zeitung*, 5 [1900], 12), "Romantisch" (*Allgemeine Schweizer Zeitung*, 5 [1900], 96), "Romantik und Neuromantik" (*Rheinisch-Westfälische Zeitung* [Essen], December 14, 1902, No. 991), and "Neuromantik" (written in November 1899, published in *Eugen Diederichs. Selbstzeugnisse und Briefe von Zeitgenossen* [Düsseldorf, Köln: Diederichs, 1967], pp. 107–109) were either remnants or offshoots of this intended book.
14 (Leipzig: E. Diederichs, 1899), 84 pp.

In this maiden venture a languid narrator depicts his exotic island and mysterious forest retreats, his lonely castles, enchanting parks, and ornate chambers. He communes with his muse, consorts with ethereal maidens, and burns his incense on the altar of beauty. Sporadic renewed contact with the profane world is followed by despair and regret, and in turn, by an urgent reaffirmation of aestheticism. All is removed in time and space, a dream world pervaded by melancholy and enveloped in a perfumed atmosphere. Colors are rich, sounds soft, and choice language flows facile. This was the ideal world that Hesse espoused, and the aestheticism that he cultivated while in Tübingen.

Hesse had written his mother on February 20, 1899, to say that a publisher was interested in *Eine Stunde hinter Mitternacht*. He had added disparagingly: "However the manuscript does not appear to me to have any business possibilities; it is something for very few readers, and will undoubtedly never have much of a market." [15] Hesse proved right. Of the 600 copies printed only 53 were sold the first year. R. M. Rilke's sympathetic review was the only heartening public response: "In its best spots it is something necessary and very personal. His awe is honest and deep, his love grand and its feelings are pious. The work stands at the edge of art." [16] The public's indifference piqued Hesse. His mother's outspoken moral aversion hurt him deeply and infuriated him. [17] But neither was able to discourage or to dissuade him. He only became more determined than ever to become a writer.

KIRCHHEIM UNTER TECK

Hesse began his apprenticeship at Heckenhauer's in Tübingen on October 17, 1895. He became an assistant in the shop on October 2, 1898, and continued in that capacity until July 31, 1899. Before leaving

15 Unpublished letter in the Hesse-Nachlass, Marbach a.N.

16 *Der Bote für deutsche Literatur* (Leipzig), 2 (September 1899), pp. 388–389.

17 Hesse's parents, his father in particular, were severely moralistic. Both looked askance at *belles-lettres*; literature was too much of this world. Appalled by *Eine Stunde hinter Mitternacht*, Marie Hesse made an immediate and fervent appeal to her son: "Shun your fever muse as you would a snake; she it is who crept into paradise and who to-day would still like to poison thoroughly every paradise of love and of poetry. . . . O my child flee from her, hate her, she is impure and has no claim to you, for you belong to God. . . . Pray for grand thoughts and a pure heart. . . . Remain chaste! . . . There is a world of falsehood where the base, the animalistic, the impure is considered beautiful. . . . My dear child, God help you and bless you and save you from this!" (unpublished letter, June 15, 1899, in the Hesse-Nachlass, Marbach a.N.). Hesse never forgot

The Petit Cénacle in Tübingen. From left to right: Otto Erich Faber, Ludwig Finckh, Hermann Hesse, Carlo Hamelehle, and Oskar Rupp (Tänzer, Ugel, Lauscher, Hamelt, and Ripplein in *Hermann Lauscher*).

The Heckenhauer Bookshop in Tübingen, at the time of Hesse's apprenticeship.

for Basel in September to assume a similar position in the R. Reich bookshop, he spent ten memorable days in little Kirchheim unter Teck. Here he rejoined his close friend and fellow budding writer, Ludwig Finckh, and the remaining members of the *petit cénacle* of students that he had joined in Tübingen.[18] The setting was idyllic, the weather was fine, and all were in holiday spirits. Hesse had hardly settled in the Inn at the Sign of the Crown before he and his company of young romantics, all in love with love, began to pay court to the innkeeper's two charming nieces. Hesse quickly fell under the spell of Julie Hellmann, the younger of the two nieces. He wooed her chivalrously with flowers and verse, won her heart but not her hand, and then left for Calw and Basel. Hesse immediately began an ardent correspondence with her, but he never returned to Kirchheim. And although the two continued to correspond intermittently until the late 1950s,[19] they did not meet again, and for the last time, until 1928 when Hesse chanced to give a reading in Heilbronn. Their brief encounter in Kirchheim did, however, have its lasting literary consequences. It was this idyllic interlude that found poetic expression in Hesse's fantasia, *Lulu* (1900) of *Hermann Lauscher*, and that Ludwig Finckh recalled fifty years later in his *Verzauberung*.[20]

---

this painful letter, and he was never quite able to forgive his parents for their perpetual prudish moralizing (see unpublished letters to his sisters in the Hesse-Nachlass, Marbach a.N.: to Marulla, July 4, 1920; to Adele, spring 1926, February 1934).

18 Otto Erich Faber, Carlo Hammelehle, Oskar Rupp, and Wilhelm Schöning.

19 Their unpublished correspondence is in the Schiller-Nationalmuseum. Marbach a.N.

20 (Ulm: Gerhard Hess, 1950), 136 pp.

3

A Retreat from Aestheticism

BASEL 1899–1904

SOCIAL DEBUT AND LITERARY SUCCESS

Hesse spent almost five years in Basel. It was a busy and fruitful period. He began his job as an assistant bookseller at R. Reich's bookshop on September 15, 1899. His profession was satisfying enough, but long hours in the shop and few holidays left him with neither enough time nor energy for his literary career, and no opportunity for travel. By the end of 1900 he was anxious for a respite. With enough savings to tide him over for some months, and assured of a new position in late summer, Hesse left Reich's at the beginning of February 1901. He returned to Calw at the end of February, delighted that he was finally able to relax and to write as he pleased. Hesse wrote the first four of his many brief recollections of childhood in Calw during these weeks immediately preceding his first trip to Italy.[1]

Hesse left for Milan from Stuttgart on March 25, visited Genoa, Spezia, Pisa, Florence, Bologna, Ravenna, Padua, and Venice, then returned to Calw on May 19, and to Basel later in the summer. His diary notes, rewritten soon after his return from Italy and published by the *Basler Anzeiger* that autumn, were the first of his many travel

---

1 *Der Kavalier auf dem Eis, Der kleine Mohr, Hotte Hotte Putzpulver,* and *Der Sammetwedel* (see Prose IV: 13a, 13b, 18b, 34).

reports (*Reisebilder*).[2] On September 1, 1901, back from Basel following a brief August vacation in Vitznau, Hesse began to work for the antiquarian E. von Wattenwyl.

In Tübingen Hesse had lived in relative seclusion. In Basel he began to seek more human contact. He now made a determined effort to learn the art of living with and not apart from his fellow humans in order to escape the ever more painful loneliness of prolonged uninvolvement. Soon after his arrival he became a frequent guest of some of Basel's culturally prominent families. He was a regular visitor in the home of Dr. Rudolf Wackernagel, state archivist and historian, where he became acquainted with a number of historians, philosophers, theologians, and architects.[3] He was also a welcome visitor in the home of the philologist Dr. Jakob Wackernagel, enjoyed a standing invitation to Pastor La Roche's musical evenings, and appreciated the hospitality of the mathematically prominent Bernoulli family.

Nor was it long before Hesse again became romantically involved. In the spring of 1900, while still writing *Lulu* (February to June), his paean to Julie Hellmann, he fell in love with Elisabeth La Roche, the daughter of Pastor La Roche and the Elisabeth of his love poems of 1900 to 1901, of Lauscher's *Tagebuch 1900*, and of *Peter Camenzind*. And when the hopelessness of this shyly pursued love became apparent, Hesse began his more successful courtship of Maria Bernoulli.

Although his circle of friends and acquaintances was thus considerably extended in Basel, Hesse himself remained essentially an outsider who felt distinctly uncomfortable at social gatherings. Like his sensitive and somewhat gauche Peter Camenzind, he was far less at home in a crowded drawing room than with an intimate friend or two in a tavern, or alone out in nature. And for him, just as for Camenzind, the outdoors gradually became an important part of an essentially lonely way of life. He was happiest when hiking in the area around Basel, boating on the Vierwaldstätter See, or wandering through the Berner Oberland on one of his frequent weekend excursions.

In June 1902, Hesse's eyes began to trouble him more than usual. He had been exempted from German military service in 1900 because

2 "Stimmungsbilder aus Oberitalien," *Schweizer Hausfreund*. Beilage d. Basler Anzeigers, 16 (September-October 1901).

3 Among these, Heinrich Wölfflin, Karl Joël, Alfred Bertholet, Adam Mez, and Heinrich Jennen.

Elisabeth La Roche,
the Elisabeth of *Peter Camenzind*.

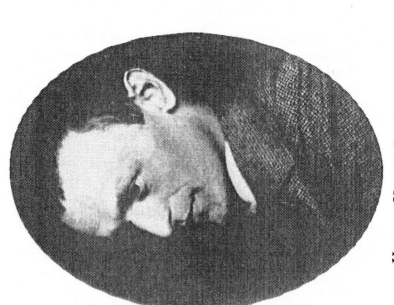

Hermann Hesse in Basel, 1903.

of poor eyesight. By the end of August 1902, severe eyestrain and prolonged headaches compelled him to take sick leave. He left at once for a much-needed rest in Calw and did not return to Basel until the beginning of November. On April 1, 1903, Hesse started on his second trip to Italy. He followed much the same route he had taken in 1901, was accompanied part of the way by Maria Bernoulli and a Miss Gundrum, and returned to Basel on April 24. During the next few days he was finally able to give the finishing touches to his first novel. He had begun to write *Peter Camenzind* in November 1901 but had progressed very slowly until toward the end of 1902. The work was sent to Samuel Fischer on May 9 and was promptly accepted for publication. An abbreviated printing in the *Neue Rundschau* was scheduled for the autumn of 1903 and book publication for January 1904.

Since Hesse's literary success now seemed assured, there was no longer any need for him to continue to work for von Wattenwyl. In September he quit his trade for good and became a full-time author. While Hesse spent the autumn of 1903 and the winter and spring of 1904 in Calw writing *Unterm Rad* and his monographs on Boccaccio and St. Francis of Assisi, Maria Bernoulli, to whom he had become engaged late in the spring of 1903, began to scour the countryside around the Bodensee for an appealing rural retreat. Both had had their fill of sophisticated city life. After much searching, Maria finally managed to find an old and very simple farmhouse for rent in the appropriately secluded and picturesque village of Gaienhofen on the German side of the Untersee. They were married in Basel on August 2, 1904, and began their Rousseauesque experiment in Gaienhofen soon thereafter, with grand expectations.

Hesse's writings both burgeoned and evolved during these years in Basel. An examination of the major publications might best be prefaced by a perusal of his then prevailing literary inclinations and of his spreading intellectual and philosophical interests. Such a preface would have to involve naturalism, Friedrich Nietzsche, Jacob Burckhardt, and Arthur Schopenhauer.

NATURALISM

In Basel, Goethe and the German romantics, particularly Novalis, Hoffmann, Tieck, Eichendorff, Heine, and Brentano continued to be Hesse's favorite writers, and Jacobsen, Maeterlinck, Dante, Hofmannsthal, Keller, Storm, Meyer, Spitteler, and Fontane continued to interest him. Jakob Böhme now began to intrigue him, while cult-conscious Stefan George, whom he discovered a few months after his arrival in Basel, repelled him from the outset. In time, Hesse learned to respect George but never to appreciate him.[4] Naturalism, too, was never to appeal to Hesse. His attitude toward the movement became fixed as early as 1895. He was willing to acknowledge the talents of such of its representatives as Hauptmann, Ibsen, Turgenev, and Zola, but he saw no future for the movement as a whole. He questioned its theory of art and ridiculed its exclusive preoccupation with social problems. Naturalism was too sordid and nihilistic, and not art-conscious enough for Hesse's liking.[5] His antipathy persisted in Basel; he now avoided naturalists as much as possible. And since most of the Russian writers with whom he was acquainted (Pushkin, Lermontov, Gogol, Turgenev, Korolenko, Dostoevsky, and Tolstoy) were in his mind closely or loosely associated with naturalism, his aversion spread quickly to Russian literature in general: it suddenly seemed too heavy, too gloomy, and too devoid of culture. Even Tolstoy became unbearable. His *Resurrection* (1899), which Hesse read reluctantly, left him deeply depressed; its atmosphere was distinctly unwholesome. For a time Turgenev alone continued to afford him some degree of reading pleasure.[6] However, Hesse soon revised his disparaging appraisal of Tolstoy and his compatriots, and by 1906 he regretted the paucity of Russian literature available in German translation.[7] During the First World War he steeped himself in Tolstoy, the best representative of all that was truly Russian;[8] and a veritable passion for Dostoevsky, genial poet-prophet and forerunner to Freud, culminated in the writing of *Blick ins Chaos* in 1919. And by 1921 Hesse ranked Russian *belles-lettres* of the nineteenth century with the best of world literature.[9]

FRIEDRICH NIETZSCHE, JACOB BURCKHARDT, AND ARTHUR SCHOPENHAUER

Hesse probably began to read Nietzsche in the spring of 1895, while still in Calw; the man never ceased to intrigue him. His im-

4 See letter of May 19, 1962, *Briefe* (1964), p. 551.

5 See letters written in 1895, *Kindheit und Jugend vor Neunzehnhundert* (1966), pp. 443–444, 451–452, 482–483, 489, 498.

6 See Lauscher's *Tagebuch 1900, Gesammelte Schriften* (1957), Vol. 1, p. 192. Hesse began to read Turgenev in the summer of 1892; this was probably his introduction to Russian literature.

7 See "Neues vom Inselverlag," *Neue Zürcher Zeitung*, September 12, 1906, No. 253; "Die grossen Russen," *März*, 3, iii (1909), 495.

8 See "Vom Geiste Russlands," *März*, 9, ii (1915), 118–119.

9 See "Russische Literaturgeschichte," *Wissen und Leben*, 15 (1921–22), 692.

mediate fascination waxed strong in Tübingen, then waned gradually in Basel, and it was an enchantment that remained all the while in the shadows of Goethe and the romantics. It was also one of decidedly mixed feelings. Hesse's enthusiastic acclaim of Nietzsche the artist alternated with supercilious disparagement of Nietzsche the philosopher. The philosophy of *Also sprach Zarathustra* was to him as dated as its word artistry was unique. Nietzsche's aesthetic approach to life appealed to him enormously, but he flatly rejected Nietzsche's "master morality." And with Hesse's disenchantment with aestheticism and its less than splendid isolation, with his growing desire in Basel for more human contact, his passion for Nietzsche quickly subsided. The first encounter at the turn of the century was primarily an exciting experience. It was not until the *Demian* period that Nietzsche became a formative factor in Hesse's life and a powerful thrust in his art.[10]

In Basel, Hesse also fell under the spell of Jacob Burckhardt, the historian who replaced Nietzsche as a guiding light in the second half of his life. He had already read *Die Kultur der Renaissance in Italien* at the beginning of 1898, and had been very impressed.[11] In Basel, he continued his avid reading of Burckhardt. The intellectual circles in which he moved were still dominated by Burckhardt. The historian quickly became Hesse's guide through Italy's past.[12] Later in life Burckhardt's view of history was to confirm Hesse's emerging belief in the temporality and relativity of human institutions, in the permanence of the human spirit, and in order and meaning beyond the apparent chaos of reality; it was also to help open his eyes to civilization's interaction of politics, religion, and culture, to the ultimate insufficiency of such areligious and apolitical purely cultural institutions as Castalia, and to the necessary interplay of *vita contemplativa* and *vita activa* in human affairs. Wise and benign Pater Jakobus of *Das Glasperlenspiel* (1942) was Hesse's token of respect and gratitude. Pater Jakobus is to Josef Knecht much what Burckhardt became for Hesse in the thirties.

10 For Hesse's attitude to Nietzsche during his years in Tübingen and Basel, see: letter of June 15, 1895, to Dr. E. Kapff, *Kindheit und Jugend vor Neunzehnhundert* (1966), p. 491; unpublished letters in the Hesse-Nachlass (Marbach a.N.) to Johannes Hesse (June 15, 1896), Karl Isenberg (June 12, 1897), to his parents (September 10, 1897; February 12, 1898); see also letters five and six of *Briefe an Elisabeth* [1900–1902], unpublished autograph in the Hesse-Nachlass.

11 Unpublished letter (March 30, 1898) to his parents. In the Hesse-Nachlass, Marbach a.N.

12 For Burckhardt's influence upon Hesse at the outset of the century, see Hesse's "Ein paar Basler Erinnerungen," *National-Zeitung* (Basel), July 4, 1937, No. 301.

A letter written to his father on June 12, 1892, indicates that Hesse was already then at least vaguely familiar with Schopenhauer. Writing to Dr. E. Kapff on June 15, 1895, he alluded disparagingly to a slight anthology of pessimistic writings that was titled *Nirwana* and included some remarks by Schopenhauer.[13] And in another letter sent to his father on June 15, 1896, he admitted that he was still scarcely acquainted with Schopenhauer.[14] Allusions to Schopenhauer in Lauscher's *Tagebuch 1900* (May 30) and in Hesse's recollections of Basel (1937) suggest that Hesse probably did not read *Die Welt als Wille und Vorstellung* until his last year in Tübingen and that he continued to concern himself with Schopenhauer during his first year in Basel. In any case, it is apparent from the earliest of these references that the initial impression Schopenhauer made upon him was neither deep nor favorable: in 1895 Schopenhauer was decidedly too pessimistic for Hesse, and in 1900 he did not sound quite authentic. Hesse's interest in Schopenhauer reawakened some four years later when he became preoccupied with the religions of India.[15] This interest simmered for years and did not climax until Nietzsche's influence on him gradually subsided following the writing of *Demian*. Only then, and particuarly during the spring, summer, and autumn of 1919, was Schopenhauer to have any real impact upon Hesse's thought and way of life.

HERMANN LAUSCHER: AN AESTHETE'S WORLD

In Tübingen, Hesse had proved to himself that he was a writer; in Basel, he managed to convince the public. *Hinterlassene Schriften und Gedichte von Hermann Lauscher*, ostensibly edited by H. Hesse, appeared in December 1900.[16] This was the first of a number of times that Hesse resorted to this type of subterfuge. When he published his *Demian* in 1919, he used the pseudonym Emil Sinclair. In 1927, he purported to be the editor of *Der Steppenwolf*, a manuscript left to him by a vagrant Harry Haller. And in 1943, he appeared as the editor of *Das Glasperlenspiel*, the biography and literary remains of Josef Knecht, another manuscript that had fortuitously fallen into his possession. Hesse's reasons for this artifice varied from instance to in-

---

13 *Kindheit und Jugend vor Neunzehnhundert* (1966), pp. 218, 488.
14 Unpublished letter in the Hesse-Nachlass, Marbach a.N.
15 See "Über mein Verhältnis zum geistigen Indien und China," in Adrian Hsia, *Hermann Hesse und China* (Frankfurt a.M.: Suhrkamp, 1974), p. 303
16 (Basel: R. Reich, 1901), 83 pp.

stance. In 1900, his considerations were both personal and practical. Hesse obviously felt that the recollections, diary excerpts, and poems of *Hermann Lauscher* were too intimate to be published undisguised, and he was also convinced that only some such literary device could justify and make acceptable a publication in book form of the stray elements that *Hermann Lauscher* comprises. Hesse abandoned this subterfuge when a supplemented edition of the book was published in 1907.[17]

Lauscher's medley of prose and poetry was written from 1895 to 1901. *Meine Kindheit*, recollections of childhood in Basel (1881–1886), written in late 1895, is our only example of the beautifully simple and sober narrative style that Hesse had managed to achieve before he began to assume the heroic pose of a suffering aesthete and to cultivate the purple prose of *Eine Stunde hinter Mitternacht*. In *Die Novembernacht*, written in the spring or summer of 1899, Hesse ably affects the pseudo-sophisticated banter and morbid cynicism characteristic of student circles as he recalls a disastrous night of carousing in the taverns of Tübingen with his student friends.

Lulu, written from February to June 1900, a transfigured recollection of Hesse's delightful ten days in Kirchheim unter Teck in August 1899, is undoubtedly the most significant of his works preceding *Peter Camenzind*. In its form is displays an unsuspected structural virtuosity. The commonplace visible world and a wondrous fairy-tale realm are not merely juxtaposed but adroitly fused. And in its substance it reflects what had become and was to remain the characteristic pendulating rhythm of Hesse's life, and foreshadows the bliss and agony of the consequent never-ending tensions. Harry Haller's crisis, his emergence from a lonely retreat, his renewed contact with life, and his subsequent return to his ascetic dedication to things of the spirit is in its essence prefigured in Lauscher's brief encounter with life in Kirchheim and his return to a lonely retreat, to his art and to the more ideal world of his imagination. Both protagonists swing from isolation to contact, from the ideal to the real, and from spirituality to sensuality. In this regard, *Der Steppenwolf* is nothing other than an extremely complex variation on a theme struck clearly for the first time in *Lulu*, but already faintly audible in the reveries of *Eine Stunde hinter Mitternacht*.

An embryonic Harry Haller, almost obscured by the pomp and

17 (Düsseldorf: Verlag der Rheinlande, 1907), 189 pp. *Lulu* (1900) and *Schlaflose Nächte* (1901) were added to the original publication.

circumstance of *Eine Stunde hinter Mitternacht* and just discernible through the misty romanticism and rather abstruse allegory of *Lulu*, assumes a clear outline in *Tagebuch 1900*. Lauscher emerges a potential Steppenwolf, like Haller a sensitive misfit, primarily an observer of life and not a participant, an extreme individualist dedicated to the ideal and disdainful of the real. He is torn by Haller's yearning for human involvement, knows his renunciation, and indulges in his self-laceration. Though troubled by gnawing doubt, he keeps reaffirming his belief in his aestheticism just as Haller continues to reassert his faith in his cultural ideals and his Platonism following periodic bouts with doubt. Lauscher's presentiment of a humor born of strength and not of weakness, associated with an acceptance of and not a recoiling from the trying consequences of idealism, becomes Haller's pursuit of that most genial of human possibilities. Lauscher is the troubled aesthete Hesse was in his early twenties and Haller is the distraught idealistic artist-intellectual that Hesse became in his late forties. It is essentially only a shift in ideology that separates the Lauschers from the Hallers.

That Hesse was still wending his way through *Eine Stunde hinter Mitternacht*'s garden of sweet sentiment is even more clearly evidenced by Lauscher's *Letzte Gedichte*, written in the summer and autumn of 1900, and *Schlaflose Nächte*, written in 1901. Assuming the guise of a minstrel-knight and striking a familiar sentimental heroic pose, Lauscher holds forth in song steeped in the melancholy of distant worship, unrequited love, and lost youth. And like the narrator of *Eine Stunde hinter Mitternacht*, Lauscher communes with his beautiful pale muse in their midnight solitude far removed from the profane world. Their concerns are his art, beauty, and eternity. There is much indulging in bittersweet recollections and weltering in nostalgia. Sighs are ready and tears copious. Theirs is an aesthete's world of harps and broken strings, of moonlight, nightingales, shadowy arcades, and sumptuous snow-white castles, and all continues to be couched in the flowery rhetoric of *Eine Stunde hinter Mitternacht*.

In his introduction of 1900, Hesse termed *Hinterlassene Schriften und Gedichte von Hermann Lauscher* "Documents of the peculiar soul of a modern aesthete and eccentric." This characterization is just as appropriate for the supplemented edition of 1907 as it was for the original publication, and *Eine Stunde hinter Mitternacht* could hardly be described more aptly. The aestheticism of *Eine Stunde hinter Mitternacht* reflects the early stages of Hesse's first adult adjustment to life, and *Hermann Lauscher* was his last reaffirmation of an approach to life he knew he had to give up if he was ever to escape a loneliness that was becoming progressively more painful. *Hermann Lauscher* was a finale to *Eine Stunde hinter Mitternacht* and not a prelude to *Peter Camenzind*, not Hesse's first attempt to win for himself "a piece of the world and actuality" as he contended in 1941.[18]

POETRY

Hesse's second book publication of poetry appeared in November 1902. Of the 166 poems in *Gedichte*, 13 were written before 1899 and the remainder between 1899 and the summer of 1902. *Gedichte* is the poetic counterpart to *Hermann Lauscher* that *Romantische Lieder* is to *Eine Stunde hinter Mitternacht*. *Romantische Lieder* had escaped the attention of both the critics and the public. *Gedichte* quickly placed Hesse among the leading neo-romantics of the day. A supplemental edition was published in 1906.[19] Repeated reprinting of this second edition and two new editions published as late as the fifties attest to the popularity these poems have enjoyed.

While still a youngster, Hesse began to give little autograph collections of his poems to favorite relatives and close friends. Eight of his earliest collections are still extant.[20] These date from 1892 to 1897, each includes from 3 to 39 poems, and only 6 of the 126 poems involved have ever been published. In Basel, Hesse not only continued this practice, but managed to supplement his meager income by branching out into a little business venture. In October 1900, he began a *Notturni* series of poem collections; 25 autograph copies of the original *Notturni* collection of 10 poems were sold to friends and well-wishers for 10 marks apiece. These were not ordinary duplicates. He varied the number of poems from copy to copy, and often revised poems while recopying them. New collections for the *Notturni* series were prepared to order until 1902. Unfortunately only 7 of all the *Notturni* collections have been located;[21] 17 of the 68 poems in these 7 autographs have not yet appeared in print.

Hesse continued this private selling of his poetic wares throughout his lifetime. A *Zwölf Gedichte* series, collections in typescript or

18 "Geleitwort," *Eine Stunde hinter Mitternacht* (Zürich: Fretz & Wasmuth, 1941), p. 11.

19 (Berlin: G. Grote, 1902), 196 pp.

20 Six are in the Schiller-Nationalmuseum, Marbach a.N.; the remaining two are in private possession (see Poetry V-C: 1a-1h).

21 Two are in the Schiller-Nationalmuseum, Marbach a.N., the other five are in private possession (see Poetry V-C: 2, 2a, 3, 4, 4a, 5, 6).

handwritten, with or without original watercolors, and rarely duplicated, was introduced in 1918 and quickly became and remained his
standard sales item. Over the years, he must have sold some 120
of these collections. After 1945, the returns were used primarily for
charity. Hesse also continued to the end of his life to honor a wide circle of friends and acquaintances with his gift collections of autograph
and typescript poems. These, too, were rarely duplicated and were
also often embellished with watercolors. The later manuscript collections, whether intended for friends or customers, include only a few
unpublished poems. Like the earlier collections, however, they do
have many poems that differ in title or text or both from their counterparts in the *Gesammelte Schriften*, and they do help to date many of
Hesse's poems more accurately than otherwise possible.

PETER CAMENZIND: A BITTER TASTE OF REALITY

Hesse's art began and remained closely personal. Protagonist
and author are generally inseparable. Many of his tales reflect his
inner self almost to the exclusion of any interaction with the physical
world. Fewer reflect both his inner and outer circumstances. *Peter
Camenzind* (1903)[22] belongs to the latter. Camenzind's aspirations and
disappointments, his inclinations, problems, and efforts to resolve
these were by and large Hesse's. So too, but for minor deviations, was Camenzind's general course of life. Hesse's Calw became
Camenzind's Nimikon; his mountainous Vierwaldstätter See, Camenzind's Alps; his Maulbronn, Camenzind's secondary school; and his
Tübingen, Camenzind's Zürich. Hesse's first trip to Italy became
Camenzind's excursions to Florence. Hesse had encountered Camenzind's Erminia in Florence and Camenzind's Elisabeth was Hesse's
Elisabeth La Roche. Hesse's association with Basel's academic and art
circles became Camenzind's exposure to modern culture. History's
fascination for Camenzind was Jacob Burckhardt's effect on Hesse, and
Camenzind's interest in the novelle of Renaissance Italy and his fondness for legends were Hesse's latest literary concerns. Camenzind is
the lonely outsider and intransigent individualist that Hesse remained
in Basel, and his distant worship of women, fondness for children,
and predilection for solitude were Hesse's. At his blackest moments
Hesse also disparaged his art and, like Camenzind, doubted the wisdom of his choice of vocation. And again, like his hero, Hesse sought

22 (Berlin: S. Fischer, 1904), 260 pp.

solace in wine, a Rousseauesque refuge in nature, and found a new ideal in the love and service exemplified by St. Francis of Assisi. *Peter Camenzind* reflects the initial stage of the new approach to life that Hesse began to cultivate in Basel. He had become disenchanted with aestheticism; it suggested pathology and was essentially a dead-end street. Just to be a beauty-conscious artist living with his dreams was no longer enough. He had also to become a life-conscious human being living with his fellow men, if for no other reason than to escape his agonizing loneliness. Hesse's ideal became Camenzind's, and Camenzind's inability to realize this ideal was Hesse's own failure to do so. As of the completion of *Peter Camenzind* in May 1903, Hesse's new approach to life had been relatively unsuccessful. His old habits and inclinations persisted. The Lauscher that lurks under Camenzind's swashbuckling rugged exterior is the moody, romantic, timid, and asocial Lauscher that lingered on in Hesse. Like Camenzind, Hesse managed to establish more contact with others but very little meaningful involvement. The *ars vivendi* and the *ars amandi* continued to elude him just as they elude his hero. Camenzind's decision to turn his back upon the world and to renounce women was also Hesse's decision. And had Hesse not completed his *Peter Camenzind* before Maria Bernoulli became a distinct new possibility in his life, the novel might well have ended in a rather traditional happy manner. Camenzind would probably have retired to Nimikon not as a bachelor but with a bride, looking forward to the same happiness that Hesse expected when he married and settled in Gaienhofen.

In Hesse's earliest works ornate style accords with aesthetic concerns. In *Peter Camenzind* a disillusioned aesthete's new style of life found its expression in a corresponding new style of art. Shades and airy worlds now yielded to living people in actual situations and involved in real events. Hesse's prose assumed an appropriately more sober and more narrative style. His emotive adjectives and adverbs became less profuse, his abstracts less common, his imagery less choice, and his narration less punctured by rhetorical questions and exclamatory outbursts. But Hesse, the writer of vignettes and episodes, hardly emerged a full-blown story teller. Camenzind's story is less a smooth continuum of evolving action firmly anchored in space and time than a series of loosely juxtaposed recollections with interposed self-contemplation, nature description, and social comment. Camenzind's spotty memory also leaves unaccounted for time fissures in his narrative, and his recollections are unevenly developed. He brushes by his formative years in high school, then lingers over a flower incident related to his first infatuation. His trip to Italy reads like a detailed guide for tourists, while his walking tours across France and through southern Germany are barely mentioned. He expands upon his brief sojourn in Assisi but chooses to give no more than passing attention to his dissolute interludes as an editor in Germany and as a correspondent in Paris.

Nor did Hesse the romantic emerge a full-fledged realist with his *Peter Camenzind*. His characters are more commented upon than described in realistic detail. They are real enough, but felt rather than seen. His settings, too, are real but they also never emerge clearly visible. Nimikon is any Alpine community, his cities are little more than names, and his houses, apartments, and rooms are just dwelling places. Even his detailed nature settings are appropriate general backdrops more than specific situations realistically depicted. Nature is to Camenzind what it has always been for romantics: a mirror for his moods and a setting for his protracted reflections. And Camenzind can rhapsodize about clouds as romantically and as effusively as Lauscher does about his favorite lakes.

In Hesse's new prose there is therefore much both in form and substance that harks back to *Eine Stunde hinter Mitternacht* and to *Hermann Lauscher*. The blending of realism and romanticism in his art reflected their blending in his own life. This close relationship between the circumstances of Hesse's life and the matter and manner of his art was to continue to the end of his career.

UNTERM RAD: A PURGING OF PAINFUL MEMORIES

Unterm Rad, Hesse's second novel, was written during the autumn of 1903 and the winter of 1904. It was published by the *Neue Zürcher Zeitung* in April and May 1904, but did not appear as a book until 1906.[23] This was Hesse'e contribution to the tendentious literature fashionable in German letters at the turn of the century. Like most of the school novels and dramas involved,[24] *Unterm Rad* was a severe indictment of the adult world. Parents, teachers, and pastors are upbraided for their lack of understanding of and sympathy for their wards, and for their smugness, incompetence, and hypocrisy.

23 (Berlin: S. Fischer, 1906), 294 pp.
24 E.g., novels by Emil Strauss (*Freund Hein*, 1902), Robert Musil (*Verwirrungen des Zöglings Törless*, 1906), and Friedrich Huch (*Mao*, 1907), and dramas by Frank Wedekind (*Frühlings Erwachen*, 1891), Arno Holz (*Traumulus*, 1905), and Georg Kaiser (*Rektor Kleist*, 1905).

The young are woefully neglected or systematically victimized. Only the thick-skinned escape relatively unscathed. The sensitive and gifted are brushed aside or ground under.

Hesse's somewhat overstated social comment was more fashionable than original. It was also a means more than an end. Hesse was less intent upon exposing social institutions than upon purging himself of painful memories and venting latent anger. His painful memories and anger related to the first major crisis in his life, to the mental anguish and indignities he suffered from 1891 to 1895. What he had endured over a period of four years in Maulbronn, Bad Boll, Stetten, Cannstatt, and Calw, was ascribed to Hans Giebenrath and his close friend Hermann Heilner, confined to Maulbronn and Calw, and extended only over some sixteen months. Brevity and cohesion obviously necessitated this concentration of his social criticism. The resultant unfavorable reflection upon Maulbronn must have troubled Hesse no little, for his painful school memories were primarily associated with Bad Boll, Stetten, and Cannstatt and not with Maulbronn. For six of his eight months spent in Maulbronn he was actually content with the school and appreciative of his teachers. Indeed, Maulbronn left Hesse with some of the fondest memories of his youth.[25]

Despite much exercising of poetic license, Unterm Rad remained even more closely autobiographical than Peter Camenzind. Like Hesse before him, Hans Giebenrath takes the state examination in Stuttgart in mid-July, spends his seven-week summer vacation in Calw, then proceeds to Maulbronn in September. Here he is put into Hellas, the very dormitory to which Hesse had been assigned. Hesse's friends and teachers, many of their names only slightly disguised, became Giebenrath's friends and teachers. Giebenrath takes the same courses as Hesse had taken and is just as fond of Homer, Latin, and history as Hesse had been. His friendship with Hermann Heilner had its precedent in Hesse's friendship with a much-admired Wilhelm Lang. He also receives the same pommeling at the hands of a fellow student that Hesse had suffered.[26] Giebenrath is the relatively docile and studious lad Hesse had been in Göppingen and had continued to be in Maulbronn until his unexpected truancy. But temperamental and self-assertive Hermann Heilner is also Hesse, particularly the rebel-

25 See "Der Brunnen im Maulbronner Kreuzgang" (1914), Am Weg (Konstanz: Reuss & Itta, 1915), pp. 43–49.
26 For Hesse's friendship with Wilhelm Lang and his scuffle with O. Knapp, see Kindheit und Jugend vor Neunzehnhundert (1966), pp. 148, 171–172, 194–195.

lious Hesse of Bad Boll, Stetten, and Cannstatt. Like precocious Hesse before him, Heilner had also rendered the essay portion of the state examination in verse. He also plays the violin and writes poetry as Hesse had done in Maulbronn, and his French leave was Hesse's. Giebenrath's eventual mental and physical exhaustion and his return to Calw recalled Hesse's own breakdown and withdrawal from Maulbronn. His headmaster is also just as pleased to be rid of a troublesome ward as Hesse's had been. And Giebenrath's subsequent apprenticeship in a machine shop harked back to Hesse's own apprenticeship in the Perrot tower-clock factory.

Hans Giebenrath and Hermann Heilner together tell Hesse's story of 1891 to 1895, just as Peter Camenzind and his close friend Richard together tell Hesse's story of 1901 to 1903. The gauche inhibited misfit Peter is what Hesse was at the time, and affable, carefree, and happy Richard is the man of the world Hesse aspired to become. Richard's death was Hesse's symbolic recognition of the hopelessness of this hope. His aspiration died with Richard, and he, like his Peter, was left to make the best of what he was. Giebenrath, too, is what Hesse was, and Heilner is the person he had to become if he was to make anything of his life. The former's demise and the latter's survival were Hesse's symbolic depiction of an actual change in his life. The hopeless Giebenrath in him died with Hans's suicide and the promising Heilner in him emerged and went his independent way. This double self-projection in the guise of intimate friends was to become a common literary device in Hesse's prose. Of his future couples, the protagonist is almost always what Hesse thought himself to be, and the close friend is almost always what Hesse would have liked to be, or had to become to fulfill himself. The protagonist consistently remains what he is when his friend is merely what he himself would like to be, or becomes what his friend represents when this change is necessary for his self-realization.

In *Peter Camenzind*, Hesse was anxiously intent upon accounting for his immediate mode of life, was not averse to indulging in fancy, and paid too little attention to craft. In *Unterm Rad*, he turned to recollection to unburden himself of unpleasant memories, chose to remain more mindful of fact, and became more conscious of his art. This shift in concern from the present to the past, from imagination to almost pure memory, and from unconstrained to conscious craftsmanship probably accounts for the stylistic differences between the two novels. Less agitated, Hesse was now able to avoid some of the pervasive deadly seriousness and most of the sporadic rhapsodic rhetoric of

Peter Camenzind and to achieve a surprisingly sober narrative manner. Pruning his memories skillfully and curbing his imagination, he managed to attain better technical control of his material. Hesse's narrative in *Peter Camenzind* meanders vaguely and capriciously and ends rather hopelessly. In *Unterm Rad*, it evolves smoothly and predictably, is unmarred by time gaps, uninterrupted by repetition or digression, and concludes convincingly.

Like *Peter Camenzind*, *Unterm Rad* is essentially a psychological study. Hesse's characters continue to have little visibility, and the outside world, though it now assumes a greater physical reality, continues to be little more than an appropriate backdrop for inner drama. This was to remain a distinctive feature of Hesse's narration.

In his earliest prose, Hesse had willingly yielded to the fascination of beautiful language. He began to resist this attraction in *Peter Camenzind*. He all but overcame it in *Unterm Rad*. Hesse now began to practise economy of language and to emphasize ordinary words, more common expressions, unsophisticated figures of speech, and syntactic simplicity. Only one nature setting in *Unterm Rad* was left marred by distended language and overburdened by colorful adjectives (Chapter II), the narrative sections are almost laconic, and Hesse's social comment is as terse as it is caustic.

OTHER PROSE WORKS AND DRAMA

Hesse's literary activity in Basel extended far beyond his books. From late 1899 to August 1904, he must have written close to seventy short stories, verse dramas, brief literary studies, nature sketches, recollections, and travel reports. Some thirty-five of these items were published in the leading newspapers and literary periodicals of Germany, Switzerland, and Austria while Hesse was still in Basel, and fifteen others appeared in later years.[27] Thirteen items were rejected by various publishers in 1902 and 1903, and four other manuscripts were never submitted for publication.[28]

27 See Prose IV: 6a–44; Prose IV: 47, 53, 56, 68a, 80b, 90, 91, 92b, 98, 160, 431, 896, 897, 906, 932.

28 Six of the thirteen manuscripts are now in the Hesse-Nachlass, Marbach a.N. (see Manuscripts X: 10, 17, 21, 25, 26, 27); the remaining seven have not yet been located (see Manuscripts X: 428). The other four manuscripts are also in the Hesse-Nachlass (see Manuscripts X: 7, 13, 429b, 429c).

4

Domesticity

GAIENHOFEN 1904–1912

A ROUSSEAUESQUE EXPERIMENT

Hesse and his wife began their Rousseauesque experiment in Gaienhofen with a happy flurry of activity. The austere half-timbered farmhouse into which they moved had been built during the Thirty Years' War. Animals were still kept in the stable section of the house. The living quarters had been vacant for some time and were in bad repair. The Hesses labored for weeks before their new home became livable. Tranquil domesticity followed. Hesse returned to his writing and sought his diversion in nature, and Maria tended quietly to her household affairs and found her pastime in music and photography.

In March 1905, Ludwig Finckh joined the Hesses in Gaienhofen. The two writers became close neighbors and remained inseparable friends for the next seven years. They spent much of their leisure time swimming, fishing, and scouring the Untersee region in boat and on foot. Their odd dress, playful escapades, and irregular way of life first startled then began to amuse staid Gaienhofen. And with the passing of the years the newcomers gradually became an accepted, if eccentric, part of the local scene.

Hesse's first son, Bruno, was born in December 1905. It soon became apparent to both parents that their simple little farmhouse could not serve their purposes much longer. Although neither was any longer particularly enchanted with Gaienhofen, they decided to buy a plot of ground and to have a house built suited to their needs. In the autumn of 1907, Hesse moved his family into its new home on a knoll overlooking the village and the lake. The area's first villa boasted all the conveniences that the farmhouse had lacked: a bathroom, run-

Farmhouse in Gaienhofen. Hesse lived here from 1904 to 1907.

The house built for Hesse in Gaienhofen in 1907. He lived here until 1912.

ning water, a wine cellar, a darkroom for Maria's photography, ample space for a large family, a maid, and guests, and a huge garden. The Spartan simplicity for which Hesse and Maria had settled in 1904 had obviously lost its appeal. Their second son, Heiner, was born in March 1909.

Hesse's fondest wishes had come true. He had become a fêted writer, had a wife and children, a home and garden, his income was good, and his future looked promising. He enjoyed the "piece of the world and actuality" denied his Peter Camenzind. But happiness was more elusive than success. Wishes come true were dreams shattered. As the novelty of his new way of life in Gaienhofen wore off, Hesse became more and more convinced that he had given up too much for too little. His new responsibilities began to weigh heavily on his shoulders. Life gradually became a drudgery. He was obviously not ready for marriage and least of all for mismarriage. Unfortunately, Hesse could not have chosen a more unlikely partner in life than Maria Bernoulli. She was not only nine years his senior but just as strong-willed, as self-preoccupied, and as set in her ways as he. Neither was suited to the other. He was too temperamental for her, and she too placid and withdrawn for him. He resented her self-sufficiency and she his flightiness. She was too dour and he too moody. She showed too little interest in his writing, and he was too disinterested in family matters. Neither seemed to appreciate the needs of the other and both were hypersensitive to slight. Eventual alienation was inevitable. Gradually they began to go their separate ways. Maria became progressively more preoccupied with her home, children, and music, and Hesse devoted himself to his writing and his garden, cultivated a wide circle of friends, and found an outlet for his increasing restlessness in travel.

But for his association with a small group of students, Hesse had kept to himself in Tübingen. In Basel, he had frequented academic circles. During his years in Gaienhofen he associated primarily with artists. He received numerous visitors, and he himself was a frequent guest. Alexander von Bernus, Bruno Frank, Wilhelm Schäfer, Emil Strauss, Ludwig Thoma, and Stefan Zweig were among the many writers with whom Hesse now became well acquainted.[1] Thomas Mann remained on the edge of this circle. He and Hesse had been introduced to each other by Samuel Fischer in April of 1904 but neither had been taken with the other and each had subsequently kept his

1 Others were Emanuel von Bodman, Paul Ilg, Alfons Paquet, Jacob Schaffner, Wilhelm von Scholz, and Wilhelm Schussen.

Hermann Hesse in Fiesole, 1906.

Hermann Hesse
in Munich, 1907.

distance. A polite correspondence did finally begin early in 1910,[2] however, their close and lasting friendship did not evolve until after Mann's emigration from Nazi Germany in 1933.

While Hesse appreciated his fellow writers, he actually preferred to associate with painters and composers. They were his diversion. When he settled in Gaienhofen, the Untersee area was just beginning to attract painters. Many of these visitors soon became his friends, Otto Blümel, Max Bucherer, Ludwig Renner, and Fritz Widmann, among the first. Hesse added Cuno Amiet, Olaf Gulbransson, Hans Sturzenegger, and Albert Welti, among others, to his circle of painter friends before he left Gaienhofen, and later, in Bern and Montagnola, he extended his circle to include Gunter Böhmer, Alfred Kubin, Louis Moilliet, and Ernst Morgenthaler.[3] It was also in Bern, when he was on the verge of a nervous collapse, that Hesse himself finally took to painting. What began as therapy in 1916 remained a fascinating pastime for the rest of his life.

Music was many things to Hesse and life without it was unthinkable. Chopin was a young aesthete's ecstatic diversion, Mozart was a troubled middle-aged Harry Haller's consolation, and Bach became an old man's reminder of the inherent order and meaningfulness of life. Even as a child, Hesse loved to listen to the church organ. As a youngster he learned to play the violin. Music became a private retreat. In Basel, he was a regular guest at Pastor La Roche's musical evenings. He and Maria Bernoulli were drawn together by their mutual love of music. Soon after he moved to the Untersee, Hesse struck up friendship with Alfred Schlenker, Othmar Schoeck, Volkmar Andreä, and Fritz Brun, musician-composers through whom he was able even in remote Gaienhofen to keep abreast of contemporary music and to maintain contact with the concert world. The composers Ferruccio Busoni, Edwin Fischer, Hermann Suter, and Justus Wetzel joined this coterie of music lovers when Hesse moved back to Switzerland.

Hesse's interest in painting and music and his lifelong association with painters and musicians left a decided imprint upon his writ-

2 See *Briefwechsel: Hermann Hesse–Thomas Mann* (Frankfurt a.M.: Suhrkamp, S. Fischer, 1968), 239 pp.

3 Hesse's painter friends in Gaienhofen also included Gustav Gamper, Bruno Goldschmitt, Ernst Kreidolf, Erich Scheurmann, Rudolf Sieck, Karl Stirner, Robert Weise, and Ernst Würtenberger. After Gaienhofen, Hesse also struck up friendships with Alexandre Blanchet, Karl Hofer, Hans Purrmann, and Niklaus Stoecklin.

Gaienhofen where Hesse lived from 1904 to 1912.

Ludwig Finckh (1876–1964)
and Hermann Hesse
in Gaienhofen.

ings. Many of the major and minor characters of his tales are painters and musicians. Painting and music are common themes in his essays and poetry. From 1918 on, he began to add watercolors to many of his manuscript collections of poems; he also illustrated several of his book and pamphlet publications.[4] Hesse wrote congratulatory and commemorative essays for painters and musicians and dedicated poems to many of them.[5] He contributed appreciative introductions to the publications of his painter friends and attempted librettos for his composer friends.[6] They, in turn, designed jackets and covers for his books, illustrated his texts, and set many of his poems to music.[7]

Despite Hesse's spreading interests, life in Gaienhofen became progressively more trying. He was decidedly disenchanted. His loneliness continued, he resented the loss of his bachelor's freedom, and his retreat was confining. General dissatisfaction and a growing desire to get away from it all became insatiable wanderlust. Hesse began to admire and to envy almost every vagabond who chanced to pass through Gaienhofen. To make a distressing situation as bearable as possible he yielded to his urge to roam. During these years Hesse traveled more than during any other period in his life. Spring walking tours through northern Italy, summer mountain-climbing excursions and winter ski vacations in Switzerland, concert visits to Zürich, Basel, and Bern, lecture invitations to major centers in Germany, Austria, and Switzerland, and regular business trips to Munich followed one another in rapid succession. But his determined efforts to make the best of his circumstances on the Untersee proved futile. His restlessness only increased. It appeared to him that he had no choice

4 For more about Hesse's watercolors, see Joseph Mileck, *Hermann Hesse and His Critics* (Chapel Hill: The University of North Carolina Press, 1958), pp. 95–97, 301.

5 See Prose IV: 188, 250, 597, 631, 648, 829, 836, 858; Letters VIII-B: 85; Poetry V-D: 8, 110, 353, 360, 448, 813, 844 and others.

6 See: Hesse as an Editor VII-B: 6, 7, 14, 22, 23, 28, 33, 34, 35; Prose IV: 648. Hesse wrote librettos for at least four romantic operas while in Gaienhofen. Nothing came of them. *Der verbannte Ehemann* was based upon and written soon after the facetious tale *Anton Schievelbeyn's ohnfreiwillige Reisse nacher Ost-Indien* (January 1905). *Bianca* [1908–09] was probably the text written for but never used by Othmar Schoeck (see "Erinnerungen an Othmar Schoeck" [1935], *Gesammelte Schriften* [1957], Vol. 4, p. 654). *Die Flüchtlinge* [1910] was put to music by Alfred Schlenker. *Romeo [und Julia]* was written for Volkmar Andreä in January–February 1915. Two versions of each of these librettos are in the Hesse-Nachlass, Marbach a.N. (see Manuscripts X: 429/d, 429/f, 429/g, 429/h).

7 Hundreds of Hesse's poems have been set to music by both professionals and amateurs (see Joseph Mileck, *Hermann Hesse and His Critics* [1958], p. 304). Reinhold Pfau's exhaustive *Bibliographie der Hesse-Vertonungen* has not yet been published; it is now in the Schiller-Nationalmuseum, Marbach a.N. For a selected list of *Vertonungen* see *Hermann Hesse: Musik* (Frankfurt a.M.: Suhrkamp, 1976), pp. 233–261.

but to continue to heed what he chose to term "the voice of life," take him wherever it might.[8] This inner urge, the guiding thrust in his life since his childhood crisis, now began to draw him down strange and even lonelier paths.

At the beginning of the century, Hesse had become acquainted with and impressed by Gusto Gräser, a long-haired, shaggy-bearded poet, sculptor, and painter, nature lover, pacifist, and vagabond-outsider, a self-styled social critic and prophet in tunic and sandals. Restless ennui induced him in 1907 to join Gräser and his vegetarians briefly in their retreat on Monte Verità near Ascona. Here he lived naked and alone in a primitive hut, slept on a stone floor wrapped only in a blanket, fasted for a week, and lay buried in earth up to his armpits for a whole day. His body toughened, but he did not find his hoped-for release from physical aches or psychological stress. He returned to Gaienhofen and his family, persuaded that Gräser's literal reversion to nature was not the solution to his own life's problems.[9] In the meantime, Hesse had also become a student of theosophy, had then turned to the religions of India, and after his experiment on Monte Verità he discovered Lao-Tse and Confucius. His growing interest in the Orient, however, only added to his general discontent and restlessness.

Accompanied by the painter Hans Sturzenegger, Hesse left for Ceylon, Sumatra, and Malaya on September 5, 1911, not six weeks after his wife had given birth to their third son, Martin. His trip was both a flight and a quest. Marriage, Gaienhofen, and vulgar, pleasure-seeking materialistic Europe, already severely taken to task in *Peter Camenzind*, had become too much for him. He needed a change of environment, and he vaguely expected to find the spirit of India, a more innocent community of man, and answers to his personal problems. Hesse was impressed by the vast primeval jungles teeming with exotic life, the simple natives in their primitive villages, and the ornate temples. But he was also appalled by the prevalent poverty and filth, and depressed by idolatrized and commercialized Buddhism. Suffering from dysentery and exhausted by the oppressive heat, Hesse returned to Europe without visiting India proper as

8 "Lindenblüte" (1907), *Gesammelte Schriften* (1957), Vol. 3, pp. 758–759.

9 For Hesse's account of his stay on Monte Verità, see "In den Felsen. Notizen eines Naturmenschen," *März*, 2, ii (1908), 51–59. Concerning Gräser and his followers, see A. Grohmann, *Die Vegetarier-Ansiedlung in Ascona und die sogenannten Naturmenschen im Tessin* (Halle: Marhold, 1904), 63 pp.; Jakob Flach, *Ascona* (Zürich/Stuttgart: Classen, 1960), 60 pp.

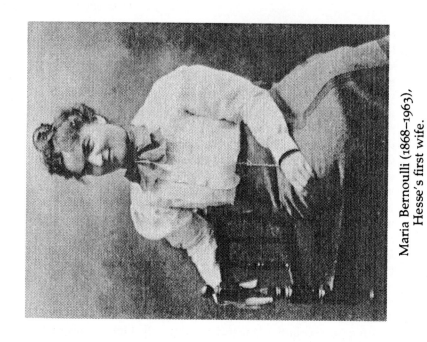

Maria Bernoulli (1868–1963),
Hesse's first wife.

Hermann Hesse in Gaienhofen
about 1909.

he had planned. India's wisdom had eluded him, he had found no cradle paradise, and his personal problems remained unresolved. His trip had been little more than a purely physical experience. It was not until his *Siddhartha* period (1919–1922) that he had his first meaningful spiritual encounter with the Orient.

By the middle of December, Hesse was back with his family and more or less ready to take up where he had left off three months before. But it soon became apparent to him and to Maria that they had exhausted Gaienhofen. Their experiment had lost all meaning and attraction. Both were convinced that a return to the city was not only necessary for their oldest son's schooling but might also be salutary for their crumbling marriage. Since Maria was homesick, they decided to return to Switzerland. On September 5, 1912, they settled in a spacious and elegant seventeenth-century country house near Schloss Wittighofen on the outskirts of Bern. Here they hoped to enjoy both the privacy of the country and the benefits of the city.

SWABIAN TALES

Gaienhofen marked a new chapter in Hesse's life, a new period in his career, and a new phase in his writing. With the book publication of *Peter Camenzind* in 1904, an unknown aspirant suddenly became a celebrity. That same year his maiden novel was awarded the Bauernfeld Prize of Vienna, the first of Hesse's many literary awards. Where previously there had been no real market for his work, demand now quickly threatened to exceed supply. Rejections were infrequent and most of his material was in print within three months of completion. Preceding Gaienhofen, Hesse's art was personal and lyrical; he wrote many musical poems, his prose was highly poetic, and all revolved about his person. With his marriage and increased concern with everyday life, he became decidedly more prose conscious, his concerns became deliberately less subjective, and he began to cultivate a more down-to-earth style. The *Novelle* now became his favorite medium of expression and Gottfried Keller his mentor.

When Hesse wrote *Unterm Rad*, he not only purged himself of painful school recollections but also evoked treasured memories of Calw. Previously, he had concerned himself only sporadically with his birthplace. Now Calw, alias Gerbersau,[10] became a persistent

---

10 The name derived from one of Hesse's favorite fishing spots in Calw, the tanners' meadow along the Nagold. Hesse began to use the pseudonym in his recollections of 1901.

preoccupation and gave his art a fresh impetus in a new direction. This little provincial community was his wonderful world of childhood. He had been familiar with its every nook and cranny and had known almost every youngster, apprentice, tradesman, shopkeeper, and schoolteacher. Here he had been part of a social complex and not yet the lonely outsider he later became. In Gaienhofen, this world—this *Heimat*—transfigured in Hesse's memory, soon became the very stuff of his art: a mythicized community reminiscent of Keller's Seldwyla.

Hesse wrote the earliest of his many recollections of Calw in the spring of 1901.[11] These were written in the first person and recount personal experiences. More recollections followed in 1903 and the first half of 1904.[12] With these, Hesse began to alternate between the first and the third person and to shift from the personal to the observed. His recollections became longer and more fictive. Literature emerged from what had begun as simple recall. This was the situation when Hesse settled in Gaienhofen. For the next eight years he managed to turn this literary possibility to good advantage. A steady flow of *Novellen* kept his coffers replenished, and the ranks of his reading public kept swelling. But by 1912 Hesse had lost most of his interest in Gerbersau and all his enthusiasm for Gaienhofen. He had exhausted a genre, and an experiment in living had failed. He left both behind when he settled in Bern. Calw, however, continued to fascinate Hesse until the end of his life. The Gerbersau *Novellen* had by no means exhausted his memories. After 1912 he reverted to the first person, and his storytelling, with rare exception, again became simple recall.[13]

Literally, Gerbersau was the Calw of Hesse's memory. In his imagination and in his *Novellen*, it became a prototypal everyday world of ordinary human beings. Like Keller, Hesse was an astute observer of his fellow man and had an eye for life's little comedies and paradoxes. He, too, was partial to the fringe elements of society, to vagabonds, fops and old derelicts, young scamps, naïve idealists and ne'er-do-wells, the atypical, the errant, and the lost. His array of misfits and eccentrics is as motley as Keller's and he exposes their foi-

---

11 *Emma Meier, Hotte Hotte Putzpulver, Der Kleine Mohr*, and *Ein Knabenstreich* (see Prose IV: 13a, 13b, 18b, 34).

12 *Karl Eugen Eiselein, Aus Kinderzeiten, Garibaldi*, and *In der alten Sonne* (see Prose IV: 19, 25, 38, 56).

13 It was only when Hesse returned to his *Knulp* in 1913, the second part of which had been written in 1907, that he reverted to his Gerbersau mode of narration.

bles, frailties, and idiosyncrasies with a Kelleresque dash of healthy humor and touch of gentle irony. He may moralize where Keller prefers to leave well enough alone, but like his esteemed predecessor, he rarely condemns.

Not all the recollective *Novellen* that were written in Gaienhofen deal specifically with Gerbersau and its natives. In some, Calw and its surrounding countryside seem only to provide some of the local color, and others hark back to Hesse's schooldays in Maulbronn and Cannstatt. [14] All these tales, however, are closely related in both matter and manner, and together with *Unterm Rad* they represent the Swabian period in Hesse's career, that lull before the storm when he chose to adjust, to look to the past, and to tell traditional stories. Most of these stories were widely published in newspapers and periodicals and favorably received. Fifteen were republished in *Diesseits* (1907), *Nachbarn* (1908), and *Umwege* (1912). Twelve of these fifteen were later revised and published again in two new collections in the early thirties. [15] Revisions were purely stylistic. To achieve greater narrative concentration he simply disposed of a lot of trivial ornamentation. Tediously long introductions and nature descriptions were abbreviated, and intrusive asides, whimsical elaborations, and excessively sentimental passages were omitted. Characters and plot remained untouched.

Diesseits (1907) is the least homogeneous of Hesse's original three collections of tales. *Die Marmorsäge*, sent to the *Westermanns Monatshefte* on March 25, 1904, is a tragic love story vaguely reminiscent of Keller's *Romeo und Julia auf dem Dorfe*. In *Aus Kinderzeiten*, sent to the *Deutsche Rundschau* on April 26, 1904, Hesse recalls a playmate's death. *Heumond*, probably completed in February 1905, and *Der Lateinschüler*, written from January to July 1905, depict touching schoolboy encounters with love. And in *Eine Fussreise im Herbst*, written in the autumn of 1905, a young poet makes a sentimental journey home in the vain hope of recapturing some of the glow of a love long past.

Nachbarn (1908) is Hesse's only collection of tales that deals exclusively with the natives of Gerbersau. In *Karl Eugen Eiselein*, first published in the *Neue Zürcher Zeitung* in December 1903, a supercilious young would-be poet learns humility and becomes a competent and contented grocer. *In der alten Sonne*, completed in March 1904, is

14 See Prose IV: 32, 69, 178, 181; 55, 6β.
15 Six tales were revised from 1928 to 1930 and published in *Diesseits* (1930); six more were then revised and published in *Kleine Welt* (1933).

Hesse's most Kelleresque tale. The poorhouse derelicts of Gerbersau could have been natives of Seldwyla. The antics of Hürlin, a crusty bankrupt manufacturer, and of Heller, a malicious and ingeniously lazy erstwhile ropemaker, are as poignantly humorous as the escapades of Manz and Marti, the pathetic old codgers in *Romeo und Julia auf dem Dorfe*. *Garibaldi*, sent to the *Neue Rundschau* on September 1, 1904, is Hesse's recollection of an odd-looking and mysterious streetsweep who had intrigued him in his youth. In *Walter Kömpff*, published by *Über Land und Meer* in December and January 1907 and 1908, a respected grocer becomes eccentric, finds religion, then hangs himself. And in *Die Verlobung*, published by *März* in September 1908, a timid and meticulously garbed clerk manages successfully to stammer his way politely through life.

Like the tales of *Diesseits* and *Nachbarn*, those of *Umwege* were neither dated nor arranged chronologically. In *Der Weltverbesserer*, written about 1906, a naïve young aesthete and intellectual, easily duped by every culture charlatan and crackpot social reformer, is brought to his senses by his love for a determined and practical-minded young woman. In *Die Heimkehr*, published by the *Neue Rundschau* in April 1909, a retired, prosperous manufacturer returns to his native Gerbersau to settle down, is appalled by the pettiness and maliciousness of the town, and leaves with a maligned widow to start life anew elsewhere. In *Ladidel*, published by *März* in July 1909, an affected dandy, disheartened student of law, and petty thief finds his true calling in the barbershop. *Emil Kolb*, probably written in the spring of 1910, recounts the story of a cobbler's son who dreams of wealth and standing, becomes an embezzler, and ends a jailbird. And in *Pater Matthias*, submitted to the *Neue Rundschau* on December 31, 1910, an errant monk is content to exchange his stifling monastic retreat for a temporary prison cell and a waiting widow.

All the protagonists of Hesse's Swabian *Novellen* are males, and whether young or old, schoolboys, tradesmen, shopkeepers, manufacturers, or intellectuals, these males, with rare exception, are cut from essentially the same cloth. Under their often rough exteriors they are weepy romantics who find comfort in nature and in solitude, self-conscious dreamers who can assume airs, vain introverts, bashful lovers, and timorous dilettantes of life forever going astray or simply drifting with fate. Like Lauscher, Camenzind, and Giebenrath before them, they are inept in their human relationships and have inordinate difficulty finding their places in life. Their fathers are consistently shadowy background personages who do little more than indulge or admonish them. The father figure in Hesse's works never transcended this pale stereotype. The women in the *Novellen* contrast sharply with the men. They are made of sterner stuff, have come to terms with themselves, and are better able to cope with life. Whether mothers or sweethearts, they are mature, strong, patient, practical, prudent, and resolute. They take the initiative in love and are the directive and stabilizing force in the male's life. They continued these roles until 1930. Hesse had idealized woman in *Eine Stunde hinter Mitternacht* (1899). He maternalized her in his Swabian *Novellen*. He was to mythicize her in *Demian* (1917), to glamorize her from *Klein und Wagner* (1919) to *Narziss und Goldmund* (1928), and then to ostracize her in *Das Glasperlenspiel* (1942). Obviously many of Hesse's problems revolved about woman. To trace his radically changing attitude toward woman is to follow the erratic mainstream of his life.

Like *Peter Camenzind* and *Unterm Rad*, the Swabian *Novellen* are personality portraits, with Hesse's characteristic minimal interest in physical attributes and in action. In the earlier of these tales, he accords nature her usual appropriate backdrop role and, as usual, renders her more animate than visible. Natural detail continued to be more enumerative and evocative than organized and depictive, and nature continues primarily to mirror and to accentuate moods. In the later tales, nature almost ceases to be a mood-inducing literary device; nature settings are less common, less burdened by excessive ornamentation and less animated. The relatively sober prose of *Unterm Rad* was continued in the *Novellen*. Hesse's language now approached the idiom of everyday as closely as it ever would in his fiction. He avoids poetic imagery and rhythms as much as possible, and uses adjectives and adverbs sparingly and unobtrusively; he carefully shuns anaphora, parataxis, and alliteration, common devices before *Unterm Rad* and again after the Swabian *Novellen*. His dialogue, once anaemic and stilted, assumes actuality, ranging from restrained parlor conversation to the swaggering jargon of apprentices, and from the timid utterances of first love to blustering verbal exchanges that would have been a credit even to Keller. Like Keller, too, Hesse achieves actuality in his dialogue without recourse to dialect.

The months Hesse had spent in Perrot's tower-clock factory had left him with a wealth of cherished memories—grist for his literary mill. The machine shop and the fortunes of master, journeyman, and apprentice became a favorite theme within the framework of his Swabian tales. During 1902, *Peter Camenzind* had progressed slowly and laboriously. A second major project, a traveling artisan's book (*Hand-*

werksburschenbuch), competed for Hesse's interest and time. In this second novel, he planned to depict the world of the artisan; it was to be the autobiography of a machinist, Peter Bastian, and his recollections of his friend Quorm, a legendary vagabond journeyman. Hesse never realized his plan. Toward the end of 1902, he put aside Bastian's unfinished story (*Peter Bastians Jugend*) in favor of *Peter Camenzind*. Hesse did not return to his Bastian/Quorm theme until early 1904, probably prompted to do so by the machine-shop chapter of *Unterm Rad*. He wrote a brief pear-stealing episode from the life of Quorm in February or March and followed it with an even briefer excerpt from Quorm's diary that autumn.[16] This is all that ever came of Hesse's *Handwerksburschenbuch*.

However, what Hesse had tried in vain to depict in a novel found readier expression in a series of separate tales. In *Aus der Werkstatt*, sent to the *Neue Freie Presse* in November 1904, a testy master and a short-tempered journeyman come to blows. A harassed sensitive machinist slits his wrists and bleeds to death in *Der Schlossergeselle*, sent to *Simplicissimus* in February 1905. *Ein Erfinder*, sent to the *Neue Freie Presse* in May 1905, recalls an inventive journeyman who renounced marriage for his machines. In *Das erste Abenteuer*, published in *Simplicissimus* in March 1906, a naïve apprentice is pleasantly startled by the amorous overtures of an attractive and wealthy young widow. And *Hans Dierlamms Lehrzeit*, completed on February 21, 1907, recounts another callow apprentice's first flirtation and resultant brush with death. Although all these tales were widely published in German, Austrian, and Swiss newspapers and periodicals until the thirties and three continued to appear sporadically until the late fifties, Hesse did not include a single one in any of his many collections of short stories. He was convinced of their documentary worth but also remained aware of their questionable literary value.

In the meantime, Quorm lingered on insistently in Hesse's memory. He gradually became less artisan than artist and more mystic-philosopher than rogue and finally emerged as Knulp, a plebian Don Quixote and a prototype of the post-*Demian* heroes. *Knulp*, the middle chapter of the novel, was written in the latter part of 1907, *Vorfrühling* was finished in May 1913, and *Knulps Ende* was added in mid-1914. What in 1902 was merely to be "a bit of German folklore"[17]

16 See *Prosa aus dem Nachlass* (Frankfurt a.M.: Suhrkamp, 1965), pp. 96–109.
17 "Vorbemerkung des Autors" (Peter Bastians Jugend), *Prosa aus dem Nachlass* (1965), p. 46.

culminated, after many years, in a view of life that evolved but was never abandoned, and in the depiction of a life style that remained close to Hesse's heart to the end.

ITALIANATE TALES

In the middle of May 1895, Hesse wrote Theodor Rümelin that he was as yet hardly acquainted with Italian literature. In a letter written to Dr. Ernst Kapff on July 18, 1895, he professed a great love for Boccaccio, Petrarch, and Tasso, admitting at the same time that he had yet to read these authors.[18] Hesse's allusions to Ariosto and to Dante in *Eine Stunde hinter Mitternacht* suggest that he read *Orlando Furioso* and *Vita Nuova* during his first two years in Tübingen.[19] It was not, however, until his fuller exposure to Jacob Burckhardt in Basel, and under the influence of his frequent host, Italophile Dr. Rudolf Wackernagel, that Hesse began to occupy himself seriously with Italian literature. In keeping with his growing aversion to aestheticism, his interest now quickly shifted from Ariosto's romantic epic and Dante's love poems to the more earthy novelle of Boccaccio, Sacchetti, Bandello, and Firenzuola.[20] These novelle became his models for a series of Italianate tales. Four were sent to various periodicals and newspapers in March and April 1902. All were rejected, none was ever published, and only the first two of these manuscripts are still extant.[21]

It was not until the autumn and winter of 1903 and 1904, while in Calw writing *Unterm Rad*, that Hesse again found time to cultivate his interest in the Italian Renaissance and to explore its novelle for his own purposes, this time to much better advantage. He completed three tales by February 1904, and each appeared in print that same year.[22] *Boccaccio*,[23] a biography narrated in the piquant manner of its subject's novelle, together with an appended brief appreciation of *Il*

18 *Kindheit und Jugend vor Neunzehnhundert* (1966), pp. 463, 506.

19 *Gesammelte Schriften* (1957), Vol. 1, pp. 27, 33, 56.

20 Giovanni Boccaccio (1313–1375), *Il Decamerone*; Franco Sacchetti (1335–1400), *Il Trecentonovelle*; Matteo Bandello (1485–1561), *Novelle*; Agnolo Firenzuola (1493–1543), *Ragionamenti d'amore*.

21 *Der Kleideraustausch, Voluntas pro facto reputatur, Der schlaue Erzähler*, and *Gesandte von Casentino* (see Manuscripts X:21, 26, 428/d, 428/e). The first two manuscripts are in the Hesse-Nachlass Marbach a.N.

22 *Donna Margherita und der Zwerg Philippo, Des Herrn Piero Erzählung von den zwei Küssen*, and *Eine Galgengeschichte aus dem zwölften Jahrhundert* (see Prose IV:33, 29, 35).

23 (Berlin und Leipzig: Schuster & Loeffler, 1904), 75 pp.

Decamerone, was written during the next four weeks. Other interests then diverted Hesse's attention from the Italian Renaissance, and once he was settled in Gaienhofen, the Swabian *Novellen* took precedence over the Italianate tales. Hesse did, however, manage to write two more of these stories in 1907, and the last in 1909.[24] These, too, were published.

Renaissance Italy is the setting for most of these exotic tales. Hesse was also mindful of the matter, the manner, and the emotional content of the Italian novella. Anecdotal accounts of men bold and ladies fair, of jousts and campaigns, of minstrels and dwarfs, mirroring the vicissitudes of fortune and the fortunes of love, are related in a mannered language suggestive of times long past, and range from the farcical to the tragic and from the witty to the erotic.

Literature of the Italian Renaissance remained a lifelong interest for Hesse. What had begun as an inspiration and model in 1902 became a recurrent theme in Hesse's many literary essays, reviews, and editorial work from 1904 to the mid-thirties and continued to be a source of pleasure until the last few years of his life. Boccaccio's *Il Decamerone* remained the center of this interest. Italian literature following the Renaissance held little attraction for Hesse. He was only mildly impressed by Goldoni, Gozzi, Leopardi, and Carducci, and but for d'Annunzio, not at all taken with the twentieth century.

LEGENDS

In April 1904, just one month after completing his *Boccaccio*, Hesse began a monograph on St. Francis of Assisi. A brief biography, some legends, Hesse's translation of *Laudes Creaturarum*, and a survey of St. Francis's impact upon the Italian Renaissance, all written in the simple and appropriately aged language and the fervent manner of traditional hagiography, were submitted for publication on May 13 and were in print soon thereafter.[25] This startling juxtaposition of Boccaccio and St. Francis was not just indicative of a romantic's diverse interests in the past, but was also, more subtly and more significantly, reflective of the disparate inclinations plaguing Hesse, and a veiled anticipation of the sinner-saint protagonist characteristic of

---

24 *Chagrin d'amour, Nach einer alten Chronika*, and *Lydius* (see Prose IV:88, 142, 167).

25 *Franz von Assisi* (Berlin und Leipzig: Schuster & Loeffler, 1904), 84 pp.

his tales from *Klein und Wagner* (1919) to *Narziss und Goldmund* (1928). Hesse's preceding protagonists are commonly rather one-dimensional saintly figures who prefer, as had their author, not to acknowledge the sinner in themselves. It was only when Hesse was prepared in bold self-confrontation to recognize not only the St. Francis but also the latent Boccaccio in himself that his sinner-saint protagonist emerged.

St. Francis meant little or nothing to Hesse before he moved to Basel. A saint was not likely to attract his attention during his rebellious years in school and at home, and in Tübingen his apprenticeship and diverse literary pursuits left him with little time for or interest in religious matters. A favorable passing reference to St. Francis in Lauscher's *Tagebuch* of April 7, 1900, suggests that in Basel such was no longer the case. And Lauscher's subsequent detailed equating of his aestheticism with religion and of the aesthete with the saint (May 13, 1900) clearly shows that Hesse's innate religiosity had again become a foreground concern. Religion and *belles-lettres*, incompatibles for his severely moral parents and conflictive interests for himself, had to be reconciled, and his immediate resolution was simply to equate them. It was upon this equation that Peter Camenzind's paean to St. Francis, and that Hesse's own identification with the saint in his monograph of 1904 are predicated.

For Hesse, St. Francis was a dreamer-poet awed by the beauty of creation, a troubadour-mystic in accord with the self, the world, and God. He was essentially an aesthete-saint, and as such, both a kindred spirit with whom Hesse could readily identify, and an ideal to which he could aspire. Nietzsche's morality had repelled Hesse as much as his aestheticism had attracted him. St. Francis, in contrast, represented a welcome synthesis of Hesse's moral heritage and his aesthetic inclinations. His interest in Nietzsche waned as rapidly as his attraction to St. Francis waxed. Hesse's renewed espousal of Nietzsche during the *Demian* years was intense but again quite brief. St. Francis, on the other hand, never ceased to haunt him.[26] His shadow lingers unmistakably behind the heroes—typically aesthetes, sinners, and potential saints—of most of Hesse's major tales. His conversion, with its joyous discovery of the oneness, the beauty, and

26 Hesse's "Aus der Kindheit des heiligen Franz von Assisi" (1919; see Prose IV:400) and his reviews over the years of works about and translations of St. Francis reflect this lingering interest (see Reviews IV-A:251, 337m, 382, 726; also Prose IV:624a).

the meaningfulness of life, prefigures those luminous moments of grace that the more fortunate of Hesse's post-*Demian* protagonists enjoy and that Hesse himself was to experience sporadically.[27] Indeed, much of Hesse's prose can be put into the category of secularized hagiography.

A special attraction to St. Francis soon became a general attachment to hagiography, just as Boccaccio quickly led to Sacchetti, Bandello, and Firenzuola. Hesse's simultaneous preoccupation with legends and novelle, partner effects of a general romantic interest in times past and places removed and nurtured by a more specific interest in Burckhardt and the Italian Renaissance, continued almost to the end of his years in Gaienhofen. He wrote eight legends from 1904 to 1912.[28] Each is narrated in an elemental, slightly archaic language and in a manner both naïve and pleasantly facetious. Some are located in Egypt and Palestine, others in Italy and England, and all deal with early Christendom, with anchorites given to prayer, fasting, and to self-flagellation in their desert wilds, ascetics tempted by demons, tormented by temptresses, and aided by beneficent angels, virgins dedicated to God, and worldly monks indulging their appetites. These *vitae* were widely published in newspapers until the early thirties, and all but one were included in Hesse's *Fabulierbuch* (1935).

THE MIDDLE AGES

Like the Italian Renaissance, the Middle Ages were for Hesse a veritable treasure trove of fascinating, warmly human tales. Hagiography was but one of the many appealing facets of this literary heritage. Latin literature centered around Cäsarius von Heisterbach's *Dialogus Miraculorum*, and the *Gesta Romanorum* was another. What began in Tübingen as pleasurable reading became an interest in translation, and then spilled over into editorial work. Hesse began to translate Heisterbach as early as 1899, some of the tales translated were published in 1908, and others in 1921. In 1914 he edited J. G. Th. Graesse's translation of the *Gesta Romanorum*, and in 1918 he included

---

27 ". . . a great deal has to be seen, lived, thought, felt, and suffered . . . for one to be able, in a small manifestation of nature, to perceive God, the essence of things, the mystery of life, the linkage of opposites, the great oneness." "Aprilbrief" (1952), *Gesammelte Schriften* (1957), Vol. 7, pp. 817–818.

28 *Der Tod des Bruders Antonio* (1904–1905), *Legende, Legende vom Feldteufel, Legende von den süssen Broten* (1906), *Legende vom verliebten Jüngling, Vater Daniel, Legende von den beiden Sündern* (1907–1909), and *Üble Aufnahme* (1912). See Prose IV:112, 76, 121, 122, 100, 215, 166, 211.

some of its items in his anthology, *Aus dem Mittelalter*. In 1925, selections from the *Dialogus Miraculorum* and the *Gesta Romanorum* were combined in another of Hesse's anthologies, *Geschichten aus dem Mittelalter*, and in 1926 he edited *Märchen und Legenden aus der Gesta Romanorum*.

Hesse's fondness for hagiography and Latin literature soon became a spreading interest in things medieval. He turned his attention to the epics and poetry of Middle High German, discovered the jest books (*Schwankbücher*) and the chapbooks (*Volksbücher*), familiarized himself with medieval art, philosophy, and life. From the beginning of the century to the mid-thirties he rarely missed an opportunity to review a publication about the Middle Ages. At first, the period was for Hesse very much the apotheosized *âge d'or* it had been for his romantic predecessors at the beginning of the nineteenth century. Medieval monastic life then became a particular fascination and eventually a treasured symbol. It was to this symbol that Hesse resorted in both *Narziss und Goldmund* (1928) and *Das Glasperlenspiel* (1942). In Goldmund's waning Middle Ages and Knecht's Middle Ages reborn, monastery and life at large became Hesse's timeless citadel of the spirit in characteristic interplay with the evanescent world of matter.

GERTRUD: AN EXERCISE IN SELF-JUSTIFICATION

The brief narrative and not the novel characterizes Hesse's eight years in Gaienhofen. A restless flow of interests and frequent but brief bursts of inspiration found their readiest expression in his Swabian *Novellen*, his Italianate tales, and in his legends; these publications, in turn, assured him a necessary and steady income. Inclination and need militated against prose of greater breadth. Of the various novels he attempted during these years he was able to complete but one, and this only after two earlier abortive efforts. According to a letter sent to Theodor Heuss on November 17, 1910, *Gertrud* was written in the winter of 1908 and 1909.[29] It was published as a book the following year.[30] This became the least popular of Hesse's novels. He himself was and remained displeased with it. He was not disappointed when it went out of print in 1927 and regretted its republication in 1947.

Gertrud was as much a self-appraisal coupled with an assess-

29 See *Gesammelte Briefe 1895–1921* (Frankfurt a.M.: Suhrkamp, 1973), Vol. 1, p. 184.

30 (München: A. Langen, 1910), 301 pp.

ment of life as *Peter Camenzind* had been. Each of these novels was a response to an urgent psychological need. Narrative in both was essentially an argument supportive of an intended or an already chosen way of life. Camenzind's story was primarily intent upon accounting for the asocial withdrawal briefly courted by Hesse after his futile efforts in Basel to become sociable. And in *Gertrud*, Hesse was eager to account for his adjustment to life in Gaienhofen. Despite Hesse's cultivation in Gaienhofen of a more impersonal mode of storytelling, the inner world of his violinist-composer Kuhn, like Camenzind's, remained intimately personal, and Kuhn's outer world, albeit decidedly more fictive than Camenzind's, continued to draw freely upon the personal for its filler detail. Konrad Lohe, Kuhn's fourth-grade teacher of Greek, was testy Professor Schmid, Hesse's fourth-grade teacher of Greek in Calw. Kuhn begins to play his violin at the age of twelve, Hesse had begun just before his twelfth birthday. At sixteen, music becomes for Kuhn the passion writing had become for Hesse by the same age. Hesse had written his first love poems during his last two years in school, and Kuhn composes his first love songs during his last year in school. Kuhn's parents are as concerned about their son's choice of profession as Hesse's had been about his determination to become a writer. His father is much that Hesse's father was. His interest in butterflies was Hesse's, as was his brief preoccupation with theosophy. Kuhn's opera was undoubtedly Hesse's *Bianca*, the libretto written for but never used by the composer Othmar Schoeck.[31] And Hesse's own troubled marriage served as a model for the mismarriage of Kuhn's close friends Heinrich Muoth and Gertrud.

Kuhn is the person Hesse had been in Basel, the lonely misfit-observer knocking timidly on the door of life, and he becomes Hesse the disenchanted artist-bourgeois of Gaienhofen desperately intent upon making self-acceptance possible and life palatable. To this end, Hesse and his spokesman Kuhn embrace a fatalistic philosophy of life, evolve a Nietzschean theory of art, argue a Schopenhauerian conception of love, and advocate, as had Camenzind, a St. Francis of Assisi adjustment to it all: fate is responsible for the inalterable circumstances of life, loneliness and suffering are the *sine qua non* for creativity, love between man and woman is essentially a flighty, brutal, and painfully demeaning passion, and social love with its commitment to service is man's ultimate solace. These postulates en-

31 See Manuscripts X:429/f.

able Kuhn, as they did Hesse, to relieve himself of all responsibility for his sorry lot, to resign himself to the sweet torment of his calling, to quell the amorous thrusts of life, and to find an acceptable rapport with his fellow humans. Nature and wine, Camenzind's refuge and comfort, were no longer deemed necessary recourses. Author and protagonist managed to achieve, if not an ideal, at least a functional adjustment to the self and to life.

Like *Peter Camenzind*, *Gertrud* is more portrait than story. The meager narrative is again only loosely anchored in space and time, is again fragmented by protracted dialogue, chronic rumination, and epistolary and verse inclusions, and again terminates rather than concludes. However, where Camenzind rambles along for eight chapters, Kuhn organizes and edits his reminiscences. An introductory comment on man and fate is illustrated by seven chapters of recollection and expounded upon in an epilogue. Each chapter of the story proper is centered about a major event or encounter. In the six years between the two tales, Hesse had obviously acquired much better technical control of his material. He had also achieved a more disciplined use of words. Unlike Camenzind, Kuhn does not try to impress or overwhelm his readers with verbiage. His syntactically simple language is not charged by frenetic outbursts, burdened by adjectives and adverbs, or conspicuously adorned by figures of speech. On the other hand, Hesse's physical world continues to lack plasticity. Settings are never particularized and characters are only vaguely visible: interiors are but indistinct incidental situations, communities are just geographical locations, even nature, once rhapsodically extolled, has become part of this skimpy insignificant staging, and people are primarily the impressions they make on Kuhn. All is still an inner drama of emotions and reflections and all again revolves about a protagonist estranged from life. Indeed, Kuhn's story is essentially Camenzind's in variation. Troubled Camenzind and carefree Richard are what Hesse was and what he wished he were. Renunciative Kuhn is again what Hesse was or thought himself to be, and self-indulgent Muoth, what Hesse could but dared not be. In each novel, this double self-projection dominates the scene. The supporting cast is reduced to pale supernumeraries, to stock in trade. Camenzind's Rösi Girtanner has her counterpart in Kuhn's Liddy. The painter Erminia becomes the actress Marion. Brigitte, the one woman who loves and would marry Kuhn, recalls Camenzind's Annunziata Nardini. And beautiful stoical Gertrud, Kuhn's inspiration and ideal incarnate, is but a variation of Camenzind's idealized Elisabeth.

OTHER PROSE WORKS, POETRY, AND FRAGMENTS

Hesse's prose in Gaienhofen went far beyond his Swabian *Novellen*, Italianate tales, his legends, and his *Gertrud*. The literary essays, diary-like recollections, ruminations, short stories, nature sketches, and travel reports that in Basel were frequently submitted to leading newspapers and periodicals but often rejected, were now regularly contributed and rarely refused. Many of these stray items were later included in various collections of miscellany; about thirty-five, however, have yet to appear in book form.

Prose was obviously Hesse's favorite medium of expression in Gaienhofen. His continued unsuccessful flirtation with the theater left only three inconsequential librettos and a fragment verse drama in its wake. None of these still extant manuscripts was ever published.[32]

Romantic poetry continued to lie close to Hesse's heart but now that he had found a niche in life, it no longer flowed as freely as it had in Tübingen and Basel. From 1895 to 1902 he had written some 380 poems. From the summer of 1902 to the end of 1911 he wrote only 185 or so;[33] about 24 of these poems have yet to be printed.

Like his romantic antecedents, Hesse left many unfinished works. It all began with his vague plans for a novel while still in Calw in the spring of 1895. In Basel, three major tales came to grief in rapid succession. What promised at the beginning of the century to be Hesse's first novel ended as an untitled and still unpublished two-chapter fragment.[34] *Julius Abdereggs erste und zweite Kindheit*, begun enthusiastically soon after the publication of *Hermann Lauscher*, faltered before the end of 1901. The Bastian/Quorm tale suffered a similar fate in 1902. In Gaienhofen, following *Peter Camenzind* (1903) and *Unterm Rad* (1904), Hesse's novels again ran into difficulties. Two fragment versions of *Gertrud*, written in the winters of 1906–1907 and 1907–1908 respectively, preceded the final version of 1909. Inadequacy more than flagging interest left *Berthold* a three-chapter fragment in 1907. Hesse was simply not equal to the narrative demands of a ranging tale of

32 See Manuscripts X:429.

33 Fifteen of these were added to the second edition of *Gedichte* (1906), fifty-five others appeared in *Unterwegs* (München: Georg Müller, 1911), 58 pp.; eleven became part of *Aus Indien* (Berlin: S. Fischer, 1913), 198 pp.; sixteen more were included in *Musik des Einsamen* (Heilbronn: E. Salzer, 1915), 84 pp.; and sixty-four others were published only in newspapers and periodicals.

34 See Manuscripts X:7.

adventure within the framework of the Thirty Years' War. Broad literary canvases were never to be his forte. *Aufzeichnungen eines Herrn im Sanatorium*, another novel, faltered and failed in 1909 or 1910. *In einer kleinen Stadt*, yet another unfinished novel and one more of Hesse's depictions of Gerbersau, probably also belongs to the period between *Gertrud* (1909) and *Rosshalde* (1913).

More fragment novels were to follow in Bern and in Montagnola. *Das Haus der Träume* was begun in 1914. It was interrupted by the outbreak of the First World War, quickly lost most of its initial attraction, and was never resumed. *Aus Martins Tagebuch* was left a torso in 1918, and *Einkehr* was probably broken off just before Hesse left for Ticino in the spring of 1919. *Aus dem Tagebuch eines Wüstlings*, a portent of things to come in *Der Steppenwolf*, terminated abruptly in February 1922 with Hesse's initial brief creative urge, and *Aus dem Leben eines Zauberers*, an intended fantastic novel, only got as far as its autobiographical introductory *Kindheit des Zauberers* of 1923. Content would suggest that *Rembold* was written in Montagnola soon after *Kurgast* (1923). In the remaining years of his life, Hesse selected his literary ventures much less impulsively and pursued them much more tenaciously. Only two more major tales were to remain fragments: two attempts notwithstanding, the eighteenth-century *Lebenslauf* of 1934 never was finished and never did become part of *Das Glasperlenspiel*; and *Bericht aus Normalien*, a social satire and ironic self-depiction, petered out with its straggly introduction of 1948.

A miscellany of abortive efforts accompanied these major fragments. *Deutsche Romantik*, undertaken in the spring of 1899, progressed unfavorably and was soon abandoned. An untitled verse drama, begun in 1904, was left a two-act fragment in 1907 or 1908,[35] and *Heimkehr*, Hesse's sole prose drama, never got beyond its first act in January of 1919. Only a series of plans and tentative introductions attest to Hesse's ambitious editorial undertaking of 1924 and 1925.[36] Many untitled fragmentary literary comments and plans, stray bits of stories, strands of recollection, brief and lengthy accounts of dreams, and numerous poetry fragments have also survived; and with Hesse's lasting penchant for self-chronicling, diary and autobiographical fragments were inevitable.[37]

35 See Manuscripts X:429/i.
36 See Manuscripts X:424.
37 See Manuscripts X:43, 50, 110, 112, 153, 175, 186, 201a, 202, 252, 274a, 294, 397, 426, 427; X-A:5/1–5/3, 5a/4, 7/22, 7/23; X-B:11a/2, 11a/9, 11a/23, 11a/25; Poetry V-D:578, 885a–1190.

TRANSLATIONS

In December 1891, while still studying in Göppingen, Hesse proudly informed his parents that he was translating a segment of Ovid's *Metamorphoses* into German hexameters and was enjoying it.[38] What began as a schoolboy exercise remained a sporadic pastime for three decades. In 1899, Hesse translated a goodly portion of Heister-bach's *Dialogus Miraculorum*. Early in 1902 he wrote *Der Kleidertausch, Voluntas pro facto reputatur, Der schlaue Erzähler,* and *Gesandte von Casentino*, all something between translations and adaptations of tales by Bandello and Sacchetti. He translated Verlaine's *Mon rêve familier* in November 1901, and St. Francis of Assisi's *Laudes Creaturarum* in the spring of 1904. A short tale (*Eifersucht*) by Hugues de Roux followed in 1910, a novella (*Toto*) by Gabriele d'Annunzio in the spring of 1912, and a travel sketch (*Kongo*) by P. Isnard later that same year. He wrote two free renditions of Shakespeare's *Romeo and Juliet* at the beginning of 1915, translated an essay (*Die einsamen Liebenden*) by Jean B. Lurçat in the autumn of 1919, and a fable (*Die Blinden*) by Voltaire in June 1922. Save for Ovid, the Italianate tales, and Shakespeare, each of these translations was published.

HESSE AS A REVIEWER AND EDITOR

Despite family, active outdoor life, travels, burdensome correspondence, periodic depression, and his chronic eye ailment, Hesse managed to add two other dimensions to his literary activities in Gaienhofen. From January 1900 to April 1901, he contributed an occasional brief review to the *Allgemeine Schweizer Zeitung*. For the next two and a half years he was too engrossed with his writing proper to pursue this budding interest, but in December 1903 he began to review books for the *Neue Zürcher Zeitung* and he continued to do so, albeit irregularly, until the end of his life. In September 1904, he also became a staff reviewer for *Die Propyläen* (Beilage zur *Münchener Zeitung*); his contributions appeared here regularly from the autumn of 1904 until 1917, then again from 1930 to 1934. More reviews were published in *Die Rheinlande* from October 1904 to 1909 and in *Der Schwabenspiegel* (Wochenschrift der *Württemberger Zeitung*) from 1909 to 1933, and from 1904 to 1912 a scattering appeared in at least eleven other newspapers and periodicals. Many of Hesse's most impressive

---

38 See *Kindheit und Jugend vor Neunzehnhundert* (1966), p. 145.

reviews were written for the *Neue Rundschau* from 1909 to 1936 and his greatest concentration of brief reports was published in *März* from the beginning of 1907 to the end of 1917. In an introduction to his review essays for *Die Propyläen*, Hesse clearly charted the course he expected to follow as a literary critic. He intended to draw attention only to those new publications that impressed him favorably and that suggested some promise of survival. He had no desire to become a traditional professional reviewer taking issue with authors and dispensing literary verities. He saw little purpose in drawing attention to influences, in categorizing writers, or in exposing their flaws. His would be the role of a sympathetic intermediary, intent upon guiding his readers by according worthy books the attention they merited. He would characterize works succinctly and comment upon the unique in both substance and form, avoiding all literary bickering and verbal niceties.[39] Hesse reiterated this statement of policy many times in the decades to follow; as a critic, he rarely deviated from it.

Hesse's initial emphasis upon contemporary German literature quickly became a general interest in European literature past and present, and this, in turn, ended in a budding preoccupation with world literature even before he left for Bern. His initial primary interest in literary matters also spread rapidly to a general interest in art and religion, and after Gaienhofen, to a concern with politics, psychology, philosophy, history, and biography. His hundreds of reviews, some detailed and others very brief, afford an excellent survey of German letters with particular emphasis upon the twentieth century, a good insight into world literature, and a revealing focus upon the culture of both the Occident and the Orient. These reviews also reveal a well-read autodidact, his panorama of shifting interests, and his changing attitudes and beliefs. The cultural impact of these many reviews published over a period of sixty-three years in more than fifty of the better-known periodicals and newspapers of German-speaking Europe, must have been considerable.

Reviewing was for Hesse a necessity, an obligation, and a diversion. It meant added income, was a public service, and it helped to allay the restlessness and the agony of the lulls in his creativity. He turned to editorial work for these same personal and cultural reasons. From the beginning, these secondary involvements were filler-

---

39 "Über neuere Erzählungsliteratur. Ein Vorwort zu künftigen literarischen Monatsberichten," *Die Propyläen*, 1 (September 16, 1904), 771–772.

commitments consigned primarily to the troubled lulls between major works.

In May 1906, Albert Langen managed to persuade Hesse to join him, Kurt Aram, and Ludwig Thoma in founding a new literary-political periodical. This was Hesse's first editorial undertaking. Bimonthly *März* was to be a positive counterpart to *Simplicissimus*. Hesse served as a co-editor from its first issue in January 1907 until flagging interest and the growing demands of his art induced him to resign toward the end of 1912. He continued, however, to contribute his usual flow of reviews until the end of 1917. Though in complete agreement with the periodical's crusade against the despotism of Wilhelm II, the militarism of the empire, and against Prussia's junkerdom, Hesse chose to confine his activities to its literary sections. He was not yet prepared to become embroiled in the social and political problems of his day.

5

War and Awakening

BERN 1912–1919

A PSYCHOLOGICAL CRISIS

Hesse's trip to the Orient was largely a physical ordeal and not the enlightening spiritual experience he hoped it might be. His move to Bern in September 1912 in the hope of resolving some of his problems proved to be an equally abortive venture, merely another physical response to a persistent psychic malaise. The city was musically alive, its environs were attractive, and Hesse appreciated the aristocratic reserve of the Bernese, but the novelty of change quickly wore thin and life resumed its unhappy course.

The birth of Martin Hesse in July 1911 did more to extend than to close the growing rift between the parents. Subsequent events in Bern soon widened this rift beyond repair. In March 1914, an ill-advised inoculation for diphtheria left Martin severely ill. His slow convalescence and extreme irritability were too trying for both Hesse and his wife. To ease the added tensions, Martin was put into a foster home in Kirchdorf; he grew up there.[1] The outbreak of the First World War left an already unsettled Hesse badly shaken. He soon found himself at odds with popular sentiment and maligned by militarists and pacifists alike. Maria's increasingly bizarre behavior became cause for concern. The death of his father in March 1916 added an acute sense of guilt to his growing despair. Physically and emotionally exhausted, he now sought relief in psychoanalysis. A traditional rest cure in Locarno and Brunnen early in 1916 had been of

---

[1] Martin lived with Johanna and Alice Ringier from 1914 until 1927 when he began his apprenticeship in an architectural firm in Thun. His interest then shifted to photography. He plied his new profession in Bern until his death in October 1968.

The house on Melchenbühlweg, Bern. Hesse lived here from 1912 to 1919.

Hermann Hesse, his son Heiner, and his wife Maria in the garden of their home on Melchenbühlweg, Bern.

little avail. Toward the end of April, Hesse left for Sonnmatt, a private clinic near Lucerne. Here he was referred to J. B. Lang, an analyst who had been one of C. G. Jung's students. He was able to return to Bern at the end of May after some electrotherapy and but twelve three-hour analytical sessions. Sixty more visits to Lucerne took place from June 1916 to November 1917.[2] Some of Hesse's anxieties were dispelled, he learned to cope more ably with his frustrations, and he slowly emerged from his deep depression.

Hesse's personal encounter with psychoanalysis had a profound effect upon his life and art. It provided him with the incentive necessary to appraise himself and his adjustment to life, and afforded him the insights needed to begin his long inward path (*Weg nach Innen*), that tortuous road that he hoped would lead to self-knowledge and ultimately to greater self-realization. It also gave him the strength to tear up his roots and to begin all over again when everything he had once cherished crumbled about him. Previous self-quest had always terminated in self-evasion. Like his Lauscher, Camenzind, and Kuhn, Hesse had been less inclined to seek, than first to justify his aestheticism, then to fix his attention and hopes upon nature, and subsequently to lend approbation to his passive adjustment to life. Previously he had not wanted to know enough and had been inclined not to act. Now he was determined to know and was prepared for drastic action. Introspection, once primarily a blissful indulgence, soon became a merciless self-analysis.

WATERCOLORS

Hesse first turned to painting in the summer of 1916, when writing became distasteful to him and music unbearable. A modest beginning in Bern became a passion later in Montagnola. He painted hundreds of little watercolors in the summer of 1919 and hundreds more during the immediately following summers. Many of these were exhibited in Basel in January 1920, some that March in Lugano, and others in Winterthur in January 1922, and even the *Allgemeines*

2 Josef Bernhard Lang (1883–1945) became and remained a close friend until his death. He was gifted, but was also a troubled eccentric whose promising career was never realized. When things personal and professional went from bad to worse over the years, he gradually became more and more dependent upon Hesse. By the forties, the initial roles in their friendship were completely reversed. Most of Hesse's letters and postcards to Lang are in the possession of Mrs. Alfred Bolliger, Hans Huber Strasse 12, Zürich. Ninety-five unpublished letters written by Lang to Hesse from 1918 to 1944 are in the Hesse-Nachlass, Marbach a.N.

Lexikon der bildenden Künstler (Leipzig) took note of them in 1923. Hesse became so fascinated by this pastime that he actually began to flirt with the notion that he might some day put aside his writing in favor of painting. This remained wishful thinking, but Hesse's new interest remained a lifetime diversion.

Hesse's watercolors are widely dispersed. Many were used to illustrate the numerous manuscript collections of poems he sold or gave away as presents from 1918 on; many were sent to friends as greetings, and some were sold to art dealers; portfolios of them were left to his sons; and a large brimming carton accompanied the Hesse-Nachlass to Marbach am Neckar. Relatively few of these paintings have been reproduced.[3]

Hesse was a writer by compulsion and a painter by choice. Writing was blissful agony, painting unadulterated joy. His pen explored life's shadows, his brush exposed its lively colors. One medium suggests a man at odds with himself and the world, the other, a man content and grateful. Hesse's paintings are for the most part pastoral scenes: peacefully clustered houses either graphically detailed or skimpily outlined, mountain landscapes delicately blurred in contour, rolling hills and scattered dwellings surrealistic in their distortions, and placid lakes, luxuriant gardens, graceful trees, and wayside chapels, all depicted in a disarmingly naïve manner. Rural Ticino was transfigured by poetic license and a concert of animated pastel colors.

THE FIRST WORLD WAR AND POLITICS

When the First World War broke out in the summer of 1914, Hesse found himself in a quandary. He was nationalistic enough to sympathize with his fellow Germans, but he abhorred violence. Political causes had never appealed to him, but now he could not in good conscience continue to remain uninvolved. In late August he reported to the German consulate in Bern and volunteered for military service. He was rejected because of his age, poor eyesight, and family. In

3 See: *Elf Aquarelle aus dem Tessin* (München: O. C. Recht, 1921), *Aquarelle aus dem Tessin: Zwölf farbige Bildtafeln* (Baden-Baden: W. Klein, 1955). *Mit Hermann Hesse durch das Jahr* (Frankfurt a.M.: Suhrkamp, 1976), *Zum Hermann-Hesse-Jahr 1977: Ein Kalender mit zwölf Aquarellen* (Frankfurt a.M.: Suhrkamp, 1976), and *Der Maler Hermann Hesse* (Frankfurt a.M.: Suhrkamp, 1977). Some paintings were used to illustrate Hesse's own publications, others to illustrate the publications of his friends, and still others have appeared in newspapers, periodicals, and sundry publications. For more details see Joseph Mileck, *Hermann Hesse and His Critics* (1958), p. 301.

Hermann Hesse about 1916.

early October he tried to enlist in Stuttgart but was again turned
down. Since it was unlikely that he would ever be conscripted, Hesse
placed himself at the disposal of the Germany embassy in Bern for
civilian service. In mid-1915 he was assigned to a department in Bern
engaged in caring for German prisoners of war (*Kriegsgefangenenfürsorge*). Here he and Professor Richard Woltereck organized a book-
distributing center (*Bücherzentrale für deutsche Kriegsgefangene*). For
three and a half years Hesse solicited books, and funds with which to
buy books, for the many German prisoners of war in the Allied countries and for internees in Switzerland. The enterprise was remarkably
successful.[4] To extend this service, Hesse helped to found a weekly in
1915 and a Sunday supplement in 1916; he served as co-editor of the
former until the beginning of 1919 and of the latter until the end
of 1917.[5] These slim journals were neither intent upon news nor concerned with political matters. Their scattering of poems, short stories,
and anecdotes was primarily to remind the prisoners of war that they
were not forgotten and to afford them some diversion. It was also
expressly for this purpose that Hesse together with Woltereck edited
two series of books in 1918 to 1919.[6]

Hesse's own publications during the first year of the war gave the
Germans just as little reason for offense as his practical contribution to
their cause. He was an ardent advocate of peace and he disparaged
war, but he also made amply clear that his sympathies lay with Germany. Only rabid militarists could possibly take issue with Hesse's
war poems. Twenty-five of his twenty-seven poems dealing specifically with the war were written from August 1914 to May 1915, and
the remaining two in 1917.[7] Most of these are personal expressions of
anxiety and of empathy, prayers for peace and utterances of hope.
Some mirror a peculiar ambiguity of mild acclaim and disclaim.
Others equate warfare with life; the heroism and the spirit of sacrifice
that ensure war its victory are also the vital factors in the battle of life.

---

4 From January 1916 to November 1918 alone, almost half a million volumes were
sent to internment camps in France, Hesse's main area of responsibility. For this ser-
vice, Hesse was awarded "the Red Cross Medal third class—Upon the order of his
Majesty the King" (presumably Wilhelm II of Württemberg).
    5 *Aus der Heimat. Sonntagsblätter für die deutschen Kriegsgefangenen und Internierten*.
Its first and only issue appeared in October 1915. It was replaced in January 1916 by *Der
Sonntagsbote für die deutschen Kriegsgefangenen*. A supplement, the *Deutsche Internierten-
Zeitung*, was added that July. See Hesse as an Editor VII-C:2, 3, 4.
    6 The *Bücherei für deutsche Kriegsgefangene* and the *Heimatbücher für deutsche
Kriegsgefangene*. See Hesse as an Editor VII-A: 14, 15.
    7 More than half of these poems are included in the *Gesammelte Schriften* (1957).

Germany itself is never taken to task and, in at least two instances, the sentiment of the traditional German war-poem is unmistakable.[8] Some of these poems were included in most of the major anthologies of war poetry published in Germany in 1914 and 1915.[9] Hesse wrote no war stories, but in 1914 and 1915 he did review a few war novels that he considered well worth reading. These reviews, too, gave his compatriots no cause to question his patriotism. Martin Lang's *Feldgrau*, the memoirs of a young soldier on the western front, was permeated by a touching love of homeland and its people.[10] Albert Leopold's *Im Schützengraben*, an account of trench warfare in Poland, was the edifying work of a true soldier.[11] In each of these cases, relatively innocuous patriotic sentiment was sympathetically appraised. But so too, upon occasion, were books that were decidedly chauvinistic. The fatherland could have received no more beautiful gift than Max Scheler's *Der Genius des Krieges und der deutsche Krieg*, an aggressive, nationalistic affirmation of a war against English materialism and imperialism.[12] And Eduard Wechssler's *Die Franzosen und wir*, a less than impartial survey of French opinion, corroborated France's extreme nationalism and its youth's general hatred of Germans.[13] No one could, and no one did, take issue with any of these, or with either of the only two other of Hesse's reviews of war literature.[14]

Nor did any of the several essays in which Hesse commented upon current events during the first year of the war occasion any untoward reactions. In fact, the ambiguity of his political posture precluded any decided response, whether of approval or of disapproval. *O Freunde, nicht diese Töne*, written in September 1914 and published in the *Neue Zürcher Zeitung* on November 3, typifies this ambiguity. Warfare is deprecated, and as usual, peace on earth and goodwill among men are espoused. Hesse's main argument, however, was di-

8 *An den Kaiser* (Prolog zur Kaiserfeier der deutschen Kolonie in Bern, [January] 1915) and *Den Daheimgebliebenen*, written in February 1915 (Poetry V-D:805, 710).

9 E.g.: *Deutsche Dichter-Kriegsgabe*, ed. Leopold Klotz (Gotha: F. A. Perthes, 1914), 166 pp.; *1914, Der deutsche Krieg im deutschen Gedicht*, ed. Julius Bab (Berlin: Morawe & Scheffelt, 1915), Vol. 1, 286 pp.

10 *März*, 9, i (March 27, 1915), 286–287.

11 *Neue Zürcher Zeitung*, October 17, 1915, No. 1386.

12 *März*, 9, ii (May 22, 1915), 167–168.

13 *März*, 9, iv (December 31, 1915), 260.

14 Max Ludwig's *Die Sieger*, *Neue Zürcher Zeitung*, August 24, 1914, No. 1253; Erich Everth's *Von der Seele des Soldaten im Felde*, *Neue Zürcher Zeitung*, December 12, 1915, No. 1697.

rected less against war itself than against intellectuals and artists who chose to enter the fray, whether in enthusiastic participation or pleading protest. The former could only extend international enmity from politics into the realms of thought and art, and the supplications of the latter were futile. Intellectuals and artists would do better to look to themselves, to continue to nurture their humane supranational values, and to leave war to the politicians. Only their strict neutrality could prepare the way for eventual reconciliation and a better Europe. In spite of this plea for neutrality and internationalism, Hesse was careful to assure Germans that he was German, that he was in sympathy with Germany's cause, and that he was not one to repudiate his fatherland in its need.

In *Tagebuchblatt*, sent to *Zeit-Echo* (Munich) on November 23, 1914, and published soon thereafter, Hesse tried to account for this ambiguous stance. He did not belong to those whose commitment to the war was a spontaneous untroubled response to duty, or to those whose involvement was based on sheer delight in violence and destruction, but to the unsettled and wayward, to those who abhorred the war yet were thrilled by its German victories. His head and heart were obviously not in accord and Hesse was not averse to admitting as much. Nor was he about to assume a less ambiguous posture. *Kriegslektüre*, first published in *Die Zeit* (Vienna) on March 14, 1915, was by and large an extension of the split sentiment of *O Freunde, nicht diese Töne*. The war was a horror but also a humanizing communal experience, a coalescent, and an equalizer. It wreaked havoc but it could also usher in a better world. Again, Hesse both disclaimed and acclaimed war and, as usual, he took care to laud the German soldier fighting for the fatherland.

In each of these first three essays, Hesse carefully avoided extended comment on the war and prudently refrained from apology and incrimination. His introduction for *Zum Sieg* (Stuttgart, 1915), a rankly chauvinistic pamphlet for the battlefront, marked an unexpected departure from this discretion. War as such was still reprehensible, but Germany's war against the Allies now became a righteous crusade against money-minded powers intent upon world domination. England and France had to be vanquished. Germany would find her rightful place in the sun.[15] It was her destiny to prepare the way

---

15 "We no longer want to be that poor ideal Germany that had many poets and thinkers but no money and no power and no voice in world affairs. We intend to be part of the action in the future. . . ." "Einführung," *Zum Sieg: Ein Brevier für den Feldzug* (Stuttgart: Die Lese, 1915), p. 7.

for a world in which human concerns would replace business interests and hate would yield to love. This apologia must have dispelled any lingering doubts about Hesse's persuasion. His identification with Germany in *O Freunde, nicht diese Töne*, had obviously been no idle protestation.

All this was quickly forgotten or went unheeded when on September 15, 1915 the *Leipziger Neueste Nachrichten* published an article in which Hesse's patriotism was called to account, his talent questioned, and his person insulted.[16] This unexpected public censure was occasioned by a comparatively innocuous remark that Hesse had chanced to make in a letter to the Danish author and critic Sven Lange and which the latter had chosen, without permission, to include in an article published in *Politiken* (Copenhagen) on September 9, 1915. Hesse's response, an open letter sent to the editor of *Der Kunstwart* (Dresden) on October 23, was admirably contained, indeed, almost apologetic. He had been misunderstood. The first half of his remark to Lange was meant to be ironic ("I have not succeeded in adjusting to the war literarily . . ."), and the second half was complimentary (". . . it is my hope that Germany may in the future impress the world not only with its weapons but above all in the arts of peace and in the practice of a supranational humanity"). Protest notwithstanding, the seeds of suspicion were sown and more was soon to come.

Alerted by the *Leipziger Neueste Nachrichten*, superpatriots began to scrutinize Hesse's every subsequent publication, determined to take even better advantage of their next opportunity to press their case against him. The occasion presented itself when Hesse's *Wieder in Deutschland* (mailed on October 3) appeared in the *Neue Zürcher Zeitung* on October 10, 1915. In the latter part of September he had made a trip to Stuttgart and environs to tend to matters relating to the *Kriegsgefangenenfürsorge* and had recorded his impressions upon his return to Bern. He had also included what he assumed were rather harmless prefatory remarks:

> I had not been home in Germany for a long while. Outer circumstances had first held me back, and then, when the war went on, I too became more liable for military service and was afraid that I would not be allowed back after a visit. By the time I too was called up for service I had long previously accepted a job in connection with the prisoners of war and in association with various

16 Hesse was termed "internally poverty-stricken and stunted"; his critic assured him "that he was not fit to be one of the architects of the cathedral of future German art."

Swiss organizations, and was not compelled to exchange this more attractive and more peaceful work for military service. This vague unguarded preamble was Hesse's undoing. Disparagement now turned to rank invective. In *Ein deutscher Dichter* published in the *Kölner Tageblatt* on October 24, an author once widely esteemed became a smirking draft-evader, a cunning coward, and a renegade, too concerned about the eventual reconciliation of the combatant nations and too little troubled by his fatherland's ordeal.[17] This anonymous diatribe was quickly reprinted and quoted in newspapers throughout Germany. Almost overnight and for all too little reason, Hesse found himself pilloried far and wide. His detractor had seized upon his unfortunate introductory remarks and had chosen to ignore the body of his article. Hesse had actually been deeply impressed by the morale, the general deportment, and the solemn dedication of the Germans. So much so, indeed, that he would willingly have donned a uniform had he been requested to do so, despite his continued compunctions about warfare.[18]

Hesse was quick to defend himself. In his *In eigener Sache*, published by the *Neue Zürcher Zeitung* on November 2, he sharply reminded his irresponsible critic that he had in fact volunteered for military service but had not been accepted, that he was engaged in wartime work with the army's express approval, and that his greater interest in peace than in war was in accord with the Kaiser's own sentiment. Hesse's protestations were as ineffectual as the few voices raised in his defense.[19] Fellow artists repudiated him, professors rep-

17 "Every decent German has to blush with shame when he hears that a hitherto 'Knight of the Spirit' is boasting about his shirking of duty and sly cowardice, and is actually making fun of the fact that he has succeeded at this critical time in snapping his fingers at his fatherland and its laws. . . . Nowhere does Hesse utter a word of sympathy and concern for his fatherland . . . glorious Swabia and its people can no longer be proud of such a son." "Ein deutscher Dichter," *Kölner Tageblatt*, October 24, 1915, No. 610.

18 "In short, I immediately find confirmed what so many have told me: Germany has changed, Germany is calmer, more dignified, more serious, better behaved. . . . I listen and bow before the power of this noble seriousness abashed and deeply moved. . . . Were I to be taken away tonight, I would certainly ask as ever that I not be required to kill, would as ever look upon rifle and bayonette as questionable and evil inventions, but I would go along, and in the pull of fate and storm of necessity, put aside completely all interest in my own lot." "Wieder in Deutschland," *Neue Zürcher Zeitung*, October 10, 1915, No. 1348.

19 Among the few who vigorously defended Hesse and his patriotism were Theodor Heuss, future *Bundespräsident* ("Hermann Hesse der *vaterlandslose Gesell*," *Neckar-Zeitung* [Heilbronn], November 1, 1915, No. 255), and Conrad Haussmann, prominent liberal statesman in Swabia ("Hermann Hesse," *Der Beobachter* [Stuttgart], November 2, 1915).

rimanded him, journalists denounced him, bookdealers complacently informed him that writers of his political views no longer existed for them, and many old friends, revelling in their newfound patriotism, suddenly discovered an undesirable degenerate in their midst.[20] Hesse had become a traitor to the cause, and as such, was unceremoniously relegated to the black list of dissenters, the enemies of the fatherland, defeatists, and alarmists.[21]

Though he was extremely perturbed by this unwarranted calumny, Hesse's loyalty to Germany remained unaffected. His work in Bern continued uninterrupted, as did his correspondence with German soldiers on the battlefront, and his efforts to improve Germany's image in the neutral countries. He continued to speak warmly of his fatherland, to laud its soldiers, and to believe that Germany was rightfully seeking its place in the community of nations.[22] And as late as December 9, 1915, he was still calmly able to inform a Norwegian journalist—whom he had just disabused of his notion that only the Germans were resorting to offensive propaganda—that Germany would come to the fore militarily and economically just as surely as she had done culturally.[23] Hesse's loyalty to, and faith in, Germany were still unshaken.

In the meantime, misunderstanding and ill will began to spread on yet another front. Hesse was not a militarist but he was also too aware of history and too much an individualist to become a real pacifist. War was a long-standing part of life and was not about to be banished from it. Pacifists were as likely to achieve peace on earth as a congress of scientists was likely to discover the philosopher's stone. In this regard, Hesse had much more faith in the exceptional indi-

20 "Kurzgefasster Lebenslauf" (1924), *Gesammelte Schriften* (1957), Vol. 4, pp. 476–477. See also Friedrich Epping, "Hermann Hesse und der Krieg," *Hamburgischer Correspondent*, 38, No. 24 (November 21, 1915).

21 "Weltgeschichte" (1918), *Gesammelte Schriften* (1957), Vol. 7, p. 123.

22 See "Wir und die Feldgrauen an der Front. Brief ins Feld" (December 7), *Neues Tagblatt* (Stuttgart), Weihnachten 1915.

23 In an article published in *Tidens Tegn* (Christiania, autumn 1915), Bernt Lie took Germany to task for inundating Norway with insipid propaganda. Hesse upbraided Lie for his lack of impartiality ("Offener Brief an Bernt Lie" [end of October], *Frankfurter Zeitung*, November 5, 1915, No. 307). Thereupon Lie conceded that England and France had also sent their share of propaganda to Norway ("Eine Antwort an Hermann Hesse" [November 26], *Frankfurter Zeitung*, December 17, 1915, No. 349). Hesse concluded his rejoinder with this prediction: "In the world at large Germany will succeed with its weapons just as in the past it has succeeded with its music, its literature, and its philosophy. And I feel certain that in its preoccupation with weapons and economy it will not neglect the arts and other areas of culture." "Zu Bernt Lies Antwort" (December 9), *Frankfurter Zeitung*, December 17, 1915, No. 349.

vidual than in organizations.[24] War and its agony were also immediate physical realities and called for compassionate practical response and not for the verbiage of starry-eyed idealists. Hesse first gave expression to this sentiment in *Den Pazifisten*, sent to *Die Zeit* (Vienna) on October 5, 1915, but not published until November 7. He briefly lauded the pacifists for their ideals, then roundly reproached them for their obsessive promotion of their convictions and for their inability to perceive the need for more action and less talk, for their inordinate concern about the world of tomorrow and their contrasting lack of interest in the immediate alleviation of the suffering around them: "something was wrong, was rotten, rigid, and dead in this ideal." These views were reiterated in *Brief aus Bern* (mailed on October 8) which appeared in the *Frankfurter Zeitung* on October 13.

Hesse's criticism of the pacifists and their organizations perplexed many of his friends and astounded most of his detractors. It had been widely assumed that he was himself a pacifist or at least a fellow traveler. *Wieder in Deutschland* roused the ire of rabid patriots. *Den Pazifisten* and *Brief aus Bern* provoked the pacifists, and Hesse was soon subjected to the acrimony of the former and to the reproof of the latter. Among the first of the pacifists to take issue with him was an old admirer, the literary critic Adolf Saager. His *Das Wirken der deutschen Pazifisten* (December 1915) assured Hesse that most pacifists were not the idle utopians he assumed them to be and that many, like Hesse, were quietly responding to the practical needs of the day, countering malicious anti-German propaganda abroad, and preparing the way for a peaceful settlement of the differences between Germany and the Allies.[25] Alfred H. Fried, Europe's leading pacifist at the time, was far less patient than Saager. His *Hermann Hesse und die Pazifisten* (January 1916) rebuked Hesse for his misinterpretation of the pacifists, deplored his ignorance of their activities and goals, accused him of glibness, and questioned his sincerity.[26] A judgment too unqualified had only managed to evoke a response too incontinent.[27]

The pacifists' criticism of Hesse was perhaps as unwarranted as the nationalists' denunciation. Hesse was as anxious that Germany

24 See "Von den Pazifisten (Antwort auf den Brief von Herrn Dr. Saager)," *National-Zeitung* (Basel), January 4, 1916, No. 5.

25 *National-Zeitung* (Basel), December 30, 1915, No. 621.

26 *Die Friedens-Warte* (Zürich), 18 (January 1916), 20–22.

27 Regarding Hesse and the pacifists, see also Hermann Hesse, "An die Pazifisten" (December 3), *Die Zeit* (Wien), December 7, 1915, No. 4742; Johanna Friedjung, "Hermann Hesse und die Pazifisten," *Die Wage* (Wien), 18 (December 11, 1915), 687–690.

win the war as the most loyal of her patriots and he wanted peace as much as the most passionate of the pacifists. But he was also something of an apostate. Though anxious for victory he could not approve of war, and though anxious for peace he could not approve of the pacifists. On the one hand he abhorred violence, and on the other hand he had little faith in organized effort. These deviations were enough to make Hesse a decided *persona non grata* in both camps.

In *O Freunde, nicht diese Töne* (September 1914), Hesse had appealed to his fellow writers to emulate Goethe in their adjustment to the war:

> Goethe was never a bad patriot, even though he wrote no national poems in 1813. But his delight in things German . . . was surpassed by his delight in things human. He was a citizen and a patriot in the international world of thought . . . he stood so high that the destinies of the nations no longer attracted attention for their individual significance but only as minor movements of history as a whole.[28]

Impressed by this humanitarian appeal, but also unfamiliar with his German colleague's less-publicized writings of the time, Romain Rolland paid Hesse a rare compliment in April 1915: "But of all German poets, he who has written the serenest, the loftiest of words, the only one who has maintained a truly Goethean attitude in this demonic war, is . . . Hermann Hesse."[29] This tribute was clearly premature. Aspiration had yet to become reality. In fact, during the first year and a half of the war Hesse proved quite unequal to the demands of this ideal neutrality. He was still too involved in the fortunes of Germany and too unsure of himself and of his values to realize this Goethean blending of patriotism and supranationalism.

By the beginning of 1916, Hesse was so distressed by the swell of disapproval from so many unexpected sources and for so little reason that he sought refuge in seclusion and silence. He continued to tend to his duties in Bern but his writing tapered off sharply and for a year and a half he refrained from all social comment. He stopped reviewing war books, wrote no more war poems, no longer countered his detractors, made no further effort to influence the German public, and ended his printed encouragements to the soldiers on the front. The lull that set in was a period of resolute reconsideration and incubation, the beginning of what Hesse was later to term his awakening

28 *Gesammelte Schriften* (1957), Vol. 7, p. 48.
29 Romain Rolland, *Au-dessus de la mêlée* (Paris: Ollendorf, 1915), p. 128.

(*Erwachen*) and his transformation (*Wandlung*). Now, for the first time in his life he began seriously to take stock of himself and of the world. The world was not what it ought to be, but his own house was also not in order. He had made his comfortable peace with this world and had in his complacency helped sustain a social order and culture that had become rotten. His way of life had to be changed, established habits of thought and old attitudes and convictions had to be sloughed off. A breakthrough in Hesse's life was imminent.

The public had no inkling of this pending breakthrough until *Gruss aus Bern* (July 20, 1917)[30] appeared in the *Frankfurter Zeitung* on August 2, 1917. An indecisive apologist for his country and for himself now became a resolute censor. Like most authors, he had compromised himself. He had used society for his benefit and had allowed society to use him for its purposes. He had been silent or acquiescent when he should have been sharply critical. Each of the remaining four war essays that Hesse wrote in 1917 made it clear that this was no longer to be the case. Hesse emerged a determined Jeremiah. Whereas he had once been able flippantly to proclaim, "Since we are engaged in shooting, let's shoot" (*O Freunde, nicht diese Töne!*), he now had but one passionate desire, the immediate and unqualified termination of the purposeless slaughter (*An einen Staatsminister*, August 7). Once willing to acknowledge an ideological justification for the war, he now recanted. Indefinite continuation of hostilities could only bring economic ruin and cultural decline to all participating nations and hasten the advent of a morally and intellectually bankrupt bureaucratic military state (*Im Jahre 1920*, November 8). In 1914, Hesse had merely been troubled by the hypocrisy of the fair-weather friends of internationalism, and disturbed by the prevalent boycotting of foreign art. By 1917, he was prepared not only to remind German intellectuals of their shameful neglect of their own humanizing art (*An einen Staatsminister*) and to confront them with the more serious hypocrisy of their sentimental lip service to Christianity (*Weihnacht*, December 12), but also to condemn statesmen and generals alike for their blatant lies (*Soll Friede werden?* December 24). Well-meaning intellectuals berated in 1914 for their vain intercession—"As though an artist or man of letters, even the best and most celebrated, has anything to say in matters of war"—were now exhorted to action: "Let us bestir ourselves! Do let us make known in every possible way our readiness for peace!" (*Soll Friede werden?*).

---

30 Unless otherwise indicated, parenthetical dates of the war essays now commented upon are the dates the articles were mailed for their first publication.

Four more jeremiads, somewhat less acrid in tone and less aggressive in nature, followed before the war ended. The future looked inauspicious to Hesse. He imagined that in the completely militarized state of 1925, the relatively cultured and humane pre-war man would be a relic of the past, and all those who were no longer of any use to the cause would simply be liquidated (*Aus dem Jahre 1925*, written at the beginning of 1918). Looking into the more distant future, Hesse envisaged the final, foolishly heroic days of warfare, God's ultimate disgust, a second deluge, and the beginning of a new age in which the tragically comic European with his destructive intellect would no longer be a threat, but would serve only as a warning from the dim past (*Der Europäer*, January 30). In his *Traum am Feierabend* (February 18), he merely indulged in pleasant reverie, imagining nostaligically what he would most enjoy if the war were over and he were free to do as he pleased. And in *Gedanken* (written in the summer of 1918), an exegesis of the Sixth Commandment, Hesse reminded his readers that only a spiritual rebirth could ultimately lead to peace on earth.

Hesse continued this moderate berating and exhorting in the immediate postwar period. In *Weltgeschichte* (November 12) he cautioned against the traditional tendency to overestimate the significance of the external world of newspapers, politics, and wars, and to remain oblivious to the greater reality of the inner world, and warned against the irresponsible shifting of allegiance from old to new political ideologies without the necessary prior and corresponding inner changes. In *Das Reich* (written on December 4), he reminded Germany of the cultural heritage she had thoughtlessly renounced for material wealth, political power, and war, and advised her to begin her regeneration with self-analysis and self-acceptance. Hesse continued to dwell upon this theme of acceptance in *Der Weg der Liebe* (December 5). Germans were admonished to put aside all their self-righteous indignation, their hatred and thoughts of revenge, to cease their theatrical worship of heroism, and to counter their adversity with love and a religious acceptance of fate. Only in this manner could the trust and goodwill of the rest of the world be regained.

This gradual shift of attention from the international and national plane to the level of the individual, and from the outer to the inner world, culminated in *Zarathustras Wiederkehr* (January 20, 1919), the most impassioned and direct appeal that Hesse ever made to German youth. Published anonymously, for fear that it might otherwise be ignored, and put into a Nietzschean guise to make it immediately attractive, this manifesto was a bold and unequivocal challenge. Youth was enjoined to discontinue all traditional escapist activities: to cease

its childish wailing and gnashing of teeth, its concern for and identification with the fatherland, its pursuit of power and material
things, and its eager promotion of social and political causes. These
were only self-blinding, cowardly exercises in futility and not meaningful action. The individual was henceforth to concentrate solely
upon himself, to learn to accept and to be himself and thereby to accept and to live his fate, for each person was his own fate. This alone
was true action and true action and suffering were inseparable. Each
had to learn to suffer and thereby to live, for to live was to suffer. And
only in agonizing loneliness could the individual expect to live his
own life, be his own fate, and die his own death. A nation of hypocrit-
ical children was exhorted to become a nation of honest men. Hesse
was hopeful. A new age could be in the offing.

After *Zarathustras Wiederkehr*, Hesse's continued appeal to German youth to go its painful inward way (*Brief an einen jungen
Deutschen*, September 12, 1919) was anticlimactic, as too was his continued censure of the Western world's persistent disregard for the
Sixth Commandment (*Du sollst nicht töten*, probably written in September 1919), and his reiteration of Zarathustra's emphasis upon self-
living (*Chinesische Betrachtung*, December 10, 1921). Except for the
faintest allusions to politics and war in *Weltkrise und Bücher* (February
11, 1937) and in *Blatt aus dem Notizbuch* (written in March 1940), Hesse
now lapsed into silence and did not begin again to address himself
publicly to Germany until after the Second World War.

Most of Hesse's war essays first appeared in the *Neue Zürcher
Zeitung*. They were never widely reprinted in Germany. After 1915
and until the end of the war, German newspapers simply chose to ignore Hesse's comments on social and political matters. Fifteen of
these articles were included in *Betrachtungen* (1928);[31] and these fifteen together with four others later became part of *Krieg und Frieden*
(1946).[32] *Betrachtungen* did little more than stir up bitter memories and
evoke more calumny,[33] and *Krieg und Frieden* met with silent disapproval.

Until 1914, Hesse had been decidedly less conscious of the social
and political world around him than of art and the immediate circumstances of his own life. Like many other German intellectuals of
the day, he had preferred to leave politics to the politicians and the

31 (Berlin: S. Fischer, 1928), 333 pp.
32 (Zürich: Fretz & Wasmuth, 1946), 266 pp.
33 E.g., Gustav Hecht, "Offener Brief an Hermann Hesse," *Deutsches Volkstum*,
11 (1929), 603–611.

world to itself. It took the war to startle him from his retreat and to involve him in current events. However, neither his initial ambiguous exhortations nor his subsequent acrid remonstrations were those of a zealous reformer of political or social institutions. They were essentially a hopeful humanitarian's moral appeal to the individual. Hesse was far less interested in the transformation of society than in the regeneration of man. To focus on society was to deal with symptoms and he was determined to get at causes. Institutions were only as humane as the individuals who sustained them. All had to begin with the individual and Hesse had faith in the intrinsic goodness of man. It was this determination and faith that conditioned his approach to war and to politics, that persuaded him against world improvement (*Weltverbesserung*), and that permitted him to advocate both self-improvement (*Selbstverbesserung*) and self-will (*Eigensinn*). These two concepts were not incompatibles but inseparables; the former was inconceivable without the latter. *Eigensinn* became a cardinal virtue. It implied an awareness of and an honest response to the self. To respond to inner rather than to outer dictates was to be oneself, and this could only mean to improve oneself, and in turn, society.[34] These convictions crystallized during the period of Hesse's awakening. They underlie his war essays and they found their strongest immediate literary expression in *Demian* (1917).

Hesse championed a spiritual reform, and the individual was his starting point. All else would follow of its own accord. To the skeptics who were prone to ridicule such an approach to the world's ills, he could only reply: "whoever so desires, may laugh at it and call it 'sentimental rubbish.' But as for him who experiences it: his enemy will become his brother, death will become birth, disgrace honor, misfortune destiny."[35] Hesse's convictions fell upon deaf ears and his expostulations only aroused animosity. In many quarters his words were casually dismissed as *Humanitätsduselei*, the idle chatter of a naïve idealist.

DEPARTURE FOR TICINO

But for his wartime service, psychoanalysis, and painting, Hesse might not have retained his sanity when the world at large denounced him and his own private world was beyond salvage. Ma-

34 See "Eigensinn" (December 1917), *Gesammelte Schriften* (1957), Vol. 7, pp. 194–200.
35 "Krieg und Frieden" (summer 1918), *Gesammelte Schriften* (1957), Vol. 7, p. 120.

ria's behavior had become progressively more eccentric. She became psychotic in October 1918 and was hospitalized until March 1919. Bruno and Heiner were placed in a boarding-school, and Hesse was left to fend for himself in an empty house. Released from his wartime job in March of 1919, Hesse immediately settled his affairs in Bern and in April left for Ticino to begin his life anew. With this, his marriage, in effect, ended. Late that summer Maria was again hospitalized. The following January, the two youngsters were put into a foster home in the Schwarzwald. Three months later, Bruno was sent to Oschwand, where he grew up in the home of the painter Cuno Amiet, and that May, Heiner was enrolled in a boarding-school in Kefikon.[36] This ended Hesse's active role as a father.

Marriage and domesticity had obviously not agreed with Hesse. His Rousseauesque adventure in Gaienhofen ended in tedium and frustration and his life as a Bernese country gentleman became a nightmare. As of the spring of 1919 he found himself without wife, children, home, and job, and with little income, but he was free again and freedom was exhilarating. What he had long suspected he now knew.[37] Though a writer who needed his loneliness and his dreams, he had settled for a hearth. Though a nomad at heart, he had tried to become an established member of society. He had again played a role and had again violated himself. Neither aestheticism nor *embourgeoisement* had served Hesse well. He was now determined just to be himself, come what may.

MAJOR PUBLICATIONS

All considered, Hesse's six and a half years in Bern were fruitful. *Rosshalde*, begun on July 10, 1912—while Hesse was still in Gaienhofen—was completed the following January, and published in early 1914.[38] *Vorfrühling*, written in May 1913, and *Das Ende*, completed by July 24, 1914, together with *Meine Erinnerung an Knulp* of late

---

36 Bruno became a painter and still lives in Oschwand. Heiner, an interior decorator, lives in Küsnacht.

37 Hesse diagnosed his situation most ably as early as 1918: "I wanted to be what I was not. To be sure I wanted to be a poet, but at the same time also an ordinary citizen. I wanted to be an artist and a man of fantasy, but at the same time also to be a man of virtue and to enjoy a home. It took a long time before I knew that one cannot be and have both. . . . I increased the world's guilt and agony by violating myself, by not daring to go the route of salvation. The path of salvation does not lead to the left and not to the right; it leads into one's own heart, and there alone is God, and there alone is peace." "Bauernhaus" (1918), *Gesammelte Schriften* (1957), Vol. 3, p. 388.

38 (Berlin: S. Fischer, 1914), 304 pp.

1907, were published as a book in 1915.[39] *Das Haus der Träume*, a three-chapter fragment in which Hesse envisaged an ideal twilight of life, was written in the spring of 1914.[40] *Musik des Einsamen*, a new collection of poems,[41] was printed in late 1914, and a second edition of *Unterwegs* appeared in 1915. *Am Weg* was also published in 1915 but only three of its miscellany of tales, ruminations, and recollections were written in Bern.[42] A troubled lull in creativity followed this auspicious beginning. Hesse wrote a mere three fairy tales and some eighteen poems from the spring of 1915 to the autumn of 1917. *Schön ist die Jugend* appeared in 1916 but both of its fictionalized recollections predate this lull.[43] *Demian*, written in September and October 1917 but not published until the spring of 1919, marked the end of this literary drought and the vigorous beginning of a new chapter in Hesse's art.[44] *Märchen*, seven tales written from 1913 to 1918, appeared in the spring of 1919,[45] and *Kleiner Garten* a collection of eighteen essays, tales, and recollections, ten of which were also written from 1913 to 1918, followed in late 1919.[46] *Wanderung*, a medley of watercolors, poems composed from 1911 to 1920, and reflective travel recollections written during 1918 and at the beginning of 1919, was published in late 1920.[47] *Kinderseele*, a psychologically penetrating recall of a theft of figs at the age of twelve, was written between December 1918 and February 20, 1919.[48] *Zarathustras Wiederkehr*, Hesse's appeal to the youth of Germany, was ready for publication on January 20, 1919, after only two or three days of frenzied writing,[49] and the first act of *Heimkehr*, a soldier's return from the war, was finished by January 24, 1919;[50] *Sinclairs Notizbuch*, comprising twelve essays and tales, ten of which were written in 1917 and 1918, was published in 1923.[51]

ROSSHALDE: FAILURE AND NEW POSSIBILITY

Rosshalde depicts an infelicitous marriage. The story drew heavily upon the circumstances of Hesse's life and reflects what Hesse be-

39 *Knulp: Drei Geschichten aus dem Leben Knulps* (Berlin: S. Fischer, 1915), 146 pp.
40 *Der Schwäbische Bund*, 2 (November 1920), 92–114.
41 (Heilbronn: E. Salzer, 1915), 84 pp.   42 (Konstanz: Reuss & Itta, 1915), 87 pp.
43 (Berlin: S. Fischer, 1916), 118 pp.   44 (Berlin: S. Fischer, 1919), 256 pp.
45 (Berlin: S. Fischer, 1919), 182 pp.
46 (Leipzig & Wien: E. P. Tal & Co., 1919) 143 pp.
47 (Berlin: S. Fischer, 1920), 117 pp.
48 *Deutsche Rundschau*, Vol. 181 (November 1919), 177–200.
49 (Bern, 1919), 39 pp.
50 *Vivos Voco*, 1 (April-May 1920), 461–474.
51 (Zürich: Rascher & Cie, 1923), 109 pp.

lieved to be the predicament of the artist vis-à-vis life. Veraguth is the temperamental individual that Hesse was, the lonely romantic who lived in dreamy anticipation, was quickly sated by realization, and carefully nurtured his chronic disillusionment. Adele is the same staid and humorless personality, the same possessive mother and unresponsive wife that Maria was. Their mismarriage was Hesse's: each is disenchanted with the other, both are lonely and embittered, neither can or will respond to the needs of the other, each is at odds with the self and with life, and both know only resignation and renunciation. But *Rosshalde* is not just a story of marital incompatibility, it is a demonstration of marital impossibility. It was not only Hesse's frank confession of the failure but even more of the folly of his attempt in marriage to achieve an intimate relationship with life and to find a place for himself in society. People such as Veraguth and he were temperamentally unsuited for this kind of intimacy and security. Hesse had become convinced that the artist was essentially an observer and a creator; to try to be a participant, and to be in and of life, was to play a role and not to live himself. Any marriage for the artist was therefore *per se* mismarriage.[52] Veraguth's mistake had been Hesse's and, like Hesse, he had only compounded his error by long resigning himself to it. His predicament was Hesse's and its ultimate drastic resolution became Hesse's.

Lauscher had chosen to pass life by, Camenzind and Kuhn had dared to knock timidly on its closed doors, and Veraguth had vainly tried to force an entrance. Lauscher had settled for aestheticism, Camenzind for nature, Kuhn for resigned retirement, and Veraguth, left an embittered recluse by his initial Kuhnian approach to life, eventually decides to settle for nothing less than himself. The first three of these resolutions had been Hesse's own responses to life, each had been bolstered by a particular philosophy, and none had long stood the test of actual living. Veraguth's resolve, on the other hand, quickly became and remained the major thrust in Hesse's life

---

52 Hesse himself provided an excellent commentary on Rosshalde in a letter written to his father soon after the novel was published: "The novel . . . marks at least a temporary departure from the most difficult of the practical problems that have preoccupied me. For the unhappy marriage with which the book deals is not at all founded upon a wrong choice, but has more accurately to do with the 'artist and marriage,' with the question as to whether an artist and thinker, a man who is not only intent upon living life instinctually but primarily upon observing and recording it as objectively as possible—as to whether such a person is at all capable of marriage." Bernhard Zeller, *Hermann Hesse in Selbstzeugnissen und Bilddokumenten* (Reinbek bei Hamburg: Rowohlt, 1963), p. 70.

and the focal concern of his art. This, like all preceding resolutions, derived from yet another reappraisal of the self and of life and was supported by yet another philosophy, by a new conception of fate.

Until *Rosshalde*, Hesse's protagonists characteristically assume that everything in life happens or does not happen to them. They neither realize nor want to recognize that they themselves are actively involved in this happening or not happening. As such, adjustment to life's given circumstances is their primary and common concern, and minimal involvement their ideal. They drift with fate, comforted by their dreams and confirmed by their philosophies. The occasional exception is quickly disabused of his views to the contrary and quickly ceases to act otherwise. The brash young hero of *Die Marmorsäge* (1904) would cut his own path through life but is soon compelled meekly to accept what fate held in store for him. Knulp alone is allowed to expound and to maintain intact a contrary view of life and to go his own way with impunity (*Meine Erinnerung an Knulp*, 1907). Hesse has his vagabond philosopher argue the novelty and uniqueness of the individual, his basic self-sufficiency and autonomy, his essential aloneness, and his potential holiness. Fate for Knulp is not intrusive but inherent. He is not adrift in and subject to the forces of an alien world, but is his own world. Life is not an adjustment to outer caprice, but a simple living of the self.

These were intellectual flirtations whose challenge Hesse was obviously not yet prepared to meet. As evidenced by *Gertrud* (1909), this shift from outer coercion to inner thrust was short-lived. Kuhn's theory of outer and inner fate, of the inexorable and the Schillerian sublime, was merely a formulary conceptualization and restatement of the still prevailing views of Hesse and his protagonists. Until his concluding decision to leave family, home, and false identity behind him and to begin life anew, Veraguth belongs to this constellation of timorous bystanders; until then, he is an unmistakable blood brother to the Lauschers, Camenzinds, and Kuhns, and his story is only a variation on their theme. With this decision, Veraguth begins where Knulp had left off. To seek happiness in marriage had been folly and his attempt to live Kuhn's credo—to fashion his own inner fate by accepting life's trying circumstances with as much equanimity as possible and by seeking his consolation in art—had only left him a pitiful wretch. He had sought something not intended for him and had been too weak to extricate himself from an alien situation. He would now seek his own medium and try only to be himself. He recognizes belatedly what he had long refused to acknowledge: that he is by nature an outsider and an observer, that art is his destiny, and not just his consolation, and that loneliness is his element and not something to be feared. Reluctant acceptance of outer circumstances yields to joyous self-acceptance, and bitter renunciation will become self-realization. Where formerly Veraguth had groped hesitantly, he will now strike out boldly and vigorously. India, his immediate destination, will not be a cradle paradise for the man but a sober challenge for the artist.

Knulps Ende (1914) was both a continuation and a confirmation of this trend of thought. Knulp has lived the kind of life Veraguth proposes to live. With death approaching, he begins to wonder whether a socially more acceptable life might not have been more commendable than his self-centered vagabondage. However, in his hallucinatory conversation with God, he manages to convince himself that all had been for the best: he was as God had fashioned him and had lived as God had intended he live. For Hesse, life was no longer social expectation but self-obligation, and no longer what happens or does not happen to the individual and his adjustment to these circumstances, but the individual happening and his adjustment to himself. The individual was now his own possibilities and limitations: his own fate and responsibility. It was incumbent upon him to be himself. *Demian* was in the offing.

From *Peter Camenzind* through *Gertrud* to *Rosshalde* Hesse's world became progressively more circumscribed, his cast dwindled and action decreased. All gradually became situation, portrait and inner drama, description, comment and dialogue. The epic waned and the dramatic emerged. A novice also slowly became a skilled craftsman. Hesse had permitted Camenzind to ramble as he roamed. He had compelled his more sedentary Kuhn to select and to organize his recollections with some care. He assumed direct responsibility for Veraguth's story. This shift from the first to the third person undoubtedly helped him achieve and maintain the emotional distance necessary for the careful craftsmanship that characterizes *Rosshalde*.

In its concentrated treatment of theme and its careful composition, the third of Hesse's artist novels approaches the controlled artistry of drama. It is more the work of a playwright conscious of the classical unities than of a lyrical storyteller. The setting is the estate Rosshalde, the action is confined to one summer, and all revolves around Veraguth, his wife Adele, and his sons Pierre and Albert. Locale digressions are minimal, the past is revealed in the terse retrospective manner of drama, and supernumeraries are limited to

Veraguth's friend Burkhardt, his servant Robert, and a nameless doctor and nurse. The tale's eighteen structural divisions are scenes more than chapters. Dialogue prevails and intermittent narration approaches stage-direction comment. An expository introduction is followed by eight brief chapter-scenes that revolve about Veraguth's plight and his friend's catalytic visit, and conclude with his decision to leave for India. The next eight sections, equally brief, focus upon Pierre and his illness, and end with his demise. Only Veraguth's terse epilogic ruminations follow. A situation rife with tension, minimal action alive with steadily mounting suspense, and this tightly organized drama-like structure afford a distinctly dramatic experience. But for Hesse's lack of enthusiasm for the stage, *Rosshalde* might have become a laudable two-act play.

The language of *Rosshalde* is as ably controlled as its structure. It is far removed from Lauscher's effeminate effusions and Camenzind's rhapsody, and is much more contained than the relatively sober expression of *Unterm Rad* and *Gertrud*. By *Unterm Rad*, Hesse had become aware of the necessity of verbal restraint; with *Rosshalde*, he emerged a master in verbal discipline. His words in *Rosshalde* are ordinary, adjectives and adverbs are used discreetly, and ostentatious literary devices are more avoided than ever before. Sentences are longer than in previous works, constructed with more care, and cleaned of all verbal dross. And dialogue, stilted in Hesse's preceding novels, is lively and real. Language once flabby is now sinewy, and what had been murky verbosity is now eloquent simplicity. Effect had become art. Hesse himself was amazed by the artistry of *Rosshalde* when he reexamined the novel in 1942, twenty-six years after he had last read it: "I thought I would find a kind of elegant kitsch. But such was not the case. The book pleased me, it stood its test. . . . There are many things in it that would be beyond me today. . . . I had at that time achieved the height of my handicraft and technique and have never gone beyond that."[53]

Rosshalde is inner not outer drama, just as *Peter Camenzind* and *Gertrud* are odysseys of the spirit and not adventures of the flesh. In each case, the physical world as such was for Hesse incidental and was accorded minimal necessary attention. Rosshalde is not located geographically, nor rendered visible. Physical detail, as usual is sparse, catalogued rather than related, and far more suggestive than

53 Part of an unpublished letter written to Peter Suhrkamp on January 15, 1942. In the Hesse-Nachlass, Marbach a.N.

depictive. The exterior world in Hesse's prose commonly has more purpose than independent meaning; it is essentially functional, providing a necessary and often enhancing setting. In *Peter Camenzind*, nature is not only the framework in which Camenzind lives and has his being, but it also symbolizes a world more ideal than that of civilization. In *Rosshalde*, manor house, park, and isolated atelier are Veraguth's actual environment, and they also symbolize the plight of artists vis-à-vis life. Like preceding protagonists, Veraguth is psychologically real, even tangible, but again only faintly visible, and Hesse's supporting cast continues to have as little visual reality and as little independent meaning as his settings. In Veraguth and Burkhardt, Hesse also resorted to his usual double self-projection: the trapped and troubled artist Hesse was, and the contented foot-loose and fancy-free person he longed upon occasion to be. And like *Peter Camenzind* and *Gertrud*, *Rosshalde* does not conclude but ends abruptly, and again at a critical juncture; a new and more meaningful way of life is proposed but left untested. Just as in these preceding novels, Hesse took his protagonist no farther than the point he himself had reached in his own experience and thought.

DEMIAN: EMANCIPATION AND QUEST

A PSEUDONYM

At the outset of 1919 Hesse asked Samuel Fischer to consider for publication an unusual tale by an unknown and sick young Swiss author, Emil Sinclair. Thought a wily old publisher, Fischer was readily taken in by this literary hoax. Hesse had good reason for resorting to this subterfuge. His name had become a liability: anathema for older Germans and ancient history for future-oriented postwar youth. If he was to be read and heeded, he had no choice but to publish anonymously or under a pseudonym. Hesse preferred a new name; it was not only excellent camouflage but was also an appropriate symbol for the new man he had become. And the name Emil Sinclair was particularly appealing to Hesse since it could also be his modest memorial to the friend and patron of his beloved Hölderlin.[54]

54 Hesse first used this pen name in print for two of his wartime glimpses into the future: "Im Jahre 1920," *Neue Zürcher Zeitung*, November 15, 16, 1917, and "Der Europäer," *Neue Zürcher Zeitung*, August 4, 6, 1918. Two other of his social comments appeared under the name after the publication of *Demian*: "Aus dem Jahre 1925," *Neue Zürcher Zeitung*, May 20, 1919, and "Gespräch mit dem Ofen," *Vivos Voco*, (January 1920), 254–255. All of these, a few excerpts from *Demian*, and seven other related items written from 1917 to 1920 were subsequently published as *Sinclairs Notizbuch* (Zürich: Rascher & Cie, 1923), 109 pp.

Hesse's boldly innovative new tale caused an immediate stir in the literary world. It could not have been more relevant in matter or manner, or more timely in publication. Much to Hesse's embarrassment, his genial protégé was forthwith awarded the Theodor Fontane Prize for Literature. He had gambled and had won far more than expected. Hesse returned the award to its donors, since it was intended only for first novels, and publicly admitted to his ruse in mid-1920, shortly after Eduard Korrodi, a discerning literary critic for the *Neue Zürcher Zeitung*, had deduced that Sinclair could only be Hesse.[55] Sinclair ceased to be listed as author with the book's seventeenth printing in 1920. *Demian* remained the rage for almost three years, a veritable bible for German youth.[56] It was youth's world that was depicted, youth's concerns and bewilderment, its apprehensions and its aspirations. And youth found new hope in Hesse's proposed new way of life. Youth had discovered a leader and was grateful, and Hesse found himself unexpectedly in the vanguard of what promised to become a social upheaval of no mean proportions. But youth also proved to be fickle when confronted by the more flamboyant and less demanding political ideologies of the twenties.

AUTOBIOGRAPHICAL MATRIX

Demian returned, as had *Unterm Rad*, to Hesse's critical formative years. *Unterm Rad* had been an emotional experience, a reliving and purging of painful memories extending from 1891 to 1895. *Demian* was an intellectual experience, a reexamination of the years 1887 to 1897 with the help of psychoanalysis and in terms of Hesse's incipient determination to be himself. Disparate though these tales are, each was as dependent upon the inner and outer circumstances of Hesse's life as the other. Each is intimately autobiographical. The family circle in *Demian* is a familiar one. Ten-year-old Sinclair is the sensitive and unruly youngster Hesse had once been. He, too, has a stern father with whom he is at odds, a gentle mother to whom he is attracted, and an older and younger sister, both of whom are better behaved than he. Sinclair's home with the escutcheon above its arched entrance is the house on Bischofstrasse in which Hesse had lived for a number of years and which he associated most intimately with his childhood; the heraldic hawk alone was fancy and not memory. Sinclair's "light

---

55 Ed. Korrodi, "Wer ist der Dichter des *Demian?*" *Neue Zürcher Zeitung,* June 24, 1920, No. 1050, and "An Hermann Hesse den Dichter des *Demian*," *Neue Zürcher Zeitung,* July 4, 1920, No. 1112.

56 See Klabund, "Allerlei," *Neue Rundschau,* 31 (1920), 1109; Gerhart Sieveking, "Hermann Hesse und wir Jüngsten," *Neue Zürcher Zeitung,* February 22, 1921, No. 276.

world"—home and immediate family, characterized by cleanliness and goodness, love and peace, prayer and duty—is Hesse's cloistered world of childhood, and this childhood paradise had ended for him as it does for Sinclair, with a growing awareness of, and a painful involvement with, seductive and profane life at large, the "dark world" as Hesse chose to call it in 1917. The streets through which Sinclair strolls, the river and bridge where he loiters and the school he attends are the Calw Hesse had known and had never forgotten. Sinclair's tormentor Franz Kromer had probably been one of Hesse's ruffian acquaintances in Calw, perhaps the same scamp who appears as Oskar Weber in *Kinderseele* (1919). His mentor Demian must surely have derived from the chimerical companion to whose every beck and call imaginative Hesse had responded as a youngster, and whom in recollection Hesse was wont to call his little man, spirit or imp, angel or demon ("Männlein, Geist oder Kobold, Engel oder Dämon").[57] Demian is Sinclair's projected alter ego and the irresistible little man was a projection of Hesse's impulses and curiosity. A Freudian id had become a Socratic *daimon*. But Demian is a recollection not only in his function but even in his person. He is very much what Hesse remembered of one of his fellow students in Maulbronn. Like his model Gustav Zeller, he is tall, strong, aloof, and superior, more man than boy, a keen observer of human nature, a student of hypnosis, and a holder of unorthodox religious views.[58] A forceful guardian and lofty example emerged from an irresistible apparition and an impressive classmate.

Like Hesse before him, Sinclair has a lengthy course of instruction in religion, is confirmed in the spring, and following his summer vacation, begins his secondary-school education in the autumn. The *Gymnasium* in St. is obviously the *Gymnasium* Hesse had attended in Cannstatt and Sinclair's experiences here are a detailed recall of Hesse's. Hesse had boarded with one of his teachers and Sinclair does likewise. He is as lonely, confused, and unhappy as Hesse had been, derives just as little comfort from his studies as had Hesse, and assumes the same protective aloofness to which Hesse had had recourse. Worldly-wise Alfons Beck corrupts his younger friend Sinclair just as a dissolute twenty-year-old acquaintance in Cannstatt had led young Hesse down the primrose path. Sinclair becomes the rebellious cigarette-smoking sot that Hesse had become, and he, too,

---

57 "Kindheit des Zauberers" (1923), *Gesammelte Schriften* (1957), Vol. 4, p. 458.
58 See *Kindheit und Jugend vor Neunzehnhundert* (1966), pp. 129–130, 172.

is left ill and at odds with himself and the world, welters in despair, is tortured by his conscience, and flirts with suicide. Like Hesse before him, he borrows money freely, is soon heavily in debt, and manages in one way or another to squeeze money out of his parents. Like Hesse's many years earlier, Sinclair's father is informed of his son's errant ways by his concerned housemaster, visits the school, berates his offspring, appeals to him in vain, and in desperation, just as Hesse's father had, threatens to have him put into a correctional institution. Sinclair's first love recalls Hesse's; he is as much in love with love as Hesse had been, and he worships his older Beatrice as much as Hesse had venerated his older Eugenie Kolb in the summer of 1892. And Sinclair's years at the University H. are Hesse's years at Tübingen: he, too, finds quarters on the outskirts of the town, remains a self-preoccupied loner, is fascinated by Nietzsche, and is just as unimpressed by his studies and student life as Hesse had been by academia in Tübingen.

In the Beatrice affair, an earlier experience was linked with a slightly later situation. In Sinclair's encounter with Pistorius, a later experience was associated with a much earlier situation. Pistorius was not some mystagogue whom Hesse chanced to meet in Cannstatt, but his eccentric analyst Dr. Lang of Lucerne. His library with its many Latin, Greek, and Hebrew titles was Lang's, as too were his antiquarian interest in religious myth, his preoccupation with the God-Devil deity Abraxas, and his Jungian interpretation of Sinclair's dreams. His conversation with Sinclair undoubtedly drew heavily upon Hesse's therapy sessions with Lang, and under his influence, Sinclair learns to respect himself and to heed his thoughts and dreams just as Hesse had. Of course, Pistorius is not Lang any more than Beatrice is Eugenie; both were more inspired by their prototypes than patterned after them. Hesse never copied, he recreated. Unlike Pistorius, Lang was a Catholic and not a Protestant, nor was he given to alcohol, and his avocational interest was painting and not music; he was also younger than Hesse, and unlike Pistorius, he became a lasting friend.

Although *Demian* scans its author's life from 1887 to 1897 and adds a touch of 1914 to 1917, it is not autobiography as such. Hesse's past and present were only the matrix of his art. His recollection was always selective and his imagination remained vivid. Maulbronn was bypassed in *Demian* and Hesse's apprenticeship in Calw went unmentioned; the former had been sufficiently exploited artistically in *Unterm Rad* and the latter obviously had no place in Hesse's world of 1917. Colored by time and modified by intent, Hesse's selected memories of 1887 to 1897 were blended with personal experience and political events of 1914 to 1917, imbued with his latest concerns, and artistically shaped by his contact with psychoanalysis. Memory and immediate situation, previously poeticized in Hesse's art, were mythicized in *Demian*. The personal became universally typical.

A NIETZSCHEAN ICONOCLAST

Rosshalde ends optimistically. Veraguth is prepared to seize fate firmly by the forelock: to terminate his timorous adjustment to life and to be what he is. Knulp lives what Veraguth only espouses. But neither Veraguth nor Knulp ponder the demanding implications of this new way of life. *Rosshalde* breaks off before its protagonist can give the matter much thought and *Knulp* glosses over it. The two tales represent the enthusiastic and ingenuous initial stage of Hesse's conversion to a new ideal. From 1915 to 1917, his thinking progressed much further. The ideal acclaimed in *Rosshalde* and only romantically illustrated in *Knulp* was now carefully weighed. *Demian* emerged from this afterthought.

The ideal that must at first have been a tremendous relief for Hesse soon became an almost intimidating challenge. To espouse a new approach to life was one thing, to realize it, quite another. To live the self involved more than just self-acceptance. Prior emancipation from traditional religion and morality was necessary, as too, the cultivation of a personal ethos. Hesse responded to these necessities much in the spirit of the man whom in Tübingen he had discounted as a philosopher and whose master morality he had disparaged.[59] A withdrawn, comparatively mild-mannered traditionalist at odds with himself and the world became a thoroughly Nietzschean individualist, iconoclast, and moralist. Hesse had always been an individualist but had never been able or willing to accept the full consequences of his individualism and had not been averse to compromise. He had tended to be more mindful of the expectations and comforts of society than responsive to the self, and had become something of a socialized outsider. Self-consciousness now became defiant indi-

---

59 "It is too bad about him. He ought to have written a master aesthetics. That would be more valuable than his master morality." "I am not one of Nietzsche's followers. The essence of his philosophy . . . that is, his murder of morality, does not much affect me since my view of things, my religion, is pious but quite free of morality." "I believe that Nietzsche the philosopher is not at all going to last long." Excerpts from unpublished letters written to his father (June 15, 1895), Karl Isenberg (June 2, 1897), and his parents (February 2, 1898) respectively. In the Schiller-Nationalmuseum, Marbach a.N.

vidualism. He would no longer adjust, society had to change, and it would change, for the Western world was in decline and a new culture was in the offing. In the meantime, responding to his self-will (*Eigensinn*) and not to herd-will (*Herdensinn*), Hesse would follow Nietzsche's path of individuation through cold ethereal realms, prepared not only to accept but to extol loneliness and suffering in the manner of the Nietzschean elect. Ours was a world of and for the herd man (*Herdenmensch*), a dated society. A better world of tomorrow could be ushered in by an enlightened few girded for a Nietzschean transvaluation of values. Christianity, now almost as suspect to Hesse as it had been to his mentor, became the focal point of this transvaluation, just as it had for Nietzsche: its God was wanting and its myths were questionable, its morality was for the many and the weak, and its values were of doubtful merit. Thanks to Christianity both the here and the beyond had become an unnecessary and trying duality of incompatibles. A religion with a deity both God and Satan and a morality beyond absolutist good and evil, a credo appreciative of wholesome self-love and tolerant of self-expression and self-realization, would be more in accord with the nature of things. The old had to and would give way to the new: a new God, a new morality, a new man, and a new world. This Nietzschean sentiment found its immediate expression in *Demian*: a novelesque depiction of Hesse's own emancipation from traditional belief and thought, and of the crystallization of his own ethos. In his Sinclair, Hesse himself emerged the man of tomorrow. No longer encased in tradition, he, like Sinclair, was ready finally and only now to live himself—like a fledgling perched and ready for flight. Veraguth proceeded as far as Hesse himself had gone by 1913. Sinclair was taken to the point Hesse had reached by the autumn of 1917. As usual, Hesse would not venture beyond his own experience.

INNER STORY EXTERNALIZED

Although Hesse's pre-*Demian* tales are by and large inner biography, they are located in a real world, albeit more evoked than depicted, and though his preceding protagonists live in the private retreat of emotions and reflection, they do, even if but minimally, relate to real people. In *Demian*, inner biography becomes virtually self-sufficient and protagonist communes almost solely with himself. Sinclair's inner story is externalized. A landscape of the soul is imposed upon and almost blots out the world and people proper: concepts assume human form, psychic experiences are rendered visible, and actuality in turn is conceptualized. The resultant intricate interplay of highly elusive symbols defies satisfactory interpretation.

Demian is Sinclair's Socratic *daimon*, his admonishing inner self, but he is also a Jungian imago, Sinclair's mental image of the ideal self, and is also the reflective culturally unconditioned alter ego Sinclair must become before he can begin to live himself: a *daimon*, an imago, and an alter ego become a guiding analyst, a guru, or a guardian angel. *Frau Eva* is Sinclair's all, and the all. She is his Jungian anima, the soul, the unconscious with which his conscious must establish rapport in the process of individuation, and she is also his ideal, the self-realization that will come with self-living: anima and ideal become inspiration and guide, potential lover and spiritual mother. And beyond the self, *Frau Eva* is life in all its fullness, heaven and earth, good and evil, an actualized Magna Mater reminiscent of Revelations' Daughter of Zion, and mankind's origin and destiny.

Both Demian and *Frau Eva* are concepts thinly actualized. The remaining personnae are actuality clearly become concepts. All are more universally typical than real, more representation than being. Sinclair himself is not just *a* son intent upon being what his parents are, but *the* son who wants to remain within the family fold, not just *a* son who leaves home and tradition behind, but *the* prodigal son who does not return to the fold, nor just *a* rebel and *a* self-seeker, but *the* rebellious self-seeker. Mr. and Mrs. Sinclair are not just *his* parents, but timeless parents, *the* stern father and *the* loving mother. Kromer is not just *a* young rascal who chances to bully and to blackmail Sinclair, but everyman's violator; he is also a personification of evil, the devil's emissary or Satan himself, a projection of a suppressed part of Sinclair, of latent and forbidden inner thrusts, a haunting Jungian shadow or Freudian id. Wayward Alfons Beck is simply Kromer the timeless tormentor become Kromer the timeless seducer. Beatrice's very name betrays her true identity; she is obviously not just *a* young woman whom Sinclair idolizes from a distance, but idealized woman. Sinclair's teachers are everyman's institutionalized source of learning. Pistorius is the seeker's guide, confidant and warning, and Knauer is the seeker's own eventual troubled young ward.

Hesse's cast includes only those who are part of Sinclair's inner world. His situations and action relate just as intimately to that inner world. And all is again rendered typical and timeless by a careful exclusion of particularizing detail and a close association with the Bible. Sinclair's place of birth is *any* community. His parental home is *the* parental home and all it implies: childhood paradise, innocence and harmony, goodness and faith, love and respect. This is the child's "light world" and is a counterpart of God's kingdom. The world at large, the threatening and forbidden "dark world," is every child's tempting mystery and a reflection of Satan's realm. Sinclair's encounter with Kromer, the fictive apple theft, and the painful consequences are clearly a variant of every youngster's first brush with evil and consequent loss of paradisiacal innocence, and all this is prefigured in Eve's plucking of the apple and man's fall from grace. The schools that Sinclair attends are every institution of learning where information is dispensed and doubts are sewn, and Sinclair's doubts, his preoccupation with Cain and Abel and the thieves on the cross, are reflective of man's timeless doubts about religion and morality. Sinclair's months of dissolute living, his family's concern and his own disgust and despair, and his subsequent elevating platonic love for Beatrice are the classic experiences of adolescence; they are also only a variation of the prodigal son's riotous living and repentance. Pistorius, whose counsel and consolation encourage Sinclair and give direction to his self-quest, *the* seeker of new belief who must settle for old myth, and Knauer *the* errant fledgling seeker who is helped by and in turn helps Sinclair, are not only the possibilities, the failure, and the error that every seeker risks, but also the comfort and aid he can expect in his inner struggle. And Sinclair's inner struggle, his emancipation from the old and his groping for the new, and the elation of his success, is every seeker's agony and bliss, is Jacob struggling anew with his angel and reveling in its blessing. The University H. is any institution of higher learning in any town, and the war in which Sinclair takes part could be any promising social upheaval, another apocalyptic vision.

Not all the action of *Demian* is the actual conceptualized. Since Demian and *Frau Eva* are concept actualized, their actions and Sinclair's interaction with them are primarily psychic experience externalized. Demian's disposing of Kromer is Sinclair's own mental neutralizing of his tormentor by acknowledging and accepting the evil that he represents. This shifting of attitude from rejection to acceptance is anticipated and rendered visible by the dreams in which Sinclair is first violated, unwillingly and much to his displeasure, by Kromer, and then similarly tormented, quite willingly and much to his delight, by Demian. Sinclair's encounter with Kromer is his first encounter with evil. The forbidden not only intrudes upon him from the outside, but asserts itself simultaneously from the inside. He begins to lie, feels wickedly superior to his father, and takes neither parent into his confidence. He is convinced he has established an alliance with the devil and is sorely troubled by his sinful behavior. His immediate subconscious response—his dream of a blissful family boating holiday—is to try to blot out the reality of evil and to return to the purity and security of childhood. But Kromer and all he represents cannot be wished away. Not only can Sinclair not simply turn his back upon his own and evil at large, but actual theft quickly follows initial braggadocian lie, and scorn for his father soon becomes murderous hatred. This hatred finds transferred dream-expression in Sinclair's subsequently attempted knife-assault upon his father, an act instigated by Kromer. This second effort to cope with evil is as abortive as the first. Kromer the evil prompter and Sinclair's repugnance are the projection and futile rejection of Sinclair's own forbidden feelings and impulse. Demian's, that is, Sinclair's alter ego's replacement of Kromer in this nightmare, and Sinclair's blissful, albeit anxious sufferance of the continued violation of his person, evidence a third and more successful subconscious effort to come to terms with evil. Rejection becomes acquiescence, and this is made possible by Sinclair's acceptance of Demian's, that is, his own incipient unorthodox conception of sin and sinner and his acclaim of society's traditionally condemned and ostracized Cains, the very personifications of evil. Sinclair is thereby able to identify with the elect and independent Cains, and to condone his own socially forbidden impulses. A repugnant Kromer who represents evil and its traditional torment and rejection becomes an acceptable Demian who offers the release of an enlightened view of life's inescapable realities. After but two such dreams, Kromer replaces Demian—reflective of a relapse into traditional morality—and Sinclair again becomes a reluctant victim. And in actual life Kromer indeed resumes his plaguing of Sinclair, but only until Demian finally confronts him boldly and disposes of him for good, that is to say, until Sinclair himself consciously grapples with, reevaluates, and absorbs the inner and outer evil that Kromer symbolizes.

This is the first of Sinclair's many assimilations. Alfons Beck and Beatrice follow in rapid succession. And when all that Pistorius and Knauer represent is also absorbed, they too are left in Sinclair's wake. Demian is the last of Sinclair's absorptions. His death is not an end but a beginning. With it, Sinclair has become his projected better self, the self-seeker finally fully emancipated and ready to live himself. And had Hesse continued his tale, Sinclair's union with *Frau Eva* would have been the final absorption, a symbol of his ideal fully realized: self-realization, the culmination of self-living; or a Jungian individuation, the integration of the conscious and the unconscious. Psychic experience rendered visible is artfully extended to a novel interplay of dreams and paintings. Sinclair's dream of the heraldic hawk, which Demian compels him to swallow and which then proceeds, to his horror, to devour him from the inside, his painting of the hawk bursting out of its shell, and his mailing of the painting and Demian's cryptic acknowledgment of its receipt externalize his evolving thought and his changing attitude. Sinclair has swung from the light to the dark world, is at home in neither and has begun to flirt with a third possibility, a complete emancipation from this dichotomy of incompatibles. This breakthrough evolves vague and forbidding in his unconscious; vacillation ends in reluctant and timorous acceptance. This musing in the unconscious assumes symbolic form in Sinclair's dream. Demian, his better self, is associated with this new possibility, indeed, forces it upon him. When Sinclair ingests the bird and it, in turn, begins to devour him, he becomes the bird; he, like the hawk, is now prepared to break through the shell enclosing him: the Christian-bourgeois ethic. But all this begins to become clear to Sinclair only with some afterthought, some communion with his better self, that is, only after he turns to Demian and receives his curt explanation. Sinclair's progression from the dark and vague imagery of dream to the clear and detailed imagery of painting mirrors his progression from unconscious rumination to conscious reflection. And what began as apprehensive desire in the hidden recesses of his mind gradually becomes determined conscious wish: Demian no longer has to impose himself upon Sinclair (the forced eating of the escutcheon), Sinclair turns to Demian for continued help (the mailing of the painting).

The dream in which Sinclair is embraced by his mother under the bright sign of the hawk, his painting of this recurrent sex fantasy, and his burning of the painting and ingestion of its ashes are thought process similarly externalized. Sinclair begins to move from emancipation from, to emancipation for. A new ethic involving a new conception of deity now evolves vague and forbidding in his unconscious, and again his musing first finds expression in dream symbolism and then seeps into the conscious level of his mind. Months of reflection under the tutelage of Pistorius culminate in Sinclair's acceptance of an ethic embracing both good and evil and in the recognition of Abraxas, the god of both good and evil. For Sinclair, the

Christian-bourgeois ethic clearly revolves around sex, his own immediate concern. In the past, he had associated sex with Kromer and
Beck and the "dark world" or with Beatrice and the "light world."
Neither alternative had been satisfactory. His persistent dream mirrors his quandary and is rooted in an incipient and insistent subconscious desire to resolve this dilemma. The dream-figure embracing
Sinclair is not just mother or lover, prostitute or angel, man or
woman, devil or god, but both and all; the embrace is not just horror
or delight, sin or worship, guilt or innocence, animalistic or spiritual,
evil or good, agony or bliss, but both and everything; it also suggests
incest and self-adulation, homosexuality and heterosexuality, and the
experience fills Sinclair with both longing and fear. Sex could be all
these things with all these reactions, and all that is should be accepted. Dichotomy of incompatibles could become dichotomy of
compatibles. Sinclair's eventual painting of his dream-figure symbolizes his full consciousness of this new ethic. When he swallowed
the hawk he became the iconoclast it connotes; his eating of his painting's ashes is his full acceptance, his absorption of all that the image
implies: the new ethic and its related deity. Sinclair's cerebral breakthrough was complete; he was free. Now, he had only to shift his goal
from Abraxas, who too could only become another distractive myth,
to himself and *Frau Eva*.

As straight narrative, *Demian* is thin fare. A brief series of encounters over a period of ten years is recollected in eight loosely related chapters. These confrontations are not particularly exciting, and
their sketchy depiction is burdened by exposition. The story lacks actional evolvement, generates little suspense, and its apocalyptic ending is abrupt and frustrating. Its characters are unidimensional: they
have no physical reality and little psychology, their movement is
somnambular, and their dialogue is wooden. The world in which
they live has just as little substance, like a stage stripped of its prop-
erties: cities, streets, houses, and parks are merely concepts; lively
nature is no longer part of the human scene, and but for the animated
yellow and blue associated with the hawk that seems to hover over
the setting, everything basks in light or is shrouded in darkness. All is
only vaguely anchored in time and space. *Demian*'s questionable
merits as straight narrative are hardly enhanced by a pervasive mystification: by extrasensory perception, thought transference, the contemplation of fire, a mystical interpretation of dreams, mysterious
appearances and disappearances, white magic, yoga, and by a climactic prophetic clairvoyance. Hesse's introductory characterization of

this unseemly mélange of the vaguely real and the fantastic is certainly appropriate: "It [the story] smatters of nonsense and confusion, of insanity and dream. . . ." Taken literally the tale is just that. But Hesse was intent upon anything but realistic fiction; to judge it as such is to misjudge it. His immediate purpose was a novel form of inner biography, and in order to detract as little as possible from Sinclair's inner story he chose to skeletonize his outer story. The occult was not introduced for its own sake or for novel effect, but to deemphasize the visible world even further. This dimming of the physical world was as deliberate and as successful as Hesse's artful exploitation of biblical imagery and concepts.[60] Thanks to these literary techniques, Sinclair's inner story emerges clear and his simple tale becomes mythic: a story of youth's timeless quest for the self, mirroring man's typological course from childhood innocence, through doubt, sin, agony, and despair, to a hoped-for ultimate second innocence, his humanization (*Menschwerdung*) as Hesse was to call it in *Ein Stück Theologie* (1932) [61]

IMPRINT OF PSYCHOANALYSIS

Psychoanalysis not only changed Hesse's way of life, it also lent new dimensions to his art. His prose, which had been more or less traditional in both matter and manner, now became highly original and distinctly modern. Psychoanalysis may not have provided Hesse with startling new insights but it certainly did make possible a more organized understanding of himself and of the creative process, and it obviously afforded and suggested new modes of literary expression. Self-observation in his art assumed an unmistakable psychoanalytic character, the psychoanalyst's preoccupation with the conscious and the unconscious and with psychological complexes and processes became Hesse's concern, and from these interests and the common techniques of psychoanalysis, new literary devices were fashioned. Few of Hesse's tales after 1916 were left untouched by this new exposure. Its imprint upon *Demian* is classical. Hesse's search for the self now became a distinct Jungian process of individuation involving dissolution and birth and culminating in a general affirmation of every-

---

60 In its free use of biblical concepts, its numerous references to biblical figures, and its dependence upon biblical imagery, *Demian* is a veritable religious tract—his *Revelations* for youth. For an excellent study of Hesse's indebtedness to the Old and New Testaments, see Theodore Ziolkowski, *The Novels of Hermann Hesse: A Study in Theme and Structure* (Princeton: Princeton University Press, 1965), pp. 87–145.

61 *Gesammelte Schriften* (1957), Vol. 7, p. 389.

thing that is. All who cross Sinclair's path are on one level Jungian projections and all Sinclair's encounters on this level are Jungian confrontations with the unconscious. Sinclair's progressive absorption of these projections is the Jungian process of assimilation in man's quest of his integrated self. Jung's process of individuation, the confrontation with and the integration of the unconscious, became a means for Hesse, a novel literary device for portraying the human predicament. Jung's recourse in analysis to both dreams and paintings probably suggested yet another novel literary device, Hesse's linkage of dreams and paintings to depict psychic process. In Pistorius, even the analyst became a literary function. And of course, Pistorius himself is clearly a Jungian: his theory of the unconscious of the individual and the collective unconscious of mankind is Jungian, as too is his interest in Abraxas and in the occult, and his interpretation of Sinclair's dreams. *Demian* was definitely written in the shadow of Jung. Freud stood nearby. Sinclair's nostalgic dreams of a paradisiacal family boating and his Kromer nightmare are clearly Freudian constructs: symbols of a yearning for prenatal security, and of an oedipal parental relationship. Hesse's paraclinical interest in Sinclair's sexuality, from childhood through puberty and adolescence to manhood, with its emphasis upon love for mother and hatred for father, fear and suppression of desires, sexual fantasies and temporary successful sublimation of insistent urges, and his redundant return to this theme in Knauer's suppression of sexual urges and his resultant sexual nightmares, undoubtedly also derived from Freud.

Hesse's art bears the indelible imprint of psychoanalysis, but only its imprint. His tales never became merely applied Jungianism or Freudianism. He was too independent a thinker to become either a Jungian or a Freudian and too much an artist merely to write psychological tracts. In his usual eclectic manner he borrowed from both analysts and from others whatever appealed to him and whatever he could use to advantage, and as usual, whatever he appropriated was modified to accord with his bent of thought and to suit his purposes. Hesse did not begin to practice a new art, he simply integrated psychoanalysis into his art as he did with all experience.

SIGMUND FREUD AND CARL GUSTAV JUNG

Hesse's introduction to psychoanalysis predates his friendship with Dr. Lang. In his *Biographische Notizen* (1923) he states that he had become acquainted with the field in 1913 or 1914.[62] Two letters of June 1914 in which E. Jung (probably a relative of C. G. Jung) tried to interest him in the subject and to impress upon him its literary possibilities clearly imply that Hesse had not yet read any of the analysts.[63] His review of E. Löwenstein's *Nervöse Leute*, written late in the autumn of 1914, indicates definitely that he was by then familiar not only with Freud but also with Alfred Adler.[64] Hesse must therefore have begun to occupy himself with psychoanalysis in the second half of 1914. An intellectual curiosity became a personal concern when his marriage continued to deteriorate and his nerves to fray. He was probably well versed in the writings of many of the major analysts before he began his analytic sessions with Dr. Lang in April 1916. Under the influence of the latter, Freud together with Adler, P. E. Bleuler, and Wilhelm Stekel receded into the background and Jung became Hesse's primary interest and left his unmistakable mark on *Demian*. However, Jung's primacy seems to have been short-lived. *Künstler und Psychoanalyse* (1918) would suggest that, for Hesse, by the middle of 1918 Freud was again the master and Jung but one of his several outstanding pupils.[65]

Hesse became a staunch supporter and defender of Freud with his very first contact with psychoanalysis. Freud was synonymous with psychoanalysis, and this new science had much to offer. His theories could be questioned in detail but not in principle. He could be maligned by friend and foe but not discounted. Hesse was always ready to upbraid those who failed to render him due recognition, and to take issue with his many lesser detractors. This relationship to Freud is already evident in Hesse's review of E. Löwenstein's *Nervöse Leute*: "He [Löwenstein] relies entirely upon Dr. Adler in Vienna, however fails to mention that Adler himself is indebted to Sigmund Freud for all his fundamentals. Freud and his psychoanalysis have embittered opponents, and to be sure Freud's method is still burdened with personal prejudices, but the road to diagnosing and curing nervous states was pointed out by him, and that can hardly be doubted any longer." These were Hesse's first printed remarks about Freud and about psychoanalysis. His reference to Freud's embittered opponents suggests that he may already have read some Jung or at

62 *Eigensinn* (Frankfurt a.M.: Suhrkamp, 1972), p. 23.
63 These unpublished letters (June 20, 29, 1914) are in the Hesse-Nachlass, Marbach a.N.
64 *Die Propyläen*, 12 (1914), 186.
65 *Gesammelte Schriften* (1957), Vol. 7, pp. 137–143.

least have known of him and of his secession from the Freudian school. In any case, it is likely that he had already become acquainted with some of Jung's minor publications before he read his *Wandlungen und Symbole der Libido* (1912) in 1916 or 1917 while being treated by Dr. Lang. According to Jung, it was also at this time that Hesse and he first met. It was also only during this period that Jung enjoyed more of Hesse's attention and interest than Freud. By mid-1918, Freud had regained his precedence and Jung had assumed the supporting role he continued to play in Hesse's thinking; the sentiment and terminology of *Künstler und Psychoanalyse* (June 1918) is as Freudian as the symbolism of *Demian* is Jungian.

What was only apparent in 1918 became obvious in Hesse's subsequent references to Freud and to Jung. His review of Freud's *Vorlesungen zur Einführung in die Psychoanalyse* is decidedly more eulogy than appraisal.[66] Freud was the genial founder of a new and already well-established science, a man of wit and modesty endowed with a rare ability to express himself clearly and precisely. Jung, in contrast, was only one of the foremost of those analysts who were intent upon making a philosophy of Freud's science. Their efforts were commendable but any exploitation of Freudian theories and simultaneous rejection of Freud was something less than proper. Freud could be corrected but his unique place in psychoanalysis could not be usurped. Hesse's review of Freud's *Über Psychoanalyse: Fünf Vorlesungen in Worcester* is just as laudatory.[67] There was no better introduction to psychoanalysis. Jung is not even mentioned. This extolment of Freud continued in Hesse's review of his collected works.[68] Freud was one of the truly great scientists of the day, a clear logician and powerful intellect boldly intent upon exposing life's mysteries, and Jung was the only other analyst whose influence extended beyond the psychoanalytical guild. Hesse obviously thought very highly of Jung, but he always reserved his warmest praise for Freud.

As a reviewer, Hesse accorded Jung's works decidedly less attention and less favor than Freud's. *Psychologische Typen* alone enjoyed his unreserved praise.[69] The book definitely furthered psychology as a science, afforded revealing insights into history, religion, and culture, and was of significant practical value. Commenting upon *Über die Energetik der Seele*, Hesse chose only to remind his readers that

66 *Vivos Voco*, 1 (June 1920), 588–589.
67 *Vivos Voco*, 1 (June 1920), 589.
68 "Erinnerung an Lektüre," *Neue Rundschau*, 36 (September 1925), 966.
69 "Ein paar schöne Bücher," *Vossische Zeitung*, August 28, 1921, No. 404.

Jung was the most outstanding of Freud's students.[70] And in his review of *Wirklichkeit der Seele*, a collection of psychoanalytical essays to which Jung had contributed, Hesse carefully couched praise in reservation and censure.[71] In his philosophical approach to psychoanalysis, Jung had done much to advance man's understanding of the psyche, but Freud had done even more. Jung was excessively professorial, and his mockery of Freud's theory of sublimation was regrettable. Jung was and remained for Hesse only one of Freud's most brilliant students.

Hesse's admiration of Freud was enthusiastic and enduring, his deference to Jung was never quite unqualified. He was honestly impressed by both the empiricist and the romantic. Only his consistently reluctant acclaim of Jung is suspect. Hesse seems never to have met Freud and their correspondence was limited to a few brief exchanges.[72] Theirs was not a personal relationship. On the other hand, he did meet Jung in 1916 and again in 1921, and did correspond with him, albeit only sporadically, from 1921 to 1950.[73] That Hesse stopped seeing Jung after only a few analytical sessions in May 1921, and that he never again sought his company, suggests that Jung as a person may have roused his antipathy, just as the professorial tone of Jung's writings was later to irritate him, and just as the presumptuousness of Jung's response to an inquiry about their relationship would surely have piqued him had he chosen to read it. In his reply to Emanuel Maier, dated March 24, 1950, Jung stated explicitly that Hesse's knowledge of gnosticism had come from him through Dr. Lang, that Hesse was indebted to him for his *Demian* and partially obliged to him for *Siddhartha* and for *Der Steppenwolf*.[74] Hesse's response to Maier was much more discreet but it was also rife with innuendo. Like his sentiment of the past, it both extolled and demeaned, and its veiled condescension again suggests something less than sympathy:

> Since I am a friend of discretion, I did not open Jung's letter. I was analysed in 1916 by a doctor-friend who was in part a student of Jung's. At that time I became acquainted with Jung's *Transfor-*

70 "Dezembergedanken," *Dresdner Neueste Nachrichten*, December 9, 1928.
71 "Über einige Bücher," *Neue Rundschau*, 45 (September 1934), 325–326.
72 Only two postcards sent by Freud to Hesse in 1918 and 1936 were found in the Hesse-Nachlass, Marbach a.N.
73 Only one (September 1934) of Hesse's letters to Jung seems to have survived (*Briefe* [1964], pp. 126–128). Six (1919, 1922, 1934, 1936, 1950) of Jung's letters appear in C. G. Jung, *Letters* (Princeton University Press, 1973), Vol. 1, pp. 37–38, 170–171, 173–174, 220, 563, 573–574.
74 *The Psychoanalytic Review*, 50 (Fall 1963), 15.

mations of the Libido; it impressed me. Later I also read books by Jung, but only until about 1922, since analysis later no longer interested me very much. I have always respected Jung, nevertheless have never been as impressed by his writings as by Freud's. Jung probably wrote to you that I had a few analytical sessions with him about 1921, in connection with a public reading I gave as a guest of his Zürich Club. There too he made a good impression upon me; but at that time I began to realize that any real relationship to art was beyond analysts; they lack the necessary wherewithall for this.[75]

This general confirmation of Hesse's past sentiments would surely have annoyed Jung just as much as had Hesse's earlier reviews. The touch of antipathy underlying these remarks would hardly have escaped his notice. Hesse maintained this polite deference to the end. In 1955, upon the occasion of Jung's seventy-fifth birthday, he dedicated part of a poem to him, graciously appending "Greetings and congratulations for C. G. Jung in old fondness and respect."[76] And in August 1961, he wrote Miguel Serrano, a mutual admirer, that with Jung's death he had also lost something irreplaceable.[77]

Antipathy and sympathy aside, Hesse was much taken by the work of both Freud and Jung. His primary allegiance to one or the other is ultimately of no great moment. Both analysts left their imprint on him. That Hesse would be partial to psychoanalysis was almost inevitable. From the beginning, thoughts and emotions, imagination and dreams, and attitudes and desires had intrigued him more than the visible world. Even his earliest tales can be characterized as psychological studies. Interest in psychoanalysis was only a natural extension of this marked proclivity for introversion. Hesse's prewar psychologizing was largely descriptive. It was based on intuition, observation, and on his reading of *belles-lettres*, and it was colored by Nietzsche and Schopenhauer. His efforts to go beyond simple description were few and distinctly in the style of the late nineteenth-century. The doctor whom Camenzind consults about his general depression can only advise him to associate more freely with people. The exceptional in young Giebenrath is accounted for by an ironic allusion to Nietzsche's association of biological degeneration and hypertrophy of the intelligence. In *Freunde* (1907–1908) Hans Calwer's

75 *The Psychoanalytic Review*, 50 (Fall 1963), 16. Hesse's letter is not dated.
76 "Seele beugt sich und erhebt sich," *Neue Zürcher Zeitung*, July 24, 1955.
77 Miguel Serrano, *C. G. Jung and Hermann Hesse* (London: Routledge & Kegan Paul, 1966), p. 32.

loneliness and disillusionment are simply attributed to neurasthenia. Troubled Kuhn is informed by the theosophist Lohe that he, like so many other lonely and unhappy young people, is suffering from a touch of moral insanity, extreme individualism, or fancied loneliness. And in *Haus zum Frieden* (1909–1910), an eccentric young writer's extreme despondency is attributed to predisposition, inner fate, and to a character weakness. This antediluvian manner of psychologizing ended with Hesse's introduction to psychoanalysis.

PSYCHOANALYSIS AND LITERATURE

Although psychoanalysis was only a brief passion for Hesse, it did remain an abiding interest. He was attracted by the subject in 1914 and was most taken by it from 1916 to 1922; he continued sporadically to read analytical writings until the mid-thirties and never lost interest in interpreting his own dreams.[78] It was from *Demian* (1917) to *Narziss und Goldmund* (1928) that psychoanalysis left its most obvious mark on Hesse's fiction. His semifictive *Kurgast* (1923) and *Die Nürnberger Reise* (1925) bask in psychoanalytical thought, and both his published and unpublished diaries from 1916 to 1927 are replete with references to psychoanalysis.[79] The psychological bent of many of Hesse's miscellaneous essays and of almost all his literary studies written during this period, and his reviews of most of the major publications of Freud and Jung from 1920 to 1934 evidence this same engrossment; psychic processes, a psychological assessment of his fellow writers, and the psychology of art were now foremost concerns. Psychoanalysis had virtually become a way of thought.

Hesse wrote *Künstler und Psychoanalyse*, his only essay dealing exclusively with psychoanalysis and its relationship to literature, in June 1918. It was his critical assessment and warm acknowledgment of the new science. He believed that psychoanalysis had already done much to define, clarify, and organize psychic experience and had rightly both confirmed and corrected Nietzsche. It could most certainly be applied to good advantage in literary interpretation; it could

78 Hesse remarked upon his dreams as late as May 1962: "You know that I also upon occasion count dreaming among those things that I call experience. Without having broken with Freud and Jung, I have really become tired of wanting to understand and to interpret dreams—exceptions granted—and have returned to the naïve and childlike manner in which the artist observes the world, and also the world of dreams, as appearance, as picture, as an experience of the eyes and of the senses, or as a grotesque play of thoughts." "Brief im Mai," *Neue Zürcher Zeitung*, May 27, 1962, No. 2120.

79 See Prose IV:334, 440, 601; Manuscripts X:426/i–426/oa.

also be misused by critics intent primarily upon proving that artists are essentially sick. Psychoanalysis, personally experienced, could restore a troubled writer's faith in himself and in the value of his activity, could afford a more fruitful contact with the unconscious, the inexhaustible source of his creation, and could help him honestly face and accept all that is repressed in him. But psychoanalysis of itself cannot make a writer. Writers would continue to be the intuitive dreamers they have always been, and they would err to try to apply the technique of psychoanalysis in their art. This remained more or less Hesse's sentiment. Some of these views were later qualified, others were elaborated upon, but none was ever retracted.

Returning to the theme of psychoanalysis and literature in *Unsere jüngste Dichtung* (1920),[80] Hesse noted that the younger generation of writers in Germany had not yet really benefited artistically from the influence of Freud and his science. In *Aus einem Tagebuch des Jahres 1920*,[81] he dwelt upon the close relationship between the personal purpose of his essentially autoanalytical art and the general intent of psychoanalysis; both activities could lead to an acceptance of life's chaos. In *Erinnerung an Lektüre* (1925),[82] he began to doubt whether Freud's rational analysis could actually plumb the mysteries of life, and in *Die Nürnberger Reise* (1925), he deplored the fact that psychoanalysis was still far too academic. By 1930, Hesse had become exasperated by the prevalent misapplication of psychoanalysis in literary criticism; he gave vent to his ire in *Notizen zum Thema Dichtung und Kritik*, written in July 1930.[83] To equate works of art with the sundry dreams and fantasies of any common neurotic, and to attempt to psychoanalyze their author by interpreting them in the manner of an analyst, was naïve and presumptuous. To account for a masterpiece by simply tracing it to the same psychic disturbances responsible for any other emotionally disturbed person's neuroses was only to equate artists and psychopaths and to reduce literature to mere symptoms of disease. These were the machinations of dilettante critics become pseudo analysts and such assertions were neither literary criticism nor psychoanalysis. This dilettante analysis was basically deprecatory, could shed no light upon the aesthetic value of a work of art, and could contribute little to biography or to the psychology of art. Hesse was of the firm opinion that this sin against both art and

80 *Vossische Zeitung*, June 30, 1920.
81 *Corona*, 3 (1932), 208.
82 *Neue Rundschau*, 36 (September 1925), 966.
83 *Neue Rundschau*, 41, ii (December 1930), 769–773.

psychoanalysis was not condoned by Freud or any other responsible analyst.

ART AND DISEASE

As a young man, Hesse must have been anything but in sympathy with the prevalent tendency at the turn of the century to associate genius with insanity and art with disease. What Schopenhauer had contended and Heine had believed, what Nietzsche had elaborated upon and Max Nordau had carried to ridiculous extremes, had become common knowledge in literary circles, stimulating to some and disturbing to others.[84] Hesse was among those disturbed. The first clear indication of this is his snide allusion in *Unterm Rad* (1903) to Nietzsche's ennoblement through degeneration ("Veredelung durch Entartung"). This uncalled for aside suggests annoyance, and rings very defensive. Hesse's association of creativity and suffering in *Gertrud* (1909) and then again in *Rosshalde* (1913) would imply that he had in the interim become more receptive to Nietzsche's theory of art. His suggestion that the emotionally troubled young writer in *Haus zum Frieden* (1909–1910) senses intuitively that his art is a by-product of his illness, tends to confirm this. Deep down and reluctantly, Hesse himself had probably long believed what his young writer senses. His earliest protagonists would verify this. They are all degenerates in Nietzsche's sense of the word: all are physically flawed or psychologically scarred or both, and all are refugees from life, for whom art is a retreat and a compensation. Hesse's heroes exemplify what he himself would not admit.

Though post-war Hesse confronted this issue more openly, he continued to be on the defensive, often resorted to more mockery than argument, and eventually evolved theories closer to his own heart. When high-spirited, he could admit of a close relationship between genius and insanity, and art and disease but, when despondent, he commonly dismissed these associations and proceeded to disparage the normal and mediocre representatives of life. This shifting attitude, obvious defensiveness, and deliberate offensiveness became Hesse's immediate way of disposing of a painful probability. Feeling that his own self-justification was at stake, he carefully avoided unqualified commitment. Irony, ambiguity, and hyperbole

84 Arthur Schopenhauer, *Die Welt als Wille und Vorstellung* (1819); Heinrich Heine, *Die Romantische Schule* (1836); Friedrich Nietzsche, *Menschliches, Allzumenschliches* (1878–1880); Max Nordau, *Entartung* (1892–1893).

suited this purpose. In *Phantasien* (1918), Hesse responded to the issue in just such a fashion: ". . . if genius is insanity, and if every accomplishment of a writer or painter or composer is nothing other than the convulsive attempt to compensate in another field for a deficiency in his being, his life, his character, then the 'normal human being' is the person who is free of such compulsion, that is to say, the person who possesses no gifts."[85] The statement was carefully couched in the noncommittal conditional, and Hesse immediately added that the remark was for him true both ironically and literally. In the remainder of the essay, ironic truth wanes and literal truth waxes and culminates in an indirect acknowledgment of Nietzsche's theory of art, in a vision of the ideal as opposed to the real writer: "[the author] who commonly has no need to sublimate repressions of whatever sort, who dwells in himself confident and happy . . . who is not driven to virtue by necessity, and whom no inner weakness compels to seek compensation in works of art. . . ." Like Hesse, Klingsor often thinks that art is really only "a substitute, an arduous and ten times too expensive substitute for neglected life, animality, and love," and like Hesse, he also tries to convince himself that art is not just a substitute but an independent activity as valid as any other (*Klingsors letzter Sommer*, 1919). A new theory of art was to sprout from this seedling thought. In *Kurgast* (1923), Hesse began to admit unhesitantly, indeed with a touch of bravado, that he was a psychopath. The term had lost all its opprobrium for him, had in fact become a mark of distinction. Used of artists, it was no longer a sickness that implied something less than the normal, but something more. Psychopathy was the agony of the uncompromising gifted, a side-effect of fruitful sublimation. Hesse boldly reversed the widely accepted cause and effect relationship between disease and art. For Nietzsche's ennoblement through degeneration (*Veredelung durch Entartung*) he proposed to substitute degeneration through ennoblement (*Entartung durch Veredelung*). And in this way Hesse now (1924) accounted for Hölderlin's fate:

> Translated into the language of current psychology, Hölderlin's summons would run something like this: Let the noble man not put his instinctual life too one sidedly under the domination of instinct-hostile spirituality, for every piece of our instinctual life not successfully sublimated will in the course of suppression occasion severe agonies. This was Hölderlin's personal problem, and he succumbed to it. He cultivated a spirituality that violated

85 *Vossische Zeitung*, August 20, 1918.

his nature; his ideal was to leave all that is common behind him
. . . he strove for an exemplary spiritualization that miscarried in
the attempt.[86]

This was just as true of Novalis and even of Nietzsche (1924).[87]

It was this essentially Freudian understanding of the term sublimation that Hesse expounded upon in a letter he wrote to C. G. Jung
in September 1934.[88] He himself preferred to use the word only where
there was a culturally fruitful deflection of basic drives. Unlike analysts, he also considered this manner of sublimation successful
and highly laudable even when thinker or artist became pathological
in the process. Illness was the risk of art, cure was the benefit of
psychoanalysis. But psychoanalysis also posed a risk, not, however,
because it might cure artists of their neuroses and thereby remove the
cause of or a supplemental thrust in their creativity, but because it
might persuade some to put aside their art for the sake of emotional
health.

Having made "degeneration through ennoblement" of "ennoblement through degeneration," Hesse proceeded to resolve what in
his mind had become the "philistine bourgeois theory that genius is
always related to insanity."[89] Genius was not absolutely linked or
synonymous with insanity but could easily succumb to it, and again,
not because it was something less, but something more than the normal. Like neurosis, insanity was only another risk run by the gifted
and not an inherent part of their constitution.

MÄRCHEN

In *Lulu* (1900), Hesse depicted two worlds: drab everyday life,
and the wondrous realm behind this curtain of appearance. Provincial
Kirchheim, with its Inn at the Sign of the Crown (*Gasthaus zur Königs-
krone*), the innkeeper and his wife, attractive Lulu, the poet Lauscher,
his entourage of young romantics, and their odd philosopher-friend
Drehdichum, provides a realistic setting for the Kingdom of Ask, with
its King Ohneleid and his opal castle, Princess Lilia and the harp Sil-
berlied, the garden of lilies and the fountain Lask, the snake Edel-
zung, the witch Zischelgift, a dwarf prince, a stolen talisman, and
the philosopher-clown Haderbart. But Kirchheim and Ask are actu-

86 "Über Hölderlin," *Gesammelte Schriften* (1957), Vol. 7, p. 278.
87 "Nachwort zu Novalis," *Gesammelte Schriften* (1957), Vol. 7, pp. 280–281.
88 *Briefe* (1964), pp. 126–128.
89 "Nachwort zu Novalis," *Gesammelte Schriften* (1957), Vol. 7, p. 281.

ally not two different worlds, nor are Lulu's and Lilia's two different stories. Ask and Lilia are only Lauscher's projected inner vision of Kirchheim and Lulu. This magic realm behind life's ephemeral and lackluster façade was for Hesse not only the real world, but also both art's inspiration and its substance. Lauscher lived and moved in Kirchheim but had his being in Ask, in the realm of his imagination. Combining recollection and poetic vision in a bifocal depiction of reality, he was able to write a fairy tale (*Märchen*) in the manner of *Der goldne Topf* and fittingly dedicated it to E. T. A. Hoffmann.

Lulu was the first of Hesse's many *Märchen*, and surprisingly enough the only one written before he settled in Bern. More would likely have followed in Basel but for his growing aversion to aestheticism. He first curbed his romantic proclivities and then found more acceptable expression for them in his Italianate tales (1902–1909) and his legends (1904–1912). Hesse did not return to the genre until after he had completed *Rosshalde* in January of 1913. For the next five years *Märchen* were the same filler activity that the Italianate tales and the legends had been in Gaienhofen. Three were written in 1913, two in 1915, two in 1916, three in 1918, another followed in 1921, and Hesse's last *Märchen* was written in 1932. All these tales first appeared in newspapers or in periodicals, seven of them were assembled in the book, *Märchen* (1919), another was added to the collection's second edition (1946) and yet another to the third edition (1955).[90]

Like most of Hesse's art, *Lulu* is poeticized autobiography. The story derived from an actual situation and a personal experience, and its incorporated philosophy of life with its associated theory of art was Hesse's effort to lend approbation to his own withdrawal into aestheticism. Each of the *Märchen* that followed was in its own way as intimately personal as *Lulu*. In this regard, they are all more fact and less fancy than the traditional *Kunstmärchen*. However, they are also Hesse's most impersonal expression of the personal. Intent upon giving the personal its least intimate expression, he properly chose a narrative form traditionally reserved for fantasy and myth. In *Lulu*, with its Hoffmannesque blending of the actual and poetic vision, the personal is refracted but is still discernible. In the later and much more original *Märchen*, where Hesse chose to forego the actual and to depict only his poetic vision, the personal either becomes mythic or is almost blotted out by the fantastic.

---

90 (Berlin: S. Fischer, 1919), 182 pp.; (Zürich: Fretz & Wasmuth, 1946), 214 pp.; (Berlin: Suhrkamp, 1955), 193 pp.

In *Der Weg zur Kunst* (February 4, 1913),[91] the first of the *Märchen* written in Bern, the poet Han Fook leaves family, friends, and fiancée to join a "master of the word" in his secluded bamboo hut in the mountains, there to perfect his art. He becomes the poet his master is, but only after a lifetime of lonely dedication and trying renunciation. Returning to his home, he finds that all whom he once knew are no more. He is left even more estranged than he had always been, but he is now at peace with himself and content with life. In *Märchen* (September 10, 1913), a callow young flutist sets out on his journey through life, mindful of his father's parting admonition that he regale his fellow humans only with joyous song. His encounter with a pretty maiden is happy but brief, and his distressing downstream odyssey with a somber minstrel-helmsman is long and enlightening. A novice has again met a guide and model and a frivolous romantic becomes a master of authentic and poignant song, and again it takes a lifetime.

Like Han Fook, Hesse was from the beginning more an observer than a participant; for him, too, life held its attractions but art and solitude were his preference. Fook's reluctance to marry and settle down before perfecting his verse were Hesse's second thoughts about his own adjustment to life and art; he had also begun seriously to wonder whether he, like Fook, would not have to free himself from life's involvements and dedicate himself wholly to his art, if he was ever to become more than just an ordinary popular writer. And like his disenchanted flutist-minstrel, Hesse had learned that life and love were not a romantic song and dance but a dark vale of torment and a torture; he had also begun to sense that but for his agony life would have no glow. Like his protagonist become mature and resolute, Hesse was now also prepared to captain his own ship and to sing of life as it actually was. But all that was personal was rendered mythic in these *Märchen*. They were rooted in Hesse's life, and immediately they are the stories of Han Fook and of a particular flutist, but essentially they are archetypal depictions mirroring the artist's inclinations, needs and aspirations, the demands of art, and the relationship between life and art.

In *Augustus* (September 30, 1913), Hesse proceeded from the story of the artist and of art to the story of man. Augustus's mythic path of life leads from the innocence and harmony of childhood

---

91 Unless otherwise indicated, parenthetical dates of the *Märchen* are those of submission for publication. Hesse customarily submitted his shorter prose works a few days after their completion.

through the joy and the eventual tedium of chance fortune, the agony and ultimate despair of sin, and the redemptive suffering of adversity to the selfless childlike contentment that may come with age. Hesse himself was still caught in the maelstrom of life; like Augustus the sated worldling, he had his fill of material things and worldly pleasures and pain, and dreamed nostalgically of his lost childhood paradise. Hesse had also begun to look forward to a second stage of innocence, when he, like Augustus, could affirm himself and all he had been and life at large for all it was, and when he would be content just to love and to serve. With the passing of his childhood and youth, Hesse lost what he termed his *Heimat*. This cradle paradise quickly became a haunting refrain in both his prose and poetry. He had sought to recreate this lost *Heimat* in his aestheticism, and for many years he had assumed it could be found again only in death. By *Augustus* it had become a possibility in life itself. Augustus's second innocence is still more a regression to an earlier state of harmony than progression to a higher level of grace, but it does anticipate this third stage of life to which most of Hesse's post-*Rosshalde* protagonists aspire, and where, if only sporadically and briefly, they are able to experience the oneness and harmony of the self and of all life. This tripartite story of man that began to evolve in *Augustus* was to receive its most fascinating mythic expression in *Siddhartha* (1922) and to be expounded upon in *Ein Stückchen Theologie* (1932).

Hesse's *Märchen* of 1913 are life mythicized. His *Merkwürdige Nachricht von einem andern Stern* (written April 22 to 24, 1915) and *Das Märchen von Faldum* (November 5, 1915) are social comment mythicized. In his poems, reviews, and essays of the time, Hesse was both an internationalist, a humanitarian who tolerated war, and a pacifist who looked forward to a German victory. His two *Märchen* of 1915 are free of this ambiguity; they represent an intermediate stage between Hesse's initial ambiguous stance and his later active anti-war campaign. Two stars are juxtaposed in *Merkwürdige Nachricht von einem andern Stern*: one on which humane traditions are cultivated, religion is practised and peace prevails, where life is valued and beauty is appreciated, and where reason is respected and love and happiness are experienced; and another star that knows only fear, hatred, jealousy, and despair, where wars are waged incessantly and battlefield murder is officially condoned, and where the countryside is left strewn with unattended cadavers. The latter is clearly our world as Hesse saw it, rendered mythical, and the former is the mythicized ideal world ours could be.

Hesse's social comment in *Das Märchen von Faldum* is less direct and more dispassionate. An archetypal society, peopled by typical humans, all anxious either to possess what they do not have or to be something other than they are, proceeds along its typical course from growth to decay and extinction. Observing the human community within the context of time and in philosophical perspective, Hesse was prepared to acknowledge that the vagaries of any society, including ours, were ultimately of no great moment. Time was the great leveler; all would eventually crumble and be forgotten. Hesse's juxtaposition of the actual and the ideal in *Merkwürdige Nachricht von einem andern Stern* was a statement of regret and disapproval; in his social comment of *Das Märchen von Faldum* he only sought some private consolation in the notion that ultimately all worlds, ideal or otherwise, were marked by time. Under the circumstances, it might be best, like the violinist of Faldum, just to try to blot out the noisy world from one's life, or like his young companion, to become only a silent observer and listener. Hesse decided in favor of the latter when his maligning by the *Kölner Tageblatt* on October 24, 1915, quickly became a widespread general repudiation; he withdrew into semi-seclusion at the beginning of 1916 and did not resume his social comment until mid-1917.

Hesse proceeded next to make myth of both the process and the stuff of psychoanalysis—of his own analytical experience. Little of any significance is known about this experience beyond the fact that Hesse was treated by Dr. Lang from April 1916 to November 1917. Lang's records would have been revealing, but these were destroyed by his daughter after his death. And Hesse's diaries of that time could throw considerable light upon his psychic ills, Lang's treatment, the doctor-patient relationship, and upon his convalescence, but these are still inaccessible and furthermore extend only from November 1916 to August 1918.[92] However, a modicum of this no longer or not yet directly available information can be gleaned from a few of Hesse's tales. *Der schwere Weg* (June 23, 1916) and *Eine Traumfolge* (November 5, 1916) afford brief glimpses of the initial stage of Hesse's psychoanalysis, and *Demian* (written in September and October 1917) and *Iris* (January 18, 1918) provide veiled reviews of the experience and reflect some of its results.

In *Der schwere Weg*, Hesse's protagonist leaves the comfort and warmth of a flower-strewn valley and reluctantly follows a patient

92 See Manuscripts X:426/l, 426/la.

and solicitous guide up a precipitous crevice to a high rocky peak basking in the burning glare of the sun and in the cold blue of the sky. He is unsettled by an ominous black bird perched in a stunted tree and croaking the word eternity, and is horrified by an all-enveloping loneliness and emptiness. When bird and guide plunge from the peak and vanish in the ether, he follows, and after an agonizingly blissful tumble through space, he comes to rest on the breast of his mother. This startlingly Kafkaesque allegory was written at the end of May while Hesse was still undergoing his initial intensive analysis at the clinic Sonnmatt. It is clearly a mythic portrayal of this first stage of his treatment. Hesse must have begun his arduous inward trek with the same apprehension that his protagonist begins his tortuous ascent, and his relationship with Lang must have become just as strained as the latter's relationship with his guide. Like his protagonist's, Hesse's ordeal must have been excruciating and also broken only by brief spells of relief, and he, too, must quickly have realized that there was no return and to stop could only be more painful and disastrous than to continue. Lang probably encouraged his faltering patient, disabused him of his illusions about himself and life, helped him to make his own decisions, and roused in him the will to pursue his self-quest regardless of the ultimate consequences, very much in the manner of the guide helping his ward proceed from desperation to determination. Hesse's protagonist's ascent to the mountain's peak was his own successful breakthrough: he had overcome his innate fear of psychoanalysis, and the initial agonies of his analytical self-quest had not intimidated him. His protagonist's tumble into the void of heaven was Hesse's own plunge into the uncharted space of his unconscious. And Hesse's venture, like that of his protagonist, took him to the breast of his mother: to the Magna Mater she symbolizes, to the primordial allness of life as manifested in himself.

Dreams were always a treasured experience for Hesse. In early life, his daydreams were a pleasant retreat from a world not to his liking; with his introduction to psychoanalysis, his nightdreams became his windows to the soul, and in later years he took delight in the surrealistic playfulness characteristic of many dreams. Hesse made art of his earliest reveries (*Eine Stunde hinter Mitternacht*, 1899), a literary device of dreams (*Demian*, 1917), and dreamers of most of his protagonists. He recorded many of his dreams, learned to interpret them psychoanalytically, and even published some. He also recognized that this interest could become a confining fascination and took care not to become what he disparagingly termed a dream writer ("Traumliterat"). [93] Of the actual dreams that Hesse may have written down before his analytical treatment, only two were published and no others have survived. [94] With Hesse's personal involvement with psychoanalysis an innate general interest in dreams became a studied concern. Dreams were now more carefully recalled, more often recorded, and closely analyzed. Under Lang's tutelage, Hesse himself soon became practised in dream interpretation. This absorption continued until his interest in psychoanalysis began to wane early in the twenties. Most of the many dreams recorded during these critical years are no longer extant, and only a few, among them the series of *Eine Traumfolge*, have appeared in print. [95] In the years following, the dream world continued to delight Hesse but never again to fascinate him. The seriousness of dream interpretation gradually gave way to sheer pleasure in the fantasy and humor of dreams. It was not until after the Second World War that Hesse began again to publish a few of the more unusual of his dreams. [96]

Der schwere Weg is the mythicized first stage of Hesse's analytical treatment. His initial agonizing misgivings are depicted in vivid detail; his subsequent euphoric plunge into the maternal abyss of the self is only mentioned. A return to Magna Mater, to elemental life in himself, was clearly still only a vague anticipation. Many psychological tangles had first to be unraveled and that was to involve dreams. This next stage of Hesse's psychoanalysis—his plunge into the self that had only been broached in *Der schwere Weg*—is reflected in *Eine Traumfolge*. In this sequence of dreams, Hesse has his being beyond the barriers of time and space, the real and the imaginary blend in

93 "Traumgeschenk" (1946), *Gesammelte Schriften* (1957), Vol. 4, p. 826.

94 *Singapore-Traum*, a religio-erotic dream experienced in a movie house of Singapore in the autumn of 1911, and *Der Traum von den Göttern*, a premonition of worldwide destruction six months before the First World War actually began. *Gesammelte Schriften* (1957), Vol. 3, pp. 803–810, 927–931.

95 See also *Traum am Feierabend* and *Ein Stück Tagebuch*, written in the winter and spring of 1918 (*Gesammelte Schriften* [1957], Vol. 7, pp. 113–117, 143–149). *Aus Martins Tagebuch* (1918) comments on an allegedly very significant dream but the dream itself is not recounted (*O mein Heimatland*, 9 [1921], 84–86). One dream is included in *Aus einem Tagebuch des Jahres 1920* (*Corona*, 3 [1932], 192–209). But for these, only a number of still unpublished dreams recorded from May 16 to October 6, 1918, and from May 10, 1919 to December 1, 1920, and now in the possession of Bruno and Heiner Hesse respectively (see Manuscripts X-A:5/2, 5a/4), seem to have survived.

96 One of these is in *Aus einem Notizbuch* (1937), another in *Traumgeschenk* (1946), two more appear in *Traumtheater* (1948), another in *Schreiben und Schriften* (1961), and two in *Brief im Mai* (1962). See: *Hortulus*, 1 (June 1951), 38–41; *Gesammelte Schriften* (1957), Vol. 4, pp. 825–830, Vol. 7, pp. 802–809; *Neue Zürcher Zeitung*, August 15, 1961, No. 2986; *Universitas*, 17 (1962), 835–840.

another Kafkaesque surreality, and all is emotionally charged. In the presence of a seductive and elusive dark-haired strumpet, Hesse is humiliated and infuriated by two suave young fops smirking at his shoeless feet. He proceeds gleefully to pommel one of his healthy tormentors with an enormous soft red slipper until all his hatred turns to love and until his adversary lies prostrate and thankful at his feet. Elated, Hesse unleashes a furious storm with but a signal of his hand and then rescues his elusive temptress from the resultant flood, only to have her change into a child and then simply vanish from the scene. Hesse luxuriates briefly in the bliss of childhood innocence, then finds himself hovering lonely and terrified on a tiny platform immediately above an enticing bevy of gypsy maidens on a frail scaffold and high above the people in the distant streets below. Eager to join the young women, he begins an agonizing and endless descent, only to appear in a large and vaguely familiar dark room with a heavy lamp in hand searching sadly and in vain for something or other and refusing to be helped or consoled by his sister and brother-in-law, who fear for his sanity. Hesse's search is in vain, his maidens vanish, and he is left with longing that knows only despair. Old age approaches, his teeth begin to fall out and a knee to putrefy, he shudders at the awesome approach of death, then labors up an insanely precipitous stairway to his home and mother, hostile clinging tendrils hold him fast, his presence goes unnoticed and his cries are not heard, his mother vanishes slowly in the recesses of the garden, and he is left standing alone at its gate.

Eine Traumfolge was an actual sequence of dreams. But it was not just any sequence, nor was it just recounted, and it does more than just afford some insight into an intermediate stage in Hesse's analytical treatment. It was a carefully selected sequence of dreams, impersonal enough to be universally typical and touched up enough to become art. This dream sequence became an exposure of everyman's inner world: a depiction of everyman's sexual anxieties and ego fantasies, of his basic insecurity, timorousness, and latent violence, of the ambiguity of human emotions, and of the universal fascination of childhood's paradise, the pervasive fear of old age and of death, and man's innate yearning to return to his mother and to the allness and oblivion she connotes. In his *Eine Traumfolge*, Hesse managed to mythicize the most private and most personal of man's experiences, and with it, he added yet another item to his list of novel *Märchen*. The rest of Hesse's recorded dreams remained on the level of reportage.

Iris is *Augustus* retold in a more autobiographical vein, rendered more psychological, and records a slightly more advanced stage in Hesse's thinking. Each of the tales depicts the tripartite story of man. The latter (September 30, 1913) was clearly recounted by an author not yet familiar with Freud or Jung and the former (January 18, 1918) shows the distinct impact of Hesse's exposure to psychoanalysis. The externals of the mythic course of Augustus's life were purely fictive; only its progression of inner experience was Hesse"s. Anselm's story was a mythicized review of Hesse's own life, both inner and outer. His paradisiacal garden was Hesse's memory's childhood paradise. As a child, Hesse had been just as contentedly self-absorbed and as happily engrossed in nature's multiplicity of wonders as Anselm. The flowers and butterflies, birds and tiny lizards in his mother's garden had been as much a part of himself as they are a part of Anselm, and for him, too, life had been a joyous synesthetic experience. Disenchantment and tedium, strife and bewilderment follow Anselm's childhood paradise, much as they had Hesse's. His garden gradually loses its magic, life its wholeness and glow, and he his contentment. Just as they had for Hesse, puberty and adolescence bring unpredictable periods of shy withdrawal, brash waywardness, and moody rebelliousness, and eventual diligent application is also rewarded with a successful career. Like Hesse before him, Anselm is sent away to school while but a youngster, returns home regularly and briefly until his mother's death, then is absorbed by life and career, only to be left disenchanted with both and given to loneliness and unhappiness. In this plight, Anselm becomes attached to a friend's sister, just as Hesse had in Basel. He and Iris are as little attuned to each other as Hesse and Maria Bernoulli ever were. Iris, like Maria, is older than her suitor would have liked her to be; she is also just as set in her ways and as self-preoccupied, as hypersensitive and withdrawn, as fond of music and as disinterested in her suitor's ambitions and pursuits as Maria had been. And Anselm is just as troubled and as impetuous, as dubious about and at the same time as desperately intent upon marriage as Hesse had been. Despite his doubts and her qualms, Hesse and Maria had married and were still suffering the consequences of their mismarriage. The Anselm-Iris relationship is resolved more appropriately and to mutual advantage. A wise Iris declines marriage and sends her distraught Anselm—as Hesse undoubtedly wished in retrospect that Maria had done to him—in search of a wondrous dream he had lost with his childhood. In Anselm's quest, Hesse imagined what his life could have and might still become. Anselm surrenders himself to his memories, neglects then gives up his calling, becomes a vagabond both feared and loved, ridiculed and held in awe, then a childlike old eccentric for whom the world of appearance gradually recedes and loses all attraction and meaning as his inner world expands and eventually engulfs him. In this absorption, Anselm finally recalls his long-forgotten dream, a vision in which he enters the gorge-like purple calyx of one of the irises in his mother's garden and is drawn down a radiant stamen-lined path into the magic depths of the flower's soul, into the realm behind appearance, and into elemental oneness and eternity. What had once been only a premonition and a dream now becomes reality. In the recesses of a forest, Anselm stumbles across a narrow cleft in a wall of rock leading down into the heart of a mountain. He enters the spectral portal only to find himself proceeding down the familiar stamen-flanked path to the bliss of his purple iris's hidden depths. However, Anselm's is not a regression to the innocent harmony he had enjoyed with the physical world as a child, but a progression from the discordant and ephemeral outer world to the noumenal oneness of his inner world. His, unlike Augustus's, is not a lost paradise regained but a new paradise found. This was the second innocence, the third stage of life to which Hesse began to look forward after his analytic treatment.

Hesse's next two *Märchen* mirror his awakened interest in painting. In *Märchen vom Korbstuhl* (January 20, 1918)—an amusing anecdote more correctly designated "eine Erzählung" in many of its republications—an aspiring novice artist, obviously Hesse himself, tries in vain to paint an old wicker chair, is infuriated by the chair's nonchalant comments, and then concludes that he might better return to writing, to his first love. *Der Maler* (March 18, 1918), on the other hand, though published but once as *Märchen vom Maler*, is as Hessean a *Märchen* as any of the items included in the collection *Märchen* (1919).

In *Der Weg zur Kunst* (1913) and *Märchen* (1913), Hesse had told the story of the artist and of his art. In *Der Maler* he turned to the artist and to the reception of his art. Albert's predicament is as mythic as the timelessly typical course of Han Fook's life, and the mythic is again rooted in Hesse's own life. With his first paintings, self-conscious self-expressions as presumptuously heroic as Hesse's early prose, Albert looks forward expectantly to a rewarding rapport with a responsive and appreciative world. Like Hesse's his dream comes to naught, his response is withdrawal, and his hope is to experience again his childhood's blissful interplay and oneness with nature. This second dream is realized but even its only brief euphoric spells of realization leave Albert cloyed, fearful of extinction, and rent by a frantic desire to live. Childhood paradise quickly becomes for him as meaningless a response to the harsh realities of life as it had been for Hesse. Years pass before Albert returns to his easel, now to paint passionately, intent only upon seeing and painting and with no regard for reception. And though now generally considered quite mad, he and his paintings suddenly become the latest rage in art circles. But Albert's enthusiastic public sees in his paintings only what it chooses to see and not what he had intended to and had actually painted. He is perplexed by this lack of communication, withdraws again, continues happily to paint, but his work is never again exposed to public view. Albert's return to this art was Hesse's passionate new beginning with *Demian*; his sudden fame was to become Hesse's renewed acclaim of 1919. And had Hesse's newfound popularity been based on the misconceptions underlying Albert's notoriety, he, too, might have chosen, at least temporarily, to withdraw and to ply his art in obscurity. But for this difference, Hesse's own experiences are clearly reflected in Albert's development as an artist and the public's reception of his work, and Albert's story is just as obviously that of all too many artists. As a callow and pretentious young man, it is the artist's customary and not undeserved lot to be ignored by the public upon whose very accolades he is both intent and dependent. And it is the dedicated mature artist's common lot to be extolled but also to be misunderstood by a whimsical public whose acclaim no longer particularly interests him. In both cases, withdrawal is the usual response.

In the last two of Hesse's *Märchen*, the personal is less mythicized than both fantasized and playfully poeticized. *Piktors Verwandlungen* (written in September 1922) depicts a hopeful shade entering paradise in quest of the tree of life and of happiness. The newcomer converses with wondrous trees, a malicious snake, and a brilliantly plumed bird, encounters a bevy of exotic flowers, some nod and laugh and others only smile, some are intoxicated by their own fragrance and others sing their many-colored songs, and one engages him in tantalizing flirtatious play. Piktor is possessed by anxious longing and a presentiment of bliss. The colorful bird becomes a beautiful flower, a glittering butterfly, and then a red-tinged crystal whose magic powers transform Piktor into a stately tree, at his own request, prompted by paradise's devious snake. Trees had always suggested equanimity, strength, and dignity to Piktor, and he had often wished to be one.

He is reasonably happy, but only until he realizes years later that he has become immutable while all else is caught in a magic stream of metamorphosis, and that immutability inevitably ends in grief. A lonely and disillusioned Piktor now begins to age, to lose vitality, and to become a very distressed tree. But fortunately a young blond maiden comes traipsing through paradise, becomes enamored with Piktor and he with her, and both willing, the two are united by the very carbuncle whose magic powers had years previously turned Piktor into a lonely man-tree. Now all is well. A flagging Piktor is miraculously rejuvenated. A despondent half-tree becomes a joyous androgynous whole-tree, a contented part of eternal becoming. In search of the tree of life and happiness, Piktor himself becomes a happy tree of life.

Piktor and his paradise were obviously Hesse the painter and the paradisiacal retreat he had found in Montagnola and environs. Piktor had departed this life and Hesse had left a way of life behind with his departure from Bern, and both had looked forward to new life and to some happiness. That Piktor should elect to become a tree was anything but happenstance. The solitary tree had become Hesse's symbol for the genial lonely outsider intent solely upon living what he is.[97] Hesse had chosen to emulate this ideal when he settled in Montagnola; he figuratively became a tree and was content. By 1922, however, he had clearly begun to have second thoughts about his new adjustment to life. Isolation and aloneness had immediately proved invigorating and unusually fruitful; *Klein und Wagner, Klingsors letzter Sommer*, and a segment of *Siddhartha* had been written in quick succession, from the summer of 1919 to early 1920. Euphoria had then given way to depression and Hesse, like his Piktor, had begun to imagine that he was fossilizing and that life was passing him by. Piktor's blond companion was blond Ruth Wenger, Hesse's second wife. They had chanced to meet in the summer of 1919. He had been attracted to her immediately but a considerable difference in age had dissuaded him from courting her. However, by 1922, plagued by loneliness, he had begun to entertain fond hopes, and these hopes found their covert expression in Piktor's happy union. Unfortunately Hesse was not to experience Piktor's subsequent bliss.

Unlike most of Hesse's shorter tales, *Piktors Verwandlungen* was never submitted to any periodicals or newspapers. It did not appear in print until 1925 and then only in a limited edition of 650 copies.

97 See "Bäume" (1918), *Gesammelte Schriften* (1957), Vol. 3, p. 405.

And it actually remained unknown to the public until it was published again as a booklet in 1954, and then as a supplement to the new edition of *Märchen* in 1955. The tale's intimacy, and the use to which he put his little fantasy, account for its hesitant and belated publication. It not only depicted a particularly sensitive private relationship but had also been written expressly for Ruth Wenger. Immediate and wide publication would have been less than discreet. However, Hesse did feel free to make private use of the tale, the same use he had begun in 1918 to make of his *Zwölf Gedichte* manuscripts, and again largely for reasons of income. From 1922 to the late 1950s, at least forty-two of these manuscripts were prepared, handwritten or typed, with or without little watercolors, and never duplicated. Most were sold to Hesse enthusiasts for 200 to 300 Swiss francs apiece, some were given to close relatives, and a few to intimate friends.

Hesse's attachment to nature was intimate and long. Nature was his childhood wonderland and his boyhood playground; she became for him the refuge she is for his Peter Camenzind, and the source of solace and spiritual rejuvenation she is for his St. Francis of Assisi; her ephemeral beauty was a poignant reminder of man's mortality, and her authenticity exemplified Hesse's conception of self-will (*Eigensinn*) and his associated ideal of self-living. Nature was also a lasting creative inspiration, remained a common theme in Hesse's writing and painting, and became his most characteristic backdrop and metaphor. Water is primordial matter, rivers are life in all its flux, and fish a prehuman stage in evolution; forests are preculture and the roving wolf is man's instinctual self; gardens are a paradise, flowers and butterflies epitomize life's lasting beauty and its evanescence, and birds are associated with the soul; nature's seasons are man's stages of life and night is the mother- and day the father-principle; trees are life's stoic outsiders, mountains its imperturbable observers, and clouds are the blue flower of Hesse's early romanticism, a symbol of man's eternal longing and of his soul's endless quest for a *Heimat*.

Nature was uninhibitedly anthropomorphized, and Hesse readily identified with its every aspect. Until the First World War, he and his protagonists related most commonly to drifting clouds, the solitary tree then became an intimate kindred soul, and it, in turn, gradually yielded its favored place to the free and elusive bird. Sinclair's emancipation (1917) from the Christian-bourgeois ethos is compared to a hawk's bursting out of its eggshell; Klein's mind (1919) soars forth on wings in its inner quest; Klingsor (1919) is Gina's strange rare bird;

Siddhartha (1922) briefly becomes Kamala's caged warbler; Harry Haller's soul (1926) is an anxious lost bird; Goldmund (1928), a migrant eagle, avoids all snares, and nests often but never long. In *Pfarrhaus* (1918) [98] Hesse's soul can become one with a bird, Goldmund wishes he were a woodpecker, and Leo of *Die Morgenlandfahrt* (1931) is anxious to learn bird language. In *Vogel* (May 20, 1932), the last of his *Märchen*, Hesse actually became a bird.

Vogel was a small and rather nondescript bird, nevertheless quite unique and bewitching, not particularly colorful nor a songster of any note but still imposing in his own peculiar way, praised by many and disparaged by others, seen by few and known by fewer, yet much inquired about, primarily by strangers, and particularly after his disappearance. In his absence, Vogel quickly became the object of rumor and a subject for legend, a celebrity who attracted the attention of intellectuals and brought notoriety to his native Montagsdorf. Zealous scholars whose contradictory and obscurant theories about Vogel were probably responsible for his withdrawal, were also likely some day simply to explain him and the legends about him away entirely.

In *Piktors Verwandlungen* Hesse had fantasized his *affaire de coeur* with Ruth Wenger, in *Vogel* he fantasized his relationship with his readers and particularly with his critics. Vogel is the same playful self-depiction that Piktor was. He had lived in the vicinity of Montagsdorf and was a subject of conversation from Careno to Morbio; Hesse had settled in Montagnola in May 1919 and was soon well known from Carona to Morbio. One legend would have Vogel be an enchanted Hohenstaufen Kaiser—a whimsical allusion to the Swabian branch of Hesse's ancestry. According to another legend, Vogel had once been a magician and had lived with *Ninon die Ausländerin* in a red house on nearby Snake Hill; Hesse had always imagined himself a magician of sorts, he had married Ninon née Ausländer in 1931, and they had settled down in a red villa on the hilly and snake-infested outskirts of Montagnola. Ninety-year-old Nina who had often gathered herbs on Snake Hill was widow Nina, a local poverty stricken crone whose simple company Hesse had learned to appreciate over the years. And Mario, one of the few old-timers who could remember when Vogel still flitted about Montagsdorf, was Zio Mario, an elderly farmer with whom Hesse had chatted occasionally when he still lived in his bachelor quarters in Montagnola. [99] It is to

98 *Gesammelte Schriften* (1957), Vol. 3, p. 401.
99 See "Besuch bei Nina," *Berliner Tageblatt*, June 26, 1927, No. 298, and "Nachbar Mario," *Berliner Tageblatt*, September 20, 1928, No. 445.

these quarters in pretentiously baroque and run-down Casa Camuzzi that Klingsor's palace ruins allude. Klingsor and Piktor are only past self-disguises and Leo is Hesse's alter ego of *Die Morgenlandfahrt.* Sehuster, one-time mayor of Montagsdorf, and his money-minded nephew Schalaster, a major source of information about Vogel and ultimately Vogel's Judas Iscariot, may well have been a community dignitary and his grasping relative or just local acquaintances of Hesse. In any case, their droll and slightly derogatory fictive names are completely in keeping with the serious playfulness of the tale.

Montagsdorf's reaction to Vogel was the public's reaction to Hesse. Like Vogel, Hesse had known better days, had once been widely appreciated and rarely disparaged. The tide of fortune had then turned for both. With a price on his head and hunted with gun and snare, Vogel had taken to the peaceful forests or hills never to appear again, and Hesse, persecuted during the First World War and increasingly discredited by German activists in the twenties, had retired, first to Montagnola and then to his remote red villa, and was intent upon remaining in his seclusion.

From his assessment of the scholarship centered about Vogel and his legends, it is quite apparent that Hesse's attitude to literary criticism in general and to his own critics in particular was no more benign than his appraisal of his fickle public. Vogel-scholarship was premature, uninformed, and excessively cerebral. Scholars were too authoritative and opinionated, too skeptical and decidedly more intent upon murder than upon understanding and appreciation. The public might better have been left to its own devices. Vogel-scholarship was Hesse-scholarship. The already forgotten "eschatological interpretation of the phenomenon Vogel," whose author remains anonymous, probably alludes to H. R. Schmid's *Hermann Hesse* (1928),[100] a derogatory Freudian study at which Hesse had taken umbrage and which he had hoped would soon find its due place in the limbo of forgotten books.[101] Privy councillor ("Geheimrat") Lützkenstett, whose investigation of Vogel and his legends was subsidized by the ministry of culture of the East Gothic Empire ("Ostgotisches Kaiserreich") and on whose behalf an official letter of inquiry together with an offer of a reward for Vogel delivered dead or alive, had been despatched to the mayor of Montagsdorf, and whose Vogel-study eventually appeared in an East Gothic university city

---

100 (Frauenfeld: Huber & Co., 1928), 218 pp.
101 Hesse comments on Schmid and his study in "Brief an einen Bücherleser," *Dresdner Neueste Nachrichten*, November 7, 1928, No. 261.

("Ostgotische Universitätsstadt"), was E. A. F. Lützkendorf, whose *Hermann Hesse als religiöser Mensch in seinen Beziehungen zur Romantik und zum Osten*, a dissertation for the University of Leipzig, had been published earlier in 1932.[102] And Balmelli, the community clerk ("Gemeindeschreiber"; Hesse's continued play upon words) whom the Lützkenstett inquiry had amused more than anything else, was none other than Hugo Ball,[103] Hesse's close friend and fellow writer whose own *Hermann Hesse. Sein Leben und sein Werk* had appeared just a few years earlier.[104]

Märchen (1955) includes but nine items and Hesse chose to call only three of his other tales *Märchen*. He could have extended this designation to at least eight additional brief narratives without violating his conception of the genre. *Die Stadt* (June 23, 1910), a mythic history of civilization, is surely as much a *Märchen* as *Iris* (1918), Hesse's mythicized story of man. *Drei Linden* (February 2, 1912) is as infused with magic as *Augustus* (1913). *Ein Traum von den Göttern* (July 25, 1914), *Im Jahre 1920* (November 8, 1917), and *Der Europäer* (written in January 1918) are as much social comment mythicized as *Merkwürdige Nachricht von einem andern Stern* (1915). Hesse's edifying conversation with a stove in *Gespräch mit dem Ofen* (November 17, 1919) is no less surreal than his protagonist's quarrel with an old chair in *Märchen vom Korbstuhl* (1918). *Inneres Erlebnis* (January 23, 1926) is as much a mythicizing of the modern writer's ultimate inability to realize his ideal in art as *Der Weg zur Kunst* (1913) is the story of the true artist. And *Vom Steppenwolf* (November 16, 1927) is as playfully fantasized autobiography as *Vogel* (1932).

In a broader and deeper sense most of Hesse's major works written after 1916 are also *Märchen*. *Demian, Klingsors letzter Sommer, Siddhartha, Der Steppenwolf, Narziss und Goldmund, Die Morgenlandfahrt*, and even *Das Glasperlenspiel* could aptly be designated twentieth-century *Kunstmärchen*. These are Hesse's magical transfiguration of visible reality. Theirs is a surreality of dream and symbolism permeated by a fervent mysticism, rendered fascinating by the occult and the fantastic, and strongly reminiscent of E. T. A. Hoffmann's *Der goldne Topf* and Novalis's *Heinrich von Ofterdingen*. Nor is this a chance kinship. These masterpieces were for Hesse a certain ultimate in an

---

102 (Burgdorf/Hann.: W. Rümpeltin, 1932), 95 pp.
103 Ball occasionally used this playful distortion of his name in his letters to Hesse. See *Hugo Ball: Briefe 1911–1927* (Köln: Benziger, 1957), p. 152.
104 (Berlin: S. Fischer, 1927), 243 pp.

art that lay close to his heart and that he strove to emulate. It was his fond belief that life in its essence and in all its mystery and hope could be depicted only in the guise of the *Märchen*.[105]

Just as for his romantic predecessors, the everyday world never held much appeal for Hesse. Visible reality had to be transformed by fantasy, replaced by dream, or made more tolerable by vision. The *Märchen* did much to meet these psychological needs. *Volksmärchen* fed Hesse's fantasy and his dreams as a child, and the *Kunstmärchen* ultimately became a characteristic mode of expression for vision. A child-sorcerer who made a wondrous fairyland of a drab world became an author-magician who conjured up and habitually withdrew into his visions of a better man and a better world. Fairy tale (*Märchen*) and magic (*Magie*) were obviously more than just common concepts in Hesse's idiom from childhood to old age; they were a meaningful part of his way of life. Indeed, he often imagined his own life to be something of a *Märchen*. It was not without reason that Hesse titled the first of his two major autobiographies *Kindheit des Zauberers* (1923), and that this, in turn, was to be the introduction of a *Märchen*-like novel that was never written but was to be called *Aus dem Leben eines Zauberers*.[106] Even *Kurzgefasster Lebenslauf* (1924), the second and more chronicle-like of these autobiographies, ends in pure conjecture and in the magic manner of a *Märchen*: an imprisoned Hesse paints a train on one of the walls of his cell, boards it nonchalantly, and vanishes with its smoke, leaving prison and perplexed guards behind.

OTHER PROSE WORKS, DRAMA, AND POETRY

Despite the terrible stress and strain of his years in Bern, Hesse was able to continue his flow of short stories, diverse recollections, autobiographical snippets, literary studies, observations on the human condition, congratulatory articles, and travel reports. Fifty-seven of these items were widely published in newspapers and periodicals; almost half of them were later included in various of Hesse's many collections of miscellany; and the rest have never appeared in any book publications. Hesse also found time to keep extensive and as yet unpublished diaries in the summer and autumn of 1914 and

105 See "Kurzgefasster Lebenslauf" (1924), *Gesammelte Schriften* (1957), Vol. 4, pp. 485–486.
106 See Prose IV:644/2.

in 1916, 1917, and 1918.[107] With the exception of a few poems, only one other item written in Bern has never been published: an adaptation of Shakespeare's *Romeo and Juliet* written in January and February 1915. Poetically, except for his war poems, Hesse continued largely to dwell sentimentally upon the glow of childhood and the painful flow of time, upon his longing for love and the agony of loneliness, and upon the lure of autumn, the night, and of omnipresent death. He wrote some 155 poems during these years.[108] Only eight of these have yet to appear in print.

HESSE AS AN EDITOR AND REVIEWER

Hesse's editorial work spanned twenty-five years. It began with the periodical *März* in 1907, was extended to books in 1910, and terminated in 1932. He became an editor of books for the same reasons he had begun to review books, and for the same reasons he had become associated with *März*. Editing, like reviewing was rewarding busywork, it was an added source of income, a gratifying service to the literary world, and a healthy diversion when he was too troubled for writing. Although the first two books edited by Hesse appeared in 1910 and 1911, his new interest did not become a serious pastime until after he had settled in Bern and had resigned from *März*. Thirty-nine of the fifty-eight books he edited belong to his trying years in Bern.[109] Ten of these were published from 1913 to 1915. In the autumn of 1915, Hesse shifted his attention to the editing of *Aus der Heimat*, the periodical that became *Der Sonntagsbote für die deutschen Kreigsgefangenen* in early 1916 and to which, in turn, a supplement, the *Deutsche Internierten Zeitung*, was added that July. Although Hesse's association with the latter ended in December 1917, he continued to co-edit the former until the beginning of 1919. After withdrawing from the *Deutsche Internierten Zeitung* at the end of 1917, he began to edit the *Bücherei für deutsche Kreigsgefangene* and the *Heimatbücher für deutsche Kreigsgefangene*; twenty-two volumes of the first series and seven of the second were published in 1918 and 1919. *Alemannenbuch* (1919),[110] a

107 See Manuscripts X:426/k, 426/l, 426/la; X-A:5/2, 5a/3a.

108 Twenty-five were added to the second edition of *Unterwegs* (München: Georg Müller, 1915, 84 pp.), thirty-three were included in *Musik des Einsamen* (Heilbronn: E. Salzer, 1915, 84 pp.). Only eight have yet to appear in print.

109 See Hesse as an Editor VII-A.

110 (Bern: Verlag Seldwyla, 1919), 117 pp.

warm tribute to his fellow Alemannic writers, was the last book Hesse edited before leaving Bern.

The introductory or concluding remarks that Hesse generally added to the books he edited vary considerably in their length and consequence. His accompanying comments for the series publications fill but a page or less and are of little import. His separate publications, on the other hand, were usually graced by essays three to seven pages long and are of correspondingly greater significance. These are the critical appraisal and the warm acclaim of a scholar-writer intent upon informing and advocating. When dealing with a single author, Hesse almost invariably characterized both the man and the artist, commented upon his reception in Germany over the years, and added interesting asides about his own introduction to and later relationship with the writer in question. Most of the thirty-nine prefaces that Hesse wrote for publications edited by others and printed from 1910 to 1962 are orientations similar in their intimacy and scope.[111] It is obvious from remarks repeated in his introductions that Hesse considered himself primarily a guiding intermediary, a literary propagandist in the best sense of the expression.

For want of time and inclination Hesse read and reviewed progressively fewer books during his years in Bern. His rich flow of reviews for *März* decreased sharply at the beginning of 1913 and petered out at the end of 1917. He continued to honor his contractual commitment to *Die Propyläen* and to *Der Schwabenspiegel* but only until September of 1917. His contributions to the *Frankfurter Zeitung*, the *Neue Rundschau*, and even to the *Neue Zürcher Zeitung* dropped off markedly during the war years. However, once the war was over and Hesse was settled in Montagnola, he became the same avid reader and prolific reviewer he had been in Gaienhofen.

111 See Hesse as an Editor VII-B.

6
Rebel-Seeker

MONTAGNOLA 1919-1931

A NEW BEGINNING

Hesse's departure for Ticino toward the end of April 1919 marked a watershed in his life. His early dedication to art had not served him well and his subsequent venture into life had become a nightmare. What had essentially been self-evasion now yielded to self-being; self-compromising adjustment gave way to existentialistic self-confrontation. Hesse had courted this new way of life in *Rosshalde*, had illustrated it romantically in *Knulp*, and had pondered its immediate challenges in *Demian*. Mental flirtation finally became physical reality. Like his Veraguth sobered by experience, Hesse was now prepared to try to be the artist-outsider he knew he was, and like his Sinclair emancipated from the Christian-bourgeois ethic, he was ostensibly ready to live his own Nietzschean values. But like his Klein, he also learned that actual emancipation and self-realization were an almost impossible, excruciating ordeal. Nevertheless, for Hesse just as for Klein there was no turning back; he had become firmly convinced that there was no way to salvation other than that to the self: "The road of redemption does not lead to the left and it does not lead to the right; it leads into one's heart, and there alone is God, and there alone peace." [1] Hesse commonly called this road of redemption ("Weg der Erlösung") his inward road ("Weg nach Innen"). It was this taxing path to the self that he traveled doggedly in the decade following his departure from Bern, and it is this tenacious self-quest that is mirrored in the many stories and numerous essays he wrote during these years.

---

1 "Bauernhaus" (1918), *Gesammelte Schriften* (1957), Vol. 3, p. 388.

The village of Montagnola, Ticino.

The Casa Camuzzi in Montagnola. Hesse lived here from 1919 to 1931.

In his search for a country retreat in Ticino, Hesse first moved into a little farmhouse on the outskirts of Minusio near Locarno. He then spent two restless weeks in Sorengo before he finally settled for Montagnola, an old village slumbering in vineyards and wooded hills some five or six kilometers from Lugano. Here Hesse leased a four-room second-story apartment in the Casa Camuzzi, a castle-like baroque edifice built in the nineteenth century. He remained in these bachelor quarters from May 10, 1919, until August 1931. Ticino and Montagnola soon became for Hesse the source of comfort and inspiration that Swabia and Calw had once been. The luxuriant pristine landscape, narrow twisted roads, picturesque villages, primitive houses, wine grottos, weathered churches, and wayside chapels furnished exotic settings for his tales, new matter for his essays, and endless themes for his watercolors. His psychic wounds began to heal. He began to live, to ponder, and to create with vigor, abandon, and unpredictable inclination. These Casa Camuzzi years remained the most vibrant and productive period of his life; his apex both as a man and as an artist.

Until 1923, Hesse emerged only rarely and never by choice from his hermitic retreat in Ticino. His postwar royalties from Germany had little monetary value in Switzerland and, despite his simple way of life and extreme frugality, his means were soon depleted. It became a financial necessity for him to give sporadic public readings of his works. These reluctant commitments seldom took Hesse beyond Bern, Zürich, and St. Gallen, and rarely for more than a few days. It was on such a trip to Zürich in May 1921 that he visited and had a few analytic sessions with C. G. Jung. From 1923 on, Hesse left Montagnola more frequently and for longer periods of time. His lecture tours were extended to Germany and continued until the late twenties. In the spring and again in the autumn of 1923, Hesse spent a few weeks in the Hotel Verenahof in Baden seeking relief from sciatica and sundry rheumatic ailments. He returned to the same hotel at this spa almost every November until 1951. Portions of *Narziss und Goldmund*, of *Die Morgenlandfahrt*, and of *Das Glasperlenspiel*, many poems,[2] diary fragments, and hundreds of letters were written here, and *Kurgast* (1923), *Der gestohlene Koffer* (1944), and *Aufzeichnung bei einer Kur in Baden* (1949) commemorate this long association.

By 1923 Hesse also became anxious to renew old friendships in

---

2 E.g., *Verse im Krankenbett* (Bern: Stämpfli & Cie, 1927), 20 pp. (fifteen poems written autumn 1927).

German Switzerland and to reestablish his erstwhile close contact with its concert halls, art galleries, and its literary and art circles. To this end, he spent the winters of 1923–1924 and 1924–1925 in Basel, and every winter from 1925–1926 to 1931–1932 in Zürich, where Fritz Leuthold, a close friend and patron, placed a small apartment at his disposal. Leuthold, director of Zürich's Jelmoli department store, was one of several business tycoons and men prominent in various professions who began to befriend Hesse in the financially difficult twenties. This intimate circle of benefactors comprised, among others, Georg Reinhart, head of Winterthur's cotton firm Gebr. Volkart & Co., Max Wassmer, cement manufacturer and owner of Schloss Bremgarten bei Bern, Hans C. Bodmer of Zürich, musician and physician, and Friedrich E. Welti, jurist of Kehrsatz bei Bern. These patrons and their immediate families became and remained the closest of Hesse's friends. Thanks to their enthusiasm for his art, their appreciation of his person, and their ready generosity, his burdens of life were appreciably lightened. Hesse, in turn, often mentioned his benefactors in his essays, enriched their Hesseana with manuscripts and watercolors, dedicated books and poems to them, and immortalized them in his *Die Morgenlandfahrt* (1931).

Hesse had hardly settled in Montagnola before he began to strike up new friendships. The Swiss writer Lisa Wenger, her husband Theo, and their daughter Ruth, who lived in nearby Carona, joined his growing circle of friends in late July. The Wengers at once took a parental interest in Hesse, and he an immediate amorous interest in their twenty-two-year-old daughter. Ruth was flattered and pleased, but mindful of the difference in their ages, Hesse made no serious attempt to court her. Their quixotic relationship waxed and waned in the course of the next four years, survived a love affair with Elisabeth (Lisel) Rupp, a budding young writer who, like Hesse, had taken up quarters in the Casa Camuzzi,[3] and finally became an anxious courtship. What began with trepidation and faint hope ended in a brief and highly painful marriage, Hesse's second marital misadventure. The marriage was doomed from the outset: Ruth entered it half-heartedly, much more impressed by the artist than by the man; her parents acquiesced reluctantly; and Hesse himself was troubled by grave misgivings—his rational self was still convinced that he was some-

3 Lisel Rupp (Gerdts-Rupp) lived in Radolfzell, West Germany, as late as 1969. Hesse's many letters and postcards to her were destroyed during the Second World War.

Ruth Wenger (1897–),
Hesse's second wife.

Hermann Hesse, about 1920.

what less than suited to marriage.[4] Compunctions notwithstanding, Hesse terminated his marriage with Maria Bernoulli in July 1923 and married Ruth Wenger on January 11, 1924. Their paths parted only eleven weeks later.

Maria had been too old and settled in her thought and ways for Hesse. Ruth was too immature and capricious. Like Maria, Ruth was also self-preoccupied and unusually sensitive to slight, willful, and not without malice. Another clash of personalities was inevitable. That she was also a singer with strong career aspirations of her own was no help. Ruth's life had been troubled by frail health and emotional instability. Marriage only made matters worse. Life with Hesse quickly became both a physical and emotional torment for her. On the verge of a nervous breakdown, and also suffering from what eventually proved to be tuberculosis of the lungs, Ruth first returned to her parents, and was then committed to a sanatorium. Her convalescence was slow, and for almost two years she suffered repeated relapses and had to be rehospitalized a number of times. Hesse's anxious efforts to achieve a reconciliation were futile. Ruth got a divorce in April, 1927.[5]

These were Hesse's *Steppenwolf* years, the third and perhaps most desperate crisis in his life. As a youngster in Maulbronn, Bad Boll, Stetten, and Cannstatt, he had taken defiant issue with family and society; during the First World War he had been painfully at odds with the world and with himself; from the middle of 1924 to the end of 1926 his quarrel was primarily with himself. In the past, Hesse had often flirted with suicide, now self-obliteration became a masochistic passion. He was prepared to settle for death but was also possessed by a frantic yearning for sensual life. Caught between these two obsessive urges, he experienced a dramatic metamorphosis. An essentially straitlaced artist-thinker suddenly became something of a worldling. A shy outsider, most at home in his study, in the concert hall, and in nature, became a frequenter of bars and dance halls. A student of classical music learned to appreciate jazz. Hesse briefly

4 The nature of Hesse's quandary is clearly defined in a letter he wrote in mid-1923: ". . . marriage is really not something that I desire or for which I am gifted, but life and fate are here stronger than my thoughts and my wishes." Bernhard Zeller, *Hermann Hesse* (1963), p. 96.

5 Ruth Wenger was Hesse's inspiration for the fairy tale *Piktors Verwandlungen* (1922), and the subject of many of his love poems (see Poetry V-D:236, 249, 281, 410, 428, 480, 601, 624, 748, 864, 898, 931a, 958, 1042, 1043). She became Ruth Haussmann, moved to East Berlin, and is still living there. Most of Hesse's many letters and postcards to Ruth are in the Hesse-Nachlass, Marbach a.N.

became a Harry Haller, a middle-aged man kicking over the traces. Acquaintances raised their eyebrows and friends took him to task for his new life style. Hesse himself was less perturbed. He knew that this assertion of his too-long-stifled sensual self was almost inevitable, he recognized its therapeutic value, and he was also convinced that it would be no more than an interlude. And such it was. By late 1926 the crisis had run its course and Hesse emerged the better-balanced and the wiser for it.

In 1909, a fourteen-year-old Jewish girl born in Czernowitz, Rumania, wrote Hesse a letter of admiration and gratitude. Ninon Ausländer was very surprised when she received a kind response. This chance correspondence was followed by a chance meeting in Zürich in the winter of 1926. In the interim, Ninon had studied at the universities of Vienna and Berlin, had married but had also parted company with the painter and caricaturist B. F. Dolbin, and was looking forward to a career as an art historian. Their attraction was immediate and mutual. Ninon joined Hesse in his Casa Camuzzi in the summer of 1927.

CONTINUED SOCIAL AND POLITICAL INVOLVEMENT

Germany's disparagement of Hesse did not end with the war or his departure for remote Montagnola. His continued advocacy of unpopular social causes attracted new abuse. When the war ended, Hesse and Richard Woltereck merely shifted their concern from the battlefield to the homefront, and continued their fruitful editorial cooperation. If not convinced, both were at least persuaded that a disrupted and disenchanted postwar Germany would be susceptible to changes for the better, and that a vigorously programmatic periodical addressed particularly to youth could give impetus and direction to these changes. *Vivos Voco* was their response to this situation and this belief. The monthly's first issue appeared in October 1919. It heralded a new Germany and a better world, and to help usher in this better tomorrow, began immediately to champion the cause of the destitute, to focus attention upon children and their educational needs, to denounce anti-Semitism,[6] and to acclaim pacifism and internationalism. Public response was less than gratifying. Old racists, militarists, and

---

6 The stupidity of Hitler's National Socialism and the dangers of its pathological anti-Semitism were apparent to Hesse from the outset. As early as 1922, he took occasion in a book review to express his contempt for the Nazis and his concern for German youth: "A small publication, *Verrat am Deutschtum* by Wilhelm Michel, gives me occa-

nationalists took umbrage immediately, and youth's initial enthusiasm soon wilted. Though cofounder and coeditor of *Vivos Voco* and completely in accord with its liberal political attitudes and humane social aspirations, Hesse chose, just as when associated with *März*, to limit himself almost exclusively to literary contributions. Before the war, he was not yet ready to become embroiled in the social and political problems of the day, and by late 1919 he was convinced that further direct appeals to the German people by a Hermann Hesse could serve little purpose. Nothing was now left for him to do but to support the cause as inconspicuously as possible and to hope. Resurgent nationalism and spreading Communism began to dispel this hope. Hesse terminated his editorial association with *Vivos Voco* at the end of 1921. He had become convinced that Germany was not about to change and that periodicals such as *Vivos Voco* were not likely to have any appreciable effect on the national scene.[7] This was Hesse's last organized effort to help reform society. It also marked the end of his career as an editor of newspapers and periodicals.

Until the First World War, Hesse's reputation was untarnished. His *belles-lettres* pleased both young and old and his marginal association with *März* and its liberal politics went unnoticed or caused no affront. After 1914 his fortunes began an erratic ebb and flow. Official Germany had hardly branded him a traitor for his wartime essays before postwar German youth acclaimed him its spokesman and guide for his *Demian*. But youth was as unstable as the times. Its espousal of Hesse's new view of man and of his proposed new approach to life was almost as brief as it was incontinent. Only a few years elapsed before less exacting and immediately more rewarding political ideologies began to fire its imagination. Hesse's new-found popular-

sion to say a few words . . . about the idiotic, pathological anti-Semitism of the swastika bards and their many, particularly student, hangers-on. . . . Today there is in vogue among horribly misguided young Germans a kind of murderous hounding of Jews. . . . No matter whether one likes or dislikes the Jews, they are human beings, often very much more intelligent, more energetic, and better humans than their fanatical opponents. . . . Simply to set up a class of people as the scapegoat of the world's evil . . . is such a horrible degenerate act that the resultant harm exceeds tenfold the harm that may ever have been perpetrated by Jews." *Vivos Voco*, 3 (July-August 1922), 62–63.

7 Widespread remarks such as the following soon proved Hesse correct: "For that reason, our youth, our students also, do not give a damn about the pacifism propagated with such comic nervousness by them [international pacifists] and their coworker Hermann Hesse." "Ein Enttäuschter," *Oberdeutschland* (Stuttgart), 3 (February 1922), 370–371.

ity waned as rapidly and steadily in the twenties as the ranks of the young National Socialists and Communists swelled. For those of his young converts who subsequently chose to become Marxists, he simply ceased to exist. For those who opted for National Socialism, he became a favorite target of abuse, of invective as vicious as that of the worst of his arch-patriotic wartime detractors. Hate letters became common even while *Demian* was still youth's favorite catechism, and most of these were written by university students. Hesse's association with *Vivos Voco* and his championing of its internationalism and pacifism were ridiculed, his art was disparaged, and his person was maligned, all with fanatical conviction and naïve bravado.

In the hopes of countering this rapidly spreading sentiment, a classical instance of it together with Hesse's rebuttal were published in *Vivos Voco* in July 1921:

> Your art is a neurasthenic lascivious wallowing in beauty, a seductive siren above steaming German graves not yet closed. We hate these writers . . . who want to make women of men, and are intent upon reducing us to mediocrity, upon internationalizing us, and upon making pacifists of us. We are Germans and want to remain Germans forever! . . . We have a right to demand that our German writers . . . arouse our slumbering nation, and that they again lead it to the sacred gardens of German Idealism, German belief, and German fidelity! . . . For us you [Hesse] are dead; we are laughing at you.[8]

Hesse reminded his correspondent and students of similar persuasion that this blatant national conceit was the traditional refuge of the average German intellectual and that it was this German sentiment that had occasioned the wars of 1870 and 1914. Theirs was precisely the comfortable and irresponsible authoritarian ideal against which Goethe fought, by which Hölderlin was broken, which Jean Paul ironized, and Nietzsche denounced. Their swagger and rattling of sabers were only the temerity of fear and cowardice.[9] Hesse's well-intentioned rebuke was as ineffectual as his self-defense had been during the war. Continued subjection to similar indignities and waning faith in a better political future for Germany persuaded him to apply for Swiss citizenship in January 1924. He became a citizen of Switzerland on November 26, 1924.

8 "Hassbriefe," *Vivos Voco*, 2 (July 1921), 235–236.
9 *Vivos Voco*, 2 (July 1921), 238.

Though Hesse was a decidedly more familiar literary figure after than before *Demian*, his publications in the twenties were generally reviewed less widely, less frequently, and less favorably than his earlier books had been, and they were also sold in fewer numbers. His break with tradition was primarily responsible for this change in fortune. His radical view of the individual excited youth, but more briefly than it vexed a less receptive adult world; his new sociopolitical ideas left him a *persona non grata* in Germany at large; and his novel assessment of an imminent cultural decline of Europe in general, and of Germany in particular, damned him in the intellectual world. Hesse had envisaged this *Untergang* in *Demian* (1917), had commented on it in *Klingsors letzter Sommer* (1919), and had finally expounded upon it in two essays written late in 1919 (*Die Brüder Karamasoff oder der Untergang Europas* and *Gedanken zu Dostojewskis Idiot*) and published the following year as a pamphlet ostentatiously titled, *Blick ins Chaos*.

In these essays, Hesse argued the cultural decline of Western Europe, evolved a psychology of history to account for its inevitability, and used Dostoevsky to illustrate its immediacy. Every culture rests upon a particular moral-religious myth that accepts certain of man's primal urges and rejects others. Out of any cultural context, these drives are beyond good and evil. They can never be extirpated, nor forever suppressed or sublimated. When an age begins to lose faith in the myth about which its culture crystallized—and this, every age is bound in time to do—then all the inner thrusts long denied and pent up begin to assert themselves, absolutes fall by the wayside, and another civilization has almost spent itself. Hesse was convinced that the Russia of Dostoevsky's novels had already reached this stage of cultural dissolution, and that Western Europe, with Germany in the vanguard, was fast approaching it. The Karamasovs and the Myshkins—amoral hysterics, both dangerous criminals and gentle saints, uncouth drunkards and sensitive dreamers, intolerable egoists and childlike innocents—were Europe's tomorrow. But tomorrow's return to primal chaos would be not just a frightening cultural relapse, but the beginning of a new cultural cycle. Like Dostoevsky's novels, Hesse's *Demian* illustrates this decline and anticipates this rebirth. The Sinclairs, like the Karamasovs and Myshkins, are symptomatic of a waning culture, and the Demians are the heralds of a new culture.

It quickly became apparent that Germany's intelligentsia was as little receptive to Hesse's psychologizing as to Oswald Spengler's philosophizing of history.[10] His theory was forthwith deprecated, and he himself was upbraided for his enthusiastic acceptance of the cultural chaos he foresaw. His was an irresponsible response to critical times. Cultural rebirth was not to be found in passive resignation to an Asiatic ideal, but in the determined return to German Idealism. Hesse was obviously a naïve intellectual who had lost his sense of values, a perverse Pied Piper preparing the way for Eastern barbarism.[11]

Siddhartha (1922) gave Hesse's persistent critics yet another occasion to slander him for his untoward penchant for the East. They did so in their usual rousing rhetoric.[12] This vain and inane Indian reverie could only be the frothy emission of a renegade aesthete inured to the plight of his own country and to the agonies of its people. Writers of this ilk were no longer relevant, and as such, dispensable. And as the twenties waxed, Hesse became a decidedly dispensable commodity for Germany's rapidly growing number of nationalistic activists, and fair game for almost any slur. In 1926, he became a perpetrator of crimes against the fatherland because he had dared to contend in his *Erinnerungen an den Simplicissimus* that *Simplicissimus* had ceased to be of any consequence the moment it had ceased its sociopolitical exposure of Germany to engage in wartime propaganda against the Allies.[13] In May of that same year, the conservative and influential segment of the press of Hesse's native Württemberg raised a hue and cry when it learned that he had been invited to Stuttgart to take part in the annual celebration of the Swabian Schiller Society (*Schwäbischer Schillerverein*). The committee responsible for the invitation was raked

10 Hesse's view of culture is only loosely akin to Oswald Spengler's philosophy of history. Neither his theory nor his use of the term decline (*Untergang*) derive from the philosopher. *Der Untergang des Abendlandes* (1918) did impress Hesse favorably, but his own theory was fully evolved before his first reading of Spengler's book in late 1919. See "Schwäbische Betrachtung," *Der Schwäbische Bund*, 2 (November 1920), 81.

11 See: Gustav Zeller, "Offener Brief an Hermann Hesse," *Psychische Studien*, 47 (December 1920), 622–630; Gertrud Bäumer, "Medusa," *Die Frau* (Berlin), 28 (April 1921), 193–199, and "Perseus," *Die Frau*, 28 (May 1921), 225–235.

12 E.g.: "I put the story aside painfully disappointed. . . . This foolish enthusiasm for India on the part of German aesthetes . . . this pallid, anaemic imitation. . . . If he were a real writer and not an aesthete, not just a wretched literary figure, something of the scream of the times, of the groaning of his people would have to resound in him. . . . Of what concern are we to Hermann Hesse of today, of what concern is he still to us? No writer turns his back unpunished upon his people in its most bitter but deeply vibrant hour." Jörn Oven, "*Siddhartha,*" *Die Schöne Literatur*, 24 (September 1923), 331–332.

13 *Neue Zürcher Zeitung*, March 28, 1926, No. 494.

over the coals for its lack of discretion, and Hesse was dubbed a man without principles. This sentiment was reiterated and extended after the publication of *Betrachtungen* (1928) with its collection of Hesse's wartime essays. Young activists accorded the work scant attention, but old diehard nationalists had neither forgotten nor forgiven and could not refrain from renewed invective. Book and author were disposed of with dispatch and finality as the malicious blathering of a sick malcontent.[14]

Hesse himself refused to grace this swelling tide of rancor and abuse with any public response, and among his dwindling number of friends and supporters even fewer cared or dared to intercede on his behalf than had done so in 1915, and their efforts were by and large futile.[15] By the end of the twenties, Hesse was prepared silently to sever all but his publication and his intimately personal ties with Germany. He accepted his last reading invitation to Germany in autumn of 1929, and in November 1930 he resigned from the Prussian Academy of Writers, of which he had become a reluctant member in October 1926. Thomas Mann's urgent and persistent plea that he resume his membership in the academy was unavailing; Hesse was determined to have nothing further to do with official Germany.[16]

Germany had proved to be a vast disillusionment. Germans had learned nothing from experience. They had refused to acknowledge any war guilt, had suffered little remorse, and had experienced no moral regeneration. They had botched the social revolution of 1918, and their political life had continued its corrupt and infantile course. The republic was as hopeless as the empire before it. Politically and morally, Germany was still the mess she had been. Her future was bleak.[17] The rift between Hesse and Germany was obviously beyond repair long before the Nazis came to power.

PRODUCTIVE AGONY

Hesse's twelve years in the Casa Camuzzi were no doubt the most trying, but also the happiest, and certainly the most memorable years of his life. Leaving Bern proved to be an unexpected blessing. It

14 See Gustav Hecht, "Offener Brief an Hermann Hesse," *Deutsches Volkstum*, 11 (No. 8, 1929), 611.

15 E.g., Franz Schall, "Um Hermann Hesse," *Deutsches Volkstum*, 12 (No. 2, 1930), 232–235.

16 See *Briefwechsel: Hermann Hesse-Thomas Mann* (1968), pp. 11–18.

17 Hesse never hesitated in his correspondence to give candid expression to his bleak view of the Weimar Republic. Accounting for his refusal to rejoin the Prussian

was as though Hesse had finally emerged from limbo and was left tossing between heaven and hell. His bliss and agony were exhilarating. He was vibrantly alive, relished his torment, and wallowed in his bliss. All that had preceded and all that was to follow was commonplace in comparison. This was the most exciting chapter of his life and the most fecund stage of his art, a period of reckless abandon and dramatic unpredictability. In Hesse's relentless and uncompromising quest of himself, his writing now received fresh impetus and assumed new directions. Life's pale and art's possibilities were extended far beyond their previous conventional bounds. A pre-First World War traditionalist emerged an uninhibited and exciting innovator.

The summer of 1919 was a gloriously hectic one for Hesse. An unexpected surge of physical and creative vitality transfigured both his life and his art. He had hardly settled in Montagnola (May 10) before he began his *Klein und Wagner*. He could scarcely wait until he had finished his first tale (July 18) before he turned to *Klingsors letzter Sommer*. The latter was completed by the beginning of September. In the meantime, Hesse was also busy writing poetry, painting many little watercolors, wandering about the countryside, cultivating new friendships, and enjoying the wine grottos of Montagnola. The three essays of *Blick ins Chaos* [18]—*Die Brüder Karamasoff oder der Untergang Europas, Gedanken zu Dostojewskis Idiot*, and *Gespräch über die Neutöner* —followed in the autumn. Part I and half of Part II of *Siddhartha* were written in the winter and spring of 1920. Hesse then suffered a severe letdown in his work, and for about a year and a half wrote little of any consequence. He was able to resume *Siddhartha* late in 1921, completed it in May 1922, and had it published later that same year. [19]

A series of major prose publications followed in quick succession. *Psychologia Balnearia oder Glossen eines Badener Kurgastes*, the delightfully ironic psychologizing and philosophizing of an embittered rheumatic, Hesse's thinly fictional account of his two visits to Baden in 1923, was written in October of that year and published privately

---

Academy of Writers, he wrote to Thomas Mann in December 1931 as follows: "Well then: the basic reason for my inability to become part of an official German corporation is my deep distrust of the German republic. This shaky and mindless state. . . . Its courts are unjust, its officials indifferent, and its people infantile. . . . Germany failed to make its own revolution and to find its own political form. Bolshevization is its future . . ." *Briefe* (1964), 57–58.

18 (Bern: Verlag Seldwyla, 1920), 43 pp.
19 (Berlin: S. Fischer, 1922), 147 pp.

the following year; thereafter it appeared as *Kurgast*.[20] *Die Nürnberger Reise*, the acerbic memoirs of a reading tour through southern Germany in November 1925, was written that year but did not appear until 1927.[21] *Der Steppenwolf*, a surrealistic self-exposure that preoccupied Hesse from November 1924 to the end of 1926, was published that same year.[22] *Narziss und Goldmund*, begun in mid-1927 and finished at the end of 1928, appeared in 1930.[23] *Diesseits*, also published that year, is only a collection of early *Novellen* revised slightly for republication.[24] *Die Morgenlandfahrt*, the last of Hesse's major Casa Camuzzi stories, was probably begun during the latter half of 1929, finished in April 1931, and published in 1932.[25] And to these many tales Hesse added two collections of miscellaneous essays and an intimate perusal of world literature.[26] He also published a steady stream of poetry.[27]

KLEIN UND WAGNER: EXISTENTIAL ANGUISH

RUTHLESS SELF-EXPOSURE

Klein und Wagner is the story of a relatively ordinary man who had chosen to become a respectable member of society, a conscientious employee, a faithful husband, a good father, and a reliable provider. It is also the tragedy of a person who had not taken the trouble to find himself. Disillusionment, frustration, and resultant murderous impulses compel him to bolt. He embezzles a sum of money, forges documents, procures a revolver, and flees the country. Distraught, he tries desperately to assess himself and his actions, to ponder life and morality, and to become an authentic human being. His belated efforts to establish his own identity, to fashion his own values, and to live himself are futile. Long hours of excruciating thought, a bout of gambling, and a whirl of sex only add to his agitation. The blissful moments when he is at peace with himself and with life are

20 (Montagnola, 1924), 137 pp.; (Berlin: S. Fischer, 1925), 160 pp.
21 (Berlin: S. Fischer, 1927), 124 pp.   22 (Berlin: S. Fischer, 1927), 289 pp.
23 (Berlin: S. Fischer, 1930), 417 pp.   24 (Berlin: S. Fischer, 1930), 393 pp.
25 (Berlin: S. Fischer, 1932), 113 pp.
26 *Bilderbuch* (Berlin: S. Fischer, 1926), 320 pp.; *Betrachtungen* (Berlin: S. Fischer, 1928), 333 pp.; and *Eine Bibliothek der Weltliteratur* (Leipzig: Philipp Reclam, 1929), 85 pp.
27 *Gedichte des Malers* (Bern: Seldwyla Verlag, 1920), 23 pp.; *Ausgewählte Gedichte* (Berlin: S. Fischer, 1921), 89 pp.; *Italien* (Berlin: Euphorion Verlag, 1923), 23 pp.; *Verse im Krankenbett* (Bern: Stämpfli & Cie, 1927), 20 pp.; *Krisis* (Berlin: S. Fischer, 1928), 85 pp.; *Trost der Nacht* (Berlin: S. Fischer, 1929), 197 pp.; and *Jahreszeiten* (Zürich: Gebr. Fretz, 1931), 43 pp.

too few and too elusive to sustain him. Guilt and anxiety plague him, his new way of life leaves him wallowing in self-contempt, and destructive impulses once more become urgent. Klein begins to falter, and flight again becomes imperative. Since life no longer holds any attractions for him and since his own inner resources are depleted, but one week after he has taken flight, he succumbs to his long-nurtured passion for suicide. To break out of the narrow confines of the bourgeois world and to shed a role had been relatively easy. To escape the moral reaches of that conventional world and to learn to know and to be himself had turned out to be quite a different matter. Klein had simply proved inadequate to the many challenges of his bold venture.

Klein und Wagner is not the trumped up criminal story it may immediately appear to be. It is, in fact, autobiography that could hardly have been veiled more thinly, and is perhaps also the most ruthless of Hesse's many self-exposures. Klein was not just akin to his author, he is literally the man Hesse was in the spring of 1919. Their persons were indistinguishable, their circumstances of life identical, their experiences similar, and their thoughts and anxieties, grievances and hopes, and their inclinations and aversions were essentially alike. Like Hesse, a fortyish Klein had managed to establish himself comfortably in the bourgeois world: he has a livable income, is married, has children, is mindful of his civic duties and domestic responsibilities, and is just as unhappy with his lot as Hesse had been. Klein had become a bank employee and not a writer, but he had been the same conscientious functionary Hesse had become during the war. As was Hesse, Klein is a man of scholarly bent, his attachment to Schopenhauer was Hesse's, and he shared Hesse's early passion for, and later antipathy toward, Wagner. Dreams fascinate him just as they did Hesse, and the south holds for him the same attraction it had for Hesse. Klein's unhappy marriage is the mismarriage and disenchantment that Hesse's was. At a weak and desperate moment, each had settled for something short of his dreams. A domineering wife, an onerous marriage, and an excessively confining bourgeois world had in time left both seething with frustration and angry resentment, and anxious for release. It is not inconceivable that Klein's long-suppressed compulsive desire to kill both his family and himself had also plagued Hesse. On the other hand, Klein's theft and cloak-and-dagger behavior were embellishment, pure and simple. Resultantly, Klein is compelled to flee posthaste, where his prototype had left at his own pleasure. That his father had not lived to see the turn of events in his life comforts Klein as it had comforted Hesse. Klein's nightmarish train flight southward over bridges, through tunnels, and by high peaks to a little unnamed lakeside resort, was Hesse's own memorable trip through the Alps into Ticino and to Lugano. In a nearby village, Klein is touched by an Italian love song, doles out sweets to the children, and comforts a lonely innkeeper's wife. The village was Hesse's Sorengo, the ditty a then current popular song that appealed to him; Hesse habitually carried candy about with him for just such purposes; and Klein's chance sexual encounter may also have been more than just sentimental fancy. Worldly Teresina, on the other hand, was a figment of Hesse's imagination, a bit of wishful thinking, and a fictive necessity. With her, he afforded Klein a necessary partner in dialogue, and lent his tale a necessary catalyst; and with her introduction, Hesse also, and perhaps unwittingly, highlighted the essentially sexual nature of both Klein's and his own chronic problems. Without Teresina, Klein's existential agony would have remained blurred, assumed no direction, and achieved no climax, and could have degenerated into an interminable monologic monotony. While Klein's gambling spree with Teresina was fictive, it was also an actual touch of local color; their Castiglione was Campione at the edge of the lake opposite Lugano, then and still today notorious for its gambling casino. Klein's seven days of freedom with their sieges of anxiety and spasms of ecstasy were the hell and heaven of Hesse's own first few weeks in Ticino. Not able to emancipate himself from the bourgeois ethos, Klein tosses frantically between the philistine, the socialized self he had become, and his stifled real self, the human being he hoped to become, is intimidated by the past and fearful of the future, and cannot achieve any stable accord either with himself or with life. Hesse's lot had been no different. Even Klein's death had its actual precedent. His demise was of course not Hesse's, but that of the Klein Hesse had temporarily become. With timid and confused Klein's death, resolute and insatiable Klingsor was born.

FROM CONJECTURED TO ATTEMPTED EMANCIPATION

Rosshalde boldly proclaims a new approach to life supported vaguely by philosophy and illustrated picturesquely by metaphor. It is Veraguth's lot to be an artist-observer and not a man among men, to depict the garden of life and not to taste of its sweet fruits. He will be what he is and live as he was meant to live. *Demian* argues and depicts the preliminary emancipation from traditional religion and morality that is likely to be necessary for this new life style. *Klein und*

Wagner proceeds from the brash manifesto of *Rosshalde* and the optimistic cerebrations of *Demian* to actual venture. Klein attempts Sinclair's emancipation from the Christian-bourgeois ethos, and tries to live himself as Veraguth proposes to do, but fails. Klein's suppressed and omniscient real and innermost self can make itself heard but is unable, except for brief interludes, to prevail over his socialized self. Unlike Sinclair, he cannot become his Demian. Whereas actual experience almost persuaded Hesse, as it does Klein, that his new ideal was more pipe dream than possibility, a surge of faith in the essential oneness, eternity, and meaningfulness of life convinced him to the contrary. This faith found its expression in the epiphanic concluding moments of Klein's life. Given this faith, the individual had only to "let himself fall," to surrender himself to himself and to life, fully and with no regard for consequences. This faith and thought were too late for Klein, but not for Hesse. When he finally settled in Montagnola, he had already recovered from his initial depression in Ticino and was eager to put his new insight into life to the test.

In *Demian*, Hesse had made myth of autobiography. Situations, characters, problems, and action were all rendered universally typical and, to complicate matters, psychoanalytical concepts were actualized and psychic experience was rendered visible. With *Klein und Wagner*, he proceeded from this complexity of symbolism to relatively straightforward realism. Autobiography was allowed to remain immediate and actual. Conjectured emancipation on the one hand, and attempted emancipation on the other, found their most likely and perhaps most appropriate expressions.

DRAMATIC PROSE

With *Klein und Wagner*, narrative became almost pure psychic drama. Hesse had just divorced himself from the past, was still adrift, and the future was remote. All but his own inner world had ceased to have any immediacy or urgency for him. This inner world became his exclusive concern in *Klein und Wagner*. Nothing could or was permitted to detract from this concern. This determined what Klein's tale became: sustained bursts of tense indirect inner monologue, incessant and urgent comment, scanty dialogue more exposition than conversation, description both sparse and bare, all held together by a thin thread of narration. The outer world, never conspicuous or significant in preceding works, was now all but blotted out. Klein was accorded neither childhood nor youth, the world and family he flees are but points of departure, and his refuge in the south is merely a chance setting for his inner drama. Cities and villages remain concepts and none but Castiglione even bears a name. Hotels, rooms, restaurants, gardens, streets, the landscape, a park, and a dance pavilion are just that and no more. Nothing is precisely located or rendered visible. Meager detail is permitted only to evoke, not to depict and to detract. The *dramatis personae* are as inconspicuous as this setting. Members of Klein's immediate family are only references; hotel employees, fellow hotel guests, and natives are but laconic supernumeraries void of any physical and psychological reality, and even Teresina has no psychology and is accorded only enough physical detail to type her. Klein himself is not allowed to detract from his inner world; his psychic experience is profuse, but physically he remains only a pale, drawn, and craggy face.

Of Hesse's major tales, *Klein und Wagner* encompasses the shortest span of time, involves the smallest cast, and witnesses the most concentrated treatment of theme. This control and concentration of matter found deliberate and appropriate expression in the classical quinquepartite structure of drama. A day and night or a part thereof are carefully allotted to each of the tale's five chapter-acts. The first of these introduces Klein and lays bare his problem, the second, third, and fourth depict Klein's unavailing efforts to emancipate himself from the past and to begin life anew, and the fifth part, preceded by a two-day hiatus, portrays Klein's climactic suicide. Each of these chapters is a distinct link in an unbroken chain. Each chapter develops a major theme introduced in the preceding chapter, and itself introduces a second major theme, which in turn is extended in the subsequent chapter.[28] This concatenative device, together with the tale's time continuum, draws the individual parts together into an unusually tightly organized whole. In the manner of good drama, tension is never allowed to flag and suspense increases from chapter to chapter. This rapid and gripping unbroken progression from exposition to development, to climax, and even to the concluding dénouement is classically dramatic. It is also reflective of studied craftsmanship.

This conscious artistry is further evident in Hesse's deliberate blending of inner state, outer situation, and mode of narration, and this, in turn, lends additional dramatic impact to the story. All becomes immediate and vibrantly alive, past tense and reported interior monologue notwithstanding. By way of illustration, one need only

---

28 This was one of Hesse's favorite literary devices. He began to explore its possibilities as early as *Peter Camenzind* and never quite ceased to resort to it thereafter.

note the opening passage of the story. Klein's agitation and his feverish flurries of thought are highlighted by the speeding train and the receding rush of the landscape, and find appropriate expression in the rapid flow and the frantically irregular rhythm of the prose. Moments of inner tranquillity are similarly accentuated. Klein arrives at his destination exhausted, strangely expectant but also briefly at peace with himself, an enchanting landscape enveloped in twilight and alive only with fragrance and muted sound awaits him, and narration assumes an accordant slow flow and even pulsation. To lend to his prose rush and broken rhythm suggestive of stress, Hesse resorted customarily and liberally to word accumulations, clusters of prepositional phrases of varying length, strings of irregularly abbreviated clauses, successions of telegrammatic sentences, parataxis, anaphora, and to dashes, exclamation points, and question marks. To achieve the slow flow and even rhythm of tranquillity, he simply avoided these excesses.

Hesse added yet more to the drama of Klein's story by returning to his usual animation of nature. In *Demian*, nature had retired briefly from the human scene. Now she reemerged not only a mirror for moods and a setting for reflection, but a partner in act. For the first four chapters nature is an appropriate but inconspicuous backdrop. At the outset of the fifth chapter, she suddenly moves into the forestage and costars with Klein. Actual summer and the summer of Klein's life set in simultaneously. The world is rejuvenated by two days of intense heat, and now glows feverish with life. During these two days, Klein is animated by love and left feverish with passion. Nature and Klein experience their stormy relief simultaneously, then together sink into their sleep of exhaustion. Klein's sexual encounter with Teresina, itself described sparingly and discreetly, is rendered almost luridly dramatic by Hesse's more protracted and suggestive depiction of nature's own joyous orgy. Simple description becomes gripping drama.

Klein und Wagner begins dramatically, evolves dramatically, and ends dramatically. Hesse permitted himself no casual preliminaries, avoided detractive digressions, and refrained from indulging in anticlimactic afterthought. A tale became inner drama in high key. An abrupt and jolting beginning, a vortex of anxiety and urgent reflection, and a crescendo of despair climax in suicide and glorious revelation. Klein's death, itself but scantly depicted, is thoroughly dramatized by his illumination. Indeed, his epiphany itself becomes a unique manner of drama. In a long freely associative flow of highly evocative and emotive words and imagery, the ineffable insights of Klein's mystical moments of grace become fascinating visible drama. Hesse had first described similar luminous moments in a similar dramatic manner in a brief recollection written in 1913.[29] He had experienced this same divine oneness, timelessness, harmony, and meaningfulness of life while listening to Bach at an organ recital in the cathedral in Bern in September 1913. After *Klein und Wagner*, Hesse and his protagonists began to experience such moments of bliss more frequently, and this manner of dramatization became his characteristic mode of depiction.

Klein's dreams lend more drama to his story. In both *Demian* and *Klein und Wagner*, dreams and visions loom prominent. In *Demian* they became a carefully cultivated literary device—an indispensable part of Hesse's new myth-oriented, psychoanalytical mode of narration—more than an integral and convincing part of the narrative proper. Dreams and visions are primarily windows to Sinclair's soul, and milestones along his road of individuation; they are there only to reveal critical psychic states and experience, and to reflect his emancipation from a traditional ethos, and the evolution of his own values and beliefs; they were tailored to suit the narrator's purposes, and they are as unactual as their archetypal dreamer. In *Klein und Wagner*, dreams and visions are a plausible part of an actual story, rather than just a literary means. Indeed, Hesse was probably their dreamer and not just their author. Be that as it may, Klein's dreams and visions are as convincing and dramatic a part of him as his emotions, his ruminations, and his ultimate illumination. His are therefore much more credible windows to the soul than are Sinclair's.

The first of Klein's dreams (he is together with another person in a car careening wildly through a city) reveals Klein's fervent desire to escape his wife's domination, the second (an over-burdened and lonely traveller on a long and dusty marital road) exposes his marriage for the barren burden it had been, and the third (his murder of wife and children and his own suicide) depicts his resultant murderous impulses and accounts for his flight. In each of these instances, the unconscious merely accelerates the process of self-analysis. The last and much more complex of Klein's dreams is not just dramatic disclosure, but discerning diagnosis. This is no longer merely vision rising from psychic shallows, but profound dream emerging from Dionysian depths. Entering what appears to be a theater, Klein encounters a woman who resembles not only the innkeeper's wife, but his own, and even Teresina. Filled with repugnance by her massive distorted head and grotesque features, he plunges a knife into her belly, only to have a second woman, a mirror likeness of the first, sink her strong sharp claws into his neck, vengefully intent upon throttling him. This is Klein's excursion into his unconscious and it obviously takes him to the heart of his problems. The dream exposes his basic relationship with women. It now becomes apparent that Klein's problems are not the result, but are the cause of his unhappy marriage. Klein's relationships characteristically end in disaster. Realized love has always left him sick with aversion, bitterly disenchanted, tormented by self-hatred, and filled with hostility. Klein's subsequent reflection discloses why such has always been the case. Life had simply fallen far short of his wondrous youthful dreams and expectations. Woman is not what he had imagined her to be, love is a lie, and the sexes are drawn into their destructive relationship only by animal appetite, and in mutual fear of loneliness and of death. Left only with these convictions and with his shattered dreams, Klein is filled with loathing for life for what it is, and with bitter disillusionment for what it is not. Compared with this psychological insight into the self and into life, Veraguth's earlier cursory and vague philosophizing under similar circumstances is romantically naïve. In both *Rosshalde* and *Klein und Wagner*, it is not the failure of mismarriage, but the folly of marriage, that Hesse argued. Neither protagonist is suited for marriage, for any marriage. In his decision to forego further intimate involvement with life, Veraguth is content merely to refer to his destiny. In 1919, such vague speculation was obviously no longer in order. Unlike Veraguth, Klein has no more illusions about the "garden of life," and he wants to have as little further to do with it as possible. Suicide serves his purposes. Hesse himself withstood the temptation and chose to try to accept himself and life, notwithstanding. His works to follow record the failures and the successes of his efforts.

KLINGSORS LETZTER SOMMER: THE THRUST OF DEATH

DISGUISED AUTOBIOGRAPHY

Autobiography had been mythicized in *Demian* and dramatized in *Klein und Wagner*. It was fantasized in *Klingsors letzter Sommer*. Klein is what Hesse was late in the spring of 1919; Klingsor's story is a memorial to the summer of 1919. Klingsor, born on July 2, forty-two years old, and unattached, painter, poet, philosopher, and hypochondriac troubled by death, possessed by a passion for life and for art, and given to revelry and depression, is obviously Hesse himself; Klingsor's circle of friends was Hesse's; and the setting is clearly Ticino. Klingsor's unrestrained mode, frantic tempo, and intoxicating absorption of life in Castagnetta had become Hesse's in Montagnola. From the small, iron-railed stone balcony of his *palazzo*, Klingsor views the luxuriant steeply terraced garden below and the lake and mountains in the distance, just as Hesse was wont to gaze at that very view from the same little balcony of his Casa Camuzzi. With the exception of his concluding self-portrait, all of Klingsor's paintings were Hesse's own watercolors, his own fanciful paraphrasing and poeticizing of the visible world in brilliant transparent hues. Klingsor's poetry is just as Hessean in both its matter and manner. And Klingsor, like Hesse, had once made a necessary trip to the Orient, and he, too, had found nothing there that could not also be found in the Western world.

Large though Klingsor looms, he is actually only one of two self-projections. His intimate friend, the blond poet Hermann, a reserved writer of sad lyrics, is the second. Demian, unlike the second self-projection of Hesse's earlier tales (e.g., Richard of *Peter Camenzind*, or Heilner of *Unterm Rad*), has no reality of his own; he is Sinclair's externalized ideal self and nothing more. Klein's ideal self is not even externalized; it remains an inner voice. In *Klingsors letzter Sommer*, Hesse reverted to his earlier mode of double self-projection; the second projection, though shadowy, is once more as real as the first. Klingsor is what Hesse had become in the summer of 1919, and Hermann is the more withdrawn and contained person Hesse had been, the person who was to emerge again after Klingsor had spent himself. These two self-projections are appropriately equated with the Chinese poets Li Tai Pe and Thu Fu, adventurer and sufferer, respectively.

Louis the Horrible (*Louis der Grausame*), Klingsor's close friend, fellow painter, and restless inveterate traveller, was none other than Hesse's itinerant painter-friend Louis Moilliet. Like his literary counterpart, Moilliet was always an unpredictable visitor, fancied himself a gourmet, and was something of a footloose lover. He, too, was inclined in brash argument to extol man's animality and to discount his spirituality, he also painted circuses, clowns, and flagpoles, and his famous carrousel is Klingsor's favorite painting. *Der Grausame* was also Hesse's actual epithet for Moilliet: a facetious allusion to his un-

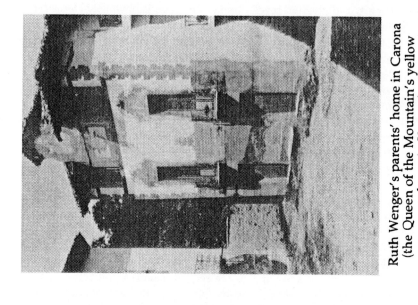

Ruth Wenger's parents' home in Carona (the Queen of the Mountain's yellow palazzo in Kareno).

Hermann and Ruth (Wenger) Hesse (Klingsor's Queen of the Mountains).

usual self-containment, and to his cultivated carefree manner and mocking tone. The Magician (*Der Magier*), the black-bearded eversmiling Armenian astrologer who carouses and contends with Klingsor, trying to disabuse him of his treasured fear of death, and who was again to appear as Jup the Magician (*Jup der Magier*) in *Die Morgenlandfahrt* (1931), was another of Hesse's close friends: buoyant, dark-haired Josef Englert, a Jew and ardent student of astrology with whom Hesse had enjoyed similar bouts of alcohol and argument, and who was also known as *Der Magier*. Klingsor's July excursion to Kareno to meet a Queen of the Mountains (*Königin der Gebirge*) was only Hesse's fantasized recollection of his own first visit on July 22 to the Wengers in Carona. The young and exotic Queen of the Mountains was Ruth Wenger, and her enchanting yellow palace with its two small balconies and a colorful parrot painted on its gable, an accurate description of her parents' *Papageienhaus* (House of the Parrot). Two barking dogs and the persistent notes of a piano tuner at work greet Klingsor's party just as they had Hesse's. Klingsor is entranced by his red-garbed Queen of the Mountains as immediately as Hesse had been fascinated by Ruth and her red dress.[30] He is also convinced, as Hesse at first had been, that he is too old for his new attraction, and that to worship was more in order than to woo. Dark-haired Ersilia's songs and turquoise parasol delight Klingsor as much as Margherita Osswald's singing and green parasol had delighted Hesse.[31] Agosto was Margarethe's husband Paolo, and the paintress and the doctor from Barengo, Klingsor's remaining companions to Kareno, were Dr. Hermann Bodmer and his wife Anny, friends of Hesse's from Sorengo. Gina the young typist with whom Klingsor is infatuated, and Edith with whom he exchanges love letters were still other of Hesse's close friends. And it is also unlikely that the various women whom Klingsor chances to encounter on his peregrinations and who attract him briefly did not also have their counterparts in actual life.

The geography of *Klingsors letzter Sommer* is just as actual as its tale is autobiographical. The setting is only slightly disguised, but enough to become appropriately remote and intriguingly esoteric. Place names, rather scarce or even entirely lacking in preceding

30 See letter to Louis Moilliet of July 24, 1919, *Gesammelte Briefe 1895–1921* (1973), Vol. 1, p. 408.
31 See letter to R. J. Humm of March 26, 1940, *Briefwechsel: Hermann Hesse–R. J. Humm* (Frankfurt a.M.: Suhrkamp, 1977), p. 91.

works, now abound, and all are playfully twisted out of recognition. Klingsor's celebrated expedition to his Queen of the Mountains begins early one morning in Barengo (Sorengo) near Laguno (Lugano). It proceeds through the valley of Pampambio (Pambio), then winds its slow course through a forest and up the steep slope of Monte Salute (Salvatore). Far in the distance Monte Gennaro (Generoso) looms imposing and unreal. The happy hikers now follow the mountain ridge to a tiny cluster of houses (Ciona), past a crumbling wayside chapel, and finally reach Kareno (Carona), just in time for lunch. Late that afternoon the party returns over Monte Salute as it had come, ambles by Palazetto (Pazzallo) to a roadside tavern and a long evening of food and revelry, then stumbles on in the dark, across fields, and by vineyards. Nearing home, the group finally disbands, and Klingsor makes his way alone back to Monte d'Oro (Collina d'Oro) and to Castagnetta (Montagnola). Everything takes place within five aerial kilometers of Montagnola, and all is recorded accurately enough to permit a retracing of the outing. Klingsor's many painting jaunts, Hesse's own, also never take him far afield, and they, too, can easily be followed. He has been to Castiglia (Castello), just to the west of Montagnola, goes with Louis to Cartago (Certenago), slightly to the north, and spends a long day in Manuzzo (Muzzano), Veglia (Viglio), and Canvetto (Convetti), a little farther to the north. Each of these little villages is within three kilometers of Montagnola.

Even Hesse's many abstruse allusions that seem to be pure meaningless fantasy can generally be accounted for autobiographically. Klingsor's mention in his letter to Louis of the hilarious tales of a certain Collofino the Rabbit Hunter from the Cathedral of Cologne (*Collofino der Hasenjäger vom Kölner Dom*) is just such an instance. The text provides absolutely no clue to this apparently absurd aside. Similar blind allusions to a Collofino occur in two of Hesse's other stories. In *Die Morgenlandfahrt* (1931) a casual reference is made to a Collofino the Smoke Magician (*Collofino der Rauchzauberer*), and in *Das Glasperlenspiel* (1942) the Latin motto was allegedly taken from a work that a certain Collof. helped to edit. In each of these instances, Hesse was simply indulging in a little private game and at the same time paying his playful respects to an old friend. Klingsor's tantalizing remark was nothing other than a facetious allusion to "The Rabbit Chase or the Deep Shadow of the Cathedral of Cologne" (*Die Hasenjagd oder der Schlagschatten des Kölner Doms*), one of a collection of very amusing anecdotes written by Josef Feinhals, an old friend who lived in Cologne.[32] That Feinhals also happened to be a cigar manufacturer and an able student of Latin accounts for his epithet in *Die Morgenlandfahrt*, for his association with Latin in *Das Glasperlenspiel*, and obviously also for his latinized *nom de plume*. Extraneous inclusions such as these indicate how extensively and in what subtle ways autobiography became part of the texture of Hesse's tales.

ANXIOUS PLUNGE INTO LIFE AND ART

Except for sporadic, brief, and unpredictable surges of euphoria, Klein remains an exceedingly troubled person. In the symbolism of *Demian*, he breaks through the eggshell that had long encased him and makes a desperate effort to fly, but a cowing past and a terrifying future make flight impossible. Continuing by and large to think and to feel as he always has, Klein is victimized by a bad conscience; this inner dissension and a fear of both life ahead and of death leave him virtually paralyzed. Too much of the eggshell remains clinging to the bird, and its wings are flapped too timorously. Klein knows only vacillating restraint where bold abandon was necessary. He is unable just to live, nor can he throw himself into the thick of life to get the painful mess over with as quickly as possible. Physically exhausted and emotionally drained, he elects to commit suicide. As he sinks into oblivion, Klein deduces that he could just as easily and might better have allowed himself to fall into life. That he had been able to surrender himself without reservation to death, to give up all willing but for his passion for extinction had made suicide unnecessary. To be able to let oneself go, was to be able to live. In *Demian*, Hesse had argued that the emancipatory stage of the new way of life he had proposed in *Rosshalde* had to be an aggressive Nietzschean process of destruction and creation. With Klein's concluding insight, Hesse proposed that the actual "living of the self" stage of his new ideal had to be a total submerging in life, Schopenhauerian in its emphasis upon will-lessness. To live oneself, following one's emancipation, one had only to give oneself unreservedly to the self and to life.

Klingsors letzter Sommer mirrors Hesse's own efforts to do just that when he settled in Montagnola, and it also indicates that to let himself fall into life proved to be much more difficult for Hesse than antici-

---

32 *Die Geschichten des Collofino: Eine Sammlung merkwürdiger Begebenheiten und rätselhafter Abenteuer, märchenhafter Schilderungen und höchst seltsamer Beobachtungen aus dem Leben von Menschen und Tieren aller Zeiten, Länder, und Zonen* (Köln, 1918), 200 pp.

pated. He and Klingsor learned quickly that to let oneself fall into life is not quite to be equated with letting oneself fall into death, that the latter is an act of desperation involving a rejection both of the self and of life, and the former can only be an act of faith, involving an affirmation and acceptance of not only the self but also of both life and death.

Klingsor tries to begin where Klein leaves off. He has also broken through the shell of traditional values and beliefs. In his case, however, there are no residual shell fragments to impede flight. Unlike Klein's, his emancipation is complete; he has managed to leave society and his socialized self behind him without any moral compunctions. He has ceased to think and to feel like a respectable member of society, lives his own morality, and nurtures his own values. He is in accord with and accepts both himself and life. He has come to terms with his immediate self and with immediate life, but not with death: neither with his own death, nor with death, the final fact of life. Haunted by the specter of death and possessed by fear, Klingsor is unable just to let himself fall into life. Klein, at odds with himself and with life, slips into death. Klingsor, at odds with death, plunges into life. Klein blots himself and life out. Klingsor tries with reckless abandon to blot out the reality of death by rushing headlong into oblivious experience. He revels in life and glories in his art, but to no avail; sex, alcohol, and painting are ineffectual weapons against death. Klingsor's life, albeit resplendent and fruitful, is as desperate an adventure as Klein's death.

Klingsor is obviously terrified by death, but as The Magician argues, he also loves death and all the agonies associated with it. And he does so for good reason. It is to death that he owes his all. Death is the positive thrust in his life and in his art. But for his fear of death, he would not live as intensively as he does and has always wanted to, and but for death he would not be the artist that he is. Thanks to death, his life is the blissful agony he actually wants it to be.

Demian explains to Sinclair that man is troubled by anxiety only when not in accord with himself, when facets of his being remain relatively unknown to and are rejected by him. In *Klein und Wagner*, this argument is extended to life at large; man is beset by anxiety only when he cannot or will not accept himself for what he is and life for what it is. Such a person can only resist and not flow with life. Klein is an instance in question: severely at odds with both himself and with the world, he is possessed by every conceivable fear, is unable to live, and cannot rightly die. Anxiety-ridden because he is unable to accept the fact of death, Klingsor is just as incapable of letting himself fall into life. This step into the void becomes possible for him only when he is finally able to come to terms fully with both life and death. This rare moment is depicted symbolically in Klingsor's struggle with his self-portrait.

Hesse is careful to explain that this self-portrait is a unique challenge, a necessary human ordeal involving Klingsor's very destiny and self-justification. All his preceding anxiety and his intoxicating flight into life and art had been fear of and flight from this ultimate task. At the beginning of his undertaking, Klingsor is still sorely troubled by the specter of death. However, once immersed in his struggle, all his longstanding anxiety vanishes and flight, which had characterized his life, comes to an end. He can now surrender himself to his portrait with ecstatic abandon and emerges triumphant.

Klingsor's painting is not just the culminating artistic experience of an exciting summer, but the crowning human achievement of his life. A lifetime of thinking, feeling, and acting the self, and a concomitant learning to know the self climax in a bold confrontation with the self and with life at large. Klingsor's painting of his self-portrait symbolizes this confrontation and his resultant affirmation and acceptance of the self and of life. The portrait is all Klingsor ever was, and ever will be, all he has ever felt, thought, and experienced, and will ever feel, think, and experience. It is his birth, life, and his death, also mankind of the past, the present, and of the future. It is all that was and ever will be: being in all its eternity. And it is to this that he yields himself without fear and without reservations.

In *Klein und Wagner*, Hesse had suggested that art was nothing but an observing of the world by a person in a state of grace. Klingsor's painting is his observation of life at just such a moment of illumination: his epiphany. He is now in accord with all, no longer suffers from anxiety, and is finally able to let himself fall into life. He manages to achieve in life what Klein had experienced fully only in death. At this critical juncture, Hesse's narration terminates in its usual abrupt manner. The next and last chapter in Klingsor's self-realization, that period when he actually lets himself fall into life, that culminating stage symbolically anticipated in his self-portrait, remains untold. As usual, Hesse took his protagonist only to the point he himself had reached, or thought he had reached. Sinclair had proceeded beyond Veraguth, Klein beyond Sinclair, and Klingsor goes beyond Klein. Siddhartha, in turn, will proceed beyond Klingsor. He alone of these protagonists is able to live fully the ideal proposed in *Rosshalde*.

After *Rosshalde*, self-living, self-knowing, and ultimate self-realization became the most persistent and the foremost of Hesse's concerns. To live oneself more fully was to know oneself more thoroughly and to realize oneself more completely. Each of the succession of major tales from *Rosshalde* to *Siddhartha* is centered about this personal challenge, each takes up where its predecessor leaves off, and together they reflect a continuous and progressively more extensive and more subtle probing of the problem. These tales are linked almost as intimately as their chapters, and in a similar concatenative manner. One or two major themes are broached toward the end of one chapter and developed in the next, which itself introduces yet another new theme or two, again to be treated subsequently; each tale, in turn, explores the theory or new possibility put forward in the abrupt termination of the preceding tale, and itself ends abruptly, broaching a new theory or possibility which is then tested in the subsequent tale. One might say that Hesse's protagonists from *Rosshalde* to *Siddhartha* live or try to live the concluding thoughts of their immediate antecedents, and think the actions of their immediate successors. Veraguth lives Kuhn's espoused life of equanimous resignation, finds it wanting, and proposes to be what he essentially is. Sinclair is intent upon realizing Veraguth's proposal, but must first emancipate himself from tradition and evolve his own ethos; having become his real self, he is prepared to be himself. Klein attempts what Sinclair is about to embark upon; self-living proves impossible with only partial emancipation, but on the threshold of death, Klein finds new hope in an envisaged will-less acceptance of the self and of life. Klingsor learns that this new approach to life, predicated upon the affirmation and acceptance of reality in its entirety, is possible only after a lifetime of intensive living. Siddhartha is accorded what Klingsor is denied; having experienced and exhausted both his spirituality and his animality, he is able in affirmation and acceptance to let himself fall into life and to enjoy the last phase of self-realization.

The major thematic linkage of these tales is reinforced by a series of subsidiary concerns that also evolve from work to work. Particularly significant among these is the theme of love and the trying polarities of the spiritual and the sensual, of time and timelessness, and of multiplicity and oneness. A young and as yet inexperienced Sinclair embraces love in all its spirituality and sexuality; for a more mature Klein, love is only sex and a flight from loneliness, a grand disillusionment, a threat, and a torture; in his interaction with women, Don Juanish Klingsor is either an old rake or a callow youth, love is one of life's flighty intoxications, a brief sexual encounter, or a passing worship; and Siddhartha knows only erotic passion or social compassion, he indulges in the former and settles for the latter. Love, that gentle, tender, benevolent, and lasting bond between man and woman, remains as foreign to these protagonists as it had been to their predecessors, and as it would be to their successors. For Harry Haller and Goldmund, love continues to be primarily a sexual experience, a necessary therapeutic diversion for the former, and a delightful steady pastime for the latter. And with *Die Morgenlandfahrt* and *Das Glasperlenspiel*, sexual love yields entirely to social love. Sinclair affirms both man's spirituality and his animality, Klein proves to be adequate in neither realm, Klingsor wallows in each, and Siddhartha experiences and transcends both. But Siddhartha's was only an ideal and not an actual resolution of the spirit-flesh problem (*Geist* and *Natur*). This polarity, for Hesse the most critical of life's many painful dualities, was to continue to plague his protagonists for years to come. In his illumination immediately preceding his death, Klein experiences a miraculous timelesssness and the essential simultaneity and oneness of all life. He now concludes that time is merely an invention of the mind, a torture instrument devised by man, and a notion that must be discarded if man is to be free. These brief asides of *Klein und Wagner* become an extended argument in *Klingsors letzter Sommer*, and a veritable philosophy in *Siddhartha*, a philosophy that argues timelessness in time and oneness in multiplicity.

INTEGRATED ART

Hesse's new and bolder approach to life brought with it a new and more vigorous stage in his creative activity. The years from 1917 to 1931 were almost recklessly prolific. Hesse now extended both the substance and form of his art far beyond their previous conventional range. The course that his writing took became dramatically unpredictable. Gradual progression had characterized his prewar work. Spasmodic transition best characterizes his art from *Demian* to *Die Morgenlandfahrt*: with *Demian*, *Klein und Wagner*, and *Klingsors letzter Sommer*, Hesse moved from psychoanalytically colored myth to psychological realism, to poetic fantasy; with *Siddhartha*, *Kurgast*, and *Der Steppenwolf*, he flitted from classical artistry to comic realism, to a fusion of fantasy, symbolism, and realism; and with *Narziss und*

Goldmund and *Die Morgenlandfahrt* he returned to German Romanticism's best tradition of story telling and to the fantasized autobiography of *Klingsors letzter Sommer*.

In Klingsor's legend, Hesse was as usual much more intent upon inner portraiture than upon narration. Description, comment, dialogue, and reported inner monologue prevail. What little real narrative there is, is confined to the preface. Actually a double portrait is executed: that which emerges as the story proceeds along its erratic course, and the unusual self-portrait of the conclusion. Hesse's characterization of the painting pertains just as much to the splintered tale preceding it: a marvelously harmonized tapestry in brilliant hues, an exercise in surrealism, a self-analysis unsparing in its psychological insights, and a ruthless, screaming confession. And what some of Klingsor's embittered opponents maintain about his self-portrait, unsympathetic literary critics could also, and with just as little cause, say about the tale itself: a product and proof of insanity, monomaniacal self-adoration, and self-glorification.

That *Klingsors letzter Sommer* is self-analysis and confession in a surrealistic vein, replete with colors and sounds reflecting and accentuating the turbulence of Klingsor's emotions and the feverishness of his thoughts is obvious enough. Immediately, however, the story seems to be anything but a marvelously harmonized tapestry, comprising as it does, ten disparate segments, jarringly juxtaposed, and assigned to one summer but otherwise only vaguely related in time: an informative preface, a study of Klingsor the man and the artist, four random episodes—a brief visit by Louis, a gay outing to Kareno, an evening of dour philosophy and wild revelry with The Magician and sundry friends, and Klingsor's sexual encounter with a peasant woman—a letter to Edith, another to Louis, a poem sent to Hermann, and a description of Klingsor's self-portrait. At first glance, this fractured structure with its romantic confusion of genres (descriptive prose, dramatic dialogue, poetry, and letters) could suggest an uncontrolled effervescence, imagination on the rampage, an undisciplined spewing forth of gaudy sentiment resulting in a hapless work of art. The tale may indeed have been written in this eruptive fashion. However, genesis notwithstanding, closer examination discloses that Hesse, like Klingsor given madly to his self-portrait, had proceeded intuitively and unerringly to produce a work of art that is anything but hapless, that is indeed a marvelously harmonized tapestry: art in which all elements of form are consonant with each other, and of which the form as a whole is in accord with the substance. The tale's untraditional, splintered structure and its lack of homogeneity—intuitive craft and not just chance—mirror and highlight the unorthodox, chaotic structure of Klingsor's lifestyle, and his inner discord. The hectic flow and the frantic rhythm of Hesse's sentences reflect and accentuate Klingsor's alternately frantic and ecstatic inner state. Nature, in turn, evocatively depicted, and excitingly animated by garish color and brilliant sound, becomes an accentuating mirror for his chronic restlessness and an appropriate backdrop for his frenzied reflections. Hesse's very language assumes Klingsor's bursting vitality and vibrates sympathetically and strongly with his persistent mania. It is vitalized by its rainbow of lively colors and its symphony of insistent sounds, its lavish similes, exotic metaphors, and startling oxymora, and by its extensive recourse to restive rhetorical questions and exclamations, and to anaphora and parataxis. Language itself is made to suffer Klingsor's agonies and ecstasies; it lends his story unusual impact and gripping immediacy. In *Klingsors letzter Sommer*, form became its own meaning. Form does not merely reinforce the content, it retells it in its own way. This is intuitively controlled artistry at its best.

SIDDHARTHA: IDEAL POSSIBILITY

INDIA AND CHINA

Klingsors letzter Sommer marked the end of the wildest and the most prolific summer of Hesse's life. His frenzy of activity subsided when autumn set in and, before winter, he had again become withdrawn, given to reflection and to plans for his next story. Part I and much of Part II of *Siddhartha* were written in the winter and spring of 1920. Dissatisfied with the chapter "At the River" (*Am Flusse*), Hesse put the novel aside in June 1920. He did not resume work on it until the end of 1921, and did not finish it until May 1922. The book appeared that October.

Like *Demian*, *Siddhartha* was basically a cerebral experience. Sinclair's tale was a reexamination of Hesse's youth in psychoanalytical terms, and Siddhartha's was a review, and a systematization and culmination of his evolving thoughts of the immediately preceding years. Neither was an artistic rendering of immediate life but of immediate thoughts and hopes. Up to "At the River" *Siddhartha* was essentially a retracing of Hesse's path of experience and of thought from *Demian* to *Klingsors letzter Sommer*, in calm reflective detachment and in an idealized mythic manner. Having dealt with Siddhartha the iconoclastic thinker and ascetic (a variation on Sinclair's theme of parental and institutional emancipation), and with Siddhartha the suffering worldling (a variation on Klein's and Klingsor's theme of self-living), having exposed his protagonist to the realm of the mind and that of the body, Hesse was at a loss for a conclusion. His vision of another Siddhartha, of one who would rise to a higher level, who would emerge a victor, an affirmer of life and all that it implied, was too dim.[33] The work had to be put aside and months of hermitic living, of meditation, and of intense preoccupation with the *Upanishads*, the *Bhagavad-Gita*, and with Buddhistic Scriptures, followed. What had been a childhood attraction to India's lore, and had become a major intellectual interest in India's religions, now became a profound spiritual experience.

As a youngster, Hesse had been as much attracted to mysterious India and its exotic religions as he had been repelled by the drabness and the severity of his parental Pietism. India suggested a desirable freedom from restraint and offered plentiful food for the imagination; Pietism knew only the evil in man and was intent solely upon an uncompromising rejection of all that is of this world.[34] In Gaienhofen, theosophy itself had bored Hesse, but it had also whetted his appetite for a more direct reading contact with India. This he first found in about 1905 in Franz Hartmann's translation of the *Bhagavad-Gita*; he then discovered Hermann Oldenberg's *Buddha*, Paul Deussen's *Sechzig Upanishad's des Veda*, and Karl E. Neumann's *Gotamo Buddho's Reden*.[35] The ultimate oneness of all reality, an underlying assumption of each of these religions, immediately fascinated Hesse, but he failed to find the wisdom he had hoped to discover. Hesse's was essentially not a quest for enlightenment, and certainly not a passion for a religious conversion, but primarily a hope for confirmation of his own still vague philosophical presentiments, a search for a school of thought in accord with his own being and responsive to his own needs. The notion of oneness accorded with his bent of thought, and as such, he quickly embraced it. As a whole, however, India's reli-

33 See "Aus einem Tagebuch des Jahres 1920," *Corona*, 3 (1932), 193.

34 "I absorbed and experienced spiritual India from childhood on just as I did Christianity. . . . India's world of religion and poetry was certainly far more enticing than this constrained Christianity, these saccharine poems, and these prevalently tedious pastors and preachers. Here no closeness oppressed me. . . . I was able to let India's first messages to me sink in without resistance, and these had a lifelong effect.' "Mein Glaube" (1931), *Gesammelte Schriften* (1957), Vol. 7, pp. 371–372.

35 Hartmann (Berlin, 3rd ed., 1903), Oldenberg (Berlin, 1881), Deussen (Leipzig, 1897), Neumann (Leipzig, 3 vols., 1896–1902).

gions proved to be too reminiscent of Pietism to be acceptable to him. Her wisdom was too rooted in asceticism, too puritanical and life-denying for Hesse's liking and his needs, and too clouded by scholasticism.[36] What he sought was not to be found in India but in China. Until his own father drew his attention to Lao-Tse in 1907, and until he read Alexander Ular's translated excerpts from *Tao-Te-King* later that same year, and then Julius Grill's translation of Lao-Tse in 1910, Hesse had never taken any real notice of the religions of China.[37] He was favorably impressed by Lao-Tse, and later in 1910 profoundly affected by Richard Wilhelm's translation of Confucius's *Gespräche*, the first of his series of Chinese classics in German. Hesse immediately became a passionate advocate of Chinese thought and belief. Of the many German translations of Chinese philosophy and literature that were published from 1910 to 1915, and again in the twenties and early thirties, there were few that Hesse did not read avidly and review enthusiastically. These translations did much to bolster his flagging spirits during the First World War, and they remained a source of spiritual sustenance until his death. Confucius, Lao-Tse, Dschuang Dsi, Mong Dsi, Lü Bu We, Yang Tschou, Liä Dsi, Mong Ko, and the *I Ging* became as much a part of Hesse's world of thought as the philosophers and religious writings of the Western world. Unlike India, China was not estranged from life, her teachings were simple and practical and not burdened by esoteric metaphysical subtleties, here life's dualities were acceptable and their poles compatible; she cultivated a wise and harmonious interplay of the spiritual and the sensual, and her thinkers suggested wisdom born of experience and tempered by humor.[38] India's asceticism repelled Hesse; China's wisdom was a confirmation of himself and all he aspired to.

36 See *Eine Bibliothek der Weltliteratur* (Zürich: W. Classen, 1946), pp. 59, 61.

37 For Johannes Hesse's views on the religions of India and China, see his: *Guter Rat für Leidende aus den altisraelitischen Psalter* (Basler Missionsbuchhandlung, 1909), 128 pp.; and *Lao-tsze, ein vorchristlicher Wahrheitszeuge* (Basler Missions-Studien, 1914), 64 pp. Alexander Ular, *Die Bahn und der rechte Weg des Lao Tse* (Leipzig: Insel Verlag, 1903); Julius Grill, *Lao Tszes Buch vom höchsten Wesen und vom höchsten Gut* (Tübingen, 1910).

38 "If India had attained things lofty and stirring in its monkish renunciation of the world, then old China had achieved things no less wondrous in its cultivation of a spirituality for which the body and the mind, religion and the everyday world do not represent hostile but friendly opposites, and both come into their own. If the ascetic wisdom of India was youthfully puritanical in the radicality of its demands, then the wisdom of China was that of a man experienced, sagacious, and not unacquainted with humor, a man not disenchanted by experience and not made frivolous by sagacity." *Eine Bibliothek der Weltliteratur* (1946), pp. 61–62.

Hesse's progression from the severe Buddhism of India to the congenial Zen-Buddhism of Japan came relatively late in life. Until 1945, nothing in his writings suggested any acquaintance with Japanese religions and philosophies. In his *Lieblingslektüre* of 1945 he alludes to Zen and equates its wisdom with that of Buddha and Lao-Tse, but fails to elaborate on his remark.[39] In a letter of 1947 to a young Japanese writer he reiterates his great respect to Zen, a school for both head and heart and with few equals in the Western world, but again chooses neither to account for this sentiment nor to comment upon the extent of his acquaintance with Zen.[40] Hesse continued to be vague about his relationship with Zen in the introduction of his privately published pamphlet, *Zen;*[41] he simply mentions that he had in the past read a number of articles and books about Zen. In any case Hesse's involvement with Zen did not peak until the appearance in September of 1960 of his cousin's, Wilhelm Gundert's, translation of the *Bi-Yän-Lu*. His preoccupation with this classic of Zen Buddhism that autumn occasioned his own *Zen*: a letter of congratulations and gratitude to Gundert, three poems inspired by the *Bi-Yän-Lu* and written in a Zen vein, and a fictitious letter ascribed to Josef Knecht and addressed to Carlo Ferromonte, in which Hesse touches lightly upon Zen and dwells on the inscrutability of the enigmatic anecdotes of the *Bi-Yän-Lu*. The paucity and tenor of Hesse's remarks about Japan's form of Buddhism clearly indicate that his belated discovery of Zen had no appreciable influence upon his thinking. Zen was confirmation and not new disclosure. In its emphasis upon the identity of essence and appearance, upon the uniqueness of the individual, and upon the incommunicability of enlightenment, Hesse found a *Weltanschauung* highly consonant with that of his *Siddhartha*.

It was not a temporary shift in inclination from China back to India, but an irresistible attraction to Gotama Buddha himself that persuaded Hesse to write *Siddhartha*. Buddhism was as questionable as ever, but Buddha the man fascinated him. He was one of history's exemplary figures, a brother to such as Christ and Socrates, and a man to be emulated. Only when his story bogged down did Hesse actually return to and steep himself in Hinduism, Brahmanism, and particularly Buddhism. What had earlier been an intellectual interest now became, in ascetic withdrawal, protracted meditation, a real

39 *Gesammelte Schriften* (1957), Vol. 7, p. 420.
40 "An einen jungen Kollegen in Japan" (1947), *Gesammelte Schriften* (1957), Vol. 7, p. 462.
41 (St. Gallen: Tschudy Verlag, 1961), 35 pp.

spiritual encounter. Hesse's coming to grips and to terms with India in 1920 and 1921 confirmed more than altered his earlier negative appraisal of her religions. However, in his renewed grappling with Buddhism, his own view of man and life evolved and emerged sharper and clearer. The ideal human possibilities he now envisaged made it possible for him to resume *Siddhartha* and to write its vital last four chapters.

AN IDEAL REALIZED

Laced though *Siddhartha* is with recondite allusions to the world of Indian thought and belief, it is anything but imperative to be an Indologist to cope with the tale. To be well acquainted with Brahmanism, Hinduism, and Buddhism, to know who Brahma and Prajapati are, what Atman is, and what Om, Maya, and Sansara signify, to be familiar with the life of Gotama Buddha and with his teachings, or to know the derivation and implication of the names Siddhartha, Govinda, Vasudeva, Kamala, Kamaswami, and Sakyamuni, can enhance a reader's intellectual enjoyment of the novel, but is unnecessary for a basic understanding of it, can be detractive, and may even be misleading. All this erudition is backdrop and not substance. The text itself provides whatever commentary is necessary. Hesse the obdurate iconoclast did not suddenly become a cheap proselytizer. He was not bent upon dissemination of information, nor upon an extolment of Buddhism and a disparagement of Christianity. *Siddhartha* was old wine in a new skin. As usual, Hesse was primarily intent upon coming to grips and to terms with himself and with life: a European immersed in Western tradition and plagued by the problems of Western man. It is from this point of view and in its close relationship, despite its Oriental setting, to all his other stories, that *Siddhartha* might best be approached.

A new way of life was proposed in *Rosshalde*, cerebrally explored in *Demian*, attempted to disadvantage in *Klein und Wagner*, and then to advantage in *Klingsors letzter Sommer*. What had become a passionate ideal for Hesse finally received its full expression in *Siddhartha*. Of all his protagonists, Siddhartha alone fully realizes this ideal: he lives himself, learns thereby to know himself, and ultimately experiences complete self-realization. However, this was not actual experience mythicized, but possibility rendered mythically, the humanly ideal depicted in a correspondingly ideal timeless manner.

Just as for Klein and Klingsor, life for Siddhartha consists primarily of two areas of experience: the world of the mind and thought, and that of the body and physical action. Klein is at home in neither realm, Klingsor lives in the intoxication of each, and Siddhartha exhausts both possibilities, and in their exhaustion, transcends them and finds himself miraculously in yet a third realm, that of the soul, that ultimate stage in being when the individual lives in complete accord with himself and with life, when he is finally able, fully and not just for chance moments, to experience the essential oneness and meaningfulness of it all. After his encounter with Buddha, and with his subsequent awakening to the realization that the incidental I of his senses ("das zufällige Ich der Sinne") is no less he than the incidental I of his thoughts ("das zufällige Ich der Gedanken"), Siddhartha, the Brahmin once dedicated to ritual and speculation and the Samana once given to asceticism, leaves the realm of the mind behind him. With his affair with Kamala the courtesan and his partnership with Kamaswami the businessman, his revelling in wealth, power, and sloth, his consequent self-disgust, life's growing repugnance, and his attempt to commit suicide, Siddhartha leaves the realm of the flesh behind him. The last phase of his life begins with his return to the river, to Vasudeva the ferryman, and to contemplation. And with his encounter with his son and his last bout with anxious love and fearful concern, Siddhartha emerges transfigured, a wise saintly figure given to his fellow humans in love and service: a paradoxical self-transcendence through self-realization. The first stage of Siddhartha's life is given to his incidental I of thought, the second to his incidental I of the senses, and the final stage to his incidental I of the soul. And with this last stage, Siddhartha will have experienced all that is humanly possible: a balanced ideal to which Hesse himself aspired but which he was not to enjoy.

Siddhartha depicts two ideals, two exemplary approaches to life based upon two diametrically opposed philosophies of life. It is the story of two Buddhas: of Gotama Buddha, an Eastern ideal, and of Siddhartha, Hesse's own ideal, a Western possibility. Their lives take similar courses and each ultimately finds his peace, but their assessments of life, their goals in life, the adjustment of each to life, and the message each leaves behind him are distinctly different. For Buddha, the physical world and life in all its involvements are Maya, a transient, painful illusion; for Siddhartha, all this is the very stuff of treasured being. Buddha's goal is a release from the wheel of Sansara, from life, its reincarnations and its incessant suffering, and a quest for Nirvana, for oblivious extinction; Siddhartha's goal is life in all its temporal agony and bliss. Buddha's is a denial and Siddhartha's an affirmation of the self. Siddhartha's message is to stand in awe of the self and of life, to embrace both for what they are, and to live fully. Buddha's message is to get these things behind one just as quickly as possible.

Despite the Orient's strong attraction, Hesse remained a Westerner. He was too thorny an individualist to become part of any organized body of thought or belief, whether foreign or native. In his wary eclectic manner he took from Eastern philosophies and religions, just as he did from their Western counterparts, only that which he understood or felt and which had a bearing upon his own life. Hesse's long and intimate association with the Orient made him fully aware of the ultimate futility and folly of Western man's quest in the East for a panacean wisdom or faith. The Orient can help Western man solve some of his problems but cannot solve them for him. This he must do himself, and can best do within the framework of the Western world. In the West's too ready embrace of the East, and *vice versa*, Hesse plainly detected too much unavailing flight into the exotic half-known. This was the sentiment to which he gave expression in *Aus einem Tagebuch des Jahres 1920, Chinesische Betrachtung* (1921), and *Besuch aus Indien* (1922), and which he reiterated in his letter of 1947 to a young Japanese author, and in his foreword of May 1955 for the sixteen-volume Japanese edition of his works.[42] Hesse had become convinced that a common heritage of timeless spiritual values and of basic truths about man and life were to be found behind the religious and philosophical trappings of the Orient and the Occident and that it was therefore superfluous to turn one's back upon the Western world. It was not for Western man to try to become a Buddhist or a Taoist, but to cultivate the Oriental art of meditation. The oneness, timelessness, and meaningfulness of life were most readily accessible in this mode of thought, too long neglected in the West. And therein lay Hesse's chief indebtedness to the East.

TIME AND TIMELESSNESS

In *Klein und Wagner*, Hesse has Klein contend that time is but a figment of the mind. The astrologer of *Klingsors letzter Sommer* argues that time is only a deception and can be thought away just as it has been thought up. Klein experiences timelessness and the resultant

42 *Eigensinn* (Frankfurt a.M.: Suhrkamp, 1972), p. 139; *Gesammelte Schriften* (1957), Vol. 3, pp. 857–858, Vol. 7, pp. 268, 462–463; Zenshū (Tōkyō: Mikasa Shobō, 1957–1959), Vol. 1, pp. 5–6.

oneness of all reality in his concluding euphoric reflections upon life, and Klingsor experiences this same timelessness and oneness while painting his self-portrait. These notions, merely broached in the summer of 1919, evolve into a mystical philosophy in *Siddhartha*. Following his attempt to commit suicide, Siddhartha becomes progressively more intrigued by the ever-changing yet never different, the ever-flowing yet always present river. At first it only puzzles him, but then further contemplative observation of its waters persuades him to conclude that there is no such thing as time. Contemplation of the river suggests only a present, no past, and no future. The river simply is. It is not a was and not a will be. It is not first here, then there, but is everywhere simultaneously: at its source, at every point along its way, and at its mouth. Contemplating himself in the manner in which he has contemplated the water, Siddhartha realizes that his very life is a river. It, too, has its source, its course, and its point of termination: birth, childhood, youth, manhood, old age, and death. So observed, his life also suggests only a present, and as such, timelessness. To contemplate life in this manner is to concentrate on essence, on the idea Siddhartha, and not just on the ephemeral manifestation of the idea, on noumenon and not phenomenon. Nor do Siddhartha's many reincarnations suggest any past or future. Siddhartha simply is. Time or timelessness depends entirely upon what the individual in his observation concentrates upon. To concentrate upon essence is to see the all synchronically and simultaneously, and to remain unaware of time. To concentrate upon phenomena is to see the all diachronically and sequentially, and to become aware of time.

Having experienced the timelessness and the implied oneness of the idea river and of the idea Siddhartha, Siddhartha proceeds a step further in his thinking as he gazes into the face of his dead Kamala. Lost in the contemplation of her countenance, he now experiences timelessness in the momentary manifestation of the idea. What Kamala was and is, is all simultaneously present before him. What he sees in his mind's eye leaves no suggestion of time. He feels only timelessness and the indestructibility of every life. Nothing is lost, nothing becomes a past. The moment or momentary manifestation is no longer a moment or momentary manifestation that will the next moment belong to a past, but is an eternity. The moment incorporates the past and the future. Was, in the sense of is no more, and will be, in the sense of is not yet, are meaningless. The moment is an eternity that reaches into the past and into the future and cancels both. That same night, contemplating himself as he had Kamala, Siddhartha experiences this same timelessness of his momentary self. Nothing was, all is. From the timelessness of his momentary self, Siddhartha now proceeds to the oneness of the momentary manifestation. If the individual at any one moment is all he ever was and all he ever will be, the momentary he is not only an eternity, but a oneness, not just a series of fragments in time but all of these things at all time. The momentary manifestation is therefore also the all, the idea; the momentary Siddhartha incorporates the idea Siddhartha. And with this conviction, Siddhartha finds full philosophical approbation for the life he has led, for his ample and intense living of the self. It is imperative to concentrate on and to experience the immediate self, as he has, for that self is the only, the whole, and the real self, and not just illusory and fleeting appearance, for phenomena are noumena.

In his ruminations, Siddhartha next proceeds from the self to life at large, from the oneness of the self to the oneness of life. About to leave for the city again in anxious quest of his wayward son, he imagines that the river is laughing at him. Peering into its waters, he notices his own image. It resembles his father. He recalls how he had forced his father to let him go among the Samanas, and how he had left never to return home. His father must have suffered what he was now suffering, and had probably died alone as he too was likely to do. His father's fate was also his. All appears to Siddhartha to be a comedy, a stupid repetition. When, together with Vasudeva, he again gazes into and listens intently to the river, he sees his father alone and mourning for his son, then himself alone and mourning for his son, and then his son eagerly pursuing his course of life, alone. Each is going his way, intent upon his goal, and suffering. The imagery still has no meaning for Siddhartha. All is still only an inane repetition. Continuing to peer at the river and listening even more intently to its voice, Siddhartha now sees a host of images, his father's, his own, his son's, Kamala's, Govinda's, the images of all those whom he ever knew or encountered, and all these faces blend and flow together, become a river hastening to its goal, become vapor, clouds and rain, and river again. Voices rise from the river, some in longing and suffering, and others in laughter, joy, and anger. The voices, in turn, blend and become one. All is a wondrous oneness, harmony, perfection. Repetition has finally become meaningful. Siddhartha now knows that each person is an integral part of the so-called past and the so-called future, that each person is a repetition of his ancestors and an anticipation of his successors, and that he is also a repetition of the human predicament, life become incarnate. All humans are therefore intimately related in a harmonious and glorious timeless oneness.

With this, Siddhartha has experienced timelessness in what appears to be time, and oneness in what appears to be multiplicity, on both the individual plane and that of life. According to this mystical mode of thought and feeling, any individual at any moment is all he ever was and all he ever will be, is what his forebears were and what his descendants will be, is what mankind was and will be, is a moment of eternity, a part and the whole. And with this philosophy, life loses its meaninglessness, aloneness its loneliness, transitoriness its painfulness, and death its fear. This is, of course, more religion than philosophy, more feeling than thought, and for Hesse in 1922 it was certainly more hope than actual experience or even conviction.

CONSCIOUS CRAFTSMANSHIP

Although *Siddhartha* traces the course of its protagonist's life from childhood to old age—unlike any of Hesse's preceding major tales—narrative continues to be minimal, and rumination, comment, description, and dialogue prevail as usual. The story is essentially a skeletal odyssey of the mind, the body, and the soul, an accounting more than a recounting, and an evolving inner more than an outer portrait. Situations, actions, and human interaction are confined to those that reflect this inner portrait, lend new dimensions to it, or occasion changes in it.

Klingsors letzter Sommer is intuitively controlled artistry at its best. *Siddhartha* is conscious craftsmanship at its best. In both instances form is perfectly consonant with and completely supportive of substance. The splintered structure of *Klingsors letzter Sommer* is in accord with its protagonist's hectic course of life. The highly symmetrical structure of *Siddhartha* is consonant with its protagonist's methodical staged self-realization. Actionally and situationally, the tale is a balanced tripartite, in keeping with Siddhartha's balanced progression from the realm of the mind, through that of the body, and to that of the soul. The first four chapters are given to things of the mind and are located on one side of the ferryman's river; the next four chapters are given to things of the body and are located on the other side of the river; and the last four chapters are given to the experiences of the soul and are located appropriately at the river's edge, between life's two extremes. Until the end of the fourth chapter, Siddhartha's story is an abbreviated variation of Sinclair's childhood and youth, his questioning of traditional institutions and his eventual leaving of the trodden paths of belief; his life among the child-adults (*Kinder-menschen*), from Chapter 5 to Chapter 8, is a temporally extended variation on Klein's belated confrontation with raw life and Klingsor's passionate last summer; and his progressive illumination in the concluding chapters is a repetition in elaborate variation of Klingsor's climactic epiphany. Siddhartha leaves Sinclair behind when he embarks upon his self-living; he leaves Klein in his wake when he elects at the last moment not to commit suicide; and he goes beyond Klingsor when he himself becomes a Vasudeva, completely in accord with the self and with life, and given to his fellow humans in love and humble service. The structural symmetry of Siddhartha's life is deliberately stressed and effectively enhanced by the structural symmetry of his tale.

The substance of the novel, Hesse's equal concern with the three areas of human experience, finds appropriate expression not only in this balanced tripartite structure, but also in the very pulsation of the tale: patterned repetition resulting in a characteristic triple rhythm. Each of the three stages of Siddhartha's life, reflective of the three realms of experience, comprises an endless series of three-beat actional patterns.

As a Brahmin, Siddhartha practises ritual and contemplation, questions it all, and then leaves the world of the Brahmins behind him. As a Samana, he cultivates asceticism, questions its ultimate value, then leaves the world of the Samanas behind him. He encounters and listens to Buddha, questions his teachings, and leaves another possibility behind him. As a young Brahmin, Siddhartha takes part in discussion, in debate, and learns to meditate. He stirs happiness in the heart of his father, pride in the breast of his mother, and love in the hearts of the maidens. But neither the love of his father, nor that of his mother, nor that of Govinda can make him happy. His intellect is not satisfied, his soul is not at peace, and his heart is not stilled. Ablutions are futile, sacrifices bring no happiness, and prayer to the gods is questionable. Three Samanas chance to appear, with dusty and bleeding shoulders, scorched by the sun, and enveloped in loneliness. Siddhartha first informs Govinda, then his father, and then his mother of his intent to join the Samanas. His father responds in silent opposition, poses three questions and makes three statements, and then gives his reluctant permission. As an ascetic, Siddhartha stands silent, smarting, and parched in the seering glow of the noonday sun until he knows no thirst or pain, stands silent, wet, and cold in the rain until his body is too numb to feel and to protest, crouches silent, staring, and motionless among thorny thickets until his blood ceases to flow, the thorns to hurt, and his body to burn. He becomes a heron, a dead jackal, and is then dismembered by hyenas and picked at by vultures, becomes a skeleton, dust, and is then blown away. It takes Siddhartha three years to conclude that this asceticism is only flight from the self, from pain, and from the meaninglessness of life. Siddhartha has three opportunities to observe Buddha before their chance encounter and brief conversation. He praises Buddha's doctrine of oneness, questions his doctrine of release, then insists that he, like Buddha, must seek his own release in his own way. Buddha for his part cautions against the conflict of words and opinions, reminds Siddhartha that many may fare better for guidance, and wishes him well. This same insistent three-beat narrative rhythm characterizes Siddhartha's life as a worldling and his subsequent withdrawal and gradual enlightenment.

Until *Siddhartha*, Hesse commonly resorted to double self-projections representing the actual and the possible. The protagonist was actuality and his bosom friend was possibility. In keeping with the three-beat pulsation of *Siddhartha*, Hesse now elaborated this favorite device. He continued to present the actual, but extended his previous alternative to three possibilities. Siddhartha is Hesse's fictivized self, and Govinda, Buddha, and Vasudeva are possibilities in life. Govinda is the self-effacing, institution-oriented person Siddhartha should not become, Buddha represents a laudable but undesirable life-denying model, and Vasudeva an exemplary life-affirming ideal. And when Siddhartha becomes this ideal, Vasudeva leaves the scene, just as Demian vanishes when Sinclair becomes his ideal self.

This three-beat rhythm of the tale's substance, structure, and action is extended deliberately to its mechanics of expression. Sentences consist of sequences of three words, three phrases, or three clauses, and often of medleys of two or even all of these triads. Common nouns frequently appear in clusters of three, proper nouns often trail two appositives, and adjectival and adverbial attributives are often twice repeated or twice extended, as too are phrases and clauses, and these, in turn, frequently begin with the same word. Sentences are often arranged in sequences of three, linked by structural parallelism and/or by a common and emphatic introductory or internal word or phrase. And upon occasion even paragraphs are triadically bunched. Visually, this patterned mode of expression is akin to an ornate tapestry characterized by many twice-repeated motifs. Musically, it suggests a composition in predominant triple rhythms.

Just as in *Klingsors letzter Sommer* and in *Klein und Wagner*, and for that matter, just as in most of Hesse's tales, inner state, outer situation, and language are again harmonized. Situation reflects and accentuates state, and expression assumes a consonant flow and rhythm. The opening paragraph of *Siddhartha* is as illustrative of this studied technique as it is of Hesse's deliberate three-beat cadence. The peaceful river setting accords with the inner tranquillity of the Brahmins who live at its edge, and the slow flow and even rhythm of the language is in keeping with the slow and even flow of the river, with the Brahmin's ritualized daily flow of ablutions, incantations, sacrifices, and contemplation, and with the correspondingly controlled flow and rhythm of their inner lives. This desired flow and rhythm of language is largely achieved by Hesse's methodically patterned mode of expression. When all is relatively peaceful, the three-beat language pattern prevails. When Siddhartha becomes agitated, outer situation changes to accord with altered inner state, and language, for its part, assumes a rapid flow and hectic rhythm. At such times, Hesse's organized three-beat clusters yield to a confusion of longer and shorter patterns, and often to a profusion of individual words. When, with the chapter "Kamala," Siddhartha leaves the relatively tranquil world of the mind for the bustling and exciting world of the senses, he is left agitated by expectancy. Outer situation and inner state accord and language becomes sympathetically vibrant. The protracted descriptive introduction to "Kamala" (the first two paragraphs of the chapter) begins with a slow but nervous and impatient two-beat rhythm, which becomes a rapid and exciting, uneven staccato of irregularly brief phrases in four- then five-beat rhythms coupled with a persistent two-beat pulsation. A tardy flow and an emphatic, methodical four-beat rhythm follows, then abruptly turns into a rough intermingling of two- and three-beat rhythms, which in turn, terminates suddenly in the original, pure two-beat rhythm, now become decidedly insistent and much more impatient with its uneven spurt of telegrammatic phrases. Both flow and rhythm of language are as tense and labile as inner state and outer situation: another instance of Hesse's conscious and sensitive craftsmanship.

Siddhartha is less a story than a depiction of the human condition and of the humanly ideal, and a sublime statement of faith in man and life. For his timeless concern and timeless avowal, Hesse deliberately and appropriately chose a mythic mode of narration: timeless matter in a timeless manner. Form was again consciously used to accentuate substance. Rather than the contemporary Western world, he favored a less time-bound Oriental world of a remote past. And even this removed setting is rendered more conceptual than actual. It is permitted no distinguishing geography, landscapes are evoked and not depicted, and interiors are accorded little more than simple reference. This timeless everywhere is fittingly peopled by humans more archetypal than actual, by figures almost void of any physical or psychological dimensions. Siddhartha's father is everyman's stern father, and his mother is everyman's loving mother; Kamala is the traditional enticing courtesan who repents, and Kamaswami, the traditional hard-nosed and harried businessman; the Samanas are the disillusioned ascetics of life, and the child-adults, its naïve indulgers; Govinda is the intimate friend and the seeker of comfort in institutions and dogma, Vasudeva is the saintly one, Buddha is the enlightened teacher, and Siddhartha is the iconoclastic self-seeker who achieves his goal. The representatives of human possibility are involved in formalized interaction, engage in ritualized dialogue, and their lives trace archetypal courses. Patterned narration and description, impersonalized dialogue, verbal and syntactic simplicity, and archaic imagery make for a priestly flow of elemental Scriptural language, a language rendered as timeless as the universally typical setting, personae, and action.

To recapitulate: timeless substance (the human condition) found consonant expression in timeless setting, characters, lives, and language; the tripartite nature of this substance (the mind, body, and the soul) found accordant rhythmic expression in triadic structure, action, and phraseology; and this harmonizing of substance and form was extended to a harmonizing of inner state, outer situation, and mode of expression. This is Hesse's conscious artistry in its extreme and at its best.

KURGAST: PENDULATION

A to-and-fro movement characterizes the lives of Hesse's protagonists just as it did his own. At the outset of his career, he and they swung between two possibilities: life and involvement with fellow humans, and art and isolation. They chose to be aesthetes devoted to art rather than members of society given to life. In their preferred isolation, they soon found themselves troubled emotionally and drawn against their will into involvement with others. Life thrusts asserted themselves, they experienced the temptations of the flesh, and in fancy if not in fact, they desecrated the realm of beauty. Author and protagonists were repeatedly subject to such crises, and after regular self-reappraisals and repeated reexamination of their adjustment to being they always resumed their dedication to art. To resolve this constantly upsetting oscillation between things of the spirit and things of the flesh, between isolation and contact, Hesse decided to marry and to settle down, to be both artist and respectable citizen, to create and to live, to satisfy both the needs of the mind and the thrusts of the senses. This only left him discontent and restless. By 1913, he and Veraguth were convinced that an artist was by definition not a participant in life, but an observer and recorder whose medium was aloneness. At this juncture, Hesse again opted for art. This did not, however, mark a return to his early wallowing in beauty, but became linked with his new notion of self-realization. In the long and lonely self-quest that followed, Hesse found himself again swinging back and forth, but now radically and more painfully than before, between isolation and contact, the spiritual and the sensual. These poles and this movement became his focal concern in his determined and protracted effort to come to terms with himself in Montagnola. During these years, Hesse's life assumed a frantic pattern. Periods of ascetic isolation, of severe devotion to his art and to matters intellectual, with resultant serious psychological problems, alternated with interludes of urgent renewed involvement with life. This swing of the pendulum, clearly reflected in *Klein und Wagner, Klingsors letzter Sommer,* and in *Siddhartha,* is expressly depicted in *Kurgast* (1923), Hesse's ironized diary and recollection of his two visits to Baden in 1923.

Physically ill and emotionally troubled after the long siege of withdrawn reflection necessary for *Siddhartha,* Hesse, the poet, loner, and protagonist of *Kurgast,* seeks relief in a convalescent home. He recalls his admission and his defensive bout of diagnostic psychologizing with the house physician, lingers superciliously over his daily trying routine of therapy and life, concentrates maliciously upon a Dutchman—a thick-skinned, wealthy, representative of the sham and repugnant bourgeois world, a normal individual with a resounding laugh, a healthy appetite, and a good digestive tract—painfully recounts his own transformation into a similar person, a philistine preoccupied with trivial physical pains and needs, given to food and cheap diversion, to mental indolence and boredom, dwells upon his sudden and miraculous psychological recovery, and then philosophizes euphorically about himself and life. This progression from an embittered, psychologizing outsider to one of the many morose and indulgent rheumatics, and then to an elated outsider become philosophical, is accompanied by a progression from arrogance and malicious benevolence to despondency and hatred, and then to humor and love, and ends in an affirmation of life's duality and man's oscillation between its poles. After only a few weeks of therapy and renewed contact with life, Hesse, physically improved, emotionally balanced, and restored in thought, is prepared to return to his isolation and his private artistic and intellectual pursuits. He is again mindful of the ultimate oneness behind reality's multiplicity, has regained faith in himself and his adjustment to life, and is convinced of the therapeutic value of humor. He is once more ready to love, to accept, and to affirm the self and life, if only until his next relapse into despondency and the next swing of the pendulum. Hesse's respite was of short duration.

In his many early allusions to the polarity of life, Hesse had always resorted casually to such words as life, art, instincts, spirit, to think, to live (*Leben, Kunst, Triebe, Geist, denken, leben*). A formulaic expression of life's dichotomy began with Klingsor's juxtaposition of the spiritual ("das Geistige") and the sensual ("das Sinnliche") continued with Siddhartha's incidental I of thought ("das zufällige Ich der Gedanken") and incidental I of the senses ("das zufällige Ich der Sinne"), and evolved into the spirit and flesh ("Geist und Natur") of *Kurgast*. This formula remained Hesse's favorite symbol for life's duality of possibilities.

DER STEPPENWOLF: BETWEEN SPIRITUALITY AND SENSUALITY

FACT BECOME FICTION

Hesse's impasse of 1922 to 1923 was mild and brief compared with his similar crisis of 1924 to 1926, the climax and turning point of which found its expression in *Der Steppenwolf* and in the novel's poetic counterpart, *Krisis*. This third major crisis in Hesse's life began when he and Ruth Wenger, his wife of but a few months, separated at the end of March 1924. Withdrawal, intensive editorial work to dull his pain, growing agitation, bitter self-hatred, a lusting for both death and raw life, and a brief plunge into the world of the senses were followed by gradual recuperation and a return to his lonely retreat, to his art, his ideals, his aspirations, and his intellectual pursuits. Hesse's *Klingsors letzter Sommer* had been a romantic rendering of the fluctuations of his ecstatic summer of 1919, his *Der Steppenwolf* was a surrealistic rendering of his latest crisis. The work was begun in November 1924, the first version was finished by the end of December 1926, and the book appeared in June of 1927.

Der Steppenwolf is not only the most novel but also the most autobiographical of Hesse's many stories. Haller's place of birth, parents, and childhood, his physiognomy, psychology, and philosophy, his feelings, thoughts, inclinations, habits, and experiences, his relationship to women, music, literature, and politics, to his age, the bourgeois world, and Germany, and his crisis, fantasies, and resolutions, were all Hesse's. Haller's birthplace, a provincial German town with a ridge behind and a river and bridge below it, was Hesse's Calw. His was the cultivated bourgeois home Hesse's had been, his stern and pious parents were just as intent upon breaking the will of their intractable son as Hesse's equally stern and pious parents had been, and they, as had Hesse's father and mother, succeeded only in twisting their son's psyche, filling him with self-dissatisfaction, and rendering him almost incapable of love. Haller was confirmed in the spring of 1891, just as Hesse had been; he experienced his first shy love soon thereafter, as had Hesse, and he, as had Hesse, enjoyed no more than shy attractions during his remaining adolescence. At the age of fifteen Haller's head was filled with Greek and Latin, as Hesse's had been, and he was possessed by literary ambitions and troubled by insistent sexual urges no less than had been Hesse. Gustav, once the wildest and strongest of Haller's schoolmates, a professor of theology who throws himself zestfully into the magic theater's bloody battle between man and machine, gleefully intent upon the destruction of our wanting world, was recollection and caricature: a recollection of Gustav Zeller, a physically imposing and assertive fellow student of Hesse's in Maulbronn, who was interested in philosophy and later became a professor in a secondary school; and a caricature of Demian, for whom Zeller had also been a model.

Haller was all that Hesse had been, and he is all that Hesse was at the time he wrote *Der Steppenwolf*. He is an aesthete, a writer, scholar, journalist, psychologist, philosopher, and a schizophrenic approaching his fiftieth birthday with considerable anxiety. As was Hesse, he is a man of medium stature and a measured gait that suggests effort, carelessly attired, politely aloof, and with short-cropped hair, sensitive and alert features, and a wistful smile. He is also a late riser, does not begin to function properly until the afternoon, and is at his best when evening sets in, suffers from insomnia, migraine, poor diges-

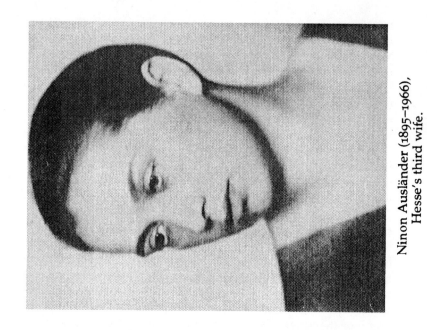

Ninon Ausländer (1895–1966),
Hesse's third wife.

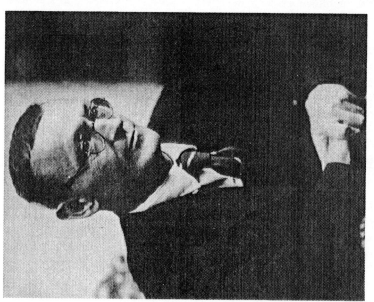

Hermann Hesse in the mid-twenties.

tion, and arthritis, wears glasses and uses a cane, is careless and irregular in his habits, consumes books, dotes on music, smokes cigars,
and enjoys his alcohol; and all this was true of Hesse. Haller, no less
than was Hesse, is basically an unhappy person, a man who is filled
with self-scorn and with disdain for others, has difficulty establishing
close relationships, has many acquaintances but few intimate friends,
hurts those whom he loves and who love him, and is constantly at
odds with prevailing public opinion. As was Hesse, Haller is a virtual
stranger in the society in which he lives, is attracted to the bourgeois
world for its industry, orderliness, cleanliness, and decency, is repelled by it for its cultural mediocrity, intellectual stupidity, and its
lifeless normality, and is emancipated from it ideologically but not
physically and emotionally. As had Hesse, Haller has become something of a sinner-saint, and his treasured isolation and independence
have also, and no less than had Hesse's, become his painful fate. Haller, as did Hesse, freely calls himself a schizophrenic, has an inordinate capacity for and derives both pleasure and strength from suffering, and flirts chronically with suicide. But he, as did Hesse, also has
his moments of blissful illumination, when all is well with the self and
the world, and as did Hesse, he customarily enjoys these sporadic
spells while listening to music, reading, creating, lost in thought, or
while in love. Haller's favorite authors and composers were Hesse's,
he shares Hesse's belief that Beethoven, Chopin, Schubert, Hugo
Wolf, Brahms, and Wagner suggest decline, and that jazz mirrors the
cultural disintegration of the Western world, and he, as was Hesse, is
both appalled by jazz and touched by its raw, honest sensuality. Haller's recollection of Gubbio and an old cypress on a nearby mountain
top was a bit of Hesse's memory, and Haller's visit to the cathedral to
listen to an organ concert and to hear an old friend sing Bach recalled
an evening Hesse had spent in Zürich's Fraumünster listening to a
similar recital and hearing again his old friend Ilona Durigo, a celebrated Bach singer. As was Hesse, Haller is sharply critical of German
intellectuals for their useless erudition, their social irresponsibility,
and for their political naïveté or indifference to politics; he is convinced, as was Hesse, that the next war is already in the offing and
that all his protestations against militarism and nationalism will be
futile; and his "O Friends, not these Tones" (*O Freunde, nicht diese
Töne*) was Hesse's first essay venture into politics in 1914. Haller is as
unfavorably disposed toward Americans as was Hesse, and for the
same reasons: Americans are enviably youthful and strong, but too
rational and ridiculously naïve in their oversimplification of life, and

obviously content with cultural mediocrity.[43] Haller's *Steppenwolf* self-characterization was also Hesse's, as was Haller's engrossment with his wolf-man split personality. His interest in the religions of India has waned, just as had Hesse's; he, as did Hesse, quarrels with Goethe's optimism in the face of life's wretchedness; and his ultimately acclaimed humor and the Immortals of the Spirit had also become Hesse's antidote against and latest hope in life. And, of course, Haller's watercolors, essays, poems, books, and his *Steppenwolf* manuscript were also Hesse's.

The course of Haller's life and career was also obviously Hesse's own. As had his author, Haller gave printed expression to his antimilitary sentiment during the First World War, was branded a traitor to the German cause, discredited as a writer, and left bereft of an income. After the war, as had Hesse, he appealed in vain to his fellow countrymen to practice patience, self-criticism, and humanity, and he, as had Hesse, continued to be subjected to the opprobrium of a nationalistic German press. As had Hesse, Haller's marriage collapsed, his wife became deranged, and a divorce followed. Just as had Hesse while preoccupied with *Siddhartha*, Haller then managed in ascetic isolation and meditation to evolve a new ideal for himself and to find some degree of peace again in a new adjustment to life, and as had Hesse's soon after *Siddhartha*, Haller's new possibility was swept away by yet another wave of loneliness, despondency, and despair. Young, beautiful, and elegant, but also troubled and difficult Erika, with whom Haller subsequently fell in love and whom he has seen only rarely for some time and seldom without an ensuing quarrel, was Ruth Wenger, whom Hesse continued to meet occasionally after their separation and never without added misunderstanding and friction. Haller's trying reappraisals of and readjustments to himself and life had been Hesse's, as had his progressively more extreme and more demanding individuation. Haller's precious isolation gradually became his confining prison, as had Hesse's, and he, as did Hesse, dreads the new self-confrontation, the excruciating rebirth, the even greater individuation and more intimidating estrangement that his new crisis in life will necessitate. Though sorely tempted by suicide, Haller chooses, as did Hesse, to go through this hell once again; as

43 Hesse's many casual remarks about the U.S.A. in his essays, book reviews, and letters are almost uniformly derogatory, e.g.: *Der Bücherwurm*, 2 (1912), 250; *Briefe* (1964), pp. 220, 298, 345, 348, 469.

did Hesse, he first becomes a habitué of nightclubs, consorts with Hermine, Maria, and Pablo, who had their actual, albeit less exotic counterparts in Hesse's life,[44] then emerges from his ordeal, dedicated anew to his ideals and prepared to continue to trudge stoically along his even lonelier road of life. Haller was clearly heir to Hesse in all but name; this he owed to the Swiss sculptor Hermann Haller, Hesse's friend and a fellow reveller of 1926.

The setting of *Der Steppenwolf* is no less actual than its tale is intimately autobiographical. The scantly depicted nameless city with its Martinsvorstadt, its market area bustling with night life, its dark and quiet ancient quarter with steep twisted streets and a grey stone wall between a little church and an old hospital, and its cozy pub the Steel Helmet (*Stahlhelm*, which actually was the inn *Zum Helm*) was Hesse's Basel. He had moved there in 1899, and there he had also spent the winters of 1923 to 1924 and 1924 to 1925; Haller too lived in the city in question twenty-five years prior to his latest visit. Haller's disorderly two-room atelier quarters in a bourgeois three-family apartment house were Hesse's mansard lodgings in Lothringenstrasse 7, and even the araucaria he so admires was no less admired by Hesse. But as the novel evolved, Zürich, where Hesse spent the winters of 1925 to 1926 and 1926 to 1927, began to impose itself upon the setting. Haller's Black Eagle (*Schwarzer Adler*), Old Franciscan (*Alter Franziskaner*), Hotel Balances, the Grand Hotel, Odeon-Bar, City-Bar, and Cécil-Bar were Zürich's sundry nightclubs, the dance locales that Hesse had begun to frequent. Zürich is also the scene of Haller's climactic masked ball.

In a letter of late January 1926 to Alice Leuthold, wife of his patron and friend Fritz Leuthold, Hesse comments candidly on his new manner of life:

> I made moderate progress in my dances. My six lessons are now over. The Boston and the blues are still a real problem for me. I think these are actually beyond my capacity, but I do believe that I can master the fox-trot and the one-step to the degree that can be expected of an elderly gentleman suffering from gout. This dancing is an attempt on my part, somewhere or other, naïvely

44 A Julia Laubi-Honegger was Hesse's Hermine. The models for Maria and Pablo have remained unknown. For a photograph of Julia, allusions and a letter by Hesse to her, and a poem associated with her, see *Materialien zu Hermann Hesses* Der Steppenwolf (Frankfurt a.M.: Suhrkamp, 1972), pp. 71–73, 76–77.

and like a child, to become part of the world of ordinary people; that is clearly its main significance for me. And that is quite important for an old outsider and eccentric.

As did Hesse, Haller takes dancing lessons, achieves some degree of skill in the one-step and the fox-trot, even manages the Boston, and he is intent, as was Hesse, on more human interaction on a simpler physical plane. In a subsequent letter written at the beginning of February and again addressed to Alice Leuthold, Hesse notes that he is about to attend his first masked ball.[45] It is also Haller's first masked ball. In this same letter, Hesse also mentions that he will be going to the ball with a number of friends, among them, the sculptor Hermann Hubacher. The latter was so impressed by the occasion that he took the trouble to record it in his memoirs, in fact, to describe it in considerable and extremely revealing detail.[46]

According to Hesse's letters, the ball in question must have taken place on February 6, and according to Hubacher's report, it was the masquerade that was sponsored annually by the artists of Zürich and that always took place in the spacious Hotel Baur au Lac. For the event in 1926, the main dance hall of the hotel was illuminated by an enormous rotating globe suspended from the ceiling and replete with dazzling lights and tiny mirrors. Of this affair, Hesse made the masked ball given yearly in the Globe Rooms (Globus-Säle) by the artists' guild. Hubacher notes that the dancing had already begun when he and Hesse arrived, not costumed, but in their evening clothes. Haller also arrives late and also in evening clothes. Hesse had at first viewed the activities rather grimly and skeptically. Haller is sullen and dejected at the outset and his first inclination is to leave. A charming Pierrette, obviously acquainted with Hesse, had settled down on his lap and had brought him to life. Young girls are anxious to nestle on Haller's lap, he, too, has a Pierrette, his Hermine, and his revelry climaxes with her appearance. Hesse and his friends had danced to the music of many bands and to the then latest popular songs. The Globe Rooms resound with the blare of a variety of orchestras, and Haller swings to Yearning, the latest American fox-trot hit. Hubacher

45 "On Saturday I am going to go to the masked ball for the Kunsthaus with some friends (Hubacher, etc.). This will be the first ball in my life. Unfortunately, it no longer has the meaning for an almost fifty-year-old man that it has for seventeen-year olds." Both letters to Alice Leuthold appear in Materialien zu Hermann Hesses Der Steppenwolf (1972), pp. 62, 64. See also Gesammelte Briefe (Frankfurt a. M.: Suhrkamp, 1979), Vol. 2, pp. 130, 131, 133.

46 Der Bildhauer Hermann Hubacher: Werke. Aufzeichnungen (Zürich: Atlantis Verlag, 1965), pp. 18–19.

recalls that their merrymaking had gone on until the wee hours of the morning, and that Hesse had had a wild time after his initial aloofness, indeed, had ended his night's gaiety by leaping on a table and dancing a sprightly solo one-step, and by scribbling verse on starched shirtfronts. Haller's crescendo of merriment also reaches into the early morning hours and climaxes with a whirl and in sheer exhilaration. Except for poetic concentration and intensification, Hesse's only major departure from actual experience in his depiction of Haller's masked ball was the night's finale. Where Hesse and his friends leave anticlimactically for the Kronenhalle and a flour-soup breakfast,[47] Haller repairs to Pablo's den to enjoy an opium fantasy. A downbeat gruel-breakfast finale obviously had no place in Haller's story. Haller's sojourn in the realm of the senses terminates with the ball and his illuminating drug trip. The ball was a highlight for Hesse but not a conclusion; he continued to frequent Zürich's nightspots until the end of March.[48] He returned to his secluded Montagnola at the end of May, and his crisis then quickly abated.

DRUGS

It is obvious from Haller's story that Hesse knew enough about some hallucinogenic drugs to be able to describe their mind-expanding effect. That Pablo the saxophonist is a drug cultist, and that Haller indulges upon occasion, and that his magic theater is a psychedelic trip, is more than manifest. However, whether or not Hesse himself had recourse to drugs for other than medical purposes during his critical Steppenwolf period is debatable. At the time, extensive experiments with mescaline were being conducted in Heidelberg by Professor Kurt Beringer; however, there is nothing in Hesse's essays, his accessible diaries, or in his letters that would suggest that he knew of this, that he himself was experimenting with drugs, or that he ever read any of Beringer's publications about drugs. It should be remembered, furthermore, that many of Hesse's works written long before *Der Steppenwolf* include passages that clearly indicate an expansion of consciousness similar to that of the magic theater. His

47 Among those who attended the ball were Othmar Schoeck, Louis Moilliet, Max Wassmer, and Hermann Haller.

48 For an insight into Hesse's winter of 1925 to 1926 see: "Ausflug in die Stadt" (December 1925), *Frankfurter Zeitung*, January 17, 1926, No. 44; "Verbummelter Tag" (March 1926), *Frankfurter Zeitung*, March 31, 1926, No. 241; "März in der Stadt" (March 1926), *Berliner Tageblatt*, March 6, 1927, No. 110; and "Die Schreibmaschine" (March 1926), *Berliner Tageblatt*, April 3, 1927.

experience of cosmic oneness and harmony depicted ecstatically in *Alte Musik* (1913) shows that a Bach organ recital could induce something akin to a psychedelic trip. Klein's religious moments of grace, those rare interludes when he is almost overwhelmed by the awesome intrinsic oneness and meaningfulness of life, are similar and similarly described spells of expanded consciousness, and these are triggered by nothing other than a peaceful twilight saunter through a beautiful countryside, by intense thought, and finally by the immediacy of death. Klingsor finds his surge of transcendent bliss in the passion of creation, Siddhartha owes his bouts of luminosity to the art of contemplation, and the experiences of both are recounted in an anoetic fashion similar to that of the magic theater. Haller himself is also able upon occasion to enjoy this manner of illumination when listening to music or given to thought, when reading or writing, and even when simply in love. And the fabulous trek to the Orient described in *Die Morgenlandfahrt* (1931) is yet another of these luminous experiences. To be sure, all this is no proof that Hesse, like Haller, may not briefly have resorted to opium or hashish or even both. It merely indicates that he could have experienced Haller's drug-induced trip without the aid of drugs. Hesse did indeed belong to the brotherhood of illuminati, but probably not to the fraternity of psychedelic freaks. His was probably not a drug-induced transcending of the self, not a chemical path to enlightenment, but a spontaneous mystical experience.

UNFAVORABLE RECEPTION

In the twenties, *Der Steppenwolf* was distinctly new literary fare. It startled the general reading public, perplexed Hesse's acquaintances, and dismayed his close friends. The arch-patriots who had become critical of him during the First World War, and the political activists who had taken umbrage with his escapist *Siddhartha*, now took him to task not only for being a poor patriot and bad writer, but also for being a man without morals. Friends and acquaintances who had become troubled by his new lifestyle and shocked by his latest poems, at once begin to upbraid him for his irresponsible aberrations, and in no uncertain terms. In the flood of letters that Hesse received from both young and old readers and new and longtime friends, *Der Steppenwolf* was criticized so severely and persistently for its sex, jazz, and drugs, that he felt obliged to account for himself, his novel, and his latest poems, not just in his private letters but also in a published statement, the postlude of his *Krisis* (1928) the novel's poetic counterpart. This rejoinder throws light upon the then inner circumstances of Hesse's life, makes clear his intent, and provides an indispensable key to the author's own understanding of his work:

> Moreover, the problem of the aging man, the very familiar tragicomedy of the fifty-year-old male, is by no means the sole content of these poems. They do not only deal with another flaring up of life's urges in a person growing old, but even more with one of those stages in life when the spirit tires of itself, abdicates, and yields to nature, to chaos, to animality. In my life, periods of extreme sublimation, of asceticism intent upon spiritualization have always alternated with periods of surrender to the naïvely sensual, to the child-like, the foolish, even to the insane and dangerous. . . . In my earlier works a large part, indeed the largest part of this shadier, perhaps deeper half of life was unconsciously passed over in silence or made more attractive. . . . I was more at home in the spiritual, and in the broadest sense of the term, than in the sensual. . . . I was a barbarian in the shimmy and the arts of the man of the world, although I knew well that these arts too are worthwhile and belong to culture. Advancing in years, and since I no longer derive any joy in the writing of things just pretty . . . I had also to bring to light and to depict this hitherto suppressed half of life. It was not easy, for it is more pleasant and more flattering to show the world one's noble, spiritualized side than the other half, at the expense of which spiritualization has taken place. Futhermore, many of my friends have also mentioned to me in no uncertain terms that my new ventures in both my life and writing were irresponsible digressions. . . . I look differently at all this. For me it is not a matter of opinions or convictions but of necessities. One cannot maintain the ideal of sincerity and always exhibit only the attractive and significant side of his being. There is also the other side. . . .

Clearly Hesse's crisis of 1924 to 1926 was new only in its intensity and in his determination to give candid expression to it. It was the most radical of Hesse's sporadic oscillations between isolation and contact, from spirituality to sensuality and back, and *Der Steppenwolf* and *Krisis* were the most painfully honest of his literary renditions of these recurrent ordeals. Compared with the poems, Haller's four-week frequenting of dance halls and trafficking with ladies of the night are rather temperate. This verse was unprecedented in its mercilessly frank spewing forth of passion too long stifled and become a raw lusting, of yearning become an agonizing scream, of self-dissatisfaction become self-laceration, of both love for and hatred of life, and of an overwhelming desire for death. *Krisis* is a brutally sincere reflection of Hesse's attempted drowning of the self in sex, jazz, and alcohol, and of his agonizing recognition that he was at best but a shy guest at life's feast and would remain a troubled stranger in the community of man. He emerged from this blissful and excruciating Bacchanalia grim but prepared to return to his lonely retreat, another necessary aberration behind him.

Hesse had Haller recount his experience in a lower key. Actuality was rendered in less strident detail and buffered by a touch of fantasy. Haller, intellectual, writer, and uncompromising idealist, too long isolated and too ascetically devoted to his mental pursuits, becomes emotionally unhinged. His aloneness has become a torment, his freedom repugnant, and all his interests and ideals questionable. This is another of his frequent crises along the road of self-realization. He is unable to continue in his estrangement, is tempted by but not prepared to commit suicide, and he will not compromise himself and join the throng, find a comfortable place for himself among the many. Humor could ameliorate his lot, but is still beyond him. He has no choice but to relax, to emerge from his isolation, and to seek relief in the world of the senses. For some four weeks, life's thrusts too long and too severely suppressed, are given free rein. He emerges from the intoxication of this therapeutic interlude still dour but ready to return to his isolation, ideals, and intellectual pursuits, and determined to continue the lonely course of his self-realization, hopeful that some day, with the help of humor, he may become reconciled to himself and to life, and that in his very process of individuation he may ultimately transcend the troubled self and life's cacophony to experience the inherent oneness, harmony, and meaningfulness behind the façade of appearance.

What was too salty for the twenties became too pessimistic for the thirties. Misinterpretation followed moral indignation. For many readers, Haller's tale became nothing more than a psychopath's self-lacerating self-depiction and his acrid assessment of Western culture. Hesse readily acknowledged that such was the case, but also repeatedly insisted that to see no more than this was to see far too little. In his many letter references to the novel and in a postlude added in 1942, he freely concedes that every reader may perceive in it whatever he desires and may take from it whatever he chooses. He also wishes, however, that more readers might note that Haller's story does not just depict sickness, distress, despair, and cultural disintegration, but ends in cure, in new hope, and in renewed faith in timeless human and cultural values and in the meaningfulness of man's aspirations and his striving. And he insists doggedly that the tale was written by a believer and not by a despairer.[49]

EVOLVING THEMES

Siddhartha accepts both his incidental I of the senses and his incidental I of thought, gives primacy to neither, and lives both to exhaustion. This was for Hesse the humanly ideal in self-realization. Haller's tale, on the other hand, depicts Hesse's actual lot, that which in self-realization was humanly possible for him. He was essentially what he had with Veraguth assumed himself to be: an observer and recorder of and not a real participant in life. Hesse's oscillation between observation and participation, between the spirit (*Geist*) and the flesh (*Natur*), was therefore never a balanced experiencing of both possibilities, not the ideal espoused in *Siddhartha*. The realm of the intellect and of art was his medium, and the realm of the senses was always an uncomfortable, albeit intriguing, seduction. And with the passing years, sensual experience gradually became for Hesse what it is for Haller: a brief and necessary therapeutic digression.

Hesse's continued concern with self-realization is both his focal consideration in *Der Steppenwolf* and the novel's major linkage with his works from *Demian* to *Das Glasperlenspiel*. A number of persistent secondary and related themes continue to strengthen this intertale thematic linkage. The notion of cultural decline, broached in *Demian*, remarked upon in *Klingsors letzter Sommer*, and about which Hesse had theorized and psychologized in *Blick ins Chaos*, is now argued in plain detail. Ours is a sick and dying world, a culture of cheap values, without religion and with no ideals, an inhumanly mechanized age of tinsel, sham, and lies, a place for politicians but not for human beings. Bourgeois society, the matrix and determinant of this culture, and a constant source of irritation for Hesse, is now also subjected to its most detailed scrutiny and most stinging excoriation. That middle-class world upon which Lauscher turns his back, with which Camenzind is at odds, by which Giebenrath is ground under, in which Kuhn lives unhappily, to which Veraguth gladly bids farewell, above which Sinclair rises, from which Klein flees, beyond which Klingsor cavorts, through which Siddhartha passes disdainfully, and by which Hesse is exasperated in *Kurgast*, is described sarcastically,

---

49 *Der Steppenwolf* (Zürich: Büchergilde Gutenberg, 1942), pp. 300–301. See also *Briefe* (1964), pp. 32, 35–37, 91–94, 149, 226.

subjected to a seering psychological analysis, and damned lustily. It is a world characterized by materialism, nationalism, and militarism, by accumulation, conventionality, and mediocrity, and by uniformity, compromise, and tedium; and its constituents are security directed and law conscious, more inclined to abide by than to be responsible for, slaves rather than masters, diligent but not creative, without geniality, taste, or worthy goals, interested in comfort and not in freedom, in moderation and not in the intensities of life, and governed in all their thought and action by the cowardly impulse of self-preservation.

Haller enjoys the same mystical interludes of grace, of blissful oneness, harmony, meaningfulness, and affirmation that Klein, Klingsor, and Siddhartha experience. However, his engrossment with the notion of timelessness assumes a new direction. For Klein, time is an invention of the mind and the bane of man's existence; the magician in *Klingsors letzter Sommer* contends that time can be thought away; and Siddhartha's contemplation does just that. Having exhausted this esoteric trend of thought, Hesse shifted his concept of timelessness from the actual to an ideal world. He now envisages a timeless realm of eternal values, peopled by *real* human beings, a community of Immortals: saints, sinners, and martyrs, artists and thinkers, and all the exceptional who manage to transcend the narrow confines of the time-bound bourgeois world. The actual world infuriates and depresses Haller; this ideal world, reflective of man's loftiest possibilities, lends approbation to his exceptional adjustment to life, gives meaning to his suffering, and spurs him onward along his tortuous path of self-realization. For Hesse, self-realization now became synonymous with *Menschwerdung*, the becoming not just of the self, but of an exemplary human being, one of the Immortals. This ideal began to assume decided precedence over the real, and the goal became more important than the way. Siddhartha's ideal way of life yielded to Haller's ideal goal of life. It is this end, this realm of timeless values, the eternal realm of the spirit that is apotheosized in *Die Morgenlandfahrt*, then realized, and in turn rejected in *Das Glasperlenspiel*. Hesse's journey from Lauscher's (*Lulu*) wondrous kingdom behind the curtain of appearance, that real world to which poets in their imagination repair for their inspiration, to Haller's Immortalia hovering above and beyond actuality was but a short step from romanticism to Platonism.

The strained man-woman relationship also continues to thread its almost predictable way through Hesse's tales. Klein is possessed by a desire to kill the women in his life, and symbolically does so, when in his dream he plunges a knife into the belly of an old hag; Klingsor's self-portrait includes a woman's breast cleft by a dagger; and in his fantasy Haller thrusts a knife into Hermine's chest. The battle of the sexes had obviously not yet ended for Hesse. Like Klein and Teresina, Klingsor and Edith, and Siddhartha and Kamala, Haller and Hermine are incapable of that love which transcends itself and binds man and woman more than just physically and fleetingly. Love continues to be a sexual encounter, a reluctant seduction, and a suspect though necessary digression.

After erotic love has run its course in *Siddhartha*, social love is introduced. Siddhartha's compassion for and service to mankind had become the latest ideal in Hesse's self-quest. However, the works to follow clearly indicate that he was no more prepared to live this altruism than he had been to follow in the footsteps of St. Francis of Assisi after Camenzind's acclaim of the latter's exemplary life of love and service. In *Kurgast*, there is much evidence of hatred, no mention of service, and considerable argued insistence that all love is self-love and that love is an efficacious immunization against enemies. In *Der Steppenwolf*, Siddhartha's love of and service to mankind become love of the Immortals and service to the spirit, and, by *Die Morgenlandfahrt*, they have evolved into a glorification of and a dedication to the timeless realm of things spiritual. It was not until Knecht's departure from Castalia to become a simple tutor to young Tito, that Siddhartha's concluding adjustment to life finally became Hesse's cultivated social ideal.

Siddhartha lives, loves, and affirms life for all it is or appears to be, for life is the all. Haller, in marked contrast, puts up with life reluctantly and hopes eventually to learn to laugh at it and to live with it, mindful of a consoling realm of timeless values hovering above it all. Siddhartha is impatient with this Platonism, and Haller finds comfort in it. Siddhartha opts for life, Haller for immortality. In terms of *Siddhartha*, *Der Steppenwolf* marks a distinct relapse. Haller is a Klein become a little older, more sophisticated, and more resourceful, but he is still as desperately at odds with himself and with life as ever. He is still far removed from the Knecht he was ultimately to become. An angry disillusioned Haller turns his back upon life; a tranquil, benign, and wiser Knecht commits himself to it.

ACTUALITY AND SYMBOLISM

Demian is a mythic account of youth's eternal quest for the self, an externalization of psychic integration, an illumination of the inner and an adumbration of the outer world, more symbol than actuality.

188 / Hermann Hesse

To approach it literally is to bypass it. *Der Steppenwolf*, in marked contrast, is a fanciful but very real depiction of a surrealistic experiencing of life, an account of a psychological crisis both personal and typical, a tale that is both appearance and implication, and that for full comprehension must be approached both actually and symbolically. Hermine, the most enigmatic of Haller's new acquaintances, best illustrates this bilevel nature of the novel.

Haller chances to meet Hermine late one night in the Black Eagle. He is despondent, desperately in need of some human contact, torn by a passion for death and an urgent longing for life, and she, an attractive and well-groomed prostitute, responds sympathetically to his plight. She is a light in his darkness. They immediately engage in a protracted conversation revolving about Haller. A dinner engagement in the Old Franciscan follows a few days later. Their initial conversation is resumed and Hermine now informs Haller that she will make him fall in love with her, and that accomplished, will order him to kill her and will expect him to comply. Haller knows what her last order will be even before she herself mentions it. In the meantime, Hermine will see to it that Haller learns how to dance, laugh, and live. Their next rendezvous takes place in a café the following afternoon; their intimate conversation continues, a phonograph is purchased, and Haller's dancing lessons begin. At Hermine's request and insistence, Haller takes her to an afternoon dance in the Hotel Balances a few days later, conversation continues to flow freely and seriously, and Haller has occasion to meet handsome young Pablo, a jazz-band saxophonist. A few days later, Haller's liaison with sensuous Maria begins, a bedroom friendship arranged by Hermine. Haller and Hermine now see less of each other. They have their last, long, and very personal conversation the day before the masked ball, and this takes place three weeks after their first dance in the Hotel Balances and about four weeks after their first meeting in the Black Eagle. At the ball, Hermine first appears as a young man, vies with Haller on the dance floor, then reappears as a Pierrette. Now she and Haller finally dance together, a passionate wedding dance, and enjoy their first ardent embrace and kisses. The ball ends in the early hours of morning and Pablo invites the two to his quarters for a climactic drug party. Emerging slightly from his drug-induced fantasy, Haller finds Hermine and Pablo sleeping naked side by side, exhausted by their sexual intercourse. He plunges a knife into Hermine's heart. Pablo awakens, covers her body, then leaves. Haller slips back into a deep daze, imagines that Mozart appears and engages him in a philosophical discourse about idea and appearance, and about the necessity of learning to laugh at the apparently real and to remain mindful only of the ideal. Haller also imagines that a trial takes place and that he is sentenced to eternal life for his misdeed. He must go on living and he must learn to laugh at life for what it appears to be. Mozart vanishes, becomes Pablo, and Pablo also chides Haller for his violence, his lack of humor, and for his confusion of the ideal and the real. And with that, Pablo picks Hermine up, she becomes a little figurine which he tucks into his vest pocket, he then vanishes, and Haller is left alone with his thoughts. Sober again, Haller is prepared to resume the game of life, to suffer its agonies and its senselessness once more, hopeful that some day he will be able, like Mozart, to distinguish between idea and appearance and to rise above it all and laugh.

Like the Sinclair-Demian relationship, Haller's encounter with Hermine is clearly symbolic; unlike the former, however, it is also, and most immediately, excitingly actual. Though this interlude in Haller's life may not always quite accord with plausibility, its basic realness remains intact. Childlike Pablo is perhaps too informed and too wise, and voluptuous Maria, too generous with her favors to be altogether convincing, and that complex Harry Haller should chance to encounter a prostitute who is nothing less than his female counterpart, and who takes him in tow without remuneration and without sex, may tax credibility, but does remain within the realm of possibility. Only Hermine's order that Haller kill her once he has fallen in love with her, and his surprising anticipation and calm acceptance of this unlikely command, appear to mar the realness of the narrative, to add a mystification reminiscent of the many obfuscations of *Demian*. But, in fact, these questionable remarks detract only from literality and not from actuality. Since Hermine insists that her death will be important both to her and to Haller, and of mutual benefit, her order must be hyperbole. For Haller to kill her, once in love with her, can only mean to terminate their affair once it has run its emotional course and has served its double purpose. So understood, it is not at all surprising that Haller anticipates and tacitly concurs with her request. Both he and his unusual female counterpart realize from the outset that theirs must be a temporary affair and not become a permanent attachment. Neither is for or of this world. Their aspirations extend far beyond it. She has her saints and he his Immortals, and both are intent upon eternity. Each can help the other temporarily, she by introducing him to the world of the senses, and he by exposing her to the realm of thought, but then both must continue their separate and lonely paths. When their relationship finally threatens to become too intimate, Hermine creates a situation that will persuade Haller to terminate their odd liaison: she gives herself to Pablo in his presence. Haller reacts jealously, becomes violent, and in his lingering drug daze imagines that he kills Hermine. More hallucinations follow: Mozart's chiding and philosophical discourse, the trial, Pablo's reappearance and his censure of Haller, and Hermine's transformation into a figurine. When the effects of the drugs finally wear off, Haller finds that both Pablo and Hermine have left. He is alone once more, and prepared again to take up where he had left off when he first met Hermine. Brief digression from his chosen path of life had served its therapeutic purpose.

The literality of the Haller-Hermine affair, but for the hyperbolic death command and its anticipation, is arguable but certainly not essential for the novel's significance or for a better understanding of it. In view of much else that takes place before Hermine's appearance, and that is literally beyond likelihood, literality becomes less attractive and extended hyperbole very persuasive. It is not only Hermine's death command but Haller's entire crisis that is hyperbolic: actuality surrealistically experienced and fancifully narrated. The novel's actuality is strictly Haller's and not everyman's. The unlikely in the tale does not derive from any intrinsic unrealness but from Haller's innate tendency to extend reality slightly beyond itself by allowing his imagination to play upon it, and his mind to prey on or to idealize it. It is his vivid imagination that is responsible for the mysterious portal in the old stone wall and for the cryptic remarks above it (Magic Theater Entrance not for Everyone—not for Everyone), on the wet pavement in front of it (Only—for—Mad—men!), and on the passing placard (Anarchistic Evening Entertainment! Magic Theater! Entrance not for Every . . .). And it is Haller's hyperactive and lucid mind that converts a chance pamphlet on whatever theme into a penetrating study of himself and of his age. Though ascribed to, the treatise was obviously not the work of one of the Immortals, and is not part of a benign conspiracy engineered by the ethereal community of Immortals to assist a floundering kindred soul. It was not written by *an* Immortal, but is thought out by *the* Immortal in Harry Haller, by Haller during one of his extended sieges of wondrous lucidity. The actual pamphlet serves only to trigger this expansion of consciousness,[50] just as Pablo's drugs induce Haller's Magic-Theater experience. Haller's im-

---

50 In *Vom Bücherlesen* (1920), Hesse comments on three categories of readers: the naïve and objective, the imaginative and thoughtful, and those who merely use a text to stimulate their imagination and to trigger their own stream of thoughts (*Gesammelte Schriften* [1957], Vol. 7, pp. 242–248). Haller obviously belongs to the third category.

mortal self resorts to the editorial we, affects a learned objectivity, identifies with the community of Immortals, and proceeds to comment on Haller's mortal self. The mortal self is helped by and must become the immortal self, just as Sinclair is guided by and ultimately becomes Demian.

Hyperbole also accounts more satisfactorily than does literality for the uniqueness of Hermine, Maria, and Pablo. Haller's vivid imagination and hyperactive mind impose themselves upon and refashion his nightclub acquaintances no less than they do his environment. They are as much Haller's creation as the world in which he moves. Hermine is idealized, Maria glamorized, and Pablo immortalized. Having idealized Hermine, having created an ideal female counterpart for himself, Haller is not only jealously angry when he discovers her naked beside Pablo, but terribly disillusioned. He realizes that the woman whom he has imagined to be his kindred soul and more is nothing other than a common harlot.

But Hermine is more than just Harry Haller's real or imagined female counterpart. She is also intimately linked to Haller's young poet-friend Hermann; she resembles him physically, is his kindred soul, and even bears the feminine form of his name. This close interlinkage of Haller, Hermine, and Hermann is perfectly plausible on the level of actuality, but perhaps best accountable on the plane of symbolism. So considered, all three are self-projections of the author: Hermann is the young poet Hesse once was, Haller is the sinner-saint Hesse had become, and Hermine is Haller's *daimon*, his guiding and admonishing better self. She, like Demian, is more experienced and resourceful than her fumbling ward, better integrated, and wiser. She appears at a critical moment in Haller's life, just as Demian keeps materializing whenever Sinclair is in distress. Both are firm but patient guides, each understands his ward thoroughly, and each is highly respected and obeyed implicitly. Demian's voice seems at times to be Sinclair's own, and Haller's own soul appears to peer at him through Hermine's eyes. As such, Hermine and Demian are similar externalizations, and Haller's and Sinclair's conversations with them are self-dialogue. However, in these projections of the self, there is a major technical difference: Demian is simply Sinclair's *daimon* palely actualized, while Hermine is Haller's *daimon* identified with an actual person. Hermine became a vibrant blending of the actual and the symbolic, while Demian remained ghostly, pure symbol.

The literality of the Haller-Hermine affair is not quite credible. Hyperbolized actuality accounts more satisfactorily for the relationship. Symbol lends an enhancing additional dimension and offers more interpretive possibility. It is in terms of both its actuality and its symbolism that this odd liaison can best be explained. What transpires need not be considered consistently actual nor entirely symbolic. Haller's socializing with Hermine and her intimacy with Pablo are best accounted for actually; their exegetic dialogues are more readily accountable symbolically. The most perplexing of their relationship's many enigmas, Hermine's death, or rather, her imagined death, is as manifestly symbolic as it is actual. Her death order is clearly hyperbole both on the level of actuality and that of symbolism. Haller and Hermine the prostitute on one plane, and Haller and Hermine his externalized *daimon* on the other, must and will terminate their relationship once Haller has fallen in love, that is, once this association has run its course and has served its therapeutic function: when, on the one hand, Haller has regained his emotional balance in his affair with Hermine the prostitute, that is, once his life's thrusts are stilled and again under control; and when, on the other hand, he has regained his mental equilibrium in his confrontation with Hermine his *daimon*, that is, once his self-doubt is again allayed and faltering belief in his ideals again bolstered. Where Hermine's death order is hyperbole both actually and symbolically, her death is imaginary on both planes. Considered actually, this imagined murder marks the termination of a real relationship between two people and Haller's return to his isolation, art, and intellectuality, having absorbed all that Hermine the prostitute represents, and again reasonably in control of his sexual impulses. Symbolically, the imagined murder marks the termination of an imaginary relationship between two people and Haller's return to his ordeal of self-realization, having absorbed all that Hermine his *daimon* represents, and with restored belief in himself and his ideals. Hermine's mock murder and disappearance is Haller's absorption of his externalized *daimon*. His better self, temporarily an outer guide, has again become a prevailing inner guide. A spiritual union takes place, the strange spiritual wedding in physical death that Haller anticipates as he approaches the last of the Magic Theater's many intriguing doors. Hermine's death is like Demian's disappearance and like Vasudeva's demise. With her absorption, Haller becomes his better self, just as Sinclair becomes his Demian, and Siddhartha his Vasudeva. Hermine's mock murder is therefore a positive act on both its actual and its symbolic plane. Haller has not yet learned to laugh at the wretched circumstances of life, at its raucous music, but he is prepared to go on, to return to his lonely ways restored psychologically by his necessary aberration, sustained by his renewed belief in the existence of a spiritual realm of timeless values, and again convinced that dedication to this realm is worth life's resultant lonely agonies.

GENIAL PORTRAITURE

In his bold exploration of literary possibility from *Demian* to *Der Steppenwolf*, Hesse steered a dramatically unpredictable course from one exciting mode of expression to another. His experimentation led him from the Jungian complexities of *Demian* to the psychological realism of *Klein und Wagner*, the fantasia of *Klingsors letzter Sommer*, the exotically stylized art of *Siddhartha*, and the ironized diary of *Kurgast*, and finally climaxed in the highly original admixture of psychological realism and symbolism, fantasy, and hallucination of *Der Steppenwolf*.

Like most of Hesse's tales, *Der Steppenwolf* offers exceedingly thin narrative fare, is left truncated, and ends on an optimistic note. There is, as usual, much accounting and little recounting, extensive dialogue and marginal involvement, copious reflection and minimal action. What little that does take place is located in a dimly sketched locality, confined to a vague period of five weeks, and revolves about an estranged protagonist engaged only peripherally with a small and shadowy cast of supernumeraries: an evening stroll, a mysterious wall, a pub, a pamphlet; a few days later, another walk, a funeral, encounter and evening with a professor-friend, the Black Eagle and Hermine; tea with his landlady the next morning; a dinner engagement with Hermine in the Old Franciscan a few days later; another tryst with Hermine the following afternoon, purchase of a phonograph; afternoon dance date with Hermine a few days later at the Hotel Balances, introduction to Pablo and Maria; a few days later Haller finds Maria in his bed and their less than three-week liaison begins; during this interval, Hermine continues to teach Haller to dance, Haller buys Maria a purse, Pablo throws an opium party for Haller and Maria and proposes his love *à trois*, Pablo attempts to borrow money from Haller, Haller has his last meeting with Hermine, and his last night with Maria; the masked ball follows and climaxes with Pablo's drug party and Haller's magic trip. This frail structure of only loosely linked events is heavily laced with expository monologue and dialogue. When Haller is not cogitating while awake, ruminating in dream, or resolving his, society's, and life's problems in hallucination, he is engaged in protracted and weighty argument with his landlady, her nephew, the young professor, Goethe, Hermine, Pablo, or Mozart. It is to this continuum of exposition and not of action that the novel owes its structural coherence. What emerges is not a traditional narrative but a detailed and psychologically penetrating study of a man, and a trenchant analysis of a bourgeois-dominated culture in decline.

As usual, Hesse the storyteller played second fiddle to Hesse the portraitist, and as usual, the portraitist preferred inner to outer depictions: the cultural to the physical world, the psyche to the body. Settings, events, and humans and their interactions are not only confined to those that bear upon these two portraits, but are also accorded minimal necessary detail. Haller's world knows no geography, his city is little more than a nameless silhouette, its much frequented pubs and nightclubs are only names, and its streets and buildings, its churches, theaters, and shops, and its library and cinema are merely reference points. The few events that take place in this skeletal setting are given short shrift. This real but only bare and dimly lit stage is peopled by real and correspondingly vaguely visible humans. Hermine is merely pale, pretty, and slender, her coiffure is boyish, and her face reminds Haller of his friend Hermann, who is not described at all; Maria has short-cropped blond hair, is blue-eyed, pretty, and voluptuous; Pablo is but a handsome, curly-haired, dark-eyed Latin dandy; and Haller's landlady, her nephew, and the young professor and his wife have even less visible reality than his ethereal and immortal Goethe and Mozart. Thoughts and feelings are primary and profuse and, as usual, potentially detractive physical attributes, but for a necessary characterizing few, were largely left to conjecture. Only Haller and his two-room atelier apartment were accorded more than Hesse's customary scant physical detail. However, this increased descriptive detail, still characteristically enumerative and not organized and depictive, was assigned to the preface, and as such does not mar the stylistic consistency of the tale proper. As for the preface, it was actually an enhancing afterthought substituted for an original, slight autobiographical introduction by Haller himself.[51] Hesse opted for the longer, more physically detailed, and matter-of-fact preface to be able to add a minor physical portrait to complement the major psychological portrait of the tractate and the tale, and then assigned his new preface to an appropriately common-place editor.

[51] Unpublished, untitled four-page autograph in the Hesse-Nachlass, Marbach a.N.

His change in descriptive technique was not a lapse or the beginning of something new, but a deliberate and appropriate deviation.

In a congratulatory article written upon the occasion of Hesse's sixtieth birthday, Thomas Mann noted that *Der Steppenwolf* was no less daring as an experimental novel than James Joyce's *Ulysses* (1922) and André Gide's *Les Faux-Monnayeurs* (1926).[52] In each of these instances, experiment was less in substance than in form. Hesse's concern with things of the spirit and things of the body, his oscillation between these poles of possibility, his flaying of twentieth-century Western culture, and his psychologizing and Platonizing were old hat by 1927. Haller's adventitious adventures of the flesh were hardly literary experiment. And literary portraits were neither new to literature nor to Hesse. The new obviously did not lie in the matter but in the manner, and not in Hesse's already familiar fusion of realism, symbolism, and fantasy, but in the multimethod of his portraiture, and in the resultant tetrapartite structure of the tale. Haller's story and that of his bourgeois-dominated culture are told not once but four times. Four complementary pairs of portraits are sketched in four distinct segments authored by three different persons. The unusually long and sober preface, ascribed to the nephew of Haller's landlady, depicts the outer man, his physical characteristics, habits, interests, and his attitudes: Haller as he appears to the bourgeois world; it also depicts this bourgeois world, its physical reality, its members, their lifestyle, and their mentality: that which this world appears to be. This prefatory perusal is extended by an inserted study, an exciting, witty, and perceptive portrait of Haller the inner man, a psychological tractate apparently penned by one of the Immortals; the treatise paints an equally incisive psychological portrait of the bourgeoisie. Haller's own records, the tale proper, afford a direct study of the whole man in action, with particular emphasis upon Haller's long-suppressed sensual self; they also afford a direct and full exposure of the bourgeois world, featuring its veiled nether regions. Haller's hallucinatory review of himself and of his life in Pablo's Magic Theater, a concluding depiction of the self, complements each of his preceding portraits; and his psychedelic reassessment of the bourgeois world and its culture confirms and complements its preceding portraits. Aligned, these four pairs of portraits afford progressively broader exposure and deeper penetration; blended, each pair different in its

52 "Dem sechzigjährigen Hermann Hesse," *Neue Zürcher Zeitung*, July 2, 1937, No. 1192.

emphasis, they furnish yet another pair: the full portrayal of a man and of a culture that Hesse had been intent upon. What in traditional portraiture could have resulted in a tediously prolonged treatise, became a tale fascinating in its exposition and unique in its structure.

Careful craftsmanship complemented novel structure. *Der Steppenwolf* was not merely assigned to three writers, but actually assumed three distinct modes of expression, each convincingly compatible with its alleged author's station in life. Like its conservative sentiment, the preface's prosaic language, clear but inarticulate idiom, awkward verbal and syntactic repetitions, and unadorned literality are what might be expected of a solid citizen with a good mind and a fair education but limited literary sensitivity and experience. The tractate is the organized, informed, articulate, and dialectically argued and parenthetically footnoted scholarly document it purports to be, it is appropriately trimmed with learned jargon and is written in the facetious tone and the casual ironic manner expected of an Immortal with a scintillating mind and practised pen, a genial soul who has transcended the human tragi-comedy. And in Haller's records, the informal recollections of a layman and the studied observations of an Immortal become the appropriate literary depiction of a sensitive artist with verbal flare. Exposition now becomes art. The actual is imaginatively fantasized, idealized, symbolized, and dramatized. Language is now more nimble and more lyrical, previously more communicative, now more evocative, imagery becomes profuse, and mode of expression assumes the intimately personal flow and rhythm expected of the highly autobiographical writings of a hypersensitive Harry Haller. Periods of tedium, of relatively little distress and no joy, find consonant expression in the lagging flow and monotonous rhythm of inordinately protracted sentences with their dragging repetitions, and their long and dangling chains of interlinked clauses and phrases. The opening paragraphs of Haller's manuscript best exemplify the extremes of this technique. In two paragraphs, counting but three sentences and numbering some 450 words, Haller languidly recounts the tedious course of one of his undesirable, placid days: a deliberate and suitably dispirited verbal rendition of sluggish monotony. In contrast, moments of bleak despair or of exciting elation find their accentuating expression in a rapidly flowing and frantically pulsating torrent of clauses and phrases, irregular in their brevity, in an emphatic rush of verbs and a hectic heaping of words, in restless rhetorical questions, frantic exclamations, and staccato repetitions, and in a liberal use of anaphora and parataxis. This restive verbal deluge is used to its best advantage in Haller's recounting of the climactic moments of the ball. The dance crests in a mad vortex, Haller glows feverishly, and the prose reflects and accentuates outer situation and inner state. Verb follows rapidly upon verb, repetition crowds repetition, and phrases and clauses whirl by. The verbal tempo becomes as frantic as the dance tempo and Haller's inner agitation. The dance ends, the fever abates, and language begins again to flow slowly and evenly.

It is not only this harmonizing of inner state, outer situation, and language, and the abundance of dialogue that lend Haller's prose its dramatic immediacy, but also a liberal use of tense interior monologue. Until *Demian*, Hesse resorted only moderately to inner speech on the story level of his many first-person narratives, and sparingly to it in his less numerous third-person tales. The protagonists of this period indulge in a good deal of rumination, but their thoughts are generally quoted, or verbally introduced, when reported. From *Demian* on, the continued monologizing of Hesse's protagonists not only becomes more extensive, but finds expression even more commonly in an unusually lively type of narrated interior monologue: in thoughts expressed in the past tense unencumbered by the normal verbal introductions to reported thought. This evolution in Hesse's narrative technique peaked in *Der Steppenwolf*. Due to the abundance of this dramatic indirect interior monologue, narrating Haller virtually becomes again the experiencing Haller, lending to his tale a gripping immediacy despite its prevailing past tense. Past tense, in essence, becomes present tense. This immediacy is reinforced by Haller's usual retention in his reported interior monologues of the time indicators of direct interior monologue, and by his frequent use of these pointers to the present even when engaged in simple narration (today, now, yesterday, tomorrow, rather than that day, then, the previous day, the next day), and also by his numerous present tense asides, and the present tense of the tractate. Thanks to these interior monologues and to these temporal devices, Haller becomes not a *was*, but an *is* with a future, and frail narrative becomes exciting drama.

NARZISS UND GOLDMUND: LIFE'S DOUBLE MELODY

THE PAST, REVIEW, AND REVERIE

By the beginning of 1927, Hesse's storm had run its course, and in the relative tranquillity of the lull that followed, a frantic par-

Ninon and Hermann Hesse.

AROSA IN
THE LATE
TWENTIES.

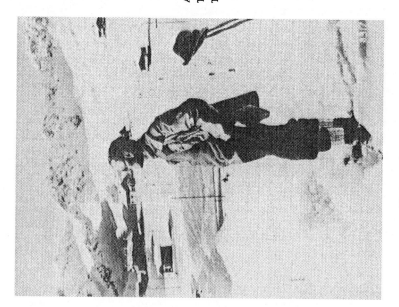

Hermann Hesse.

ticipant and acrid recorder became a composed observer and wishful dreamer, an embittered Haller was forgotten and an amiable Goldmund was enthusiastically espoused, and the dramatic tempo of *Der Steppenwolf* yielded to the more epic tread of *Narziss und Goldmund*. This marked the end of that turbulent decade during which Hesse was intent primarily upon coming to grips and to terms with himself. The many tales of this period reflect not only the anxieties, tensions, and general anguish of this undertaking, but also Hesse's dogged persistence, his unflagging hope, and his spells of elation. *Demian's* proclamation of emancipation and self-realization begins these years with vigorous aspiration and high optimism. *Klein und Wagner* mirrors the initial agonies and despair of Hesse's actual emancipation. *Klingsors letzter Sommer* documents his almost manic surrender to life and art during the summer of 1919. *Siddhartha* is the resolving philosophical lull following this flurry of activity. *Kurgast* records one of the many desperate sieges of physical pain and mental distress that Hesse suffered in the twenties: crises illustrative of the artist-thinker's conflicting need for isolation from and for contact with life. *Der Steppenwolf* depicts the most critical of these periods of depression, aberration, and renewed hope; it was also the cathartic experience that brought the relentless phase of Hesse's self-quest to its end. Center of interest was soon to shift from the self to the community. In the interim, Hesse looked to his past, reviewed his thoughts, permitted himself to dream, and wrote his *Narziss und Goldmund*. According to an unpublished letter to Helene Welti, December 19, 1928,[53] the novel was begun in mid-1927 and completed in December 1928. The book appeared in the spring of 1930.

Both *Siddhartha* and *Narziss und Goldmund* were written during lulls following considerable turbulence, and each followed in the wake of a tale contrastingly autobiographical and gripping in its immediacy. Both were as much the consequence of equanimity as *Klingsors letzter Sommer* and *Der Steppenwolf* were the effects of agitation. Regarding thought, feeling, conflict, and aspiration, Siddhartha and Goldmund are no less self-projections than any other of Hesse's protagonists, but their worlds are basically novel and their actions are largely imagined. In *Siddhartha*, there is nothing in outer detail that is discernibly autobiographical, and in *Narziss und Goldmund*, very little. Hesse's Maulbronn obviously lent its name to Goldmund's Mariabronn. It also left its physical imprint on the monastery. Mariabronn's

---

53 In the Welti-Nachlass, Schweizerische Landesbibliothek, Bern, Switzerland.

arched entrance, large courtyard, dormitories, refectories, its double early Gothic church, ornately carved choir pews, and small cloister garden and fountain are clearly recollections. Goldmund is brought to the monastery at the age of fifteen, with the expectation that he will in time become a cleric; Hesse had entered Maulbronn at fourteen and with similar parental hope. Goldmund's fisticuffs with a strong schoolmate are reminiscent of a similar tangle in which Hesse had conducted himself equally admirably and which had first received literary expression in *Unterm Rad*.[54] As had Hesse before him, Goldmund applies himself diligently in school, ruins his health, even thinks of taking French leave, becomes generally abrasive, finds solace with an intimate, and eventually loses all interest in school and studies. He leaves the sanctuary of the monastery at the age of eighteen, just as Hesse at the same age had left the shelter of home and parents. What follows on Goldmund's departure is story and not converted fact.

Narziss und Goldmund is an amalgam of pre-1914 narration and post-*Demian* thought. In his storytelling, Hesse returned to his Gaienhofen years in general, and specifically to *Berthold*, the three-chapter fragment put aside in 1908 for want of interest, inspiration, or ability. Fragment and novel are similar enough to suggest that one was the narrative springboard for the other. Both are located in South Germany and the Rhineland, and both begin as school tales. Like Goldmund, Berthold is reared by his father, has no memory of his mother or earliest childhood, and is sent to a church school at the age of fifteen to be educated for the priesthood for which he, too, is not at all suited. In both cases, studies once attractive soon become tedious, and initial spiritual concerns give way to worldly interests. Both youths are strong, handsome, and naïve, puberty proves trying for both, each has vivid sexual fantasies, and each gladly allows himself to be seduced by an older and practised young woman. Each also latches onto a slightly older and more sophisticated confidant and teacher, and both pair of intimates engage in long philosophical discussions. Though anything but a saintly Narziss, Berthold's friend Johannes is a similarly attractive young man, with the same long dark eyelashes, just as courteous in manner, shares Narziss's air of solicitous superiority, courts his high aspirations, and also awakens his ward to the realization that the church is not his calling. Both Berthold and Goldmund also fall in love with a blond-haired Agnes who pre-

---

54 See *Kindheit und Jugend vor Neunzehnhundert* (1966), p. 148.

cipitates a severe crisis for each, both murder in jealous rage, and both flee church and school for life at large, while still in their late teens. *Berthold* breaks off at this juncture. It seems as though Hesse had just not been up to the epic demands of his protagonist's subsequent adventures as a soldier in the Thirty Years' War. A discarded fragment of 1908 proved to be a suggestive narrative source in 1927, and an intended picaresque novel became a well-disguised *roman à thèse*.

But *Narziss und Goldmund* harked back to more than just *Berthold*. Its monastic situation returned to the more detailed depiction of Maulbronn in *Unterm Rad*, and much of Goldmund, of his family situation and school experiences, and even some of his relationship with Narziss, is prefigured in Giebenrath and his family situation, school experiences, and friendship with Heilner. In fact or in memory, Hesse must also have returned to Knulp, his favorite pre–*Demian* protagonist. Both are handsome vagabond-artists and childlike voluble charmers, and both sing and dance and are facile storytellers. Knulp writes poetry and plays a harmonica, and Goldmund recites verse and plays a lute. Neither has talent for work, both are footloose, and each treasures his freedom and lives his own life regardless of consequences. Both age prematurely, and both return home pale, haggard, and mortally ill. God appears to Knulp in the delirium of his illness, counters his lurking regrets, and consoles him. Mother-Eve (*Eva-Mutter*) confronts Goldmund in his hallucinations, alleviates his pain, and expunges all fear of death. As God's voice trails off, it suggests that of Knulp's mother, that of his first sweetheart Henriette, and then that of Lisabeth, the mother of his son. Analogously, Goldmund's Mother-Eve is a composite of all the women in his life. But for Goldmund's insatiable and freely exercised sexuality, he and Knulp are unmistakable birds of a feather. Indeed, Hesse's beloved protagonist of 1927 was largely a resurrected prewar ideal upon which he imposed a postwar favorite, his sensual and uninhibited Klingsor.

The origins of Narziss and of his relationship with Goldmund were no less diverse than Goldmund's derivation. His lineage began with Wilhelm Lang, Hesse's own bosom companion in Maulbronn, and his literary antecedents were legion. He and his role in Goldmund's life were prefigured in the earliest of Hesse's trail of double self-projections, and returned most immediately to *Demian*'s interplay of friendship. With *Demian*, erstwhile intimate friend and contrasting personality had become a veritable guru practised in psychoanalysis. Narziss was a return to and a slight humanizing of this Demian concept of friend, foil, and guide. Like his predecessor, Narziss is slightly older than the protagonist, is also a schoolmate, and is just as quick to take his newfound friend under his wing. Both Demian and Narziss are dark-haired and sad-faced, courteous and disciplined, deadly serious and hyperintelligent, and consciously aloof and supremely self-confident. Each is more man than boy, more scholar than student, more guide than friend, and more function than fact. Both wards are immediately fascinated by these haughty young princes among lesser commoners, and both quickly succumb to their slightly mocking solicitude. Like Demian, Narziss knows more and better than his troubled friend, is determined to awaken him to himself and to life, engages him in religious, philosophical, and moral discussions, and helps him break out of a restrictive shell, that he may find, live, and realize himself. Like Demian too, Narziss can read thoughts, is present or appears when needed, and in deep contemplation assumes an open-eyed, trance-like, rigid posture. In his being, his function, and in the mechanics of his relationship with Goldmund, he was clearly a harking back to Demian. He was to Demian very much what Goldmund was to Knulp.

Demian was borrowed from Sinclair's tale and accorded more reality, *Eva-Mutter* was simply lifted from it and rendered more clearly symbolic. Both Demian and his mother *Frau Eva* are basically concepts actualized. Their actuality is thin and pale and their symbolism is inordinately complex. Both are too many things too mysteriously veiled to be entirely satisfactory. Such is not the case in *Narziss und Goldmund*. In Narziss, Hesse resurrected only the person Demian, and in *Eva-Mutter* only the symbol *Frau Eva*. Unlike Demian, Narziss is not a disguise, not a person who is essentially but a projected *daimon* or externalized imago, but an independent reality, an actual friend and guide. *Eva Mutter* too, unlike *Frau Eva*, is not an implausibly disguised anima and Magna Mater, but pristine idea. Narziss was rendered more actual than Demian, *Eva-Mutter* became more symbol than *Frau Eva*, and *Narziss und Goldmund* emerged a tale more plausible and less murky than *Demian*.

DICHOTOMY AND ITS POLARITIES

From *Demian* to *Der Steppenwolf*, Hesse was bent on self-quest, obsessed by life's dichotomy, and absorbed by its complexity of polarities. Life and thought became a fluctuating and faltering upward progression, and began to revolve about the spirituality and animality of man, about art and life, the artist and the nonartist, about thought and feeling, erotic and social love, the transitory and the permanent, culture and the bourgeois world, appearance and the real, contact and isolation, multiplicity and oneness, and about time and timelessness. During these years, Hesse was only twice able to relax enough to review his rapidly evolving thoughts. *Siddhartha* was a meditative summation and culmination of his initial thinking, and *Narziss und Goldmund* was his calm concluding reconsideration of most of the period's major concerns.

Like most of Hesse's protagonist's, Goldmund is a man with a pressing quarrel. His dispute is with himself and with life, and his grievance is dichotomy and its many polarities. Man is male or female, becomes a voluptuary or ascetic, a dreamer or a thinker, a thinker or an artist, an artist or an ordinary citizen, a citizen or a vagabond, is caught between the sensual and the spiritual, between evil and good, and experiences joy or sorrow, and love or hatred. Thanks to this flaw in God's creation, life is a frustrating either-or and never a rich simultaneous experiencing of its diverse possibilities. This dichotomy is the critical fact of existence with which Goldmund, like his predecessors, has to come to terms. Like theirs, his whole life is governed by this challenge.

For Sinclair, dichotomy extends little beyond the duality of incompatibles inherent in Christian belief and morality, and a Nietzschean emancipation is enough to resolve his quandary. Able to cope neither with inner nor outer dichotomy, Klein elects to escape it all in suicide. Klingsor's response to life's dualities is desperate affirmation and wild revelry. Siddhartha's is a general affirmation, systematic exhaustion, and an ultimate transcending of dichotomy. In *Kurgast*, life's poles and man's swinging back and forth between them are enthusiastically acclaimed. And an embittered Haller, whose eyes are fixed on an ethereal realm beyond dichotomy, requires a touch of gallows humor to make the spirit and flesh polarity of life even tolerable. In his grappling with and resolution of dichotomy, Goldmund is something of a very human compromise between two intimidating possibilities: the magnificent ideal depicted in *Siddhartha* and Haller's heroic retreat into Platonism.

Like Siddhartha's, Goldmund's emphasis is upon life for all that it is and upon its living, and like Siddhartha, he experiences and realizes himself, and accepts death. Unlike Siddhartha, however, though Goldmund accepts life's dichotomy, he does not cease to quarrel with it. He makes his peace with himself, but not with life; God could have fashioned it better. Siddhartha traverses and transcends dichotomy, whereas Goldmund continues to be troubled by it to the end. He does not experience Siddhartha's revelatory timelessness, oneness, and meaningfulness of life, but he does achieve a very human insight into himself and life.

Like Haller, Goldmund is troubled by and quarrels with life's dichotomy, unlike him, he chooses, notwithstanding, to live life fully. For Haller, dichotomy is life's most regrettable flaw and he can only agonize in his oscillation between its poles. He turns his back upon the flawed phenomenal world to the extent he can and finds his sustenance in the perfect noumenal realm of his Immortals, endures his lesser physical self and pampers his spirituality, starves his appetites and fattens his dreams. His sporadic adventures of the flesh are but brief aberrations tolerated for their therapeutic value, minimal exposures necessary to immunize himself against life and to render secure his isolation and passionate dedication to things spiritual. In contrast, and despite his quarrel with dichotomy, Goldmund learns to revel in his to and fro between life and art, between animality and spirituality. Pendulation is life's curse, but it is also life's glory, a blissful agony to which man owes much of his achievement, and wherein alone self-realization is possible.

For Siddhartha, all is well with world and man, neither is ideal enough for Haller, and Goldmund has serious reservations about both. Siddhartha affirms reality for all it is, his life is living, and his reward is transcendence. Haller takes bitter issue with and rejects reality, his life is trying quest, and his goal is a world etherealized and man spiritualized. Goldmund questions but accepts reality, his life is to live fully and to create, and his goal is self-realization and death. Siddhartha knows no disparity between what is and what could or should be, Haller is tormented by it, and Goldmund is able to put up with it. Siddhartha feels no need to reconcile anything, for all is a reconciled oneness, Haller cannot reconcile his spirituality and animality or phenomena and noumena, and Goldmund manages to reconcile himself to life's frustrating dichotomy. In Hesse's recapitulation and synthesizing of the past, a new possibility emerged, an ideal more possible than Siddhartha's and an adjustment more attractive than Haller's: all in all, a more human coping with the self and with life.

TWO POSSIBILITIES

Like most of Hesse's major tales, *Narziss und Goldmund* juxtaposes and scrutinizes two human possibilities: the ideal possible and the dubious actual. Goldmund is obviously the possible, and Narziss the actual. Protagonist and intime are yet another variation of Hesse's customary double self-projection: Goldmund is the ingratiating artist-voluptuary he would have liked to be, and Narziss is the retiring thinker-ascetic he knew himself to be. Contrary to the implications of the title, the novel is not a balanced recounting of the lives of two protagonists, nor was it ever intended to be. From its inception, the story was to be Goldmund's. Its initial array of titles makes this amply clear: *Goldmund oder Das Lob der Sünde; Goldmund und Narziss; Goldmunds Weg zur Mutter.*[55] The final bipartite title and its sequence was an appropriate afterthought for a tale featuring dichotomy in both its substance and form, and a sensitive response to metric flow. Nor does it do the novel justice merely to consider it allegory, to argue that protagonist and friend are but flesh (*Natur*) and spirit (*Geist*) personified and that their intimate friendship only demonstrates Hesse's belief in the necessary and desirable interplay and interdependence of these poles of life. Goldmund and Narziss are not just unidimensional personifications but complex personalities. They, like all of Hesse's very human protagonists, are caught up in life's polar tug of war, and each adjusts in a manner that most accords with his psychology. Neither adjustment is without its drawbacks and each has its virtues. Goldmund swings freely and with no compunctions between sensuality and spirituality, is both a disciplined artist and a roving voluptuary, and as much at home in the monastery as in the world. His rewards are life's intensities, and the price he pays is equanimity. Narziss chooses to deny his body, to turn his back upon the world, and to cultivate things spiritual in the seclusion of the monastery. His reward is peace and its price is human warmth. Each is envious of the benefits of the other's adjustment to the self and to life, but neither can nor will exchange roles with the other. For Goldmund to live like Narziss would be a violation of the self, and for Narziss to emulate Goldmund would be to violate himself even more than he does. Though Hesse gives obvious preference to Goldmund's resolution of the dichotomy, he clearly condones both approaches to life; both are psychological necessities and not mere caprice, and both can unveil life's mysteries.

It was not given to Hesse to live and to create as spontaneously and unconcerned as Goldmund—but he could dream. Narziss, like Haller before him, was Hesse's real predicament and lot. Narziss's

55 See manuscript of the novel in the Bodmer-Hesse-Collection, Schiller-Nationalmuseum, Marbach a.N.

kinship with his antecedent is manifest. Haller's suppression of his sensuality and his Platonic rejection of the world became Narziss's chastity and monastic withdrawal from the world, his realm of the spirit became Narziss's Kingdom of God, and both have their eyes fixed on eternity. Haller is likely to continue to swing between man and wolf for some time before he is able to join his serene Immortals. What still lies between mortality and eternity for Narziss remains conjecture. Goldmund's dying reference to the impossibility of death without life smolders ominously in Narziss's heart. He is a Haller more firmly in control of himself and of life, but he is also a potential *Steppenwolf*. Narziss and Haller sacrifice themselves for a purpose and a possibility. Goldmund surrenders to actuality, simply yields himself to himself and to the rhythm of life and death. A wistful dream died with Goldmund's death, and Hesse was left with Narziss and a way of life that was immediately far less attractive, but that was in accord with his being and that promised to be far more satifying.

ART AND LIFE

Art was a concern for Hesse as persistent and almost as insistent as life's dichotomy. He was as fascinated by one as he was troubled by the other. Most of his protagonists and many of his minor characters are artists by vocation or avocation, much of the argument of their stories is focused on art, and this serial exegesis clearly traces Hesse's own evolving attitude toward and notions about art. Art was for Hesse the substitute for life it is for Lauscher, it became as wretched a profession for him as it does for Camenzind, as great a consolation as it is for Kuhn, the all-absorbing fated profession it ends up being for Veraguth, the passion it became for Klingsor, the loneliness and self-exposure it is for Haller, and Goldmund's reconciliation of life and art became a culminating ideal that Hesse nurtured but himself never realized. Each of the tales in question paints an inner portrait of an artist, and under the aegis of psychoanalysis, these studies became progressively more penetrating in their psychology. In 1918, this psychological interest in the artist began to spill over into Hesse's essays. His tales, together with these essays from 1918 to 1930, afford a composite psychological portrait of the artist and a detailed supplemental psychological theory of art.[56]

At the outset of Hesse's career, art and life were virtually incompatible and mutually exclusive areas of human experience. Like the

---

56 See Chapter 5 above, "Art and Disease."

author-protagonist of *Eine Stunde hinter Mitternacht* and Lauscher, Hesse believed or wanted to believe that true art neither derived from nor dealt with drab life at large, but was inspired by and depicted a romantically ideal world behind appearances, a realm accessible primarily in dream or poetic imagination. This wondrous world behind the ordinary world became the subject of his art. Spirituality and sensuality, too, were as incompatible for Hesse as they are for the author-protagonist of *Eine Stunde hinter Mitternacht* and for Lauscher. For him, just as for his two self-projections, seductive sensual experiences—deviations actually imagined more than experienced, and frequently alluded to but never depicted—were cause for guilt and reason for fervent atonement. Sensuality sullied, spirituality edified. For young Hesse, the world was a wretched detraction, sexuality a questionable urge, and both were heroically renounced for art and spirituality.

From *Peter Camenzind* to *Rosshalde*, and particularly in the Swabian *Novellen*, art and life were interrelated, but the bland mixture became as unsatisfactory to Hesse as his futile attempt to reconcile his sensuality and his spirituality, and to be both an artist and a respectable citizen. Life as an artist-citizen proved to be as confining and frustrating as life dedicated to beauty. From *Demian* to *Der Steppenwolf* the old cleft between art and life reappeared and widened progressively. Depicted life narrowed down again to Hesse himself, and as earlier, with primary emphasis upon inner world and not outer circumstances. But this was no return to the past. Art had once been an ornate depiction of an innocent young aesthete's dreams and sorrows, now it became a raw exposure of a wayward middle-aged artist's psychology. Sexuality, once carefully shunned in life and art, was now indulged in both. Spirituality, however, continued as always to be Hesse's true love. Sensuality remained suspect, affirmed fully in theory, but less accepted than just tolerated in fact. Hesse was a Haller and Siddhartha was a dream.

It was to dream that Hesse returned in *Narziss und Goldmund*. What he had not been able to settle satisfactorily in life, he now resolved in yet another ideal. Goldmund's tale not only again accords life at large a real role in Hesse's art, but makes life an integral part of creativity, and thereby justifies and renders acceptable the spirit-flesh dichotomy. Instinctuality, previously a detraction for the artist, now became a necessity for his art. Goldmund concludes from his experience that true art derives from life itself. To create, the artist must live and allow life's experiences to imprint their images upon his soul.

These images are the source of his inspiration and become art in disciplined application. Art is a product of both the flesh and the spirit, and exemplifies their necessary and desirable interaction and interdependence in life as a whole. This theory of art and life was Hesse's latest sentiment, and Goldmund personifies what temporarily became a new ideal following *Der Steppenwolf*. Hesse had been a troubled aesthete and a discontented artist-bourgeois, had become a wayward artist-seeker, had ended an artist-recluse with aspirations after immortality, and now he imagined himself a freewheeling, self-affirming and life-accepting artist-voluptuary.

ART AND TIME

Life's transitoriness and death became the source of anguish and fear early in Hesse's life. His first response was flight into the world of his imagination, a Lauscherean retreat into the timeless and wondrous real realm behind the ever-changing ugly façade of life's appearance. Dream's solace lasted only as long as Hesse's short-lived aestheticism, and he was left again to lament and to endure the ravages of time. Siddhartha's theory of timelessness was Hesse's second attempt to eliminate the reality of time. This second effort to anesthetize himself was as futile as the first. He had been able to imagine a life without time, and could think timelessness, but he continued to live in time. Hesse had meanwhile begun to pursue a more conciliatory approach to time. If this painful fact of life could not be wished away, it could perhaps be rendered more palatable. And this it was, when like his Knulp and Kuhn respectively, he began to recognize that life's very transitoriness heightens the appreciation of its beauties, and provides the thrust in man's creativity. These early notions evolved in greater detail following *Demian*, and received their culminating expression in *Narziss und Goldmund*. Klingsor hates and fears time and death, but he also loves them, for they are the driving impulse in both his life and his art; death kindles an appreciative passion for life, the frenzy of creativity blots time out, and his art, a veritable weapon against death, lends some degree of permanence to the evanescent. In *Kurgast*, Hesse insists that transitoriness and death are the *sine qua non* of beauty and its appreciation, and even argues that permanence could be a drab and lifeless tedium. His return to this theme in *Narziss und Goldmund* was essentially a repetition of old sentiment become more continent and modified in its emphasis. Fear of death is again the creative thrust, and Goldmund, like his predecessors, is anxious to rescue something of life from the dance of death, but he is no longer interested in making death more palatable, or in blotting out its reality, or in lauding it. Art is now simply man's attempted conquest of time and his partial victory over death and despair, and death itself ultimately becomes for Goldmund but a welcome culminating experience, an almost erotic reunion with the Primal Mother. Goldmund's life was Hesse's dream, his tranquil death had become his hope.

THE BOURGEOIS WORLD

Though generally conciliatory in his review of the past, Hesse remained adamant in his deprecation of the bourgeois world. In *Demian*, this is the world of the herd, of the cowardly weak and of their self-protecting herd morality and religion. In *Klein und Wagner*, the bourgeoisie is the stifling society of socially conditioned, self-righteous hypocrites and philistines. In *Klingsors letzter Sommer*, it is the bland everyday world of the ordinary. In *Siddhartha*, it is the world of trivial material concerns and absurd anxieties, peopled by child-adults. In *Kurgast*, it is the world of dignified appearance, fat wallets, good stomachs, and also of vulgar normality, mental indolence, and tasteless superficiality. This swell of vituperation peaked in *Der Steppenwolf*. Middle-class society is enviable in its cleanliness, diligence, orderliness, in its emphasis upon duty, and its consciousness of law, but beyond all this, it is everything that is wrong with our age humanly, politically, and culturally: empty mechanical existence, nationalism and militarism, materialism and utilitarianism. Haller's touch of ambiguity, his basic animosity, and his bitter invective carried over into *Narziss und Goldmund*. His sentiment is essentially Goldmund's. The sedentary members of society (*die Sesshaften*) are less to be envied for their well-being and self-satisfaction than to be soundly berated for their emotional and mental stagnation, their vulgarity and avarice, vacuity, petty pursuits, and easy satiety. For Goldmund to join this staid and stark world of bickering merchants, fishmongers, and tradesmen, would have been to become another artistically crippled and embittered Master Niklaus, the malcontent artist-bourgeois Hesse had himself once been. Like most of his predecessors, Goldmund is irked by and never makes his peace with the bourgeois world. Hesse himself had not done so, nor was he about to. This world was tantamount to the establishment, and the establishment was almost by definition inimical to the individualist.

VERBAL COUNTERPOINT

For Goldmund, successful art is an organized composite whose multiple parts are consonant with each other. Forehead must accord with knee, knee with shoulder, shoulder with hip, and all must be in keeping with nature and temperament. His Apostle John is a partial and his Virgin Mary a perfect realization of this artistic ideal. Goldmund's theory of art was also Hesse's, and *Narziss und Goldmund* was obviously another of his more deliberate responses to this conception. In *Siddhartha*, human possibility evolving through three areas of human experience found its conscious and accordant expression in a tripartite structure, and in action and language characterized by a three-beat rhythm. In *Narziss und Goldmund*, life's basic dichotomy with its constellation of polarities found its appropriate and just as conscious expression in a thoroughly contrapuntal manner: setting is bipartite, movement fluctuates, personae are paired, actions and attributes are coupled, attitudes are opposing, emotions are polar, and mode of expression affects a primary two-beat rhythm. Manner itself becomes matter! In *Kurgast*, Hesse had expressed the fervent desire to be able some day to give simultaneous expression to the two voices of life's melody in both the substance and form of his prose. He doubted that he would ever realize this aspiration, but would never cease trying.[57] *Narziss und Goldmund* approaches this envisaged verbal counterpoint as closely as prose ever can.

The antithetical setting of *Narziss und Goldmund* immediately focuses attention upon dichotomy and polarity. Monastery and world not only exemplify life's intrinsic dichotomy but, like Narziss and Goldmund, they are also a visible expression of the polar concepts of spirit (*Geist*) and flesh (*Natur*), about which all things human revolve. Ten of the tale's twenty chapters are properly given to the monastery, ten to the world, and Goldmund twice moves from one to the other. Each of these halves is in turn appropriately bisected. The monastic half begins in the Mariabronn of Goldmund's youth and awakening, and ends in the Mariabronn of his manhood and death. The secular half silhouettes two situations and possibilities: the bishop's city, domestication, and art; the world at large, the open road, and life. The splintered structure of *Klingsors letzter Sommer* accords with the fractured structure of its protagonist's life; the symmetrical tripartite structure of *Siddhartha* is consonant with its protagonist's systematic

---

57 See *Gesammelte Schriften* (1957), Vol. 4, pp. 113–115.

three-stage progression through life; Goldmund's confrontation with dichotomy found its correspondent expression in this balanced bipartite structural segmentation and fluctuating movement.

Life's dichotomy and the polar predicament of man are equally accentuated by the narrative itself. A father and son arrive with two horses at Mariabronn, a monastery with an entrance arch resting on double columns, with native walnut trees and a southern chestnut, and with two exceptional inmates: the old Abbot Daniel, simple and wise, and the young novice Narziss, learned and haughty. Handsome and delicate Goldmund, the student newcomer, immediately becomes attached to both abbot and novice, finds himself torn between two ideals, and soon becomes troubled and angry. It is with trepidation and expectations that Goldmund agrees to accompany Adolf and two other schoolmates to visit two young girls in a nearby village. He also declines two further invitations. As a student in Mariabronn, Goldmund becomes ill twice, is twice put into an infirmary, and twice enjoys the monastery's traditional medicinal wine. He and Narziss are opposites and complements: one is blue-eyed and has blond hair, a dreamer and a child, and the other is a dark-eyed brunet, a thinker and an analyst. Convinced by Narziss that he is neither monk nor scholar, and that he belongs to those with strong and delicate senses, to those who are at home in the garden of love and in the land of art, Goldmund's interest in learning and his enthusiasm for dispute wane and die. Goldmund resembles his once beautiful and wild mother in both figure and face. In his frequent dreams, the reawakened mother-world envelops Goldmund, suggesting not only kindness, love, happiness, and consolation, but also all that is dark and frightful, all greed and anxiety, sin and sorrow, birth and death. Twice Goldmund leaves the monastery stealthily via mill and stream, and he also has two sexual encounters with the gypsy Lise before he wanders forth into a receptive and waiting world. He wanders frantic and hungry for two days and nights through a forest alive with birds and animals, then chances upon a hovel with an old woman and a young child, a peasant and his wife, and two goats. A year or two of incessant wandering and frugal fare follow. Women and love become Goldmund's destiny, he learns rapidly and forgets little. Desire is sated as quickly as it is roused, and after each affair, Goldmund is left both happy and sad.

This mannered two-beat narrative rhythm continues to the very end of the tale. Before lapsing into unconsciousness, Goldmund leaves Narziss with a pair of statements alluding to the impossibility of death without life, and for two days and nights, Narziss watches over dying Goldmund and ponders his last words.

Matter affected mode of expression as thoroughly as it determined structure, narrative movement, choice and arrangement of cast, physical action, and emotional reaction. Dichotomy left its imprint even on the mechanics of Hesse's prose. The first paragraph emphatically establishes the two-beat rhythm that pervades the novel. The paragraph comprises two sentences, the first of these sentences consists of two major segments, and the second of these segments is introduced by a pair of parallel principal clauses and followed by two parallel clusters of five principal and subordinate clauses. This coupling of sentences and paired clustering of clauses is too patterned to be anything but design. A closer examination of syntax reflects this same design. The first segment of the first sentence consists of four syntactic couplets: two prepositional phrases that locate Mariabronn's lone chestnut tree, the tree-subject and an appositive, two more prepositional phrases that account for the southern origin of the exceptional tree, and a second appositive reference to the tree, together with a qualifying prepositional phrase. The second segment of the first sentence draws attention to the appèarance of the tree in the spring and in the autumn, and is composed of at least twenty syntactic couplets. The second sentence again stresses the foreign origin of the tree, draws attention to the contrasting reaction to it of the Latins and the natives, and consists of at least another eight syntactic couplets.

Not only syntax but Hesse's choice of words and juxtaposition of concepts was influenced by his dichotomous concern. Compounds and bisyllabics are almost obtrusive in their abundance. The first paragraph includes no fewer than thirty-two of these bipartite nouns, adjectives and adverbs. This duality is broached by Hesse's immediate allusion to the double columns of Mariabronn's arched entrance, and then made explicit by his spaced antithetical references to the chestnut and the walnut trees, the south and the implied north, the spring and the autumn, the youngsters and the prior, and to the natives and the foreigners. Matter's way is well prepared, then constantly accentuated by manner.

The entire novel is not as thoroughly mannered as its opening paragraph, but this two-beat pulsation remains the prevailing rhythm of its style. Just as in *Siddhartha*, deviation from characteristic mode of expression occurs primarily when outer situation and inner state become exceptional. In particularly novel, threatening, or otherwise exciting situations, and at times of nervous expectancy, intense anxiety, or sheer elation, pattern yields as usual to asymmetry. Sentences normally more or less comparable in length, slow and steady in flow, and even in their two-beat rhythm become an animated intermixture of longer and shorter units with gripping successions of irregularly brief clauses and phrases, liberal parataxis, emphatic repetitions, rousing word accumulations, lively exclamations and rhetorical questions, and with a resultantly rapid and fluctuating flow and decidedly varied rhythm. As usual, Hesse's language adjusts to and accentuates changing situation and state. Such is particularly evident where he recounts Goldmund's initial expectant wandering through a forest teeming with animal life, his frantic stumbling across a stark, wintry landscape following Viktor's death, his manic experiencing of the plague, his night of despair and desperation in the governor's castle, and his sieges of inspiration and creation.

Apart from its pervasive two-beat rhythm, the manner of *Narziss und Goldmund* shows the usual hallmarks of Hesse's prose. Although the tale may suggest a return to German Romanticism's best tradition of storytelling, it is anything but traditional narrative. But half of Goldmund's very short life is recounted. He arrives at Mariabronn at the age of fifteen and with no more than a skeletal past. Only the remaining sixteen or seventeen years of his life are brought into focus, and of these merely ten are actually accounted for, and then but spottily. Hesse's customary thin thread of narration is as usual repeatedly broken by time fissures, descriptions, commentary, and protracted interior monologue and expository dialogue. Goldmund's first three years in Mariabronn are skimpy narrative: he attends school, engages in a scuffle, takes part in an illicit outing, experiences two bouts of illness, gathers herbs, and is seduced by Lise. Only the first few days and the last few months of Goldmund's first year and a half in the outside world are focused upon: his night with Lise, two days and nights in a forest followed by a day with a peasant's family, and his second sexual experience; autumn months on a homestead with an old knight and his two daughters, two days in a village, birth of a child, another sexual encounter, Viktor's death, and wintry struggle for survival. The year preceding Goldmund's months on the homestead, and the year and a half following Viktor's murder are disposed of with but brief references to the passing seasons, the tribulations of the road, and to Goldmund's continued adventures of the flesh. Allusions to more affairs and to a great deal of brawling suggest that much transpires during Goldmund's next three years in the bishop's city with Master Niklaus but little is narrated. Only the first two and the last few days of this period are accounted for; all else is rumination about and dialogue involving art and life. Goldmund's subsequent four years of hunger and adventure are accorded but a brief paean to the knights of the road. Only Hesse's description of the plague and its summer of mayhem and mania, and his recounting of Goldmund's encounter with Robert, Lene, and Rebekka enjoy a touch of epic breadth and detail. But for his affair with Ágnes, his apprehension, and his rescue, and but for his briefly recalled second and last sortie into the world, and his death, Goldmund's brief return that autumn to the bishop's city and his last three years in Mariabronn are again primarily interior monologue and expository dialogue. As usual, Hesse's tale is more an airing of views than a depiction of life, more an exposing of minds than a telling of deeds, less a narrative that unravels than a portrait that emerges. And this inner portrait of Goldmund evolves more fully through a succession of expository monologues and dialogues revolving about nodal situations and episodes, just as the image of Goldmund's Primal Mother assumes detail as he proceeds along his road of self-experiencing, and emerges full flown when he has exhausted himself and life.

Goldmund's story is clearly not a traditional romantic narrative, nor is it a realistic historical novel, and it does not pretend to be either. Like *Siddhartha*, it is a simple romance, which is located in time and place removed, in which Hesse features his usual protagonist and foil who for him exemplify two human possibilities, and in which he again peruses life's polarity and again airs his evolving views. And like most of Hesse's tales, Goldmund's is anchored firmly in neither time nor space. The setting is not *the* Middle Ages, but *a* medieval world of monasteries, castles, churches, and remote villages, of monks, and priors, peasants, townsmen and knights, artisans and vagabonds, guilds, masters, and apprentices, and of vast forests, mountains, and a large river, presumably the Rhine, and the bishop's city which may be Cologne. All this is again but incidental, albeit interestingly exotic staging for life's polar drama. As such, stage property and supernumeraries are only contoured in Hesse's usual sparsely enumerative manner: evocative concepts more than visible reality. Even Goldmund and Narziss are accorded minimal necessary physical attributes; theirs, like that of all Hesse's heroes, is primarily a reality of words, thoughts, feelings, and acts.

Narziss und Goldmund's characteristic concomitant evolving of portrait and argument lends inner coherence to its twenty rather straggly segments. Outer coherence is achieved by Hesse's customary concatenative linkage of chapters. As usual, each chapter broaches the major action or theme, or both, of the following chapter and, as is customary in Hesse's novels, the last chapter ends on a suspensive upbeat: Goldmund has lived and died and his story has been told; Narziss has known only service and sacrifice, may not be able to die, and his story has yet to be told. Narziss was an anticipation of things to come in *Das Glasperlenspiel*. In 1927 to 1928 Hesse was obviously not yet prepared either to give him his merited attention or to accord him the self-justification that he so willingly grants his Goldmund.

DIE MORGENLANDFAHRT: RENASCENT AESTHETICISM

GENESIS AND LINKS WITH THE PAST

Though the years following *Der Steppenwolf* were tranquil in comparison with the preceding decade, they were not without their periodic spells of doubt and despair. In December of 1928, while putting the finishing touches to *Narziss und Goldmund*, Hesse experienced sharp qualms about his own writing and about artists and thinkers in general. He managed to convince himself that intellectual and artistic pursuits were meaningful endeavors, popular skepticism and his own compunctions notwithstanding, and concluded that he would go on writing come what might.[58] Doubts were resolutely repressed but never resolved. Lingering uncertainty coupled with a severe letdown following the completion of *Narziss und Goldmund* left Hesse extremely despondent until the summer of 1930. Too close identification with Goldmund had persuaded him that he himself had never really experienced life's intensities, that he had become an artist but not a man among men, and that art had literally absorbed his life.[59] The festering questionableness of art, the feeling of personal failure as a human being, and a renewed awareness of the general horror and futility of life itself almost occasioned another major crisis. It was this period of depression, and Hesse's usual determination to find order and meaning in chaos, that provided the impetus for *Die Morgen-*

---

58 See "Eine Arbeitsnacht" (1928), *Gesammelte Schriften* (1957), Vol. 7, pp. 304–307.

59 "I became a writer, but not a human being. I attained a partial goal, not the main goal. I have failed . . . my life is nothing other than a readiness for work. . . . The value and the intensity of my life are to be found in those hours I am productive as a writer, that is to say, when I give expression to my life's very inadequacy and desperateness." *Briefe* (1964), p. 29 (a letter of August 9, 1929).

Hermann Hesse, 1929.

landfahrt. The story was conceived in the latter half of 1929, and written from the summer of 1930 to April 1931. The book appeared at the beginning of 1932.

Like every major work after *Demian*, *Die Morgenlandfahrt* was another necessity in self-expression and another experiment in narration. It is also the most esoteric of Hesse's many elusive tales. Abstruseness of matter and narrative pyrotechnics notwithstanding, its close kinship with the past is apparent. The tale's shifting planes of reality, H.H.'s movement between the fascinating realm of the imagination and the pedestrian everyday world, are reminiscent of Lauscher's involvement with the wondrous Kingdom of Ask and with lowly Kirchheim, and most immediately recall Haller's to and fro between the actual and the ideal. Each of these protagonists exists in a tangible here, but has his reason and being in an ethereal beyond. Space- and time-bound actuality suffices for none, and all opt for a related timeless ideal. The fairy-tale world behind the curtain of appearance is Lauscher's retreat, the realm of the Immortals is Haller's hope, and the Order of Eastern Wayfarers is H.H.'s dream come true. The tale's manner is just as closely related to the past as its matter. The story itself is the threadbare fragment that most of Hesse's novels are, and narrative is as usual constantly interrupted by comment, rumination, and ceremonious dialogue. The poetic fantasies of H.H.'s eastward trek plainly recall the vagaries of Klingsor's outing to Kareno. Indeed, an abbreviated version of this excursion could have been included in H.H.'s recollections without ruffling either its substance or its style. The tale's plethora of enigmatic allusions and tantalizing mystifications are but an old and favorite literary ploy run amok, its two protagonists are Hesse's customary double self-projection, and the mock trial motif had already been explored and similarly used in *Der Steppenwolf*. Settings and characters are depicted in Hesse's characteristic evocative manner, and the rhythm and flow of language continue to adapt themselves to inner state and outer situation. And like all of Hesse's major tales, *Die Morgenlandfahrt* is life become art.

LIFE TRANSFIGURED

H.H.'s Order of Eastern Wayfarers is not just another secret society, but an elite assemblage of questers of all time and from all places. The journey is not a physical expedition, but a timeless spiritual odyssey. The East is not a geographic destination, but a psychocracy, an immaterial and timeless realm of light and wonder where soul and mind prevail, a Platonic reality beyond the wanting reality of the physical world. And this typically Hessean bent of thought is as dependent upon Hesse's life for its narrative projection as most of his tales. Autobiography had been poetically fantasized in *Klingsors letzter Sommer*, surrealistically fantasized in *Der Steppenwolf*. It was playfully fantasized, mystified, metaphorized, and symbolized in *Die Morgenlandfahrt*.

H.H.'s acceptance into the Order, his year of probation, his initiation, his participation in the Order's journey to the East, his defection after but a few months, his ten-year period of lonely suffering and suicidal despair, his months of grueling effort to recall and to record his association with the Order, and his culminating readmission into its ranks extend over some twelve years. This narrative structure was Hesse's own twelve years of quest, despair, and of new hope following his departure from Bern in the spring of 1919. The various stages of this critical period of H.H.'s life correspond loosely with the vicissitudes of Hesse's life from 1919 to 1931: H.H.'s probational year, with Hesse's initial readjustment to life in Montagnola; his eastward quest, with Hesse's months of study and meditation preceding his completion of *Siddhartha*; his painful years of apostasy, with Hesse's turbulent twenties; and his return to the Order and its master-servant ideal, with Hesse's retreat from radical individualism and his nurturing of an incipient communal consciousness. That H.H. concentrates on his long bygone trip and dwells on the immediate circumstances of his life, but only alludes to his many intervening aberrational years, is not at all surprising. The strain and gloom of these years had already been more than adequately depicted in *Kurgast, Die Nürnberger Reise, Der Steppenwolf*, and in *Krisis*. Their interludes of equanimity and euphoria, virtually ignored in Hesse's previous writings, were now taken out of their actual sequence and became the highlights of H.H.'s wondrous odyssey.

With the solemn blessing of the Order's august assembly of Superiors (*Oberen*), and mindful of its Speaker's solicitous admonition to be constant in faith and courageous in danger, H.H. forswears the temporal world of money and machines, and armed with the Order's protective ring of membership (*Bundesring*), begins his sacral pilgrimage. He and his fellow wayfarers eschew all that is of this world, live in tents, and travel afoot in groups of ten, and upon occasion singly or in couples, or as a vast throng. Apart from the journey's lofty collective aims, forbidden by oath to be divulged, each partici-

pant is immediately motivated by a private aspiration. One is determined to capture a magic snake Kundalini, another is intent upon the
treasure Tao, yet another is intrigued by the coffin of Mohammed,
their enigmatic retainer Leo has to learn the language of the birds,
and H.H.'s quest is the fabled Princess Fatme. Their crusade wends
its capricious and fractured way through places and times remote and
near: through Swabia, Switzerland, and parts of Italy, toward the
East, into the Middle Ages and the Golden Age, and into the spaceless geography and timelessness of dream and recollection. On a courageous trek through Upper Swabia, H.H. and his cohorts experience
memorable wonders. They are miraculously befriended by a St.
Christopher painted on the wall of a half-ruined chapel beside an intersection of three roads in the vicinity of Spaichendorf. On another
occasion, accosted by the Guardians of the Crown (*Kronenwächter*),
hoary and less than friendly guardian warriors of the memory and inheritance of the Hohenstaufen dynasty, they discreetly abandon their
plans to visit Bopfingen. Near Urach, an emissary of the Guardians of
the Crown puts a dreadful curse upon the expedition for the refusal of
its leaders to abet the cause of the Hohenstaufen in Sicily. The questers also manage to spy the gnome (*Hutzelmännlein*) and surmise that
the Blue Pot (*Blautopf*) will be one of their destinations. Their mean-
dering route takes them to the Bodensee, Zürich, and Winterthur, to
a triumphal reception in Bremgarten, and to the surrender of Ticino's
Montags-Dorf. Under the temporary leadership of Albertus Magnus
they travel to Famagusta across the Moon Sea (*Mondmeer*), and they
discover Butterfly Island (*Schmetterlingsinsel*) twelve lines behind
Zipangu. And leaving his troop briefly, H.H. travels back through his
life to his bride on the Upper Rhine, to friends in Tübingen, Basel,
and Florence, and to his youth, schooldays, and butterfly chases.

In compliance with their initiation oath, H.H. and his confrères
pay their humble respects to all places and memories associated with
their ancient Order. Mankind's venerated shrines, monuments,
ruins, churches, and burial grounds are dutifully visited and honored
in song and silent devotion, chapels and altars are adorned with
flowers, and the illustrious dead are celebrated in prayer and with
music. The wayfarers are both mocked and revered by the unin-
itiated, and are greeted everywhere by thankful friends. Amid the
tramways and banks of Zürich, they are hospitably received by Hans
C. steering Noah's Ark (*die Arche Noah*) through the shallows of a
sober age. In Winterthur, they are the guests of the Black King (*der
schwarze König*) in the Chinese temple one floor below Stoecklin's

Magic Cabinet. And at the foot of Sun Mountain (Sonnenberg), they enjoy the hospitality of Suon Mali, a colony of the King of Siam. But the most memorable of their festive occasions is the Order's grand celebration in Bremgarten, hosted by Max and Tilli, master and mistress of the local castle. Drab everyday is washed away by a wave of magic, the castle, park, and river bask in moonlight, glitter in the flare of fireworks, and swarm with artists and their creations, with beings supernatural and talking animals. Othmar at the piano in the great hall regales the festive throng with Mozart, Max recites a poem inspired by the happy occasion, the natives kneel in homage to beauty, and strutting peacocks scream in the gardens. Longus the astrologer keeps company with Heinrich von Ofterdingen and paints his wondrously metamorphic Greek and Hebrew characters, Louis converses in Spanish with Puss-in-Boots, and Hans Resom contemplates a pilgrimage to the grave of Charles the Great. Hugo Wolf is a restless guest, Brentano is brilliant and elfish, and inebriated Hoffmann darts chattering to and fro among the celebrants. Anselm, alone and apart, stares smiling and transfixed into the purple calyx of his iris. Klingsor glows, Lauscher is taciturne, Leo frolics with two white poodles, and Pablo, bedecked with roses and surrounded by maidens, plays his Persian flute. The fairy Armida sings at the fountain, lean Don Quixote stands solitary guard under a chestnut tree, and the Archivist Lindhorst playfully spews fire like a dragon. The animals of the forest gather in awe at the walls, sweet nymphs emerge and glitter on the rocky river bank, and festive schools of gleaming fish are fêted with cake and wine. And while the revelers sleep, a joyous H.H. slips past a knight on guard to join white mermaids in their moonlit crystal depths.

Bremgarten was the zenith of H.H.'s spiritual adventure, the dangerous Morbio Inferiore was its nadir. All is well until he and his party enter this wild and rocky gorge on the border of Italy. Their esteemed Leo vanishes without trace, unexpectedly and unaccountably, and with him, the original or a copy of the Order's treasured Charter (*Bundesbrief*). Leo's disappearance is the beginning of their end. Their loss seems irreparable, the Order quickly loses its meaning, their journey becomes questionable, and their individual missions cease to fascinate them. Dissension soon leaves the group in shambles. One by one its members drift away in despondency, and their fanciful journey ends in dismal disillusionment but a few months after its ecstatic start.

In the preamble to his journey, H.H. surmises that much or

perhaps even all of his account will appear incredible and remain incomprehensible. Credibility is most immediately strained by the narrative's outmoded derivative form. Its prototype was clearly the rather trivial league novel (*Bundesroman*) vogue in Germany during the second half of the eighteenth century.[60] The exclusive Order, its parareligious structure and atmosphere, its mysterious retreat and secret archive, its hierarchy of members ranging from the Supreme One (*der Oberste der Oberen*) to the Tribunal of Superiors (*der Gerichtshof der Oberen*), to the Speakers (*Sprecher*) and to the novices, its mystical rites of initiation, the pomp and ceremony of its festivals, its unusual journey, its Charter, ring, and its emissary Leo are all standard trappings of a genre passé. With an added burden of playful literary and fanciful personal ornamentation, a tale rather incredible also became somewhat baffling. Much of the literary bric-à-brac is immediately meaningful only to Germanists well versed in the century from 1750 to 1850, Hesse's favorite period of German literature; many of the delightful personal allusions elude all but those of the author's intimate friends who are still alive and those readers who have become serious students of Hesse; and some of the tale's puzzles died with their creator. Fortunately bygone narrative form and unprecedented display of fantasy and hide-and-seek are means and not end, and though the tale's esoteric means may be frustratingly detractive and perplexing, its message is amply clear. H.H.'s world of Eastern Wayfarers—eighteenth-century garb in fanciful adaptation—became Hesse's treasured realm of the spirit accorded a visible form, a unique symbol of life as he would have preferred it.

Despite its inherited literary paraphernalia and its unbridled fantasy, *Die Morgenlandfahrt* drew as heavily upon autobiography for its narrative content as for its narrative structure. H.H. is what Hermann Hesse at the time was, undisguised even in name. All that is revealed of his person—his background, and friends, his interests, inclinations, aspirations, and conflicts—reflects Hesse's own life. According to the cryptic information of the Order's archive, H.H. became a citizen of Calw in 1890, the same year Hesse had become a subject of Württemberg. As a youngster, as had Hesse, H.H. enjoyed chasing butterflies and spying on otters, learned to play the violin, and became an avid reader of fairy tales. As a young man, as had Hesse,

---

60 The relationship between *Die Morgenlandfahrt* and the *Bundesroman* is discussed in considerable detail by Theodore Ziolkowski, *The Novels of Hermann Hesse* (1965), pp. 255–561.

H.H. caroused with friends in Tübingen, Basel, and Florence, and wandered through the region of the Upper Rhine with an erstwhile betrothed. H.H.'s dark-haired and dark-eyed Ninon the Foreigner (*Ninon die Ausländerin*) was Hesse's Ninon, née Ausländer, the Montags-Dorf was his Montagnola. H.H.'s fellow wayfarers were also Hesse's closest friends: Jup the Magician (*Jup der Magier*), who is intent upon his fortune in Kashmir, was Josef Englert, also known as *Der Magier*, who had actually left Switzerland temporarily to try his luck in Kashmir and Bengal; Collofino the Smoke Magician (*Collofino der Rauchzauberer*) is as fond of citing from Grimmelshausen's *Simplizissimus* as was his prototype Josef Feinhals, cigar manufacturer of Cologne; and Louis the Horrible (*Louis der Grausame*), with his dream of an olive grove and slaves in the Holy Land, is very much the footloose eccentric that his model the painter Louis Moilliet was. All three of these bosom friends had appeared earlier in *Klingsors letzter Sommer*. H.H.'s motley entourage also includes Hesse's Lauscher, Anselm, Klingsor, Vasudeva, Siddhartha, Pablo, and Goldmund, and he consorts with characters out of some of Hesse's favorite literary works: with Novalis's Heinrich von Ofterdingen, E.T.A. Hoffmann's Archivist Lindhorst (*Der goldne Topf*) and Armida (*Ritter Gluck*), Cervantes's Don Quixote and Sancho Panza, Wolfram von Eschenbach's Parzival, Heine's Almansor, Stifter's Witiko, and Fatme and the Barmicides (*Thousand and One Nights*). Zoroaster, Lao-Tse, Plato, Xenophon, Pythagoras, Albertus Magnus, Sterne's Tristram Shandy, Novalis, and Baudelaire, cofounders and brothers of the Order, were all Hesse's intellectual companions. H.H. also shares Hesse's enthusiasm for Ariosto's *Orlando Furioso* and for C. M. Wieland's *Oberon*: the intrepid heroes (Roland and Hüon) of these verse romances had made the last great journeys sponsored by the Order; H.H.'s verse quotation commenting on the general lack of appreciation for tales such as his was taken from *Orlando Furioso* (Canto VII); and the Order's ring incantation was lifted from *Oberon* (Canto VII). And just as his author had been, H.H. was suicidal in despair, and writing is for him, as it was for Hesse, a necessary attempt to give expression to and to find order and meaning in the chaos of life.

H.H.'s serpentine journey and its joyous festivals are just as rooted in autobiography as his immediate person. Trek and highlights are nothing less than a fantasized amalgam of Hesse's five or six reading trips to South Germany from 1923 to 1929 and of his many festive receptions in the homes of his wealthy friends in Zürich, Winterthur, and Bern. The longest and most memorable of these trips took place in the autumn of 1925, and was recounted in wry detail in *Die Nürnberger Reise* (1925). The first half of this same journey furnished the basic itinerary for H.H.'s jaunt through Swabia. Leaving Switzerland, Hesse had proceeded via Singen and Tuttlingen to Blaubeuren. H.H. and his party follow the same general route: they halt briefly at Spaichendorf (Spaichingen near Tuttlingen), approach Urach, and assume that their journey will lead to the Blue Pot (*Blautopf*), the legendary pool of blue spring water in Blaubeuren. The chapel in ruins at an intersection of three roads ("an einem dreifachen Kreuzweg") near Spaichendorf is probably an oblique reference to the Dreifaltigkeitskirche (Holy Trinity Church) on the Dreifaltigkeitsberg (Holy Trinity Mountain) above Spaichingen.[61] The wayfarers' confrontation near Urach with the inimical Hohenstaufen Guardians of the Crown (*Kronenwächter*) is a facetious tribute to a favorite tale (*Die Kronenwächter*) by much-admired Achim von Arnim and a covert allusion to Hesse's continued hostile reception by the ultra nationalistic press in Württemberg. Their courageous traversal of Upper Swabia is but another allusion to this persistent animosity. The hill on which an old Guardian of the Crown appears mysteriously and dissuades the group from continuing its journey to Bopfingen (east of Stuttgart), is obviously Hohenstaufen, the mount between Göppingen and Schwäbisch Gmünd, on which the ancestral castle of the Hohenstaufer dynasty once stood. In *Die Nürnberger Reise*, Hesse concedes that he had agreed to give readings in Ulm, Augsburg, and Nuremberg largely because the trip would afford him an opportunity to revisit Blaubeuren and to see the Blue Pot (*Blautopf*), where according to legend and particularly to Mörike's *Das Stuttgarter Hutzelmännlein* the beautiful nymph Lau had once lived. It is Mörike's gnome (*Hutzelmännlein*) whom H.H. and his companions chance to encounter, presumably in or near Stuttgart. Their assumption that their path may resultantly lead to the Blue Pot is a reference to Mörike's cobbler Seppe and his journey to Blaubeuren after his encounter in Stuttgart with the gnome.

It is not just the Swabian portion of Hesse's reading tour of 1925 that links *Die Nürnberger Reise* with *Die Morgenlandfahrt*. Both works are also more comment on the self, age, and art, than actual or imaginary travelogue. Indeed, their common concerns and a distinct at-

---

61 This observation was first made by Siegfried Wrase in his very imaginative doctoral study, "Erläuterungen zu Hermann Hesses *Morgenlandfahrt*" (Tübingen, 1959), 205 pp.

titudinal progression from one to other would suggest that *Die Morgenlandfahrt* was to a considerable degree a fictive sequel to *Die Nürnberger Reise*. In the latter, Hesse is sorely troubled by the gross disparity between the real and the ideal, he disparages the actual world, quarrels with its money, machines, and its time, detests travel by train, and dreams fondly of the Middle Ages. All is transfigured and remedied in the fantasy of *Die Morgenlandfahrt*. H.H. discounts the real, turns his back upon the physical world and its plaguing unrealities, travels by foot, and roams at will through the Middle Ages and wherever his mind or imagination care to take him.

On most of his reading tours Hesse made it a point to renew old friendships. He abhorred public appearances but enjoyed private visits. In *Die Nürnberger Reise*, he gave a factual account of a trip and of his many visits. In *Die Morgenlandfahrt* he allowed his imagination to both mystify and enchant. H.H. recalls three memorable receptions and one major festive occasion. The receptions are tantalizing enigmas, and the festival is a brilliant romantic fantasia. Noah's Ark in the heart of Zürich with Hans C., a descendant of the sons of Noah and patron of the arts, at its wheel, might be imaginative absurdity except that the helmsman was Hans C. Bodmer whose impressive old home, The House at the Sign of the Ark (*Zur Arch*), still stands in Bärengasse, a veritable museum piece among Zürich's tramways and banks, whose nautical association invited his addition to Noah's family, and who was none other than Hesse's own old friend and patron. The flute-playing Black King of Winterthur, host to H.H. and his cohorts in the Chinese temple below Stoecklin's Magic Cabinet, was none other than Hesse's friend and yet another wealthy patron of the arts, Georg Reinhart, known to family and close associates as *der schwarze König*. Stoecklin's Magic Cabinet was a small studio that housed some paintings by Nicklaus Stoecklin, in which Reinhart himself painted, and from which a narrow staircase descended into a temple-like chamber with an extensive collection of Oriental art featuring a large bronze statue of Maya. Reinhart also played the flute. The wayfarers' reception in Buddha-strewn Suon Mali, the King of Siam's colony at the foot of Sun Mountain (Sonnenberg), continues this playful verbal refraction of actuality. The King of Siam was neither royalty nor an Oriental, but Hesse's patron Fritz Leuthold; Suon Mali (Siamese for Jasmin Garden) was not a Siamese colony, but the Leuthold household, which was actually located in Sonnenbergstrasse at the foot of Zürich's Sonnenberg; and grateful travelers, burning incense and pouring their libations among the stone and bronze Buddhas, were Hesse and other close friends of Leuthold, smoking and imbibing among his many statues of Buddha. The Leutholds had spent many years in Siam, had brought back many *objets d'art*, had christened their home Suon Mali, and were known to their friends as the Siamese.

The Order's grand festival in Bremgarten is as romantically fantastic as any of E.T.A. Hoffmann's many phantasmagorias. Hesse's blending and fantasizing of the past and the present, of fairy tale, literature, and actuality was as uninhibited as his idolized predecessor's customary erasure of the line between the real and the imaginary, and, as usual, all was intimately personal. Max and Tilli, hosts to the Order, were Hesse's old friends, the Wassmers. The castle with its towers, great hall, and grand piano, its garden and park with parrots and peacocks, its fountain under an immense old chestnut tree, and its surrounding walls, woods, and river is a sparse but accurate depiction of the Wassmer's manor house in Bremgarten on the Aare River a few kilometers outside of Bern. Othmar at the piano was the composer Schoeck, the astrologer Longus was the analyst Lang, Louis was the painter Moilliet, and Hans Resom was the writer Hans Albrecht Moser. These were some of Hesse's friends, who, like him, enjoyed both the patronage and the hospitality of the Wassmers. The presence of Hesse's esteemed Hugo Wolf, Clemens Brentano, and of E.T.A. Hoffmann blends the past and the present. The addition of his Pablo, Leo, Anselm, Klingsor, and Lauscher, and of Hoffmann's Armida and Lindhorst, Novalis's Heinrich von Ofterdingen, Cervantes's Don Quixote, and of Puss-in-Boots and mermaids fuses actuality, literature, and fairy tale. A magic realm emerges from this transfiguration of life: a visible rendition of the transcendent world of Hesse's dreams, another of his many testimonials to the reality of this other world, and a poetic memorial to the many times he was a fêted guest at the Wassmers. This festive gathering of Hesse's circle of intimate friends in Bremgarten was to continue sporadically until the fifties.

H.H.'s voyage to the East consists essentially of his trek through Swabia and the festivities in Switzerland. His several minor excursions are only alluded to, and are primarily fanciful embellishment to underscore the metaphoric nature of his journey. However, even in the most bizarre and purely imaginative of these sallies, the content remains very personal. The expedition across the Mondmeer to Famagusta under the leadership of Albertus Magnus is a veiled association with the crusades, and a clear tribute to the Swabian philosopher and theologian who had himself supported them. Moon Sea (Mondmeer) is an exotic rendition of Mediterranean Sea (Mittelmeer), and Famagusta is a Cyprian city that played a prominent part in the crusades. Albertus Magnus's listing among the founders and Superiors of the Order reflects the prominent place he had assumed in Hesse's pantheon of thinkers and artists. This linkage of the Order's pilgrimage with the crusades, together with H.H.'s repeated identification of his group with the medieval crusaders and their religious intent, and along with the Order's abundant religious trappings, was very much in keeping with Hesse's characteristic tendency to equate the artist with the saint, and art with religion. At the beginning of his career, a troubled Hesse had resorted to this identification to make his aestheticism palatable to himself; in 1930 an anxious Hesse accorded bold visibility to this association, determined to lend justification and dignity to his rejuvenated aestheticism. The discovery of Butterfly Island (Schmetterlingsinsel) behind Zipangu, Marco Polo's name for Japan, probably alludes to Hesse's own trip to the Orient, and mirrors his lifelong interest in butterflies. He had collected butterflies as a youngster, and with the passing years they had become his treasured symbols of life's transitoriness and beauty, and exotic messengers from an ideal world behind drab actuality, the very world to which the wayfarers aspire.[62] Famagusta and Zipangu, like Mondmeer and fictive Schmetterlingsinsel, were obviously chosen less for geographic reasons than for their euphony and for the esoteric remoteness that they suggest. A trip to the grave of Rüdiger and an encounter with the giant Agramant are more complimentary allusions to Ariosto's *Orlando Furioso*. The abrupt termination of H.H.'s pilgrimage in the shadows of the gorge Morbio Inferiore is an appropriately symbolic ending for a metaphoric journey that ends in depression and confusion. But even this apparently pure symbol derived from actuality. The suggestive place-name was not a genial invention but a brilliant application. A tiny community that Hesse knew quite well, and with just that unlikely name, lies in the Muggiotal between Lake Lugano and Lake Como.

The several remaining enigmas associated with H.H.'s journey are similarly accountable. The bizarre individual aspirations of the wayfarers are not just the ornamental dabs of pure fancy they may at

62 For Hesse's interest in butterflies, see: "Apollo" (1901), *Gesammelte Schriften* (1957), Vol. 3, pp. 904–906; "Das Nachtpfauenauge" (1911), *Jugend*, 6 (June 6, 1911), 617–620; "Nachweihnacht" (1927), *Berliner Tageblatt*, January 1, 1928, No. 1; "Über Schmetterlinge" (1936), *Berliner Tageblatt*, February 1, 1936.

first glance appear to be. Like almost everything else in the tale, these quests had their personal significance. H.H.'s life-goal, beautiful Fatme, is Ninon the Foreigner, and Ninon Ausländer was the latest princess in Hesse's life. Princess Fatme was but another name for the ideal woman that the Queen of the Isle of Beauty (*Der Inseltraum,* 1898), Princess Lilia of the Kingdom of Ask (*Lulu,* 1900), and Klingsor's Queen of the Mountains (1919) had once been for Hesse. This ideal had become part of H.H.'s dreams in late boyhood. It was in late boyhood that Hesse had discovered *Thousand and One Nights* and its Princess Fatme in his grandfather's library. The book remained one of his favorite collections of fairy tales, and Fatme became for him a blending of and a common designation for all its enchanting princesses. As such, the Order's card-catalogue reference to the tale of the Princess of the Stone City (noct. mill. 983) is as correct as an allusion to the tale of Princess Fatme and the poet Murakkish would have been. It also permitted yet another expression of Hesse's penchant for playful mystification. The remaining remarks on Fatme's catalogue card are similar tantalizers (princ. orient. 2; hort. delic. 07). The Fatme in question is Ninon, and she was Hesse's second oriental princess. Ruth Wenger, Klingsor's Queen of the Mountains alias Fatme of Damascus, had been the first of these two enchantresses. The last of these references probably pertains to the Abbess Herrad von Landsperg's *Hortus Deliciarum,* a twelfth-century illustrated manual of instruction for nuns. If this is the case, and should the appended 07 refer to the seventh illustration in this compendium,[63] then the conundrum was not only another playful manifestation of literary erudition, but was also a deliberate extension of Fatme's symbolism. Her association with the illustration in question—a portrayal of the Garden of Eden, of Adam, and of the creation of Eve—would identify her with the mother of mankind and elevate her to the mythic plane of Sinclair's *Frau Eva* and Goldmund's *Eva-Mutter.* Fatme would emerge a symbol incorporating both Hesse's woman beautiful and life and its living. That Princess Fatme loses her old fascination for H.H., once he is back in the Order's fold, suggests the beginning of the new stage in Hesse's own aspirations, a phase of exclusive dedication to art.

The quest of one wayfarer for the treasure Tao, of another for the snake Kundalini, and Leo's desire to understand the languages of the

---

63 Siegfried Wrase first drew attention to this possibility, "Erläuterungen zu Hermann Hesses *Morgenlandfahrt*" (Tübingen, 1959), p. 18.

birds were all Hesse's own aspirations. Most of his adult life had been a quest for the true way and the timeless and changeless essence of reality implied by Taoism's Tao. Most of the immediately preceding thirteen years of his life had also been devoted almost exclusively to the reconciliation of life's disparate poles implied by Kundalini, the snake with magic powers. Kundalini is the female principle which, according to Hinduistic Tantrism, lies coiled at the base of man's spine until it is roused in a Yoga process and compelled to move up the spinal column to the top of the head where it achieves union with the male principle. The snake's magic powers allude to the mystical experiencing of the nonduality of the absolute achieved in the transcendent ecstasy of this union of the female and male principles. Leo's desire to learn bird language was one of Hesse's more facetious aspirations. From *Demian* on, he had freely identified with birds, *Die Morgenlandfahrt* reflects a progression from identification to interest in communication, and in *Vogel* (1932), a sister fantasia, Hesse actually became an exotic feathered creature, able both to sing and to fly. H.H.'s mysterious reference to Solomon's Key (*salomonischer Schlüssel*), in connection with Leo's singular wish, is an oblique allusion to Wieland's *Oberon*. Solomon's Magic Ring makes possible the impossible for Wieland's Hüon, and Solomon's Key can do the same for Hesse's Leo. The talisman will, it is hoped, unlock the language of the birds for Leo just as it magically unlocks the door of the Mountain Queen's abode for Klingsor.

Paul Klee's presence in a group of pilgrims intent upon rescuing Princess Isabella from the Moors alludes to Achim von Arnim's *Isabella von Ägypten*, another of Hesse's favorite fantastic tales, and to Klee's actual trip to Tunisia and his proclaimed feeling of kinship with Africa. Although Hesse seems not to have known the painter personally, he was highly appreciative of his art, and looked upon him as a fellow seeker.[64] Kyffhäuser, seat of the government where the Order's Charter may have been deposited, is an allusion to the mountain in Thuringia on which the Hohenstaufen once resided, in which legend would have Barbarossa asleep, and from which the Emperor would one day emerge to unite the German peoples and lead them to victory against their enemies. This, like all other of Hesse's references to the Hohenstaufen dynasty and to the Middle Ages, owes its inclusion to the appropriate literary-legendary color that it lends to the

64 See Hesse's review of W. Hausenstein's book *Kairuan oder eine Geschichte vom Maler Klee, Vivos Voco*, 3 (November-December 1922), 224.

wayfarers' timeless Eastern trek. It was for this same reason that Hesse at the beginning of his tale associated the Order's journey with Ariosto's *Orlando Furioso* and Wieland's *Oberon*, and deliberately disassociated it with Hermann Keyserling's *Das Reisebuch eines Philosophen* (1919) and with Ferdinand Ossendowski's *Tiere, Menschen und Götter* (1923). The former's report was too much glib philosophy and poor travelogue, the latter's alleged actual adventures were but incredible fabrication, neither's voyage was a true spiritual odyssey, and both books were anything but works of art.

The pretentious voyages of Keyserling and Ossendowski accorded less with Hesse's inclinations and aspirations than did the legendary trek through Bavaria and Thuringia in 1920 of a band of idealistic and ecstatic young reformers intent upon spreading Gustav Gräser's gospel of nature, love, joy, freedom, and self-fulfillment.[65] Hesse had in 1907 briefly attempted to practise Gräser's prescribed austere natural way of living. His respect for Gräser's regimen had suffered, but his admiration for the man had remained intact and had persisted with the passing years. Though Hesse himself took no part in the Gräser-inspired ecstasy of 1920, the numerous reports of this latter-day crusade of innocents touched him deeply and left an indelible impression upon his memory. His recollections of welcoming throngs, joyous processions, flower-filled churches, and communal song and dance, all suggestive of the advent of a millenium, became filler for his imaginary trip into his own more ideal world.

AUTOBIOGRAPHY CAMOUFLAGED

With the third chapter, the center of attention shifts from H.H. the erstwhile wayfarer journeying happily through a realm beyond time and space, to H.H. the writer, alone in a large city and desperately intent upon recounting his past association with the Order and upon reestablishing contact with it. H.H.'s recollections were Hesse's past fantasized, his immediate situation was Hesse's present only slightly camouflaged. His narrative problems, his wish, and the physical setting were Hesse's recurrent struggle to give artistic expression to life, his efforts in 1930 and 1931 to regain his faith in the community of art and the intellect, and his familiar urban haunts. The nameless city in which H.H. has been living for some months is Haller's

---

65 For reports on this evangelizing tour, see: Werner Helwig, *Die blaue Blume des Wandervogels* (Gütersloh: Mohn, 1960), pp. 180–181; Walter Z. Laqueur, *Die deutsche Jugendbewegung* (Köln: Wissenschaft u. Politik, 1962), p. 133.

Basel-Zürich. St. Paulstor is Basel's medieval, Spalentor, and the nearby park where H.H. and Leo sit and chat is the adjacent botanical garden. The old city hall to which Leo draws H.H.'s attention is Basel's celebrated fifteenth-century *Rathaus*, the Paulskirche and the cathedral in which Leo prays are its Pauluskirche and its Münster, and the large museum-like building housing the Order's archives and located in a sleepy suburb-street is its Art Museum in St. Alban-Vorstadt. The two-room attic quarters in which H.H. settles to record his association with the Order were Hesse's apartment in Basel's Lothringerstrasse in the winter of 1924 to 1925. Leo lives in Zürich's Seilergraben. He and H.H. saunter along on Zürich's Gartenstrasse which leads into Am Schanzengraben, where Hesse actually wrote a portion of *Die Morgenlandfahrt* in the winter of 1931. Hesse may even have met H.H.'s unfriendly Alsatian on one of his own occasional strolls up Gartenstrasse. H.H.'s old friend Lukas was Hesse's longtime intimate Martin Lang. Like his prototype, Lukas had taken part in the First World War, had written a book about his experiences, had become an editor, and was a mild skeptic with a good sense of humor. H.H.'s visits to Lukas and their conversation about the Order and about writing were probably Hesse's recollection of similar visits to and discussions with Lang while in Stuttgart for reading engagements in late 1928 and 1929. Lukas was also Lang's actual nickname. As a budding poet and apprentice gardener, he had been a frequent guest in Gaienhofen, had helped Hesse lay out the garden of his second home with the aid of a garden manual by a certain Lukas, and had acquired the name Lukas.[66]

LEO AND THE ORDER

H.H.'s eastward trek is actuality fantasized; his immediate physical setting and his friendship with Lukas are actuality camouflaged; his relationship with Leo and his ceremonious admission and readmission into the Order are psychic process externalized in pure fantasy and playful mystification. The psychic process is one from faith and wondrous expectation, to doubt and despair, to faith regained and new hope, and the impulses in this progression are the transcendant realm of art and thought and a new personal possibility. H.H. and Leo were another of Hesse's double self-projections: the distraught individualist he actually was, and the confident master-

66 See Ludwig Finckh, "Ein Lorbeerblatt für Martin Lang," *Blätter des Schwäbischen Albvereins* (Stuttgart), 7 (July-August 1955), 71.

servant he hoped he might become. Leo had his antecedents but no actual prototype. Like Demian and Hermine, he is both the admonishing and enlightening *daimon* and the more ideal alter ego, rendered visible. And the Order is another of Hesse's ideal communities, another kingdom of the spirit accorded visibility. Admission to the Order and Leo's presence symbolize H.H.'s awareness of and faith in a noumenal reality, and represent the first stage in his progression from an anxious seeker to a blithe Eastern Wayfarer. Leo's disappearance and H.H.'s defection from the Order are tantamount to a disturbing loss of this vision and belief, a relapse to self-centered and troubled individualism, and a return to everyday reality and its agonies. Leo's reappearance, H.H.'s readmission to the Order, and Leo's ultimate absorption and displacement of H.H. promised by the double-bodied figurine connote faith restored and anticipate H.H.'s emergence as a master-servant and his selfless dedication to the transcendent world of art and thought. This was Hesse's own latest aspiration.

The Order was not just a means for transmitting this message, not merely traditional literary paraphernalia that chanced to suit Hesse's purpose. The very concept of such an Order lay close to his own heart. Hesse's early rebellion against Pietism and its denial of the world and of the self had been less a rejection than a secularization. He had rejected a denial of the self, but sectarian Pietism had left him with an aversion to the world as it is and a passion for a Kingdom of God on earth, a deep commitment to religion, and a decided penchant for exclusiveness, and these traits remained important determinants in Hesse's life and thought. Pietism had first found its secular expression in Hesse's early aestheticism: in his rejection of physical actuality and acclaim of a transcendent realm of beauty, his identification of art and religion, the artist and the saint, and in his *petit cénacle* of young romantics in Tübingen. Labels were changed, but intrinsic substance had remained intact. Hesse's continued quest for an exclusive order and a secularized Kingdom of God eventually took him to the Cains and their realm beyond good and evil, the Immortals and their icy eternity, the Eastern Wayfarers and their psychocracy, and finally to the Castalians and their oasis of spirituality. The parareligious secret societies of the *Bundesroman* were made to order for Hesse's proclivity for exclusiveness and his otherworldly bent. He had only to add a personal touch of fantasy and his own sympathy for Catholicism.

Though Hesse was never seriously tempted to become a Catholic, he had long admired and never ceased to extol Catholicism for its unity, time-honored dogma, and confessional, its hierarchy, pomp, and ritual.[67] Its pope also confirmed and epitomized his evolving master-servant ideal. This admiration and association left its unmistakable Catholic imprint on Hesse's version of an eighteenth-century secret society. The Supreme One, resplendently frocked and tranquilly seated on his canopied throne surrounded by a pyramid of obeisant Superiors, is decidedly less a Grand Master in business session with his Elders, than a secularized pope in solemn conclave with his lay cardinals and archbishops. His master-servant relationship to his flock is just as decidedly more papal than masonic. It is to this dual papal role that Leo's catalogue card alludes (Cave! Archiepisc. [overseer] XIX. Diacon. [servant] D. VII. cornu Ammon. 6 Cave!). The cryptic note is also a warning (Cave!) that Leo represents a trying ideal. The papal *servus servorum Dei* was probably Hesse's inspiration for the first part of this teaser. What the horn of the Egyptian god Ammon was meant to imply, and what, if anything, the appended numerals were to signify, remained Hesse's secrets. Leo's own name was part of Hesse's game. It is purposively papal, but why Leo rather than equally suggestive Gregory or Benedict? Leo had no actual prototype, but he did owe many of his rather unusual attributes (naturalness, independence, silent graceful walk, fondness for nocturnal wandering, love of birds, and attraction for dogs) and his name to Hesse's beloved cat Lion (Löwe).[68] Löwe latinized killed two birds with one stone: the name chanced to be appropriately papal, and gratitude was acknowledged where gratitude was due, and in Hesse's usual facetious manner.

The Order's concerns, attitudes, activities, and ultimate goal are as spiritual as its hierarchy is ecclesiastical. There is much ado about sin and suffering, contrition, grace, and paradise, humility and piety are stressed, blessings are cherished, pilgrimages and prayer are a way of life, the world is forsworn and a psychocracy awaits the faithful. All is imbued with spirituality: the secular is sanctified, and religion is secularized. When H.H. appears before the august assemblage of his betters, it is not as a wayward Freemason or Rosicrucian seeking readmission to his Order, but as a repentant confessor of venial sins, anxious for grace; his penalty—to examine his file in the Order's

67 See "Mein Glaube" (1931), *Gesammelte Schriften* (1957), Vol. 7, pp. 371–374.
68 For a convincing argument in support of this contention, see R. H. Farquharson, "The Identity and Significance of Leo in Hesse's *Morgenlandfahrt*," *Monatshefte* (Madison), 55 (1963), 122–128.

archive, that is to say, to peer into himself—is not punishment but penance; and this self-scrutiny, the double-bodied figurine, promises a spiritual rebirth. H.H. will become the priestly master-servant that Leo is.

MORE CONUNDRUMS

The remainder of Hesse's mystifying conundrums are just as personal in their content as the rest of his tale's engaging fantasies. The archive's reference for the Order's Charter (Chrysostomos, Zyklus V, Strophe 39, 8.) is almost as perplexing as Leo's catalogue association with the Egyptian god Ammon. Chrysostomos can only be St. John the patriarch of Constantinople whose eloquence earned him his epithet (golden-mouthed) and to whom Goldmund owed his name. With this allusion, Hesse added yet another admired worthy to his many other illustrious cofounders of the Order. The specific cycle and strophy references could have been sheer fancy, might be an oblique allusion to one of Chrysostomos's many treatises, or may even be a playful allusion to his mention in *Narziss und Goldmund*. It is even more tempting to believe that the numbers refer to the year 398, when Chrysostomos was made bishop of Constantinople, and to the five years before he was deposed. The three-leaf clover painted on a gold-plate that H.H. finds in Klee's archival slot is more facetious compliment than teasing mystery. The emblem accords with both the painter's name and his art. The blue sailboat and the multicolored fish on two of the leaves are the motifs in Klee's art that most appealed to Hesse. And the ingenuous ditty—As blue as snow/As Paul as Klee (*So blau wie Schnee/So Paul wie Klee*)—on the third leaf was Hesse's verbal burlesquing of the childlike quality characteristic of many of the painter's works. Klee owed his inclusion in the archive to his membership in the Order. But Hesse also knew that Klee was well represented in Basel's Art Museum, the Order's headquarters. No more than a slight acquaintance with Latin and biography is necessary to help decipher the abbreviated rubric on H.H.'s own catalogue card (Chattorum r. gest. XC. civ. Calv. infid. 49). Written freely and fully in the vernacular, this could have read: The history of the Hesses, in this case, of that Hesse who became a naturalized citizen of Calw in 1890, and who succumbed to apostasy vis-à-vis the Order during his Steppenwolf crisis of 1926, at the age of forty-nine.

COMMITMENT TO THE TRANSCENDENT

With his *Die Morgenlandfahrt*, Hesse left the review and the reverie of *Narziss und Goldmund* behind and returned to his immediate life situation and to new possibility. From *Demian* to *Narziss und Goldmund*, he was firmly committed to himself. Self-quest had become a major preoccupation with spirituality and sensuality, and a persistent concern with art and life, the artist and the nonartist, and time and timelessness. All had remained on an intimately personal level. Following Goldmund's tale, Hesse began to move from this primarily psychological to an ethical plane. His focus of interest shifted from self-concern to self-justification, and from adjustment to the self to adjustment to a community.

From *Demian* to *Narziss und Goldmund*, Hesse's protagonists swing radically between their spirituality and their sensuality—as did he. His later heroes are not spared this fluctuation, however they are no longer caught primarily between the mind and the body, but primarily between spiritual realms and the actual world, between ideality and reality—as was he. Unlike that of their predecessors, theirs is not an agony rooted in psychology, but is primarily existential and artistic anguish for H.H. and an ethical quandary for Knecht. H.H.'s anguish and Knecht's quandary were Hesse's, and his self-justifying responses to these changing circumstances became theirs. To counter his existential and artistic anguish of the late twenties and early thirties, Hesse opted for a sequestered aestheticism, and to resolve his subsequent ethical quandary, he argued an active commitment to society. Aestheticism is as natural an inclination for H.H. and as inevitable a first decision for Knecht as it was for Hesse, and understandably so. Both are cut from the same cloth as their author, belong to the Haller-Narziss lineage, to the artists and intellectuals who gladly forswear an imperfect physical world for the ethereal realm of timeless art and thought. This lineage's alienation from actuality increases from *Der Steppenwolf* to *Narziss und Goldmund*, peaks in *Die Morgenlandfahrt*, then lingers on in *Das Glasperlenspiel* until Knecht envisages a new and better possibility. Haller's eyes are fixed on a transcendent eternity but he is compelled to tolerate the world proper and to live among his lesser fellow humans. In his monastic retreat, Narziss manages to remove himself a little more than Haller from the profane world, and a little closer to immortality. H.H. has least to do with the world of ordinary human beings; he is actually privileged to consort with the Immortals in their autonomous, timeless, and spaceless kingdom of the spirit. Haller collars but does not tame his troublesome animality, and chokes in his chosen isolation. Narziss controls life's urges adeptly, and can satisfy his social needs in the narrow confines of his monastery. H.H. is able to sublimate successfully, and in his very withdrawal finds both an expansive and congenial community of kindred minds. Stifled sensuality unsettles Haller, and his loss of faith in himself, his ideals, and in his work derives from this psychological plight. Narziss's predicament is similar, but he only teeters where Haller falls. H.H.'s corresponding loss of faith and consequent despair obtain from the awful recognition that life is beyond understanding and justification, and that virtue, justice, and reason are of little consequence in human affairs. A brief sojourn in the realm of the senses is needed to restore Haller's emotional balance and his lost faith. Narziss's tenuous homoerotic relationship with Goldmund is enough both to shake him and to help him retain his balance and his faith. H.H. finds succor in private self-scrutiny, in an intense soul-searching that ends in a recognition that the arrogant, petulant, impious, and inordinately egocentric individualist that he has been, must become a humble, reverent Leo, a master-servant selflessly dedicated to the community of art and thought, if he is to make life possible and himself acceptable. It is in this consecration to the transcendent, as a servant to art, thought, and fancy, and not to man, that H.H. finds his self-justification and his hope for a future.

Hesse's renascent aestheticism, a blending of Lauscher's romanticism and of Haller's Platonism, was complete. To make his aestheticism palatable, Lauscher had associated it with religion. H.H.'s aestheticism, accorded a priestly hierarchy, garbed in sacral robes, and sanctified by piety, *is* a religion. With *Die Morgenlandfahrt*, life's vexing and fascinating polarities suddenly vanished, almost as though they had never existed for Hesse. Spirituality ceased even to acknowledge sensuality, art became life, artist left citizen in his wake, and timelessness washed time away. Demian's herd, Siddhartha's child-adults, and Haller's philistines, and the world of material things, petty concerns, and seductive distractions were no more. The voluptuous Teresinas, Kamalas, Marias, and Goldmund's succession of sexual partners, suddenly yielded to ethereal princesses, to fairies fair, and moonlit water nymphs. And Goldmund's magnanimous Magna Mater was supplanted by H.H.'s pristine Order. The actual world is no longer another possibility for H.H., but only a void into which he falls when his faith in his transcendent world wavers. His dilemma is not decision but belief. In this sense, he is back where Hesse was when he wrote his *Eine Stunde hinter Mitternacht*. The scintillating polyphony that had become characteristic of Hesse's tales reverted temporarily to the blander monophony of his earliest vignettes.

THE ULTIMATE FAILURE OF ART

H.H.'s problems revolve around the Order from which he defects and which he is anxious to rejoin, relate to life whose inscrutability, irrationality, and inhumanity have left him in metaphysical despair, and derive immediately from his inability to give satisfactory artistic expression to his past association with the Order. Art was for Hesse both calling and concern. All revolved about it. His works feature the artist's person, bare his psychology, and weigh his lot, scrutinize the creative process, and ponder art's questionable relationship with life. Art was Hesse's refuge, bane, bliss, obligation, and it was also a psychological necessity. It was a passion that deprived and rewarded, and was alternately damned and extolled.

As long as Hesse remained within the pale of tradition, he never seriously questioned the adequacy of inherited modes of narration or the efficacy of language. His literary quarrel with the past began in earnest with *Demian* and its ideological altercation with society. Emancipation from traditional narrative structures and techniques was abrupt and fairly complete, but language itself remained a source of annoyance and grievance for years to come. In *Sprache* (1917), language is indicted and the poet's lot is bemoaned. Musicians and painters are envied for their tones and colors, for their languages, which are both exclusive and universal. Writers are left with words, with society's crude, confining, and stereotyped medium of communication. The inherent shortcomings of language became a recurrent theme. For Klein, words only complicate and confuse, Klingsor is suspicious of verbal exchange, Siddhartha argues the pitfall and ultimate uselessness of words, *Kurgast* laments the inadequacy of language vis-à-vis life's polarities, and *Die Nürnberger Reise* poses the inappropriateness of traditional beautiful literary language for modern man's experiences. In his long battle with words, Hesse never turned his back upon tradition, never created an idiosyncratic idiom in the manner of a James Joyce or a Hans Arp, but he did evolve a personal use of words for life's ineffable interludes, those mystical moments of grace when all is a harmonious, meaningful oneness. Where everyday use of language could not begin to depict these spells of illumination, a dramatic free association of highly emotive and evocative images, sounds, and thoughts might at least suggest the nature of this rare experience. All the epiphanies of Hesse's post–*Demian* protagonists were rendered in this characteristic manner.

Nor could language adapted to the everyday physical world

suffice to depict Hesse's transcendent world. Like man's mystical experiences, his beliefs and his dreams—and these were life's ultimate truths and realities—were beyond actual depiction. They could at best only find symbolic expression, and this in fairy tale or poetic fantasy. Hesse had had recourse to the former in his early *Lulu*, he explored the possibilities of the latter in *Die Morgenlandfahrt*. Unlike Lauscher, H.H. is not prepared to leave his readers to their own devices. His endeavor in *Die Morgenlandfahrt* is made explicit by repeated present-tense asides and by a most unusual intermediate inclusion (the Lukas chapter), all tantamount to presenting a disquisition on the ultimate impossibility of recounting his association with a transcendent world while doggedly engaged in doing just that. To depict the transcendent is to try to narrate the past truthfully, without documentation, with faulty memory, and with little faith. H.H.'s commentary on his attempted memoirs was Hesse's acknowledgment of the ultimate failure of the writer's craft. Man's profoundest and most treasured experiences are beyond words, and his transcendent world of belief and dream is beyond even symbolic narration. And all this was by implication Hesse's wider acknowledgment of the ultimate failure of all art.[69]

H.H.'s lot is the artist's threefold agony: he experiences the tragedy of life's imperfection, that of man's frail faith, and that of art's inadequacy. Triple afflication notwithstanding, he is left unbroken in spirit. Suffering is for him the benign therapeutic experience it is for most of Hesse's protagonists. He emerges from his valley of the shadows with faith regained: not faith in life, but in his kingdom of the spirit. A novice repairs to the Order's ethereal realm, prepared to become a Superior, a master-servant à la Leo. His homage will again be to the kingdom of the spirit and not to the community of man, and the pious nurturing of art and thought will again be his service. H.H.'s recollection of Leo's remark about anaemic authors and their robust creations, while observing Leo's half of the double-bodied figurine gradually absorb his own representation, suggests that he will now not only become his master-servant better self, but will also resume his writing. Despite its ultimate failure, writing had and will continue to lend meaning to H.H.'s life. The service and sacrifice demanded by his art will also assure him some degree of immortality. He will vanish but his characters will live on.

69 Hesse elaborates on this idea in a letter of September 1932. See *Briefe* (1964), pp. 72–74.

Peter Camenzind (1903) espouses the love and service exemplified by St. Francis of Assisi. A long hiatus followed. *Siddhartha* (1922) ends his life in love and service to mankind. These were Hesse's ideals, not his realities. Pietism had left him incapable of accepting man and the world for the imperfect actualities they are. To cherish and to nurture the ideal was more in accord with his being than to love and to serve the real. Hesse was much less a Siddhartha given to life than a Haller determined to join the Immortals, a Narziss devoted to the spirit, and an H.H. committed to his transcendent world. With this lineage and in his emerging quest for a community with which he could identify and which he could serve, Hesse moved from Siddhartha's humanity to an aestheticism of the elect. The Order was Hesse's latest ideal transformation of the world, and Leo was his latest ideal self. H.H.'s none too surprising concluding doubts about his situation (the first paragraph of the penultimate chapter) indicate that he himself is not entirely comfortable with his latest adjustment to life. *Das Glasperlenspiel* was soon to show that this rejuvenated aestheticism did not sit well with Hesse either.

NARRATIVE EXPERIMENT

H.H.'s is his story, but it is also that of man and of art, and is told in the appropriate distilled and timeless manner of symbol and concept. In *Klingsors letzter Sommer*, Hesse had fantasized actuality playfully and thoroughly. In *Die Morgenlandfahrt*, he fantasized it as playfully and as thoroughly, more extensively, and to new advantage. But for introductory comment, recollected visits with Lukas, and running asides, the tale is pure protracted symbol, strongly reminiscent of Hesse's mythic *Märchen*. The Order, its trek, and its solemn conclave, like the wondrous star in *Merkwürdige Nachricht von einem andern Stern* (1915), symbolizes an ideal world, and H.H.'s own eastward peregrination, like Anselm's quest for his lost dream (*Iris*, 1917–1918), reflects man's timeless aspiration for this heaven on earth, and traces his recurrent three-stage mythic path from belief, innocence, and harmony, to doubt and sin, despair and contrition, to grace, its redemption, and paradise regained. The story of art is introduced in H.H.'s explanatory preamble, pursued in his conversation with Lukas, gradually evolves into a theory in his asides, and ultimately becomes part of the very tale responsible for broaching the theme. H.H. literally takes his reader into his workshop, exposes him to a work of art in its making, involves him in the organizational problems of the artist, and informs him of the ultimate inadequacy of narrative art. It was this exploitation of the problems and shortcomings of narration, and not fantasized autobiography or extended metaphor that marked Hesse's return to narrative experiment.

Hesse's experiment resulted in a novel bi-level narrative and temporal structure. He tells not one, but both an outer and an inner tale: that of the past Eastern Wayfarer, and that of H.H. the present defector and writer. Both the narrated past (outer story) and the narrating present (inner story) extend over but a few months, and are separated by a ten-year interval that is only alluded to. Chapters I and II deal primarily with the wayfarer, Chapter III with the troubled writer, Chapter IV with the anxious defector, and in Chapter V writer and defector become wayfarer again, and past outer story and present inner tale converge, become one, and terminate in the inconclusiveness typical of most of Hesse's prose. Both of these segments are characteristically unnarrative. As usual, Hesse was interested in depiction and argument and not simple recounting. Befitting myth, the Order's structure is skeletal, its oaths are vague, its Charter remains a mystery, and its members are an etherealized mélange of fable, history, and actuality. Its journey's geography also knows no space, events and situations are divorced from time, landscape has no characterizing contours, and place names are pure fancy or mere concepts. Little is visible enough to confine in time and space, and all narrative is too fragmentized to detract from Hesse's attempted depiction of his incorporeal and timeless transcendent world. Narrative and description were permitted to detract just as little from the art argument of the inner story as they were from the ideal of the outer. Recounting is limited to H.H.'s two brief visits to Lukas and his reencounter with Leo, the urban setting is left nameless and nondescript, churches, municipal buildings, apartments, streets, and parks are only casual reference points, and Lukas, H.H., and Leo are all less physical-psychological realities than major possibilities vis-à-vis an elusive ideal: the skeptic, the vacillating dreamer, and the believer.

In its characteristic manner, Hesse's mode of expression varies with changing situation. H.H.'s preludial comment is cast in the appropriate manner of causerie. His long, fumbling, additive sentences, plentiful interjections, casual repetitions, and insistent rhetorical questions are an excellent approximation of a preliminary collecting of thought. The fantasia that follows fluctuates brilliantly between poetic narrative thoroughly fragmented by prolonged contorted and dangling past-tense comment and brief present-tense inner-story asides, highly evocative romantic description, and the agitated recollection of Leo's disappearance and the resultant general consternation. With H.H.'s narrative impasse and his descent from the ideal to the real, mode of expression shifts to an appropriately lower key. In this diary intermezzo that succeeds his glittering fantasia, the problems of art are pondered in anxious and protracted direct inner monologue and in unadorned dialogue, and immediate sparse events are less storytelling than curt and down-to-earth simple-sentence diary recording. H.H.'s readmission to the Order and the merging of outer and inner tales occasion a corresponding converging of the poetry of his recollection and the realism of his diary.

In each of these situations, Hesse also carefully maintained his usual intimate relationship between inner state and the flow and rhythm of his language. The agitation of elation, depression, and of exciting anticipation find their characteristic expression in the alternating rapid and slow flow and frantically irregular rhythm of H.H.'s mode of recounting and ruminating: a prose comprising Hesse's customary strings of longer and shorter sentences, clauses, and phrases, laced with questions, exclamations, and parenthetical additions, and characterized by anxious repetitions, tense word accumulations, and by emphatic anaphora and nervous parataxis. The slower flow and more even rhythm of less studied expression are reserved as usual for the protagonist's moments of relative equanimity. Like all Hesse's major tales, *Die Morgenlandfahrt* was something old and something new in both substance and form, and substance, as always, found its accordant form.

OTHER PROSE WORKS AND POETRY

There is no doubt that Hesse's first twelve years in Montagnola represent the golden age of his art. His literary output now peaked in volume and variety, novelty and brilliance, and immediacy and urgency. Family problems, financial difficulties, poor health, political tensions, and a dwindling following of readers were actually more stimulating than distracting. He produced a generous flow of major tales, diverse shorter prose works, and poetry, wrote many reviews, and continued to pursue his editorial interests. Some 125 literary essays and short stories, diary fragments and autobiographical snippets, memorials and recollections, nature sketches and Hesse's usual travel reports were published in periodicals and newspapers throughout German-speaking Europe; three quarters of this mélange was included in his collections of miscellany, the remaining items have not yet appeared in any book publications. During these years, Hesse left few fragments,[70] and most of what he wrote eventually found its way into print. Hesse's new life style occasioned as great a change in his poetry as in his prose. Tradition and convention yielded to originality and individuality. Where sentiment, mood, and musicality had once prevailed, reflection, dramatic situation, and cacophony now became characteristic. Hesse's plaintive lyrics in simple traditional poetic form gave way to restive prose verse, irregular in structure, blunt in expression, and often brutal in raw sentiment. Some 167 poems were written during this period.[71]

HESSE AS AN EDITOR AND REVIEWER

Once settled in Montagnola, Hesse was quick to resume his diverse editorial interests. Editing was still the financial necessity, the cultural obligation, and the healthy diversion it had always been for him, and his involvements again came in successive waves. He was coeditor of *Vivos Voco* from October 1919 to December 1921, then turned his attention to books. He edited *Merkwürdige Geschichten* (six volumes of German, Italian, Japanese, and French tales) from 1922 to 1924, and *Merkwürdige Geschichten und Menschen* (six volumes devoted to individual German writers and to Oriental and Italian tales) from 1925 to 1926, and from the autumn of 1924 to the spring of 1925 he planned an open-ended edition of German literary works and autobiographies of the period 1750 to 1850. He was assisted in this latter venture by his nephew Carlo Isenberg. This new project almost immediately became Hesse's major editorial undertaking. His initially planned six to seven volumes (*Das klassische Jahrhundert deutschen Geistes 1750–1850*) gave way to a twelve-volume collection (*Deutscher Geist 1750–1850*) to be supplemented, if successful, first by a ten-

70 Only twenty brief introductions written in 1925 for an ambitious editorial project that never materialized (see Manuscripts X:424), six one- to four-page prose fragments (see Manuscripts X:154, 175, 186, 202, 397, 427b), a truncated twenty-one-page account of his life in Ticino (see Manuscripts X:427c), seven bits of diary (see Manuscripts X:426/m–426/r), and a fascinating forty-two-page recounting of some of his dreams from May 1919 to December 1920 (see Manuscripts X-A:5a/4) were never published.

71 Most of these were included in *Ausgewählte Gedichte* (1921), *Krisis* (1928), and *Trost der Nacht* (1929); fourteen have yet to be published.

volume series of anthologies and then by an eight-volume series devoted to individual authors.[72] Unfortunately all came to naught. Hesse's prospective publisher, the *Deutsche Verlags-Anstalt* of Stuttgart, balked when it learned that he would at the same time continue to edit his *Merkwürdige Geschichten und Menschen* for the S. Fischer Verlag. Although he had already written introductions for most of his planned volumes, Hesse chose not to seek another publisher. Not a single volume was ever published. With the collapse of his grand plan, he lost all interest in further editorial work.

Hesse's activities as a reviewer were only briefly interrupted when he left Bern for Montagnola. By the end of his hectic summer of 1919 he had again become an avid reader and had resumed his reviewing with gusto. More reviews were written during the next five years than had been in either Gaienhofen or Bern, and Hesse's interests continued to range freely from world literature to the fine arts and history, and from religion to philosophy and psychology. Hesse's greatest concentration of reviews appeared in *Vivos Voco* from October 1919 to April 1924. He contributed heavily to the *National-Zeitung* (Basel) from 1920 on, to *Wissen und Leben* from 1920 to 1922, and many other reviews were sent sporadically to more than a dozen other periodicals and newspapers. His most impressive items continued to be published by the *Neue Rundschau*.

72 See Manuscripts X:424.

7

Social Commitment

TROUBLED WITHDRAWAL

Hesse chanced to meet Ninon Dolbin while in Zürich in the winter of 1926. Their immediate friendship became a close relationship when he returned to Zürich the following winter, and that summer Ninon joined Hesse in Montagnola. Her summer's visit became an extended stay. When it seemed apparent with the passing years that their association was likely to be a lasting one, both decided that quarters more suitable and more permanent than the Casa Camuzzi were in order. Hesse's dream of another house and garden all his own would probably have remained unrealized but for the generosity of his patron-friend Hans C. Bodmer. An appropriately large and comfortable house was built on a wooded hillside not more than a stone's throw from the Casa Camuzzi and was placed at his disposal for the duration of his life. Hesse and Ninon moved into their impressive Casa Bodmer in August 1931. They were married that November.

Hesse's third and last marriage was remarkably successful. It afforded him all the security and contentment that he had sought but had failed to find in either of his previous ventures. This success was due in large part to the persistent efforts of two reasonably compatible people, mature enough to appreciate their differences, to cultivate their common interests and to curb their expectations. A turbulent life had left Hesse somewhat mellowed. He was still very much an outsider, but he was now ready and more able to come to terms with life. Ninon, for her part, was both attractive and intelligent. Unlike her predecessors, she appreciated Hesse's person no less than she revered his art. She was enough of an intellectual to share his diverse

The Casa Bodmer in Montagnola. Hesse lived here from 1931 until his death.

View from the Casa Bodmer.

religious, philosophical, and aesthetic interests, and strong enough to accommodate his hypochondria and his still acerbic impatience. She also managed to structure her life around Hesse's without sacrificing her own independence or foregoing her own interests in art history and folklore. She quickly became an indispensable companion, aid, and buffer.[1]

Hesse's life now assumed a slower flow and a more even rhythm. It became home-centered and revolved almost ritually around his writing, reading, correspondence, music, painting, and gardening. Mornings and afternoons were given to gardening, watercolors, and letters, and evenings were reserved for books, music, and writing. Before the First World War, Hesse had been an inveterate and restless traveler. He had remained restless during the twenties, but travel had gradually lost its old fascination. Once settled in his new home, his restlessness slowly abated, and trips became more ordeal than pleasure. He had made his last reading tour to Swabia in the autumn of 1929, and had spent his last winter in Zürich in 1931. Now, but for his continued late-autumn health trips to Baden, appointments with an eye specialist in Munich (January 1934) and Bad Eilsen (August 1936), sporadic and brief visits with friends in Zürich and Bremgarten bei Bern, and infrequent ski holidays in Engadin, Hesse confined himself to Montagnola and its environs. This was less a deliberate withdrawal from the world than a new adjustment to it.

Thanks to his changing inclinations, to the improved circumstances of his life, and to the chance of politics, a perennial guest again became a host. Life began to converge upon Hesse: relatives and friends became frequent visitors, devotees found their way to Montagnola in increasing numbers, and with Adolf Hitler's rise to power, Hesse was soon host and benefactor to a steady flow of political refugees. The first of these artists and intellectuals appeared in 1933 and 1934, a wave of Austrians followed in 1938 and 1939, and stray victims of the times continued to crop up in Montagnola throughout the war. This commitment, an unusually extensive correspondence with troubled friends and strangers, his brother Hans's suicide in 1935, and his own continued poor health, left Hesse almost

1 Unlike Ruth Wenger, Ninon appears to have been the subject of but one of Hesse's love poems (see Poetry V-D:87). Only three books (see Books and Pamphlets II:43/A, 65, 114) and two printed poems were dedicated to her (see Poetry V-D:600, 618), and just four amusing little lyrics were written for her (see Poetry V-D:544, 1114, 1146, 1170). Hesse apparently preferred to express his attachment to Ninon in a rich correspondence. Their letters and postcards are housed in the Hesse-Nachlass, Marbach a.N. (see Letters VIII-C:34, 34b; VIII-F:2).

Thomas Mann and Hermann Hesse in Chantarella, 1932.

chronically exhausted and depressed. The Gottfried Keller Prize of 1936 did little to alleviate this depression. He lent moral support to the degree his own psychic well-being allowed, interceded when intercession might help, and gave financial aid to the extent his shrinking royalties from Germany permitted. Too little time, energy, and interest were left for his own art. It is not surprising that Hesse took fully twelve years to complete *Das Glasperlenspiel*. Indeed it is a wonder, under these circumstances, that the novel was written at all.

POLITICS AND THE NAZIS

Hesse's postwar public involvement with social and political matters ended with Harry Haller's disparagement of the ivory-tower intellectuality, social irresponsibility, and political immaturity of Germany's intelligentsia. His wartime censure of wayward artists and intellectuals, short-sighted politicians, and narrow-minded generals had been an exercise in futility, and his subsequent advocacy of social reform, pacifism, and internationalism had been much less than rewarding. There was every reason to believe that further direct sociopolitical involvement would not only avail just as little, but would also incur an official proscription of his books and preclude whatever benign influence he might still have in Germany. Hesse again became convinced that an artist might best divorce himself from politics, tend to his art, and nurture his humanitarian ideals. To do otherwise, whether for good or evil, was to prostitute his talents and to misuse his office, and to questionable benefit. Artists were not to govern but to serve, were not society's architects but its conscience, and not its reformers but guardians of its spiritual heritage.[2] For these reasons Hesse had only reluctantly accepted Romain Rolland's invitation to take part in the international conference of liberal intellectuals held in Lugano in 1922, and for these reasons he consistently refused to join or even to lend his name to organizations of whatever ilk, and carefully refrained from becoming publicly involved with Germany's National Socialism. He had permitted the First World War to divert him from his persuasion, and to no advantage to himself, his art, or to Germany. He was not about to allow the political mayhem of the thirties or even another war to affect his better judgment a second time.

2 See *Briefe* (1964), pp. 88, 107, 110, 114, 165 (letters of 1932, 1933, 1934, 1937). This is also Josef Knecht's conception of the Castalian's place in the human community (see *Gesammelte Schriften* [1957], Vol. 6, pp. 465–466).

Careful avoidance of renewed embroilment in political and social causes, however, never became apathy or philosophical neutrality. Hesse always remained in close touch with current events, became thoroughly versed in the major European political ideologies, and continued, in his many private letters of the thirties and of the Second World War, to give unconcerned and candid expression to his decided political views: the Weimar Republic was neither new enough nor republic enough, its courts were corrupt, its officials irresponsibly blasé, its people politically infantile, and its days numbered; Germany was likely to succumb to bloody civil strife and ultimately to be bolshevized; Hitler was a mad demagogue, his National Socialism a political inanity, and all could only lead to another war.[3] But that Germany fell to the Nazis and not to the Communists, Hesse's assessments and predictions were all too correct.

Hesse's political posture served its purpose. Some readers, a few friends, and a number of close relatives took private issue with him for his public silence or for his antipathy to things German, but official Germany left him well enough alone. His poems, recollections, and stories continued to appear in many of Germany's better newspapers and literary journals, his old and new books continued to be published, and even a few literary critics and historians continued to take note of him. But for his book reviews, Hesse might not again have become a *cause célèbre*. When it became apparent that the swelling number of party-line literary critics was intent upon according favor only to those writers in sympathy with its Nazi ideology, and bent upon discrediting all others in a campaign of defamation or a conspiracy of silence, Hesse began deliberately to call attention to Catholic and Protestant authors in bad standing, and to feature German-writing Jews. The press reacted immediately. Reviews, which had until 1933 enjoyed welcome in both newspapers and periodicals throughout Germany, were suddenly anathema. By the end of 1935, all but the *Neue Rundschau* had ceased to carry them.

Hesse's continued reviews in the *Neue Rundschau* either chanced to escape the attention of potential detractors, or were noticed but deliberately ignored since it was obviously only a matter of time before the S. Fischer Verlag, like all other Jewish publishing houses, would have to sell out or be liquidated.[4] But when Hesse became associated

3 See *Briefe* (1964), pp. 57, 88, 110 (letters of 1931, 1932, 1933).
4 S. Fischer died in the autumn of 1934. In December 1935 his heirs were ordered by the Ministry of Propaganda to relinquish their ownership and the direction of the S. Fischer Verlag. The publishing house was sold to a consortium in December 1936.

Hermann Hesse in his garden, 1935.

with Sweden's *Bonniers Litterära Magasin* and began to contribute regular surveys of contemporary German literature in which he continued to feature those writers who had become silenced undesirables,[5] he was viciously assailed by *Die Neue Literatur* (Leipzig), the very prominent and thoroughly nazified journal edited by Will Vesper, writer, critic, and rabid nationalist. The first of Hesse's Swedish articles (March 1935) went unnoticed. The second (September 1935) was immediately countered by the rankest of calumny. Lily Biermer, a minor literary functionary, insisted vehemently and with full editorial sanction that a grossly distorted picture of German literature was being spread abroad, that good Aryan writers were being belittled or totally neglected while such questionable Germans as Thomas Mann, such Catholics as Gertrud von Le Fort, and particularly such odious Jews as Franz Kafka, Alfred Polgar, Ernst Bloch, and Stefan Zweig were being extolled. Hesse was unhesitantly branded a blatant Jew-lover whose probity was to be questioned and whose treachery was to be denounced:

> He is reviling all of our new German literature. . . . He acts as though Germany, new Germany, had no writers. . . . He is betraying contemporary German literature to Germany's enemies and to the Jews. . . . The German writer Hermann Hesse is taking over the traitorous role of Jewish literary criticism of yesterday. To oblige the Jews and the bolsheviks of culture he is helping to spread notions abroad that are false and damaging to his fatherland.[6]

Hesse took righteous issue with this slander in a short letter written on December 3 and published in *Die Neue Literatur* in January 1936: he was not a German national and could therefore not be considered a traitor, regardless of his literary opinions; furthermore, his was a service to and not a betrayal of the cause of German literature abroad. Neither retraction nor correction followed. Protest served only to invite caustic recrimination. An appended and anonymous editorial response immediately stamped him a treacherous emigrant hiding behind his newly purchased Swiss nationality.[7] Although

---

Peter Suhrkamp, sole director of the house since January 1936, continued to serve in that capacity until he was taken into custody by the Gestapo in the spring of 1944.

5 The original German versions were not published until 1965: *Neue Deutsche Bücher. Literaturberichte für Bonniers Litterära Magasin: 1935–1936*, ed. B. Zeller (Marbach a.N.: Schiller-Nationalmuseum, 1965), 160 pp.

6 *Die Neue Literatur*, 36 (November 1935), 686.

7 *Die Neue Literatur*, 37 (January 1936), 57–58.

Hesse now lapsed into deliberate silence and no one in Germany cared or dared to come to his public defense, Vesper himself, insisting that he was being slurred by Hesse in a circular letter, chose to continue Biermer's fanatical exposé.[8] In the April issue of *Die Neue Literatur*, he not only maintained the veracity of her accusations, but reminded his readers maliciously of Hesse's past animosity toward Germany, and contended that any German writer intent upon belying or belittling German literary achievement, as was Hesse, could justly be branded a traitor, regardless of his immediate nationality. In his concluding assessment of the case, Vesper argued his usual anti-Semitism. Hesse was a classical example of Jewry's maleficent influence, of the insidious poisoning of the German soul by Freud's psychoanalysis:

> Once and for all it must be made public that Hesse is a classic example of how the Jew can poison the soul of the German people. For if at that time, when he took no delight in the war . . . he had not fallen into the clutches of the Jew Freud and his psychoanalysis, he would have remained the German writer whom we all loved so well. The warping of his soul can only be ascribed to this Jewish influence.[9]

Vesper was obviously rankled by Hesse's continued success in Germany, and was anxious to have him proscribed. His diatribe occasioned no quarrel, but it also did not elicit enough popular approval to induce the National Board of Arts and Culture (*Reichskulturkammer*) to take any adverse action. Indeed, Hesse was not only not put on the official blacklist, as Vesper had expected he would be, but thanks to his unbroken silence, he was actually exonerated a year later by a confidential circular (May 1937) addressed to all bookdealers by Josef Goebbels' own Ministry of Propaganda:

> In opposition to announcements of a different tenor, I am expressly affirming that, in agreement with the Minister of Education and Propaganda . . . the German writer Hermann Hesse is

8 In 1932, the editorial board of the newly established *Bonniers Litterära Magasin* invited Vesper to become a regular contributor of *Literaturbriefe*, dealing with current German literature. His very first contribution was declined for its racist bombast, and his contract was promptly terminated. Arthur Eloesser replaced Vesper, and was in turn succeeded by Hesse. Rumor suggested that Vesper's defamation of Hesse was a matter of professional jealousy, and Vesper ascribed this rumor to Hesse himself. See *Die Neue Literatur*, 37 (April 1936), 241; *Briefe* (1964), pp. 152–155; and also *Neue Deutsche Bücher* (Marbach a.N., 1965), p. 152.
9 *Die Neue Literatur*, 37 (April 1936), 242.

Hermann Hesse, 1937.

Hermann Hesse, 1934.

not to be subjected any more to attacks of any sort, and that accordingly, the dissemination of his works is not to be hampered.[10]

During the First World War, Hesse had publicly taken issue with both militarists and pacifists, and had himself been spared by neither. In the thirties, public silence notwithstanding, he again found himself caught between and assailed by opposing factions. While Nazis in Germany maligned him for promoting the cause of Jewry in literature, émigré German Jews in Paris took him to task for abetting National Socialism by writing for the *Frankfurter Zeitung*. For Germans such as Vesper, he was a Jew-loving renegade German, for refugee Jews such as Georg Bernhard, editor of the *Pariser Tageblatt*, he became a Nazi-sympathizing renegade émigré. Again Hesse discreetly avoided enmeshment in protracted and futile public self-defense. In his repudiation of Bernhard's slur, which had appeared in the *Pariser Tageblatt* on January 19, 1936, he simply informed his detractors on January 23 that he was neither a fellow émigré nor a correspondent for the *Frankfurter Zeitung*, had his demurral published in the *Neue Zürcher Zeitung* on January 26, and then again lapsed into deliberate silence. Bernhard did not even acknowledge this letter, let alone retract his remarks, and no émigré came to Hesse's defense. Angered by Vesper's smear campaign, and deeply hurt by the detraction of those for whose very cause he had exposed himself to racist slander, Hesse resolved to withdraw even more from controversy, and to devote himself exclusively to his writing. The last of his many review-articles in the *Neue Rundschau*, and the last of his six literary surveys in *Bonniers Litterära Magasin* were written in mid-1936 and appeared that September.

It was Hesse's termination of his controversial reviews and his continued political silence, and not newfound favor, that persuaded the Ministry of Propaganda to issue its surprising edict of grace. Thanks to this circular of May 1937, his books continued to be published relatively unhampered, to be displayed freely, and to sell well until the outbreak of the Second World War. Thereafter Hesse's applications for publication, like those of all other condoned undesirables, were screened closely by the National Board of Literature (*Reichsschrifttumskammer*). Many of his older and politically innocuous

10 Excerpt from *Vertrauliche Mitteilungen der Fachschaft Verlag*, Nr. 23 vom 27. Mai 1937.

works continued to be printed throughout the war,[11] but rationed paper was suddenly no longer available for his new books, and showcases gradually ceased to feature any of his publications. Compromise could have assured the continued reprinting of more of Hesse's works and even the publication of some of his new books, but he would not oblige. In 1934 he chose to discontinue *Eine Bibliothek der Weltliteratur* rather than to accede to his publisher's request that all Jewish authors be deleted from the text. *Narziss und Goldmund* was reprinted for the last time in 1941 because he refused to agree to the omission of its reference to anti-Semitism and pogroms. A new edition of *Trost der Nacht* appeared in 1942 only because Hesse decided to comply with official insistence that the names of the Jews and émigrés to whom many of its poems were dedicated be stricken; he obliged, but also countered by expunging all dedications to Gentiles.[12]

The period from 1931 to 1945 was for Hesse as much the lull after, as his years in Bern had been the lull before, the storm of the twenties. Creative energy had welled in the agony of self-quest and adversity. It flagged with domesticity and advancing years. What had been dramatic novelty and abundance, now became primarily recollection and collection. New books appeared at regular intervals but these consisted largely of earlier prose and poetry.[13] And when paper for Hesse's publications became scarce, Switzerland became his major outlet. During the war, the Büchergilde Gutenberg and Fretz & Wasmuth together published a dozen new editions, new collections, and new works,[14] among them the first two of the eventual twenty-three

11 E.g.: *Peter Camenzind*, 1942, 1944; *In der alten Sonne*, 1943, 1944; *Kleine Welt*, 1943; *Schön ist die Jugend*, 1940; *Knulp*, 1943, 1945; *Musik des Einsamen*, 1945; *Demian*, 1942; *Klingsors letzter Sommer*, 1944; *Siddhartha*, 1942; *Weg nach Innen*, 1940.

12 See *Briefe* (1964), pp. 132–133, 373–374.

13 The four stories of *Weg nach Innen* (Berlin: S. Fischer, 1931, 434 pp.) were written immediately following the First World War, each of the seven *Novellen* of *Kleine Welt* (Berlin: S. Fischer, 1933, 380 pp.) predates the war, all of the twenty-three tales of *Fabulierbuch* (Berlin: S. Fischer, 1935, 343 pp.) precede 1928, and only six of the ten reminiscences of *Gedenkblätter* (Berlin: S. Fischer, 1937, 272 pp.) belong to the thirties. All but the last two of the sixty-five poems of *Vom Baum des Lebens* (Leipzig: Insel-Verlag, 1934, 79 pp.), and eighteen of the fifty-six poems in *Neue Gedichte* (Berlin: S. Fischer, 1937, 98 pp.) were written before 1931.

14 *Stunden im Garten* (Wien: Bermann-Fischer, 1936), 63 pp., a ruminative idyl in hexameters, was a forerunner of Hesse's many books published abroad. The Büchergilde Gutenberg (Zürich) published new editions of *Der Steppenwolf* (1942), *Am Weg* (1943), *Narziss und Goldmund* (1944), *Siddhartha* (1945), *Knulp* (1945), and *Kleine Betrachtungen* (1942), a new collection of six essays, of which all but one predate 1931. Fretz &

volumes of the Swiss edition of collected works: *Die Gedichte* (1942), 607 of Hesse's 1300 or so extant poems, and *Das Glasperlenspiel* (1943), the last of his novels.[15]

DAS GLASPERLENSPIEL: CROWNING SYNTHESIS

GENESIS

Hesse's many letter references to *Das Glasperlenspiel* from the time of its inception to its completion are generally rather despairing and disparaging. Mood colored his remarks. Slow progress, poor health, and German politics left him chronically dejected, and depression more often than not induced him either to exaggerate his spells of infecundity or to slight his productivity. And thanks in part to indifference and in part to faulty memory, dates are for the most part vague and perplexing or precise and contradictory. Unfortunately too, the novel's bountiful manuscripts, manuscript fragments, plans, and memoranda are rarely dated, and even then, not always reliably. While this bewildering array of often conflicting source material virtually precludes a reconstructed genesis beyond controversy, it does make possible a reconstruction that is reasonably persuasive.

Das Glasperlenspiel had its shadowy beginning in early 1927.[16] Hesse had envisaged a literary undertaking in which a person experiences the great epochs of human history in several reincarnations, a type of biography that could be both individual and archetypal. It had then occurred to him that reincarnation could be a means whereby he might also give apt expression to the stable in life's flux: to the continuity of tradition and particularly of man's spiritual and intellectual

---

Wasmuth (Zürich) added new editions of *Eine Stunde hinter Mitternacht* (1941) and *Knulp* (1944), the early fragment *Berthold* (1942), and *Der Blütenzweig* (1945), old and new poems collected in the summer of 1945.

15 (Zürich: Fretz & Wasmuth, 1942), 448 pp.; (Zürich: Fretz & Wasmuth, 1943), 452 pp.

16 Reflecting upon the genesis of *Das Glasperlenspiel* in a letter of January 1955 to Rudolf Pannwitz, Hesse remarks: "During the years that lay between the first conception and the actual start of my work on the book, and when I still had two other tasks to finish, the story, later titled *Das Glasperlenspiel*, hovered before me in changing forms. . . . These were for me years of tolerable well-being after a serious crisis in life. . . ." *Briefe* (1964), p. 437. Since the two other tasks and the severe crisis could only refer to *Narziss und Goldmund*, *Die Morgenlandfahrt*, and to the difficult Steppenwolf period, and since this crisis was over by the end of 1926 and *Narziss und Goldmund* was begun in the middle of 1927, it is reasonable to conclude—assuming his memory served him well—that Hesse first began to think about his new novel early in 1927.

life.[17] Vague possibility did not become serious consideration until soon after Hesse had completed *Die Morgenlandfahrt* in April of 1931. On the reverse side of a letter from Gebr. Fretz A. G., Zürich (April 30, 1931), Hesse refers to or briefly outlines five biographies.[18] The undated document was actually drawn up in two stages. The initial plan in ink consists only of Biographies I, II, and IV. Tales III and V were added in pencil several days or at most a few weeks thereafter. Hesse's vision of 1927 was assuming shape. As yet, these biographies have no titles and their hero is known only as X. The first of them was obviously to become *Der Regenmacher*. The second is too briefly sketched even to permit conjecture. The third is vaguely suggestive of *Der Beichtvater*. The fourth might have become Hesse's own story and that of the twentieth century; perhaps the feuilleton age depicted in the novel's introduction is all that came of this intended reincarnation. The fifth tale is unmistakably that of Knecht and Castalia, the embryo of what was ultimately to become the novel

17 *Briefe* (1964), p. 436.
18 X is born 5 *times*.
  I Rainmaker with the mothers?
    Primitive life. Minor chief ends life voluntarily as sacrifice after a drought or pestilence or earthquake. Goes into the forest (of the souls), determined to allow himself to be born again as son of a son or grandson.
  II Rebirth as grandson or great-grandson, hero. Establishes world realm.
  III Christian, knight, monk.
  IV Rebirth as present X narrating the story.
    The saga of X.
    End in Mechanei. Will (wants) *not* to be born again. However, realm and earth do not therefore die out. No longer he, but other beings, demons will enter into the bodies of his grandsons; some day these foreign grandsons will perhaps create a new world youth.
  V Future. Even less actuality, even more fantasy. Highest culture: the bead game in many categories, embraces music, history, space, *mathematics*. X is now the highest of bead game players, plays the world symphony, varies it according to Plato, to Bach, to Mozart, expresses the most complicated of things in 10 lines of beads, is completely understood by three or four, half understood by 1000s.
    However, those suffering, and the cultureless have had their fill, they shatter everything (rightly so); they consider the bead players ridiculous, and hate them.
    The intellectuals have stopped writing books instead are only preoccupied with the bead game. They have likewise also renounced well-being and success, and live only for their beautiful lifelong game, very content and without wants.
    Description of the game: "not easy to render it visible, since it is very complicated, and has furthermore not yet been invented."
Autograph in the Hesse-Nachlass, Marbach a.N.

proper; the word Castalia does not yet appear and the hero is still without a name, but the bead game, its golden age, decline, and reasons for this decline are already clearly defined. The extended outline of this fifth biography also suggests that the bead players and their realm had already begun to thrust the other conjectured stories into the background.

Obviously this plan could only have been outlined after April 30, 1931. Its precise date of composition, however, is left to deduction. Scattered and imprecise references to his latest undertaking did not begin to appear in Hesse's correspondence until 1932.[19] According to these references, and keeping in mind April 30, 1931, Hesse's initial plan must have been put together some time between May and December of 1931, probably in mid-1931. The many later letter references to the genesis of the novel clearly confirm this.

Hesse's plan of 1931 had hardly been conceived before it started to change. When the bead-game tale moved into the foreground of his interest and in plan assumed unanticipated proportions, it gradually became divorced from the initial project and seemed destined to become a separate book publication. It is specifically to this tale and not to his multistory project that Hesse refers when he mentions a new book in letters of January and July 1933 to Gottfried Bermann and Thomas Mann.[20] A letter to Thomas Mann written toward the end of 1933 suggests that another change of mind must have brought the bead-game story and the other biographies together again sometime after July: "At the same time the conception of my two-year-old plan (the mathematical-musical mental game) is expanding into a conception of a work involving many volumes. . . ."[21] The bead-game tale seems now not only to have been reunited with the other biographies but structurally to have assumed a central, dominant position; the parenthetical remark equates the tale with the whole subject. From one of many biographies, the bead-game story was to become the structural backbone of Hesse's now envisaged novel, and the remaining tales were to become appendages. This departure from an original only loosely juxtaposed series of stories marks the emergence of the more complex structure of Hesse's finished novel.

The genesis of the introduction of *Das Glasperlenspiel* was no less

19 *Materialien zu Hermann Hesses* Das Glasperlenspiel (Frankfurt a.M.: Suhrkamp, 1973), Vol. 1, pp. 8, 55, 56–57, 60, 74; *Briefe* (1964), pp. 111, 129–130.
20 *Briefe* (1964), pp. 90, 105.
21 *Briefe* (1964), p. 111.

involved than this evolution of Hesse's literary plan of 1931. Four undated versions[22] and imprecise allusions left much to speculation. Hesse seems never to have made any explicit letter references to either the first or the second version. According to a letter sent to Helene Welti on April 3, 1932, and a diary-fragment of July 1933, the first of these was probably written in March and April of 1932, and the second by that July.[23] In a typescript note to his wife, January 19, 1933, Hesse mentions a third version completed that very day.[24] By mid-1933 Hesse was convinced that this politicized third version, somewhat expanded and revised in the meantime, would have to be rewritten.[25] For his intended more expansive treatment of Knecht and Castalia, and narratively to account for the hierarchic mode of expression he had begun playfully to affect, he appropriately substituted a Castalian chronicler with access to the bead game's archives for his previous layman narrator dependent largely upon his memory. For their convincing incorporation into the novel proper, the satellite biographies became Knecht's own fortuitously preserved manuscripts. For a rejected defector to emerge a legendary hero, decadent Castalia of Knecht's day (*circa* 2200) had to become the chronicler's much later Castalia (2400), a province and order revitalized over the years by its Magister Ludi's parting admonitions and heroic example. And for both the sake of art and eventual publication, all direct criticism of Hitler's Germany was deleted or veiled. According to a memorandum of June 1934 this fourth version was completed in May and June of 1934.[26] Minor changes were made in the summer of 1934, and the work was mailed to the *Neue Rundschau* on September 8.

Like that of the introduction, the genesis of the biographies is

22 *Das Glasperlenspiel*, 29. April 1942. Autograph in the Bodmer-Hesse-Collection, now housed in the Schiller-Nationalmuseum, Marbach a.N. This includes the unpublished first version of the introduction. *Versuch einer Geschichte des Glasperlenspiels. II. Fassung.* Unpublished typescript, 15 pp. *Das Glasperlenspiel: Versuch einer allgemeinverständlichen Einführung in seine Geschichte.* Unpublished third-version typescript, 23 pp. *Das Glasperlenspiel: Versuch einer allgemeinverständlichen Einführung in seine Geschichte.* Published fourth-version typescript, 29 pp. The three typescripts are in the Hesse-Nachlass, Marbach a.N.

23 *Materialien zu Hermann Hesses* Das Glasperlenspiel (1973), Vol. 1, pp. 55, 64.

24 Unpublished note in the Hesse-Nachlass, Marbach a.N.

25 See diary fragment of July 1933, *Materialien zu Hermann Hesse* Das Glasperlenspiel (1973), Vol. 1, p. 65.

26 "The introduction that I am hereby handing over as a curiosity for keeping was written three times. . . . Since this introduction could not be printed in Germany today, I wrote a fourth, partly altered version in May and June." Montagnola, June 1934. Typescript memorandum in the Hesse-Nachlass, Marbach a.N.

hidden behind a paucity of information. Little in this regard can be said about *Der Regenmacher* that is not conjecture. It may be inferred from Hesse's plan of mid-1931 that he had already given considerable thought to his biography, but it was probably not written until the second half of 1933. Finishing touches may not have been put to it until January and February 1934. The story was sent to the *Neue Rundschau* on February 20, 1934.

Having completed or almost completed *Der Regenmacher* by late 1933, Hesse began to steep himself in German Pietism of the eighteenth century. He had apparently decided to add a sixth possibility to his original list of five biographies. A theologian of the eighteenth century was now to become one of his protagonist's later reincarnations. Most of Hesse's frequent letter references to this tale from the end of 1933 to the beginning of 1935 suggest much labor and little progress. Even as late as the autumn of 1934 no mention is made of any emerging manuscript. The Castalian chronicler's account (see *Studienjahre*) of the eighteenth-century biography that Knecht had undertaken but had never carried out was Hesse's accurate recollection of his own futile effort to make art of history. Like Knecht, Hesse had studied the lives of Johann Albrecht Bengel, Friedrich Oetinger, and Nikolaus Ludwig von Zinzendorf, and had familiarized himself with liturgy, hymnals, and church government of the eighteenth century. He too had learned a great deal, and not least, that the eighteenth century was too immediate and too well documented to be rendered in a manner accordant with the legendary nature of the other biographies. But for its actual reference to a manuscript, Hesse's account of his eighteenth-century tale in a letter written to Rudolf Pannwitz in January 1955 differs little from his chronicler's remarks.[27] Not one but two untitled and undated autograph fragments were eventually found among Hesse's collected papers.[28] They were probably written during the closing months of 1934 and the first month or two of 1935. What was to have become the last of Knecht's historical sequence of biographies was finally published as "Der vierte Lebenslauf" in *Prosa aus dem Nachlass* (1965).

For whatever reasons, Hesse was much more secretive about his successful biographies than about his eighteenth-century failure. The history of *Der Beichtvater* is as obscure as that of *Der Regenmacher*. The

---

27 See *Briefe* (1964), p. 436.

28 [*Manuscript 1*], 121 pp.; *Manuscript II des nicht vollendeten 4. Lebenslaufes*, 59 pp. Both of these autographs are in the Hesse-Nachlass, Marbach a.N.

tale may have had its origin in the third (*Christ, Ritter, Mönch*) of Hesse's five tentative projects of 1931. An undated autograph sketch on the reverse side of a letter sent to Hesse by the Verlag Ullstein on November 9, 1931, suggests that the story may already by the end of 1931 have been thought out in broad outline.[29] It is likely that this plan was then put aside in favor of the introduction, the Castalia-tale, *Der Regenmacher*, and the eighteenth-century biography, and that Hesse did not return to it until March or even April of 1936. His records indicate that *Der Beichtvater* was sent to the *Neue Rundschau* on May 28, 1936.

Even less is known about *Indischer Lebenslauf* than about *Der Beichtvater*. There is a remote possibility that it may in its genesis return to the second biography of 1931 (*Wiedergeburt als Enkel oder Urenkel, Held. Gründet Reich der Welt*). However, without any other evidence that Hesse was already dwelling on the tale at this early date or in the immediately following years, it can be assumed that he turned to it only after having finished *Der Beichtvater* in May 1936. A letter inquiring about Sanskrit names and written to Heinrich Zimmer on April 22, 1937, suggests that Hesse may not have begun to write it until February or even March of that year.[30] The tale was mailed to the *Neue Rundschau* on April 28, 1937.

According to an unpublished four-page autograph, probably written in early 1935 and eventually incorporated into the first three chapters of *Das Glasperlenspiel*, Hesse intended initially to assign these inner tales to Knecht's years in Waldzell.[31] Sometime after writing the fragment he crossed out the word biographies in its last paragraph and substituted the word poems. The stories were then shifted to the chapter *Studienjahre*. This change of words was likely to have been made only shortly before Hesse decided to add poems to his protagonist's literary residue, and this took place in the spring of 1935 before "Die Gedichte des jungen Josef Knecht" were submitted to *Corona* on May 21.

It was not until after he was done with his satellite biographies that Hesse finally returned to his bead-game tale. From the first version of its introduction (March and April 1932) to the actual writing of the first chapter of Knecht's biography (January 1938) simple contour

29 *Zwei Heilige (eventuell als Schluss eines Knechtlebens?)*. In the Hesse-Nachlass, Marbach a.N.

30 *Materialien zu Hermann Hesses* Das Glasperlenspiel (1973), Vol. 1, p. 176.

31 "Es war ihm nicht unbekannt, dass im Lauf der 5 jährigen Waldzeller Studienzeit. . . ." In the Hesse-Nachlass, Marbach a.N.

must have become rich texture. Having written an introduction, Hesse turned almost immediately to the tale itself. But desire quickly became aversion, and for the next year or so he was able to do little more than complain of an utter inability to write. Of his earliest efforts, only a fragment titled *Schluss*, typed on the reverse of a letter sent to Hesse by the *Neue Rundschau* on June 22, 1931, seems to have survived.[32] The sketch clearly indicates that the rush of adverse current events had persuaded Hesse to politicize his initial plan for a bead-game tale and to adopt a more sympathetic attitude to his beadplayers and their institution. Reference is made to an important conversation between Knecht and his country's dictator, to Knecht's refusal to place himself and his fraternity at the disposal of the state, to his final game, and to his death. Knecht's last game reflects his undying conviction in the ultimate victory of the spirit over evil worldly powers. This direct incorporation of German politics suggests that the possibility outlined must have been courted and jotted down after Hesse had injected his sociopolitical comment into the introduction at the outset of 1933 and before his diary acknowledgment of July 1933 that current events had no place in his novel. The fragment was never implemented.

Having tried in vain for more than a year to get the bead-game tale under way, Hesse put it aside and for the next almost four years concentrated on its companion stories. All the while, however, the tale continued to brew and he continued sporadically to record the more significant of his evolving thoughts. The few notes still extant disclose possibilities courted then discarded or later developed and incorporated.[33] Only after more than six years of careful nursing did Hesse's meager plan of mid-1931 finally become a story ready to be told. The telling was to take almost four and a half more years of fitful inspiration.

32 Typescript in the Hesse-Nachlass, Marbach a.N.

33 A four-page untitled autograph (referred to two paragraphs back) would indicate that the first three chapters of the biography had already begun to assume form in early 1935. An untitled two-page autograph conversation between Knecht and Desingnori ("Designori: Mein Grossvater . . ."), *Die Verschleierten*, a handwritten paragraph reference to Knecht's sexual involvement with women, a two-paragraph autograph in defense of play ("Knecht erklärt u.a.: Spielen . . ."), and a one-paragraph typescript comment on culture ("Aus einer Schrift Jos. Knecht's . . .") point to *Waldzell, Studienjahre*, and to Knecht's encounter with Pater Jakobus. *Ende des Magister Musicae* outlines what was originally in store for Knecht's old patron. The one-page autograph mentions his resignation when old and no longer equal to his duties, his subsequent humble service as a school organist, and his death while attending Knecht's first annual game. The Magister's descent from office to organ probably derived from eighteenth-century

The first of these years was Hesse's most prolific, a barren 1939 gave him good cause for growing despair, persistence was rewarded by resurgent productivity in 1940, renewed creative vitality ebbed in 1941, and the first few months of 1942 were sheer toil. Chapters 1 to 5 were written in 1938. Then for an entire year Hesse was able to do little more than agonize. The next three chapters were added in 1940. Chapters 9 and 10 were written in the first half of 1941, and the last chapter from September of that year to April 29, 1942.

Only Chapter 11, *Das Rundschreiben*, was not written in expected sequence. Both Knecht's letter and Alexander's reply were probably composed in mid-1938,[34] and quite likely prompted by the writing of Knecht's debates with Designori earlier in 1938. A copy of Knecht's letter was sent to Peter Suhrkamp that September. An extremely negative response[35] coupled with his own doubts persuaded Hesse to forego separate publication and to put the chapter aside for future revision. The whole of Chapter 11—revised letters plus a connective introduction and conclusion—was probably not put together until shortly before Hesse turned to the last chapter in September of 1941. Suhrkamp's wish of February 19, 1943,[36] to see the latest version of

---

Pastor Knecht's exchange of pulpit for organ. If such is the case, this remnant may date back to early 1935 when Hesse became convinced that his eighteenth-century biography would remain an unusable fragment. An untitled one-paragraph autograph ("Es heisst vom Musikmeister . . .") reveals that Ferromonte was originally to succeed the Magister Musicae and not just to become his deputy, and also suggests that Hesse may initially have intended to tell more of his story than he eventually did. *Schluss*, a one-page typescript (1933), envisages a Knecht loyal unto death. The fourth version of the introduction (1934) promises an exemplary Knecht, but also tragic conflict with a hint of defection. *Ende des Ludi magister*, a one-page autograph, reflects Hesse's continued uncertainty about the final chapter of his protagonist's life. Reference is made to his last game and resignation, to his parting talks with his peers, and to his departure for the outside world, there to serve as a modest musician and never to be heard of again. Like *Ende des Magister Musicae* this possibility probably also had its origin in the discarded eighteenth-century biography and may also have been written as early as 1935. Precisely when Hesse decided in favor of Knecht the tutor and his icy death remains conjecture. That Knecht's legendary end is anticipated in the first chapter would insist that the conclusion projected in *Ende des Ludi magister* had become questionable by the beginning of 1938, and that the Tito affair and Knecht's unusual demise may already have been substituted. All of these fragments are in the Hesse-Nachlass, Marbach a.N.

34 *Das Schreiben des magister ludi an die Erziehungsbehörde*. First-version autograph, 36 pp. *Das Schreiben des Magister Ludi an die Erziehungsbehörde*. Typescript of printed version, 13 pp. *Die Erziehungsbehörde an den Mag. Ludi*, 2 pp. This first-version autograph is briefer than the printed version. Each of these items is in the Hesse-Nachlass, Marbach a.N.

35 Unpublished letter of October 7, 1938, in the Hesse-Nachlass, Marbach a.N.

36 See unpublished letter by Suhrkamp to Hesse in the Hesse-Nachlass, Marbach a.N.

Knecht's letter, suggests that Hesse continued to revise this troublesome segment long after his completion of the last chapter and almost
to the day his book finally went to press.

Like its prose, the poetry of *Das Glasperlenspiel* suggests fitful
brief spells of creativity bolstered by patience and purpose. Knecht's
thirteen poems were written from December 1932 to May 1941, and all
were published separately or in clusters from December 1934 to June
1942. But for *Stufen* (May 3, 1941) all were in print even before Hesse
had finished the first chapter of Knecht's life (January 1938). There is
no specific mention of poetry in the final version of the introduction
(July 1934). At the time, only three of Knecht's poems had been written, and it had probably not yet occurred to Hesse that these and
others could eventually become part of his novel. In 1935 three new
poems were added to the original three, and together they were submitted to *Corona* on May 21 as "Die Gedichte des jungen Josef
Knecht." A seventh poem was added to this cluster before it appeared in print in late 1935.[37] The already mentioned four-page autograph written during or even shortly before the spring of 1935 and
this cover title are the first indications that poems were also to be ascribed to Knecht.

The very arrangement of the poems in this cluster publication of
1935 is revealing. It is neither chronological, according to dates of
composition, nor random, but a deliberate sequence progressing, albeit haltingly, from lament, doubt, and despair to faith and dedication to the Castalian ideal. From this it may be concluded that Hesse's
carefully arranged sequence became a formative factor in the writing
of the chapter *Waldzell* in which these poems and their progression
from doubt to faith are commented on, or more likely, that *Waldzell*
was already at that time more or less clearly envisaged and determined this arrangement of the poems. When "Die Gedichte des
jungen Josef Knecht" were supplemented in Hesse's *Neue Gedichte*
(1937) by four poems, and in the publication of the novel (1943) by two
more, the additions were not simply appended chronologically to the
original sequence but carefully inserted, disturbing the original progression from doubt to faith as little as possible.

Suhrkamp applied to the National Board of Literature (*Reichsschrifttumskammer*) for permission to publish *Das Glasperlenspiel* in

---

37 *Corona*, 5, iv (1935), 390–393. The poems were arranged as follows: *Klage*,
January 1934; *Doch heimlich dürsten wir* . . . , December 1932; *Buchstaben*, February 1935;
Zu einer Toccata von Bach, May 10, 1935; *Dienst*, April 1935; *Nach dem Lesen in der Summa
contra Gentiles*, June 9, 1935; *Das Glasperlenspiel*, August 1, 1933.

February 1942. The work was not yet finished, but the end was in sight. He fully expected that consent would be forthcoming after the usual protracted formalities. But sanction was withheld. Paper had become extremely scarce for new publications by authors not beyond all official suspicion, and since his clearance in 1937 by Goebbel's Ministry of Propaganda, Hesse had become quite suspect. When Suhrkamp's appeals for a reversal of this decision proved futile, the novel was submitted to the Fretz & Wasmuth Verlag of Zürich in November 1942. It appeared exactly one year later. Suhrkamp was not allowed to import copies for the German book market, and the book was not published in Germany until the summer of 1946.

AUTOBIOGRAPHICAL MATRIX

Autobiography never ceased to be the stuff of Hesse's art. His outer world provided content, his inner world furnished substance, his imagination spun its labile web of disguise. In his major tales from *Eine Stunde hinter Mitternacht* to *Knulp*, life was first aesthetically transfigured and then slightly poeticized. It was elevated to myth in *Demian* and *Siddhartha*, dramatically psychologized in *Klein und Wagner* and fantasized in *Klingsors letzter Sommer*, became surrealism in *Der Steppenwolf*, was romanticized and symbolized in *Narziss und Goldmund*, and transformed into metaphor, fancy, and enigma in *Die Morgenlandfahrt*. And it became the matrix for a world of tomorrow in *Das Glasperlenspiel*.

Although the last of Hesse's tales is less conspicuously personal than many of its predecessors, it is actually as, if not more, autobiographical than most of these. It not only highlights a particular period of life but also draws heavily upon all of the many preceding years. Other of Hesse's stories do as much, though on a more modest scale, but none was quite the novel exercise in self-projection that *Das Glasperlenspiel* became. In its autobiography, the book is very much like Haller's Magic Theater or Siddhartha's equally magic river. Time is cancelled, and like Haller's and Siddhartha's, Hesse's past, present, and future intermingle.

Twelve- or thirteen-year-old Knecht, pupil at the Latin School in insignificant Berolfingen at the edge of the Zaberwald, is Hesse at that same age attending the Latin school in the little town of Göppingen prior to his admission to Maulbronn near Zabergäu. Knecht is the studious youngster Hesse had then been, plays the violin, as had Hesse, and is chosen for Eschholz, one of Castalia's elite schools, as

Hermann Hesse in Bremgarten, 1943.

Hesse had been for Maulbronn, one of Württemberg's exclusive church schools. The illustrious Magister Musicae of Monteport, blue-eyed, white-haired, and only moderately tall, a man much given to meditation, Knecht's benign sponsor, confidant, and patron, is the personage, the counselor to the young, the student of musicology, and the meditative sexagenarian Hesse had become in Montagnola. The old master's belief in the inherent sanctity of man, his advocacy of self-realization, his recognition of life's opposites as the poles of life's oneness, his rejection of panacean doctrines, and his conviction that truth cannot be taught but must be lived, were Hesse's. He is also the student of dreams that Hesse was, the magician that Hesse had always wanted to be, and he had spent some time at Mariafels just as Hesse had at Maulbronn. The Magister Musicae is the man Hesse had become, just as clearly as Knecht is the boy he had been. In memory, a master returned to his youth and in imagination, he took the novice he once had been into gentle tow. Their conversations are another variation of the self-dialogue characteristic of all of Hesse's major tales.

Knecht's departure from Berolfingen for Eschholz had been Hesse's from Göppingen for Maulbronn, and most of the little known of Knecht's life in Eschholz is recollection. As had been Hans Giebenrath at the beginning of the century and Hesse before him, he is assigned to the dormitory Hellas. He fares as well as had Hesse in music, Latin, Greek, and mathematics. A frightful fire at Eschholz recalls a similar conflagration at Maulbronn. And reference to Knecht's single major misdemeanor while at Eschholz is probably an oblique allusion to Hesse's Maulbronn truancy of March 1892.

Eschholz inherited Hesse's experiences at Maulbronn, Waldzell and Mariafels bear Maulbronn's physical imprint and its mark of distinction, and the Order itself was accorded Maulbronn's monastic heritage. Waldzell, small and old, with beech forests above it, with its towers, remnants of wall, and mill-dam, its bearded citizens, plump women behind shop counters, mocking maidens, and children at play, and with its imposing Cistercian monastery become a school for the elect, is the Maulbronn of Hesse's memory. It enjoys the exclusiveness and rank in Castalia that Maulbronn had enjoyed in Württemberg, and as had Maulbronn's alumni, Waldzell's number many illustrious members.

While Waldzell owes its repute and profile to Maulbronn at large, the abbey Mariafels is indebted for its history and structural detail to the monastery proper. The abbey's preëminence over the centuries in theology, music, and politics had been Maulbronn's eminent past, and its two churches, famous chapter hall, long guest house, huge vaulted wine and fruit cellars, two refectories, and sundry particulars of its sprawling plant are the Maulbronn of Hesse's boyhood. And like Mariabronn of *Narziss und Goldmund*, Mariafels is obliged for its very name to Maulbronn: another of Hesse's customary camouflages. Mariabronn had been an appropriate mutation for a monastery much given to its veneration of the Virgin, and Mariafels was a further suitable modification for an abbey that Hesse chose to locate in rocky terrain.

Catholicism's hierarchy and papal pomp and circumstance had furnished trappings and aura for the Order of Hesse's Eastern Wayfarers; monasticism now left its equally decided impress upon Castalia's related Order. Church secularized had become a spiritual home for H.H. and his confrères; monastery secularized now became an actual home for their spiritual descendents, a model for Hesse's long-espoused realm of the spirit. The Order and Castalia became all that Hesse associated with Maulbronn and its monasticism. In their structure and function, the Order's World Commission (*Weltkommission*) and each country's own Commission (*Landeskommission*), Directorate (*Ordensleitung*), Council of Studies (*Studienrat*), and Board of Education (*Erziehungsbehörde*) approximate the general chapter, regional chapters, and the various governing layers of the Cistercian order's interlaced hierarchy. Like a monastic province, Castalia is but one branch of a world-wide order. Its assemblage of students, scholars, masters, and sundry administrators is essentially a secularized cadre of novices, monks, canons, and priors. Its Magister Ludi's election and investiture are distinctly abbatial, he presides over his domain in the monarchial manner of an abbot, and he too enjoys his congregation's Roman reverence, obedience, and filial piety. Life in Castalia is monastic in its ritual, its dedication to a cause, and in its exclusion of women; human relationships are ecclesiastically formal, monkish anonymity is imperative, deportment is servile, and language is solemn, replete with Christian concepts, and laced with Latin terminology. The Order's members are pledged to monastic poverty, chastity, and obedience, disposed to piety, and given to meditation. Its schools are like exclusive seminaries, their education is predominantly humanistic, and they provide both Castalia and the world at large with celibate scholars and teachers. Like monasteries of the Middle Ages, Castalia owes its origin to a passion for moral reawakening and cultural revival; like its prototypes, it is an island of spirituality in a sea of worldliness; and it was Hesse's belief that an eventual Castalian-like lay monasticism would become for our Western world what ecclesiastical monasticism had once been for it.

Knecht's closest friendships at Waldzell are no less recollection and self-projection than his friendship with the Magister Musicae. Carlo Ferromonte, the fledgling musicologist who is interested in old music, is particularly well-versed in the sixteenth and seventeenth centuries, and in time turns his attention to Slavic folk music, and who converses at length with Knecht about music, introduces him to such composers as Purcell and Couperin, and becomes involved with him in extended musical studies, is none other than Hesse's young nephew Karl Isenberg, a musicologist whose friendship Hesse had courted in the twenties and thirties, whom Hesse had actually invited to Montagnola in August of 1934 to help him extend his technical acquaintance with classical music, and whose interests and pursuits in music Hesse had duly noted and not forgotten. Knecht's bosom friend managed even to inherit his esteemed model's full name.

Unlike Carlo Ferromonte, Plinio Designori was not an actual prototype's name playfully Italianized, but an Italian construct determined by its bearer. Of the many names in *Das Glasperlenspiel*, Josef Knecht and Plinio Designori probably received Hesse's most considered attention. He obviously had two objectives in mind when he chose these: his protagonist's name was to reflect the master-servant ideal he had broached in *Siddhartha* and was espousing in *Das Glasperlenspiel*, and the names of his protagonist, spokesman for *logos*, and of his protagonist's complement, spokesman for *bios*, had to be appropriately antithetical. It was undoubtedly with Goethe's Meister in mind that Hesse settled upon such a direct characterization as Knecht. Josef was a more difficult, a more subtle, and also a more circuitous choice. The name was probably suggested by Thomas Mann's *Die Geschichten Jaakobs*, which had reminded Hesse of the biblical story of Joseph and his brothers, and which in turn had reminded him that he had actually chosen to call himself Joseph during his mid-teens. These associations proffered a name both appropriately personal for a self-projection and appropriately connotative for Hesse's purposes. Joseph, Jacob's favorite son, chief steward to Potiphar, and a powerful official at the court of the Pharoah, belonged to the elect, to the world's masters. His name had all the aristocratic coloration that Hesse expected of the first of his protagonist's names. Josef added to Knecht, a combination synonymous with master-servant, became an accurate characterization of its bearer and a fortunate symbol for Hesse's new ideal. Once Hesse had decided upon the name Knecht, Designori's became an obvious antithetical choice for his protagonist's complement. Plinio was as deliberate a selection as Designori. It was not only fittingly Italian but was also as patrician in its Roman associations as was Designori in its Italian meaning.

Like Peter Camenzind and Richard, Kuhn and Muoth, Veraguth and Burkhardt, and immediately like Narziss und Goldmund, Knecht and Designori are a characteristic pair of Hesse's complementary self-projections. Each of the two is, as usual, most everything the other is not: one is of this world and the other is estranged from it, one is given to the body and the other to the spirit, and one is a participant and the other an observer. Theirs is also the characteristic relationship: each is drawn to and needed by the other, each is taken with, yet wary and envious of, the other, each is both irked by and concerned about the other, and their protracted dialogues are exercises in dialectics. Unlike previous double self-projections, however, Knecht and Designori respectively are not what Hesse had been and was, and what he would rather have been or had to be, but each is what Hesse had been. Not only protagonist, as had characteristically been the case, but also complement fell heir to the personal circumstances of their author's life. Hesse's story became both Knecht's and Designori's: his schooling and career were assigned to the former and much of his private life to the latter. Only *Unterm Rad* witnesses analogous self-projections: Giebenrath is what Hesse had been and Heilner what he had become.

Protagonist and complement are two sides of a single coin, and that coin was Hesse. Knecht inherited the artist-intellectual, Designori fell heir to the man, and each reflects both the inner and the outer circumstances of Hesse's life. The family background, childhood, marriage, home, and offspring denied Knecht, were all accorded Designori and all drew heavily upon Hesse's own world. Designori's is a prominent old family of landowners and officials, and Hesse's lineage had long been distinguished for its theologians, scholars, and teachers. He is as attached to his mother as Hesse had been to his, and her death leaves him as grief-stricken as Hesse had been when his own mother had died. His father is very much the chivalrous traditionalist, and the justice-minded, righteous man Hesse's father had been; he is also a friend of the church, and he is as proud of Plinio's education in Castalia as Johannes Hesse had been pleased by Hermann's admission into Maulbronn. The father-son relationship in the Designori family is essentially what it had been in Hesse's home. In both cases, less than intimate early ties eventually become severe estrangement. Sons are perverse, fathers inflexible, quarrels wax bitter, and the family situations become almost intolerable. Designori leaves Castalia in his mid-twenties for the real world just as Hesse in Basel and at that same age had turned his back upon his early aestheticism in quest of real life. He is as disappointed in his subsequent university studies as Hesse had been unimpressed by academia while in Tübingen. His eventual marriage is a virtual copy of Johann Veraguth's which in turn had been a close depiction of Hesse's marriage to Maria Bernoulli. Partners are similarly mismatched and the results are equally unfortunate. Like Adele Veraguth, Mrs. Designori is not only the stately, intelligent, and reserved woman Maria had been, but also the troubled, wary, obstinate, and domineering wife Maria had become. And like Veraguth, Designori is both the sensitive and gifted individualist Hesse had been and the moody and long-suffering husband Hesse had become. Designori's marriage, like Veraguth's, is as charged with deep resentment and mute hostility, and as thinly veneered by anxious politeness as Hesse's had been. He, like Veraguth before him and Hesse before Veraguth, is anything but master in his own home, vies in vain for a son's favor, is left alone, lonely, and unsettled by doubt and guilt, wallows in chronic melancholy, and knows only resignation and renunciation. Veraguth eventually bolts, as did Hesse, and there is no reason to believe that Designori will not in time also break out of his stifling marital confines.

As already noted, most of the little known about Knecht's schooling in Berolfingen and Eschholz derives from Hesse's stay in Göppingen and Maulbronn. That virtually nothing is recalled of Knecht's subsequent seven years of formal education in Waldzell should be no surprise. Since his own school days had terminated where Knecht's in Waldzell begin, Hesse plainly had no reservoir of memories to tap, and preferred as usual not to account for what he himself had not experienced. He chose instead to dwell on Knecht's extracurricular preoccupation with music, philosophy, poetry, and man's physical-spiritual quandry, drawing upon the major extraprofessional interests of his own years as an apprentice and bookdealer in Tübingen and Basel.

Knecht's last year in Berolfingen, his four years in Eschholz, and his seven years in Waldzell correspond with and are dependent upon Hesse's year and a half in Göppingen, the one year he did spend and the three more he would have spent in Maulbronn if all had gone well, and his almost eight years as an apprentice and bookdealer.

Knecht's following ten years of independent study and preparation for admission into the Order equate with Hesse's journeyman years from *Peter Camenzind* (1903) to *Rosshalde* (1913), and biography continued to derive primarily from autobiography. Knecht treasures seclusion during this period in their careers as much as had Hesse, the game becomes the passion for him that writing had become for Hesse, and he achieves the widely acknowledged distinction that Hesse had gained by the First World War. As had Hesse, Knecht also extends his exposure to and knowledge of music during these years, becomes practised in fasting and meditation, and discovers the Chinese classics. However, like the preceding periods in Knecht's life, this bears not only the impress of the corresponding stage in Hesse's career but also that of his later years. Knecht writes the latest of Hesse's poetry while at Waldzell and Hesse's latest prose during his decade of independent studies. He not only inherited his author's three biographies but even his attempted fourth. In the research necessary for this attempt, Knecht becomes as entangled in Pietism and music of the eighteenth century as had Hesse, and his reasons for not writing this tale were Hesse's for never completing it.

Knecht's friendships of this period draw just as heavily upon these later years of Hesse's life. Like Knecht and the Magister Musicae, Knecht and the Elder Brother (*der ältere Bruder*) are paired self-projections, not the complementary paired self-projections that Knecht and Designori are, but projections of a self that once had been and of a later self. In Berolfingen, a gentle and wise old Hesse becomes guide and patron to Hesse an ingenuous youngster, and years later Hesse an inquisitive young man is introduced to the Orient by Hesse, a much older and thoroughly orientalized Westerner. Just as in the Magister Musicae's case, there is little of the Elder Brother that does not derive from Hesse himself. He is slender, as was Hesse, has his author's blue eyes, and wears glasses, as did Hesse. He is the eccentric outsider, the shy hermit, and the dedicated student of Oriental philosophies Hesse had become in the years immediately following the First World War. His Chinese hermitage with its bamboo grove, set in a southern mountainous terrain with terraced vineyards, was Hesse's secluded Montagnolan retreat, with its carefully nurtured growth of bamboo, hidden among Ticino's terraced vineyards. The *I Ging* was as much Hesse's favorite Chinese classic, as it is the Elder Brother's, and Hesse had become almost as versed in its oracle game as is his self-projection. The Magister Musicae of Knecht's youth is very much what Hesse was in the mid-thirties, and the Elder

Brother is what he had in years past almost become. He represented an ideal that had threaded its ever-changing but unbroken course through a lifetime. Hesse's early aestheticism and his subsequent Orientalism, Hallerian Platonism, and revived aestheticism of *Die Morgenlandfahrt* are all mutations of this persistent ideal, and his Castalian monasticism was but its latest and last expression. It was an ideal born of antipathy for the world as it is and of aspiration for a world more ideal, it involved extreme individualism, seclusion, and self-indulgent esoteric pursuits of the mind and of the imagination, and it promised problems solved and peace undisturbed. Aestheticism and Platonism proved wanting. The ideal is fully realized only in the Orientalism of the Elder Brother, and then, only to be rejected. What had once suggested heaven on earth is for Knecht the unacceptable sublime flight from existence it had become for Hesse. The Elder Brother's essentially aesthetic adjustment to life does not satisfy Knecht's vague but deep-seated urge to serve in some meaningful capacity or other, nor his yearning for a wider range of experience, nor his incipient desire for a fuller realization of his self, any more than it did sexagenarian Hesse's.

Only two other friendships of Knecht's journeyman years are accorded any attention, and these too are rooted in autobiography. Like Ferromonte, both Fritz Tegularius and Thomas von der Trave had their prototypes in Hesse's life, neither deviates appreciably from fact, and each is to Knecht what his model had been and was to Hesse. Fritz Tegularius, withdrawn and lonely aristocratic genius given to suffering, student of classical philology with a penchant for philosophy and marked disdain for history, arch individualist with little communal concern, super-intellectual tragically aware of the dubiousness of all intellectual effort, victim of frail health and emotional instability, and contentious eccentric subject to spells of melancholia and insomnia, is obviously Friedrich Nietzsche. Though much more obscurely, even the names Tegularius (tiler) and Keuperheim, Hesse's substitutes for Nietzsche and Schulpforta, are rooted in actuality. Intent upon a Latin camouflage for his student of the classics and unable to translate the name Nietzsche, Hesse found a fitting alternative in the Latinized surname of his Swabian philosopher-friend Leopold Ziegler. The derivation of Keuperheim, center for the study of classical philology and *alma mater* to Tegularius, is equally devious: Keuper was Hesse's pet name for his wife Ninon, and Ninon had become an ardent student of classical antiquity. Associatively, Keuperheim was as appropriate a substitution for Schulpforta as Tegularius was for Nietzsche.

Tegularius is a memorial to Nietzsche, the Knecht/Tegularius friendship is a literary rendition of Hesse's relationship to Nietzsche: initial attraction and aversion, years of occasional and casual contact, intimacy and dependence, and concluding transcendence. And Knecht's ultimate conviction that Tegularius is an example to be treasured but not to be emulated, that his sick geniality is self-destructive, and that his asocial individualism poses danger more than it promises hope, had become Hesse's concluding assessment of Nietzsche. The Elder Brother is what Hesse had almost become and Tegularius is what he could still but should not become. Their variant expressions of aestheticism, both once highly espoused, had become as unpalatable to him as they are to Knecht.

Thomas von der Trave's fictive disguise is even thinner than that of Tegularius. Characterization confirms what name more than intimates. The epithet is an unmistakable allusion to Thomas Mann's birthplace on the Trave River, and Knecht's cosmopolitan and urbane predecessor, practised traveler formal in manner, courteous in speech, careful in enunciation, and high-voiced, craftsman par excellence, master of irony, a Magister Ludi thoroughly versed in the game and given to ascetic severity and diligence but often and unjustly denigrated for his alleged uninspired icy rationality, is Thomas Mann just as Hesse knew him in the thirties. And the Knecht-Thomas von der Trave relationship is as deferential and ceremonious as was the Hesse-Mann friendship. Even Thomas von der Trave's closest associates were drawn from life. His teacher and predecessor, who had been a while in London, is undoubtedly Theodor Fontane, to whom Mann felt deeply indebted and who had spent considerable time in England. And Bertram, Thomas von der Trave's loyal understudy, is the scholar Ernst Bertram, who had long been something of a devoted shadow to Mann. Bertram is ostracized by Castalia's elite when they lose confidence in him, just as Ernst Bertram was being berated by German émigré writers and intellectuals for his alleged espousal of National Socialism. Knecht's appeal on behalf of Bertram was an expression of Hesse's own sympathy for his prototype.[38]

The three to four years after Knecht's admission to the Order and

---

38 Hesse gave direct expression to this sympathy in a letter addressed to a number of Bertram's former students in 1948. See *Briefe* (1964), p. 252.

before his elevation to Castalia's most exulted magistery correspond to the First World War in Hesse's career. The interim is for Knecht the hiatus of sociopolitical involvement it had been for Hesse. Knecht commits himself to a hoped-for reconciliation of Castalia and the Catholic Church, just as Hesse had committed himself to the cause of peace. Though more successful, Knecht's political venture beyond Castalia is as inherently alien and distasteful to him as Hesse's similar venture beyond the realm of art had been to him. This exposure to the world at large interrupts Knecht's treasured pursuit of the game as much as it had Hesse's passionate cultivation of art, and the interruption is as perturbing to one as it had been to the other.

For Hesse, these few years had been primarily an interval of political commitment, for Knecht they are also an important period of historical awakening. But this, too, is rooted in autobiography. Like his friendship with Thomas von der Trave, Knecht's interaction with the Benedictine historian Pater Jakobus is merely a later experience in Hesse's career transferred to an earlier period in his protagonist's life. Pater Jakobus, sage, seer, and renowned scholar, a spare elderly ascetic with a hawk-like head, long sinewy neck, sharply receding forehead, hooknose, and short chin is an appropriate assessment and accurate portrait of Jacob Burckhardt, the Swiss historian who had first attracted Hesse at the outset of the century but had not become a real factor in his historical thinking until the thirties. Jakobus is the down-to-earth historian and the forceful but polite partner in argument that Burckhardt had been, his historical interests and his emphasis upon the study of source materials had been Burckhardt's, as too had his marked disdain for philosophies of history; he opens Knecht's eyes, as Burckhardt had Hesse's, to history's interplay of culture, politics, and religion, and brings Knecht back to earth just as his prototype had helped to redirect Hesse from ideality to reality. Jakobus is revered by Knecht as was Burckhardt by Hesse, he is the major influence in Knecht's life that Burckhardt had become in Hesse's, his remark appended to Knecht's circular letter is a direct quotation from Burckhardt's *Das Revolutionszeitalter*,[39] his antipathy for Tegularius had been Burckhardt's aversion to Nietzsche, he is also the modest pianist that Burckhardt had been, and even his evenings are given to things other than readings or writing, as Burckhardt's had been. Knecht's discourses with Jakobus are but a dramatized

---

39 In Jacob Burckhardt, *Historische Fragmente aus dem Nachlass* (Berlin & Leipzig: Deutsche Verlags-Anstalt, 1929), Vol. 7, p. 426.

rendition of Hesse's renewed preoccupation with Burckhardt. He learns from Jakobus what Burckhardt had bolstered in Hesse: that the Castalias of civilization are not independent of the world at large in origin, lot, or destiny, nor autotelic, nor beyond the wear of time, that culture is but one of history's many manifestations, that life implies a recognition of both the physical and the spiritual and human affairs demand an interplay of reflection and action, and that order and meaning prevail behind the apparent chaos of reality.

In Burckhardt's, as earlier in Nietzsche's case, Hesse was drawn to an exemplary loner, and attracted to ideas that extended or confirmed his own, responded to his latest needs and inclinations, and promised a more satisfying adjustment to the self, society, and life. Burckhardt had become his latest guide and inspiration, and Jakobus was his unqualified testimonial to both the man and the historian. Hesse's appreciation of and gratitude to Burckhardt never abated. In his introduction to *Krieg und Frieden* (1946) he actually went so far as to affirm that Burckhardt's influence upon him had been third only to his home and the Orient. Nietzsche had been for Hesse the temporary fascination and agitation Tegularius is for Knecht. Burckhardt was and remained for Hesse the reverence and solace Jakobus becomes for Knecht. Nietzsche had been a necessary intermediate stage in Hesse's life and Burckhardt was necessary for its concluding stage. Nietzsche had become a yesterday for Hesse, and Burckhardt promised new possibility. The former was a dreamer with whom one could rhapsodize and the latter was a realist with whom one could live.

The eight years between Knecht's investiture and his departure from Castalia correspond to the period in Hesse's life from the end of the First World War to the mid-thirties. These are for Knecht the years of dedicated application, major achievement, severe conflict, and drastic decision they had been for Hesse. Knecht dedicates himself as whole-heartedly to the bead game as Hesse had devoted himself to his writing. His seven grand annual games are counterpart to the seven major tales written by Hesse from *Demian* to *Die Morgenlandfahrt*. As was true of these tales, each of Knecht's games is extant, each continues to be studied and cherished by the young, and all are dazzling in their thoughts and formulations, original in their rhythms, and worthy of careful stylistic analysis. Success notwithstanding, life's polar possibilities gradually become for Knecht the crucial and disturbing concern they had become for Hesse. Life begins to unsettle his Castalia as it had Hesse's private world of art and intellect, and Knecht is caught between isolation and contact, reflection and involvement, and between the mind and the body, just as had been Hesse's lot. He is left convinced, as Hesse had been, that he has become an artist but not a human among humans. He also becomes convinced that Castalia is something much less than the impeccable ideal he had believed it to be, just as Hesse had lost his exclusive faith in the timeless realm of art and thought courted in *Der Steppenwolf* and extolled in *Die Morgenlandfahrt*. Knecht's departure from Castalia was Hesse's farewell to Haller's Immortalia and to H.H.'s Order of Eastern Wayfarers, his commitment to social involvement was Hesse's final rejection of long-espoused aestheticism, and Knecht's hoped-for harmonious interplay of *vita contemplativa* and *vita activa* had become Hesse's latest and last ideal.

Supernumeraries, filler, and even Knecht's biographer drew no less heavily upon actual life than did the novel's main characters, its substance, and its content. The Castalian chronicler is not just Hesse's narrator but yet another of his many self-reflections. Though he pleads impartiality, it is quite obvious that he, as did Hesse, approves of Knecht's person, shares his thoughts, appreciates his independence, and condones his decision to leave Castalia. He believes that Knecht's step beyond the province was necessary for his well-being and self-realization, just as Hesse had begun to believe that his own further self-growth and ultimate self-justification demanded that he relinquish his sequestered aestheticism for an active commitment to his fellow man. He is also convinced that both the Order and the outside world are the better for Knecht's exemplary act, just as Hesse was persuaded that it would be to the decided advantage of both culture and life at large if artists and intellectuals, each in his own way, were to emulate Knecht's example. The chronicler's historical, philosophical, religious, literary, and musical interests were Hesse's. He is as acquainted with ancient China, classical antiquity, gnosticism, scholasticism, Catholicism, German Romanticism, and European culture of the nineteenth and twentieth centuries as was Hesse. The *Upanishads*, Lü Bu We, Pythagoras, Socrates, Horace, Abélard, Thomas Aquinas, Cusanus, Leibniz, Goethe, Hegel, Novalis, and Nietzsche were as familiar to Hesse as they are to him. He is as versed as was Hesse in European music from 1500 to 1800, believes, as did Hesse, that this wondrous classical period had already begun to decline in the eighteenth century, and contends, as had Hesse, that Bach's music is the very quintessence of Christian culture. He dedicates his biography to Hesse's Eastern Wayfarers, knows of Hesse's

Bremgarten und Morbio, alludes to the chapter "Die Musik des Untergangs" of *Klingsors letzter Sommer*, and he even quotes the very passage about music and the state from Lü Bu We's *Frühling und Herbst* that Hesse himself often cited in his letters.[40]
All of the little known of the scholar Plinius Ziegenhalss points just as unmistakably to Hesse himself. He is a literary historian, as was Hesse, and the chronicler is as indebted to him for his view of the twentieth century as he actually was to Hesse. He inherits Hesse's coinage of the designation feuilleton age, is also familiar with the expression magic theater, and his caustic assessment of the twentieth century is but a variation of Hesse's chronic disparagement of his age. Even the name Ziegenhalss was only another of Hesse's self-descriptions, a characteristically facetious allusion to his goat-like, rather long thin neck.
Like the chronicler and Ziegenhalss, Alexander, the chief administrator of Castalia, is yet another bit of Hermann Hesse. His interaction with Knecht, very much like Leo's with H.H., is in its origin essentially only the interplay of but another pair of Hesse's complementary selves, and the written and verbal exchanges between Alexander and Knecht, like those between Leo and H.H. or between any other of their author's self-projections, are basically only another of Hesse's many exercises in inner argument. Leo is the serene Eastern Wayfarer Hesse aspired to become at the outset of the thirties, and H.H. is the troubled person Hesse then actually was; Alexander is the dedicated Castalian Hesse had briefly been in the early thirties, and Knecht the defector is the ethically swayed individualist Hesse had then become. All continued as always to derive from and to center about Hesse himself.
As usual, too, even the novel's many incidental names are but veiled actuality. In his earliest works, Hesse often accorded his characters the actual or only slightly disguised actual names or sobriquets of their prototypes, from *Demian* to *Narziss und Goldmund* many of his names became fictive and decidedly symbolic, and in *Die Morgenlandfahrt* and *Das Glasperlenspiel*, actuality, wit, and sheer playfulness determined his choice of names. A Latinization of actual names became Hesse's favorite mode of facetious camouflage. His game of "guess who" begins with the novel's very motto, an excerpt from a Latin work written by Albertus Secundus and edited by Clangor and Collof. Collof. is obviously Collofino the Smoke Magician (*Collofino*

---

40 Compare *Briefe* (1964), p. 122, and *Gesammelte Schriften* (1957), Vol. 6, p. 100.

der Rauchzauberer) of *Die Morgenlandfahrt*, who in turn is Hesse's old friend Josef Feinhals, cigar manufacturer and avid student of Latin. Clangor is Franz Schall, one of Hesse's schoolmates in Göppingen, a lifelong friend and a classical philologist; it was he who in the autumn of 1932 translated into Latin the motto that Hesse himself had written in German. And Hesse's choice of the pseudonym Albertus Secundus was an expression of his esteem for and feeling of kinship with Albertus Magnus, the Swabian mystic whom he had already numbered among the more celebrated of his Eastern Wayfarers. All other Latinizations continue this very personal game of names. Lodovicus Crudelis, alias Louis the Horrible (*Louis der Grausame*) of *Klingsors letzter Sommer* and *Die Morgenlandfahrt*, is Hesse's painter-friend Louis Moilliet; his translation of old Egyptian texts into Greek and Sanskrit is but an oblique allusion to a painting trip Moilliet had once made to Africa and to his general zest for travel. Eccentric Chattus Calvensis II, author of a monumental four-volume fragment on the pronunciation of Latin in the universities of southern Italy toward the end of the twelfth century, is another of Hesse's more waggish self-portraits; Chattus is Hesse in Latin, Hesse was born in Calw, his paternal grandfather was the first Hermann Hesse in the family, and Hesse was also very adept in Latin. Knecht owes the III of his official title Josephus III to a similar playful association; since Joseph the son of Jacob had probably suggested the forename for Knecht, and since Hesse had once chosen to call himself Joseph, Knecht became the third in his private lineage of Josephs. Pater Jakobus for Jacob Burckhardt, Carlo Ferromonte for Karl Isenberg, and Tegularius for Nietzsche were born of this same playfulness.

Actual names not Latinized were otherwise playfully disguised, left untouched but for the omission of either fore- or surname, or were dispensed with entirely. Actuality shows through clearly or only nebulously and often not at all. Thomas von der Trave, as had already been noted, is as transparent a disguise as possible for Thomas Mann. Ludwig Wassermaler, an erstwhile Magister Ludi highly regarded by Knecht, is yet another of Hesse's several memorials to his painter-friend Louis Moilliet. Bastian Perrot of Calw, mechanically minded inventor of the original game with actual beads and musically gifted author of *The Apogee and Decline of Counterpoint* (*Blüte und Verfall der Kontrapunktik*), owes his name and talents to the Perrots in whose machine shop in Calw Hesse had worked as a youth and to Sebastian Bach, chief exponent of counterpoint. As already pointed out, Bertram, close associate of Thomas von der Trave, was modelled after

Ernst Bertram, scholar and long-time friend of Thomas Mann. Dubois, director of Castalia's foreign office, is indebted to Hesse's maternal grandmother for his name. The Feustel theory of the correspondence between the scale of colors and the keys of music is a complimentary allusion to a similar hypothesis maintained by Els Feustel, wife of Hesse's painter-friend Max Bucherer. In his depiction of Designori's marriage, Hesse must have remembered the like plight of Veraguth in *Rosshalde*, and it was probably from this association that Veraguth, Designori's father-in-law, derived his name. Knecht's strained relationship with Otto Zbinden, headmaster of the school in Waldzell, faintly recalls Hesse's own difficulties with the school authorities in Maulbronn. But why the name Zbinden and to whom was Hesse originally indebted for the name Veraguth? Hesse's inspiration for the Joculator Basiliensis, the Swiss musicologist-mathematician who invented a language of symbols capable of reducing music and mathematics to their common denominator was either his Swiss friend and student of music Otto Basler, or Hans Kayser a scholar and longtime resident of Switzerland who had evolved a system allegedly capable of giving expression to almost anything in mathematical-musical harmonic relationships.[41] The *Republik der Massageten*, casually mentioned by Knecht in his letter to Alexander, was Hesse's fictive disguise for Germany in a brief but bitter satire directed against his former countrymen in 1927,[42] but who was the model for that notorious republic's university professor who insisted that it was not for the country's faculty but for its general to determine the sum of two plus two? The so-called Yogi, an oddball Sanskrit scholar to whom the Magister Musicae had many years earlier turned for much-needed counsel is undoubtedly Gusto Gräser the eccentric student of Eastern religions and of Yoga whose hermitage a troubled young Hesse had visited in 1907. But who inspired Hesse's Parisian scholar, a respected but also much mocked student of Chinese philology, who, in an essay titled *Chinese Warning Cry* (*Chinesischer Mahnruf*), had made an appeal for an international language of symbols akin to ancient Chinese script? Who among Hesse's friends is the Eastern Wayfarer who had taken it upon himself to build a Bach organ as Bach would have had it built? And who is the world-famous author of our Babylonian twentieth century who, reasonably certain

41 G. W. Field first suggested that Hans Kayser might have been Hesse's model for the Joculator Basiliensis. See "On the Genesis of the *Glasperlenspiel*," *The German Quarterly*, 41 (1968), 680.

42 "Bei den Massageten," *Berliner Tageblatt*, September 25, 1927, No. 454.

of impunity, allegedly signed in one year alone more than 200 idle protests and appeals to reason, some of which he himself had perhaps not even bothered to read? Hesse's prototype for Pius XV, a pope who had attempted to institute proceedings against the bead game, was probably Pius X whose *Pascendi*, an encyclical of 1907, condemned the tampering of intellectuals in matters pertaining to faith and dogma, and Oskar, Otto, and Charlemagne, Knecht's fellow students at Eschholz, are more likely than not Hesse's recollections of Maulbronn, but what are the stories behind Gervasius the Abbot and Anton the novice of Mariafels, Petrus the student in Monteport, and the Magister Musicae's successor Ludwig, and to whom is Alexander the chief administrator of Castalia indebted for his name? The Diodorus Siculus whose account of the presumable causes of the flooding of the Nile the chronicler disparages is an obvious allusion to the Greek historian Diodorus Siculus and to his mythic history of Egypt, Silbermann is an actual organ builder of the eighteenth century, and Schwan von Boberfeld and his baroque German is a mildly mocking reference to Martin Opitz, to his cherished title and his extravagant language. But who was the model or inspiration for aristocratic and spirited young Tito, and why that name? Surely Hesse must have given almost as much consideration to Tito as he had to the names of Josef Knecht and Plinio Designori. Was the name chosen, as Designori's forename had been, for its fitting patrician connotation? Or was it derived from Titan the sun god whom Tito the sun worshipper honors in the wild sacrificial dance preceding Knecht's death? Most of the answers to these and related questions probably died with Hesse.

Geography and place names are as much obliged to actuality as persons and their designations, and as usual Hesse confined himself to the familiar. Knecht's Castalia is probably just as far removed from the distant future that it purports to portray as it is from antiquity's Mount Parnassus and the celebrated spring of poetic inspiration to which it owes its name. The setting of all the major tales excepting *Siddhartha* is either Swabia or Switzerland, or both Swabia and Switzerland as is the case in *Die Morgenlandfahrt* and *Das Glasperlenspiel*. The Eastern Wayfarers range through Hesse's Württemberg and Switzerland of the twenties, and the Castalians cultivate their intellectuality in the Württemberg of Hesse's youth extended to the Ticino of his later years: an ideal amalgam of the homeland of birth and that of choice. Hesse peered into the future but depicted the past. What he conjured up is not the likely megalopolitan technological civilization of 2200 but the rural agrarian world of the late nineteenth century. Knecht's world is one of small communities with gates and towers, of villages surrounded by open fields and forests, of monasteries with abbots and monks, refectories, and stables, of cobblers, coopers, smiths, and tenant farmers, of candles, styli, and manuscripts copied by hand, and of trains and pedestrians, but few automobiles and no airplanes. All this was treasured memory become part of an envisaged ideal.

Hesse was inclined to use place names rather sparingly. In his major tales until *Demian*, most of these are the actual names of the actual places depicted, some are one- or two-letter abbreviations of actual names, and only a few are truly fictive. After *Demian*, place names become somewhat more common. Purely fictive names continue to be rare, but letter substitutions are dispensed with and most of the commonly used actual names are now playfully distorted. And such is also true of *Das Glasperlenspiel*. Actuality shows as clearly through most of the novel's playfully camouflaged place names as it does through many of its similarly disguised surnames. As already noted, Berolfingen and Zaberwald stem from Göppingen and Zabergäu, Mariafels returns to Maulbronn through Mariabronn, and Monteport is indebted to Montagnola. Hirsland, administrative headquarters of the Order and center for lengthy exercises in fasting and meditation, derives appropriately from Hirsau, located only three kilometers from Hesse's birthplace and once a site for one of Europe's most celebrated Benedictine monasteries, or the name could be another of Hesse's oblique acknowledgments to his patrons Alice and Fritz Leuthold who lived in the Hirsland quarter of Zürich. Porta, seat of Aristotelianism and scholasticism, was Hesse's tribute to Schulpforta, once famous for its classical education. Keuperheim, center for the study of classical philology, is obliged, as already noted, to Hesse's pet name for his wife Ninon and to her interest in classical antiquity. Planvaste is a suitable descriptive construct for a school specializing in mathematics. Belpunt, the Designoris' mountain retreat, may be an equally fitting symbolic construct. In its home and in the person of Tito, the family promises an attractive bridge between Castalia and the world: a rapprochement of the spiritual and the sensual, and a reconciliation between individualism and social commitment. As such, the name would be a symbolic confirmation of Hesse's own positive view of the novel's perplexing concluding episode. Knecht experiences at Eschholz what Hesse had experienced at Maulbronn and Waldzell bears Maulbronn's physical imprint, but to what do these places owe their names, and what is the origin of Sankt Urban where Knecht studies Chinese? Hesse did not tell and the text affords too little for meaningful speculation.

The names of Knecht's appended autobiographies are no less intriguing than those of the novel proper. Unfortunately, for want of textual clues or external information, the source and significance of many of them have again all too often to be left to guess and the imagination. Each of Knecht's self-projections fittingly bears his own name or an appropriate translation of it, and in each instance the name is as much a direct characterization as in the parent novel: as an apprentice, Knecht of *Der Regenmacher* is a servant to the old rainmaker, and as his master's successor, he becomes a servant to his stone-age people; as a hermit-confessor in the wilds of early Christian Palestine, Josephus Famulus (Knecht Latinized) of *Der Beichtvater* is a servant of God and a servant to man; and disenchanted with the world, Dasa (Knecht Sanskritized) of *Indischer Lebenslauf* becomes a servant to a yogi, and as a yogi, will by example be a servant to his fellow mortals, a reminder of the illusion of the phenomenal world. The supporting casts are accorded names suggestive of or consonant with their different cultures and times, and upon occasion these names are also aptly connotative. Turu the rainmaker, Knecht's master and mentor, is probably indebted for his name to Hesse's usual playfulness and the Sanskrit word *guru* (teacher); but Turu may also be a playful disfiguration of Thor, the god of thunder. Scheming Maro, the rejected apprentice rainmaker who is intent upon Knecht's destruction, may owe his name to Buddhism's malevolent spirit Mara. Knecht's wife Ada (Adalein) in all likelihood inherited her name from Hesse's sister Adele. If nothing else, Turu, Maro, and Ada do sound appropriately old and authentic. Dion Pugil, like Josephus Famulus, is precisely what his Latin family name suggests: a pugilistic person, a severe hermit-confessor who is forever fighting demons and pommeling his penitents. Dion may be a contraction of Dionysus, and if so, the name could refer to Pugil's general incontinence or allude to a wild life preceding his conversion. All the many names in *Indischer Lebenslauf* are appropriately Indian, but with the exception of Dasa, none is readily accountable or even invites a guess. They may have been purposive choices, but they may also have been only casual recollections from Hesse's reading of such of India's epics as the *Mahabharata* and the *Ramajana*. Without author comment, no more than conjecture is possible.

In contrast with the names in *Der Regenmacher, Der Beichtvater,* and *Indischer Lebenslauf,* those in the tale that was to have become Knecht's fourth autobiography are of relatively little interest in either their origin or their use. All the numerous theologians, pastors, composers, hymnists, writers, and philosophers, discussed or merely mentioned, bear their actual names, as do all the cities and towns, except for Beutelsperg (Beitelsperg in the second fragment), the protagonist's birthplace. What is clearly Calw in description became Beutelsperg in disguise, and this was but a slight distortion of Beutelsbach (near Stuttgart), a name that in turn owes its selection to chance recollection or to accidental encounter in Hesse's extensive research for his eighteenth-century story. With the exception of the protagonist, who is again called Knecht and again for the same reasons, the nonhistorical characters bear names of no apparent significance and of indeterminate specific source. Reverend Bilfinger and Knecht's teacher Roos undoubtedly had their models in Calw of Hesse's youth, and perhaps even Knecht's sister Benigna (Babette in the second fragment), the tailor Schlatterer, and the clerk Pfleiderer were recollections, but the names themselves seem to have been no more than choices drawn randomly from memory.

Hesse's art is protean in its form, and its substance never ceases to evolve. Its sole constant is its intimate actuality. It is life transmuted, not fictively simulated. The last of his major tales is as rooted in autobiography and draws as much from general recollection as the first. Hesse's whole person, the world in which he lived, the details and rhythm of his life, his agonies, ideals, and his view of man, society, and Western civilization permeate *Das Glasperlenspiel.* Like all its predecessors however, the novel, though autobiographical, is itself not autobiography. Actuality is as usual only the stuff of which Hesse's art is made. Nor can actuality explain resultant art. However it does account for the tale's content, can throw light upon its substance, and does in some measure expose the creative process.

REALITY AND IDEALITY

Siddhartha is not just what it appears to be, nor is *Narziss und Goldmund,* and *Die Morgenlandfahrt* is no exception. Essentially, *Siddhartha* is not a depiction of India and a treatise on its religions, *Narziss und Goldmund* is not a portrayal of the Middle Ages and a tale of adventure, and *Die Morgenlandfahrt* is not an excursion to the East and an exercise in innocent fantasy. Nor is *Das Glasperlenspiel* just the vision of things to come and the memorial to an exemplary hero of tomorrow that it appears to be. Appearance notwithstanding, Siddhartha's, Goldmund's, and H.H.'s are no less Hesse's own evolving story than are Hesse's less exotic tales, and Knecht's biography is essentially the final installment of this serial projection of the self and its concerns. Setting and guise are diverse, but substance only evolved.

Rejection and withdrawal were Hesse's reflex response to the outside world, and self-preoccupation quickly became enduring fascination. The last of his tales reflects this reaction and concern no less than his first. Solipsistic Lauscher seeks better possibility in the beauty of art, and self-conscious Knecht finds it temporarily in the beauties of thought. One enjoys the splendors of the imagination, the other the adventures of the mind, and neither is much given to the needs of the body. Psychological distress and social expectation quickly made Lauscher's emotional brand of aestheticism unbearable for a young Hesse, and psychological need and social obligation soon rendered Knecht's cerebral brand of aestheticism untenable for an older Hesse. In both instances, response itself became a problem, retreat a confinement, and defection a necessity. Each time, too, individual and not social concern was the primary thrust in defection: an earlier vague penchant for greater self-expression and a later conscious passion for greater self-realization. And upon both occasions, synthesis was the compelling new attraction: at the outset, to be both an artist and a member of society, to create and to live, and at the end, to nurture both spirituality and physicality on the personal plane and to cultivate a responsible balanced social interplay of thought and action. Early reconciliation of art and life proved to be an elusive ideal, and with Knecht's premature death, late reconciliation of intellectuality and life was to remain but a promise. In its dynamics, and as reflected in *Das Glasperlenspiel*, the concluding chapter of Hesse's life marks a clear return to opening chapter: not just repetition, however, but variation on a new plane, full spiral rather than full circle.

Hesse, boy and man, was chronically at odds with life. Humans and their world were something less than they could be. This basic disenchantment with reality as it is, and Hesse's persistent dream of things better, became and remained both the thrust and the characteristic substance of his art. Discontent and dream wax, wane, and evolve as they thread their way through his tales from *Eine Stunde hinter Mitternacht* to *Das Glasperlenspiel*. In the earliest works, dream received unrestrained expression in a young aesthete's frequent sallies into a wondrous and beautiful world of the imagination, and discontent is only reflected in the dismal and noisy everyday world left behind. Dream receded and discontent unburdened itself in Camenzind's quarrel with an alien age, Giebenrath's victimization by society, Kuhn's struggle with cruel fate, and in Veraguth's grappling with his meager lot. The joyous ideal of dream reasserted itself in the heroic world of the Italianate tales, the whimsical irreality of the legends, and in the magic make-believe of the *Märchen*. Discontent and dream merged in Sinclair's painful actuality and his glowing possibility. Dream faded in Klein's agony and Klingsor's dissonance, only to resurge and to find new expression in Siddhartha's exotic Orient and his ideal self-realization. Insipid actuality and bitter discontent are Haller's unfortunate lot, and dream's treasured Immortalia hovers afar. The real then yielded again to the ideal, and Hesse's protean world of dream became Goldmund's lusty medieval reality. H.H. swings between juxtaposed commonplace life and fantastic dream, suffering the discontent of one and enjoying the euphoria of the other. In *Das Glasperlenspiel*, the world as it is became a chronicler's chaotic and culturally barren past, and ethereal dream, once Lauscher's authentic reality behind the curtain of life, Sinclair's better world of tomorrow, Haller's stratosphere of Immortals, and H.H.'s timeless psychocracy, finally became hard actuality, a utopian Castalia. But Hesse the malcontent and dreamer was realist enough to recognize that an ideal realized was but a splendid possibility exposed to the fallibility of man and the atrophy of time. Castalia's fortunes could only be that of all other human institutions. This recognition neither assuaged Hesse's chronic discontent nor dampened his persistent dreams. If anything, he had more reason than ever to look askance at so-called reality and to believe more firmly than ever that dream was man's ultimate sustenance.

While Hesse's body of evolving interests and concerns remained more or less constant, its focus changed with his periodic readjustment to himself and to life. Initial aesthetic withdrawal featured the joys and agonies associated with a callow young man's dedication to art. Subsequently ventured social adjustment shifted major attention to the painful consequences of an artist's marriage and his effort to become a solid citizen. Psychoanalysis and ensuing self-quest prompted a lengthy preoccupation with life's dilemmic polarities and man's existential anguish. And when passion for self-realization yielded to yearning for self-justification, obligation beyond the self became focal consideration. H.H.'s espousal of a master-servant ideal was Hesse's immediate response to ethical impulse. Self-justification seemed possible in a selfless dedication to the realm of art and thought. But *Die Morgenlandfahrt* was not the last link in Hesse's chain of tales, and

H.H.'s precipitate resolution was not to be Hesse's concluding comment on the artist-intellectual and life. Like most of Hesse's tales, *Das Glasperlenspiel* took up where its predecessor had broken off: *Die Morgenlandfahrt*'s ethereal realm of spiritual exclusiveness became an actual Immortalia, a concrete Castalia, and Knecht becomes the master-servant H.H. can only aspire to become. As usual, too, attractive possibility reconsidered became possibility discarded in favor of new conviction. Mounting political and social chaos in Germany and Hesse's own lingering sensuality rendered untenable what in 1930 and 1931 had been a desirable and even laudable adjustment to life. A community of elitists intent upon cultivating the mind to the exclusion of the body, and virtually divorced from practicality and the world at large, was neither in accord with nature nor responsive to the needs of society: a violation of man's physicality and an abdication of his social responsibility. A new ideal emerged. H.H.'s detached aestheticism became Knecht's responsible social involvement.

As usual, protagonist is as strong a link with the past as substance. Knecht is clearly a blood brother to his many predecessors, the last of Hesse's long lineage of kindred loners and self-seekers: aesthetes bolstered by dream and moved by conscience, saintly sufferers troubled by life's polarity, advocates of love and humble service, and severe moralists and social critics. Not person alone, but the very circumstances, path, and even outcome of Knecht's life are essentially the familiar in variation, accordant with new context, with a shift from actuality to ideality. Hesse's mental refuge of the thirties became his protagonist's reality, his Castalia: a life beyond base impulse and passion, a realm beyond politics and strife, an enclave of intellectuality, principle, and dedication, peopled by seekers of truth and guardians of cultural heritage. And Knecht's story is but the Hessean human drama reenacted in new guise and new focus.

Like most of his fellow protagonists, Knecht belongs to the elect, and like all his predecessors beginning with Sinclair, he is conscious of a calling and conducts himself accordingly. The self is, as always, central to this calling, and the self's self-realization as usual brooks no binding human bonds or confining institutional affiliations. Like most interpersonal relationships in Hesse's tales, Knecht's are characteristically politely impersonal, more reverential or patronizing than intimate, and of short rather than long duration, and like all of Hesse's marked protagonists, Knecht is most immediately drawn and committed to a community of the elite and not to the world of the ordinary. Ties with this world of the ordinary are if anything fewer and frailer than ever; Knecht knows no family, he literally leaves the world at large at the age of thirteen, does not return to it until three days before his death, and Designori is the only real link with it. The latter is the friend and foil, the counter-possibility accorded most of Hesse's protagonists. Self-fulfillment is as much the compelling and directive urge in Knecht's life as it is, consciously or otherwise, in the lives of all his predecessors, and except for a shift from high to low key and from psychological to ethical considerations, everything continues to revolve about life's polarities and to be directed toward synthesis. This change of key was inevitable with Hesse's substitution of Apollonian ideality for Dionysian actuality, and new ethical concern was but a reiteration in variation of the love and service acclaimed by a young Peter Camenzind and practised by an old Siddhartha. Nor are Knecht's departure from Castalia and his untimely death startling novelties. On the contrary. This turn of events is indeed as commonly Hessean as the chronicler's introductory disparagement of the twentieth century. Claustrophobic aversion to belonging and periodic departure, facts of life for Hesse, had become a standard feature of the Hessean scenario, the hallmark of his protagonists' quest for the self and pursuit of dream. Quest and dream in the Hessean world simply cannot brook actuality and attachment. Attachment precludes quest, and actuality by very definition falls short of dream. Castalia is Knecht's actuality and attachment and he ultimately responds as necessarily and as predictably to it as do any of his less fortunate predecessors to their lesser twentieth-century world. Having exhausted Castalia's possibilities in terms of his own person and private belief, Knecht dreams of better things to come. At this point, he, like almost every other Hesse protagonist, stands between what has been and what can be, between the actual and better possibility. This promise of things to come had become Hesse's link from novel to novel, and death, actual or symbolic or both, had become a standard feature of this characteristic thematic linkage. Knecht's outcome, like his life's circumstances and path, is therefore not innovation but repetition: a novel and expected variant of Demian's demise, Klein's suicide, Hermine's mock murder, and H.H.'s figurative death.

Knecht is the last of a long line of restless nomads, discontented seekers, and obdurate loners. The Magister Ludi in his Castalia is a Sinclair whose new world, new religion, and new morality eventually become but another confining prescribed way of life, a Klein who lets himself fall unreservedly into the stream of living only to find himself troubled by new reservations, a Klingsor whose appetites nine more lives fail to sate, a Siddhartha whose Om cloys with time, a Haller whose terrestrial Immortalia turns too frigid, a Narziss whose monastery eventually proves to be too confining, and an H.H. whose Order of Eastern Wayfarers cannot ultimately justify itself. Like Hesse, all these self-projections are in one way or another rebels and apostates. They and their author are roamers who will not be fenced in, questers who must have their quest, loners who cannot long tolerate contact, sinner-saints who revel in their martyrdom, and dreamers who feed on their dreams. Their medium is stony soil and inclement climes, and heaven itself would be their hell.

SHADES OF *Demian*

Although *Das Glasperlenspiel* and *Demian* may appear to be as different from each other as the ages that they portray are removed from each other, they are actually closely linked in both theme and narrative structure. The later novel is as unmistakably Hessean as its earlier cousin. The road from Sinclair to Knecht was twisted and tortuous but unbroken and unerring. Self-quest and self-expression began vigorously and optimistically under one pseudonym and ended calmly and contentedly under another. *Demian* depicts imperative initial self-emancipation, the intervening tales serialize self-confrontation culminating in self-acceptance, and *Das Glasperlenspiel* focuses on what in the thirties had for Hesse become the final stage of self-realization, namely self-justification. Obligation long confined to the self, then briefly addressed to the realm of art and thought in *Die Morgenlandfahrt*, had now to be extended to society at large. Hermann Hesse's faith in the artist and in art, and his detached aestheticism became Knecht's faith in man and in life, and responsible social involvement. While *Das Glasperlenspiel* features this final stage of self-realization, it does not bypass the self-quest that must precede. To be sure, self-quest is no longer the struggle *in extremis* with the self and a disjointed twentieth century, and is also no longer narrated in the high key of immediate experience, but it does return to the narrative structure pioneered in *Demian*. Like Sinclair's, Knecht's story might properly be termed exposition and nodal narrative, that is to say, an expository tale that focuses narratively on those human encounters that mold its protagonist, set the course his life assumes, fix his goals, and mark his progress. From this point of view, the Magister Musicae, Ferromonte, Designori, the Elder Brother, Tegularius, Dubois, Thomas von der Trave, Pater Jakobus, Alexander, and Tito are to

Knecht what Demian, Kromer, Alfons Beck, Beatrice, Pistorius, Knauer, and *Frau Eva* are to Sinclair.

Differ though the Magister Musicae and Demian do in person and life, they basically are motivated by common belief, and theirs is a common multifunction that follows a common course. Both are apostles of individualism, advocates of self-realization, proponents of meditation and of experiential truth, opponents of absolute belief, and espousers of oneness behind life's conflicting poles. Each is to his ward, friend and guide, thrust and sustenance, inspiration and model. Both Demian and the Magister Musicae start their fledglings along the road of self-fulfillment, recede and become hovering guardian spirits ever ready to caution, counsel, and to encourage, and then pass from the scene with purpose served. Death follows for both when wards have absorbed all that their guardians have to impart and instill by precept and example. Each dies only to live on in his protégé.

Demian and the Magister Musicae are the impulse and control that determine the courses their wards travel. All other human relationships are but milestones along these roads of self-realization. Kromer is Sinclair's first encounter with evil, Beck his bout of indulgence in sensuality, Beatrice his caper with love spiritualized, Pistorius his religious quest for answers and solace, Knauer his positive reappraisal of sex, and *Frau Eva* his ultimate goal finally in sight. Like Sinclair's, Knecht's encounters are those vital confrontations with life and the self that broaden horizons, heighten self-consciousness, and demand decisions: the consequential moments of self-becoming. Ferromonte is his experience of loyal and lasting friendship, Designori his exposure to life at large, the Elder Brother his asocial withdrawal into idyllic seclusion and esoteric pursuit, Tegularius his flirtation with unbridled individualism and pure intellectuality, Dubois and Thomas von der Trave his involvement in politics, Peter Jakobus his introduction to history, Alexander his battle between individual needs and institutional expectations, and Tito his grappling with the individual's obligation to the self and his obligation to his fellow man.

These parallels in the narrative structure of *Demian* and *Das Glasperlenspiel*, two tales otherwise as removed in general character from each other as their dates of composition, in no way warrant any suspicion, let alone any contention, that the earlier must have been a conscious model for the later. In relationship to each other, *Demian* and *Das Glasperlenspiel* are no more than the extremities of a continuum extending over a period of twenty-five years. Appearance changes drastically and unpredictably with every tale from Sinclair's to Knecht's, but central theme evolves unbroken and basic narrative structure remains intact. *Das Glasperlenspiel*'s thematic linkage with *Demian* witnesses Hesse's deliberate and dogged literary pursuit of a major personal concern. Their structural linkage is a continued adroit exercising of a narrative technique adopted in *Demian* and cultivated in variation and to good advantage in *Siddhartha, Der Steppenwolf, Narziss und Goldmund,* and *Die Morgenlandfahrt.* Self-realization and nodal narrative are as much the hallmarks of Hesse's later works as self-evasion and traditional narrative are the distinguishing features of his earlier tales.

A SEQUEL TO *Narziss und Goldmund*

Self-realization is the thrust in Knecht's existence, self-justification becomes his passion, and both impulses revolve about life's polarity. The Magister Musicae alerts Knecht to this duality, but it is Designori who impresses its reality upon him and compels him to come to grips with it. As such, the Designori friendship is the most crucial of Knecht's peer relationships, and as usual the most critical of these relationships is a double self-projection. Knecht fell heir to Hesse the artist-intellectual, and Designori to Hesse the man. The split inheritance became the stuff for another of many demonstrations of life's polar possibilities, and a final argument for synthesis.

The latest and last of Hesse's long line of antithetical double self-projections is most reminiscent of the Narziss and Goldmund friendship. Knecht and Designori are as obvious variations of Narziss and Goldmund as distant future and Castalia are of removed past and monastery. A story is retold in new guise, with but a shift in focus from physical to spiritual pole, and with the expansion of self-realization to self-justification. New guise is only thin disguise: the world in which Designori lives differs only in appearance from that through which Goldmund wanders, and both are reflections of the bourgeois world that Hesse knew and frowned upon; and an order of intellectuals, its confines, and its Magister Ludi are but a religious order, monastery, and abbot, secularized. With Hesse's shift in focus from physical to spiritual pole, protagonist became friend and friend became protagonist, world receded and retreat moved into foreground: Designori's is a skeletonized and truncated variation of Goldmund's story, and Knecht's tale is an elaborated and extended variation of Narziss's; Goldmund's expansive and variegated world became but a shadowy association with Designori, and Narziss's modest monastery burgeoned into an educational province. It was only with the injection of self-justification that Hesse's last novel assumed its own unique character: a new dimension was added to argument, a new direction was given to self-realization, and protagonist finally leaves radical individualism and aestheticism behind him.

Protagonist and friend in both *Narziss und Goldmund* and *Das Glasperlenspiel* are exceptionally gifted complements marked by destiny to pursue opposite paths of life. One is an estranged observer with a penchant for thought and a preference for things spiritual, and the other a participant in life committed primarily to the physical world. With Hesse's shift in concern from Goldmund's sensuality to Knecht's spirituality, protagonist and friend reversed their representation but remained fixed in their persons, and the interplay of their relationship continued its old pattern. Protagonists represent life's opposite possibilities, but each is blond, handsome, shy, childlike, and something of a dreamer, neither is robust, and both are younger than their intimes. Though likewise life's opposites, friends too are cast from one mold: each is attractive, sophisticated, articulate, aristocratic, and assertive, neither knows much humility, and both are slightly older and more mature than the protagonists.

Attraction between protagonists and friends is immediate and mutual: each friend senses a complement in his new acquaintance, and though somewhat apprehensive, each takes the initiative in the budding friendship; both protagonists are quite fearful, for both new acquaintances suggest temptation and danger, but both also promise an expansion of horizons of experience. Each protagonist finds not only a friend who is both attraction and detraction but also a much older guardian who is both model and inspiration: the Magister Musicae is as solicitous of Knecht's welfare as Abbot Daniel is of Goldmund's, and each of these saintly figures leaves an indelible impression upon the mind of his ward.

Both friendships begin at a comparably early and impressionable stage in life, are located in analogous situations and characterized by little action and abundant argumentation, involve mutual respect and influence and evolve dialectically, run similar courses and terminate with the protagonist's death. The initial phase of both friendships extends over some three years. During this period, friend alerts protagonist to life's polarity and to their respective polar relationship: Narziss in private discussion argues his own spirituality and place in Mariabronn and opens Goldmund's eyes to his innate sensuality and to his destiny in life beyond Mariabronn; Designori in debate associates himself with the world of flesh and blood to which he exposes Knecht whom he, in turn, identifies with Castalia and its spirituality. Both friendships evoke mutual admiration and each party of both friendships is quickly caught up in life's polar tug of war: Goldmund would become a monk like Narziss but opts for the secular world; Narziss eyes Goldmund and life at large enviously but keeps to his ascetic retreat; Knecht nurtures a kindled longing for Designori's world of flesh and blood but dedicates himself to Castalia's intellectuality; and Designori is drawn to Castalia's life etherealized but turns to life natural and naïve.

Protagonist and friend in both novels part on the best of terms after their short but rich friendship, each is persuaded that life holds much in store for the other, each goes his predestined way, and in both cases a decade transpires before their paths again cross. Narziss and Knecht remain in their institutional retreats and become their spiritual leaders, and Goldmund and Designori return to the outside world, one to become an artist-voluptuary and the other a lawyer-politician. Friendships are resumed in each case when friend chances to become a member of a commission sent to confer with the authorities of his complement's world, friends know protagonists at once but are themselves not immediately recognized, old intimacies are quickly restored, and each couple enjoys a concluding three years of fruitful interaction. In both cases, these last three years virtually take up where the first three break off. Protagonists and friends are again drawn together in mutual need and respect, protracted argument again centers about life's polarity, and each pair is still conscious of its polar constitution: an embittered Goldmund is quickly soothed by the meditative prayer prescribed by Narziss, and a despondent Designori responds immediately and favorably to the meditative observation prescribed by Knecht; Goldmund restores a vital touch of life to Narziss's ascetic lot, and Designori restores Knecht's vital contact with life; the abstract world of thought is still questionable to both Goldmund and Designori, and the outside world still holds its simmering attraction for both Narziss and Knecht.

Relationships broken off years previously not only resume their common interaction but end in an identical reversal of roles, and in the death of each protagonist. Initiative now passes from friends to protagonists: friends, once cocksure and aggressive, now stand by in doubt and in need of solace, and protagonists, once troubled and timid, become content affirmers of the self and decisive consolers.

Each protagonist finally leaves his own world, is given shelter by his friend, then suffers an accidental and early death: Goldmund returns sick but smiling to Mariabronn after his last fling and dies fully at peace with himself soon thereafter; Knecht steps joyfully out into the void of life, courts death almost immediately, and dies calmly; and death is for both but an exciting new adventure. Neither protagonist dies before he has come to terms with himself but both leave an old hope unfulfilled: Goldmund's statue of Mother-Eve remains a dream, and Knecht's harmonious interplay of life's spirituality and sensuality, sequestered observation and active commitment, remains an ideal. A concluding touch of narrative appeasement rounds out each protagonist's tale: Goldmund's death promises a compensating union with Mother-Eve, and Tito promises to be Knecht's hope realized.

Whereas each protagonist's story concludes, each friend's merely terminates. Both Narziss and Designori are left mired in the mess their lives seem to have become. Ascetic dedication to spirituality has lost its once unassailable meaning for Narziss, and the physical-sensual world has lost all its old attraction for Designori. Goldmund's dying words leave Narziss wondering whether indeed he can die without ever having lived, and renewed contact with Knecht draws Designori's attention back to the personal synthesis of Castalia and his world that he had once courted. Each friend is left on the threshold of major decision, and both may bolt their confines in the manner of the typical Hessean protagonist.

Narziss und Goldmund was, of course, no more a conscious model for Hesse's double self-projection in *Das Glasperlenspiel* than *Demian* was for the narrative structure of the novel. Both these considerations had long before become characteristic features of Hesse's mode of storytelling: Hessean narrative movement and rhythms. This peculiar nodal narrative structure had its origin in Hesse's own life; his own evolving self-realization had in retrospect become to him primarily a series of critical human encounters. And the dynamics of his inter-friend relationships derive primarily from his persistent concern with life's basic polarity imposed upon reflections of his own close friendships.

In the years following *Demian*, this autobiographically determined mode of narration became ever more pronounced and gradually spread from the protagonist's story to his complement's. This progression peaked in *Das Glasperlenspiel*. Knecht and Designori are not only projected polar components of one personality, or two sides of the same coin, but theirs are also narratively analogous tales. Each of the stories depicts a decidedly different possibility of life, one is ample and the other skeletal, but narration follows a common pattern. Both Knecht and Designori belong to the exceptional and are marked for the exceptional. Each in his own way is an outstanding student in Waldzell, one emerges the world's advocate and the other Castalia's apologist, both are a source of concern and annoyance for a headmaster who enjoys the confidence of neither, and each finds a lasting friend in his adversary. Their paths part, one gives himself to things of the spirit and the other to things of the body, and each in time fulfills his promise in the world of his inclination and choice. Knecht becomes a member of the Order, an emissary to Mariafels, and Castalia's Magister Ludi, and Designori becomes a lawyer and leading politician, establishes a home and has a family. Each enjoys all his world has to offer, but neither is content. Knecht's world is too abstract and esoteric, and Designori's is too concrete and common, the body is neglected in one and the mind in the other. Each had hoped to achieve a personal synthesis of the world and Castalia and neither had succeeded. Both mavericks have reached an impasse in their lives when their friendship resumes. Each is for the other a salutary renewed contact with life's other possibility. Designori becomes Knecht's stepping stone from Castalia to the outside world, and Knecht reopens Castalia's doors for Designori. Knecht may be a defector, and Designori may become one. In any case, Tito is their common promise of synthesis.

THE ELDER BROTHER, TEGULARIUS, AND PATER JAKOBUS

The Magister Musicae is thrust, control, and inspiration in Knecht's life, Designori is perturbing expansion, the Elder Brother brief temptation, Tegularius sharp warning, and Pater Jakobus lends perspective and ethical direction to self-realization. Each of these individuals is a loner and self-seeker cut from rare cloth: appropriate possibilities and lessons for a kindred Josef Knecht, but also yet another illustration of the extent to which Hesse's person cast its shadow over his personae. Like Knecht and Designori, the Magister Musicae and the Elder Brother are different and yet essentially the same. The former is dedicated to music, the latter is given to his Oriental studies, and both are students of meditation. The Magister Musicae is gentle and the Elder Brother thorny, but each is something of a saintly mystic, each has cultivated his spirituality to the absolute exclusion of his sensuality, and both are at peace with the self and the world. Basically, these two of Knecht's mentors differ only in their commitments: the Magister Musicae is both official and teacher in Castalia, and the Elder Brother is committed only to the beauty of his splendid isolation and his esoteric cerebrations. This is the very tempting aestheticism against which the Magister Musicae warns Knecht and to which the Magister Musicae had not permitted himself to succumb. Knecht savors this seductive possibility briefly, perceives flight and renunciation in it, and turns his back upon it. The Elder Brother's is not Knecht's way, but the encounter does engender in him that greater consciousness of the self and its unique destiny that eventually takes him to a potential self-realization beyond Castalia.

The Elder Brother's withdrawal among the already withdrawn is a benign expression of the aestheticism disparaged by the Magister Musicae. Tegularius exemplifies that Castalian hazard become a malignancy. He is Castalia at its best and worst, all that a Castalian should and should not be: a genius among geniuses and a wanting human among already too wanting human beings. As a bead-game player, Tegularius is virtuosity itself, he is also a most discerning teacher for the most advanced of Castalia's students, and a loyal friend, trustworthy confidant, and dedicated assistant to Knecht, but he is also sick in body and weak in character, prone to pervasive disbelief and subject to deep depression, volatile in mood and erratic in behavior, abrasive in relationships and irresponsible in duty, intolerant of any restraints and disdainful of all authority. The Elder Brother exemplifies individualism and intellectuality become blithely self-indulgent, Tegularius is individualism become anarchistic and intellectuality become nihilistic, both are dead-end streets for Knecht, and neither augurs well for Castalia. Each of these Castalian aberrants holds a deep attraction for Knecht, one stirs his reverence and the other his solicitude, but he quickly recognizes that neither should be emulated if he is to realize himself and Castalia is to survive.

His debates with Designori compel Knecht to reflect upon the outside world and to scrutinize Castalia, convince him that life as a whole is a dynamic spiritual-physical phenomenon, and leave him wondering why a harmonious interplay of life's polar components should not be possible for himself. But Knecht also emerges from the fray a confirmed Castalian, and with Designori's departure, the outside world ceases to be of much further concern. What is argued flamboyantly in Waldzell by Designori is reiterated calmly in Mariafels a dozen years later by Pater Jakobus. Another of Hesse's many inter-friend dramas is reenacted. Like Designori, Pater Jakobus takes the initiative in both friendship and argument: he addresses himself to and maintains a close relationship with Mariafel's reserved visitor, and repeats Designori's conviction that Castalia is but an enclave of effete aesthetes who have chosen to divorce themselves from real life. Knecht again has recourse to reference books to counter and instruct Castalia's critic, adversaries again enlighten each other and win each other's respect and affection, and each again goes his way unconverted by the other but the richer for the encounter: Pater Jakobus is apprised of Castalia's history, institutions, and its bead game, ceases to deprecate the province, and even intercedes on its behalf with the papacy; and Knecht in turn is persuaded that Castalia is a part of human history and not an autotelic institution exempt from time, and is left with an enduring curiosity about and love for the greater world beyond his province. His encounter with Designori engenders in Knecht a longing for a closer relationship between Castalia and the world and for an interplay in his own life of the principles these represent. In its own small way, Pater Jakobus's intercession with the papacy helps to promote this envisaged rapprochement of polar worlds, and his own life exemplifies something of the personal synthesis espoused by Knecht: an intellectual given to solitary reflection and a wise observer of man, but also a human among humans and a responsible participant in the affairs of man. Neither encounter moves Knecht to immediate decision and action or even deflects the course of his life, but both leave lasting impressions and desires, and these in time have a common critical delayed impact.

The Magister Musicae impresses upon Knecht his obligation to the self and to Castalia. Pater Jakobus directs Knecht's attention to his fellow man and to social obligation. The former is Knecht's guide and goal in Castalia, and the latter becomes his guide and goal in life. Pater Jakobus's view of history leaves Knecht concerned about Castalia's future, it also whets his long-latent appetite for life at large, and the old historian's social commitment attracts his admiration and pricks his conscience. This concern for Castalia, urge for further self-realization, and ethical impulse increase with the passing years and together eventually take Knecht into the attractive and promising unknown beyond Castalia.

THE INEVITABILITY OF DEFECTION

Knecht's departure from Castalia is obviously not caprice, panic, chance, or even choice, but dispositional inevitability. He, like every other of Hesse's many protagonists, is essentially a nomad nowhere permanently at home, a seeker never satisfied, and a loner intolerant of ties and plagued by life's polarity. They are all truants who refuse to be institutionalized, and their long chain of truancies has its origin in Hesse's own truancy-filled life: in his French leave from Maulbronn, his departure from family tradition, early divorce from life, flight to the East, defection from Christian orthodoxy, disassociation from Germany, and separation from family. That Knecht is not likely to be different from his antecedents becomes clear at the outset of his story. The model but also troubled and restless teenager in Eschholz points clearly to the middle-aged and model but also troubled and restless Magister Ludi in Waldzell. Boy and man, Knecht is not only dedicated to but critical of Castalia and aware of better possibility, his grappling with life's polarity begins early and never ends, and anomaly is congenitally more fascinating than rule. In short, Knecht is an outsider and potential defector from the beginning. That some of the students carefully selected for Castalia's schools should be dismissed for incompetence or inability to make the adjustment required of them leaves young Knecht deeply depressed and his faith in the Order somewhat shaken. He is persuaded that these dismissals are more Castalia's own failure than human flaws, that the dismissed are not the weak and inferior but the strong and daring, and that return to their families is not penalty or regression but a bold leap back into the real and enticing world. These outcasts become Knecht's models, Eschholz's exemplary students attract his scorn, and Castalia pales a touch before life at large. Knecht even hopes that he too may have the courage to strike out as boldly as the province's rejects, should his upward aspirations some day make that necessary. Only circumstance separates recalcitrant novice from defecting master.

Life's polar worlds but faintly etched in Eschholz become dynamic realities in Waldzell. The town itself is a composite of the profane world and of the Order's inner sanctum, a visible juxtaposition of sensuality and spirituality. The rare aura of the Vicus Lusorum, the complex reserved for the bead game, leaves Knecht in humble awe, and the community proper with its bearded burghers, stout women, and mocking maidens, its dogs and yowling children, workshops and stores, and its sundry sounds and smells, excites him. Designori's friendship worsens Knecht's predicament. Vague emotional quandary now becomes conscious argument and serious inner conflict. Knecht is sorely troubled by and argues strongly against but also tacitly concurs with Designori's contention that Castalians are an arrogant crew of priestly parasites divorced from life and disdainful of the very world that supports them. His latent attraction to this more primitive world becomes sympathy and love even while he argues Castalia's cause. Polarity, which had previously been primarily an outer fact, also becomes an inner reality in Waldzell: growing friction between Knecht's budding sexuality and his spirituality is added to choice between Castalia and life at large. Knecht's poems of the time best mirror his spreading predicament: secret longing for raw life and surfeit of dream and thought are countered by aversion to life's blind flux and a desperate quest for permanence and meaning in things spiritual, fervent profession of faith in intellectuality is cancelled by equally grave doubts about it, and joyous embrace of a personal life marked by a flow of distinct stages is followed by envisaged serene and lasting dedication to the bead game. Whereas these poems themselves reveal a very perturbed Knecht, their writing, together with Knecht's headstrong insistence upon pursuing an imbalanced course of studies, flagrant breaches of practice in Castalia, already evidence some of the rebelliousness that much later perpetrates a similar but much more serious infraction of Castalian tradition. An intransigent individualist's self-expression in each of these instances takes precedence over constraint and self-denial. Eventual defection is but the last and most momentous expression of this tenacious self-assertiveness. Knecht's acclaim of a life of rhythmic bold venture and its identification with a necessary and meaningful flux of nature are no less at odds with Castalian belief and practice than is his propensity for self-assertion. And his wistful wish for a harmonious interplay between Castalia and the outside world and between man's spirituality and sensuality clearly runs counter to the Order's political tradition of separation and its exclusive cultivation of the intellect. Wishful thinking had but to become espoused ideal for dedication to become defection. Knecht is only somewhat out of step in Eschholz. He is distinctly at variance with Castalia in Waldzell. Each of these stages takes him closer to the heart of the Order and simultaneously increases the likelihood of his eventual departure from it.

Knecht's subsequent ten years of independent study are but another step in this same direction. Left to his own devices, he becomes the nomad, seeker, and loner that he basically is. Waldzell is left behind and he goes his own elusive way, given to his own intellectual pursuits, and jealous of his own privacy. Polarity, Knecht's engrossment in Waldzell, ceases temporarily to be of much concern, and the faith in and doubts about the bead game which are but broached in the poems, now become focal concern. Suspicion that the game, art for some and religion for others, is ultimately perhaps only an exercise in intellectual virtuosity, gradually ebbs, and Knecht finally concludes that it is indeed a *lingua sacra* which makes accessible the world's innermost mysteries, and which merits his own lifelong dedication. So persuaded, he becomes a member of the Order and quickly finds his place among the elite. But suspicion only ebbs, conclusion is more self-delusion than conviction, and dedication becomes accommodation. And that Knecht is likely to strike out for new possibility when this happens is clearly reflected in the second of his conjectural autobiographies. Neither of the two hermit confessors hesitates to pull up stakes when his office loses its meaning and attraction.

Eschholz, Waldzell, and the province's period of independent study are for Knecht not only institutional frameworks that permit personal growth but also enclosures that demand accommodation. The Order itself is for him but the last of Castalia's possibilities and confines, and not a terminal goal. And for the self-willed seeker-loner that he is, it can be no different. Perpetual quest and periodic upheaval are virtually predestined. A possibility once exhausted is for Knecht, as it always was for Hesse himself, a confine rendered intolerable. And the Order becomes just that when its intellectuality wears thin and unresolved personal problems wax acute. Knecht's encounter with Pater Jakobus makes this an inevitability. Attention is directed back to polarity: to Castalia and the world, and to Castalia's cultivation of the mind and its neglect of the body. And unresolved polarity is extended from geopolitics and psychology to ethics: to a choice between sequestered celebration and responsible involvement. The Order's almost exclusive commitment to the former begins to pale beside Pater Jakobus's commitment to the latter. Knecht counters the historian's insistence that the bead game is essentially only a game, but the contention, a suspicion sowed years earlier by Designori, lingers on in his mind. And Jakobus's location of Castalia in history and time makes conviction of what had long been merely vague belief for Knecht. Mariafels is obviously no less a significant stepping stone to Knecht's ultimate secession from the province than it is an immediate proving ground for his succession to its highest office.

Like the Designori debates, the Jakobus discussions have their decided impact but elicit no immediate decision or reaction. The course of life that the Magister Musicae sets for his ward continues its unswerving upward sweep until it levels off on Castalia's highest plateau. Knecht has now only to become a practised Magister Ludi to exhaust the Order's possibilities. Anxious to prove himself, he accepts his obligations enthusiastically and soon becomes an able administrator, an inspiring teacher, and an original bead-game player. But with mastery all cloys. Functionary duties, tedious from the outset, soon become onerous, indoctrination of the advanced and gifted gradually loses its attraction, and the bead game itself becomes a questionable *summum bonum* in but a few years. Belief and fascinating novelty end in doubt and tedious repetition.

A reawakened interest in history after only one year in office redirects Knecht's attention to polarity. What had twice been pondered then put aside is now repondered and acted upon. Argument broached by Designori then extended and accorded historical context by Pater Jakobus becomes compelling conviction. Though perhaps heaven on earth, Castalia is indeed but a fragile fragment of and absolutely dependent upon the world at large, and though the sublimest of human accomplishments, the bead game is truly an esoteric art bordering upon and highly susceptible to aestheticism, and neither Castalia nor its game are beyond human perversion or even the normal assault of time. From the vantage point of his office Knecht now himself perceives clearly a dangerous and ever-widening rift of mutual indifference between the province and its patron world. Life, politics, and even education beyond its own borders have become largely a matter of indifference to Castalia, the province and its game have ceased to be of much consequence to the outside world, and interaction between the polar two has become minimal. Circumstances in Castalia itself promise that this rift is likely to grow beyond repair: intellectual universality, meditation, and wisdom have already begun to give way to specialty, compulsion, and hubris, and such characterless aesthetes as Tegularius are harbingers of worse to come. And approaching troubled times in the outside world promise just as surely to reduce the Order and its province to an expendable luxury. Knecht is convinced that this incipient inner degeneration and eventual outer rejection number Castalia's days, and that only a drastic intellectual and moral regeneration may prolong its historical moment. He also feels morally obliged to impress these convictions upon his colleagues, and is persuaded that defection may best serve his purpose. The harmonious interplay of two polar worlds, an ideal of which a student had once plaintively dreamed, becomes a necessity for which a master is prepared to put himself on the line.

Concern with polarity again spreads from geopolitics to ethics and to psychology. Although long mentor to Knecht even before his investiture, Pater Jakobus does not become his model until following the Magister Musicae's death some three years thereafter. By then, Knecht has virtually become his old Castalian patron and has experienced all that Castalia has to offer. He has exhausted one possibility and is ready for another. The Magister Musicae had been his model for self-realization in terms of the Order, Pater Jakobus becomes his model for self-realization in terms of the world at large; the former had directed Knecht to the heart of Castalia, the latter leads him to the threshold of life; dedication to the province yields to moral obligation to the community of man. Impressed by the responsible interplay of thought and action in the life of Pater Jakobus, and convinced that Castalia's ideal precludes emulation of this ethical ideal, Knecht is left no choice but to relinquish his office and to leave the province.

Like individuality, the libido has no place in Castalia's order of things. Anonymity is the ideal and sublimation the rule. Neither constraint sits well with Knecht. His self is not to be denied and his urges demand more self-expression than the province will permit. An ultimate parting of ways is inevitable from the very start. Although a thing of the past, Hesse's radical oscillation between spirituality and sensuality from *Demian* to *Der Steppenwolf* was not entirely forgotten in the thirties. Knecht is dedicated to intellectuality and has no truck with women, but he is not spared the disquieting tug of sexuality. Sexual drama is again enacted, but in low key and in a manner consonant with monastery-like Castalia. Libidinal urges first fired by the profane world in Waldzell, then stoked by Designori's defense of physical life, but immediately damped by meditation, quickly find continent and satisfactory expression in comradeship and intellectual pursuits: in Knecht's relationships with the Magister Musicae, Ferromonte, Designori, the Elder Brother, Tegularius, Pater Jakobus, the novice Anton, and even the student Petrus, and in his private studies, the bead game, and even in his eventual instructional and administrative duties. This sublimation of appetite and energy continues successfully only until Knecht has experienced, learned, and become all he can in Castalia. Once the province's possibility has been more or less exhausted and faith in its adequacy shaken, biological energies long deflected begin to reassert themselves. The Magister Ludi's waning interest in the bead game and its players after but two or three years in office is countered by his growing concern with Castalia's younger and even youngest students. This immediate and devious assertion of long pent-up urges eventually becomes forthright yearning for their more direct self-expression: Knecht's simple desire for a touch of naïve life, for substance and not just abstraction, for involvement with real humans and not just men become minds. Except for its moderation, Knecht's is Haller's psychological crisis all over again. In both cases, spirituality has been cultivated at the expense of sensuality, and in both cases sensuality finally demands its own. But where Haller lusts for life and embarks upon raw sexual adventure, Knecht merely yearns for a breath of life and becomes tutor to a child of nature.

Once Knecht has tried all that Castalia has to offer and new possibility becomes insistent, the confines of the Order turn intolerable. Synthesis, an old dream, emerges a new pursuit. Life for Knecht will no longer be Castalia or the world, *vita contemplativa* or *vita activa*, spirituality or sensuality, but Castalia and the world, *vita contemplativa* and *vita activa*, spirituality and sensuality. Since this new possibility is an impossibility within the province, Knecht has no choice but with hope to go beyond it. It is to Castalia and the world, to their historical interdependence, their rift of mutual indifference, and their necessary synthesis that he alerts the Order in his circular letter. A decadent institution must again become responsive to its basic obligation and ultimate justification: the preservation of the spiritual foundation of the world. Convinced that this is immediately possible, that Castalia itself will be the healthier for it, and that his espoused harmonious interplay of province and world can best be realized if Castalians again become for the world the schoolmasters they once were, Knecht elects to shed dignity and authority to do just that. The circular letter directs attention to the province and the world, Knecht's subsequent pleading of his cause in Hirsland dwells upon himself and his hunger for reality beyond Castalia's, for deeds, service, and suffering not yet experienced, and focuses upon his irresistible further urge for self-realization and its poignant moments of awakening. Knecht's concern about Castalia and for the world is certainly a significant factor in his decision to leave the province, but this passion for fuller self-realization is undoubtedly the ultimate determinant. It is this pertinacious self-preoccupation that persuades Alexander to brush aside the Magister Ludi's plea for respect and understanding, and to brand him a traitor to the cause even though he performs his duties in exemplary fashion to the very end, and though his resignation and departure are but an exercising of recognized privilege, and not a violation of trust or decree. Like Hesse and most every other of his outsider-protagonists, Knecht chafes at and defects, and the established order disapproves of and rejects.

CROWNING ACHIEVEMENT

Immediately, Knecht's resignation and departure from Castalia might appear to be futile warning and venture, and his icy death, the fruitless consequence of a rash and foolish response. All seems to have no apparent impact upon either Castalia or the world and to be of little avail either to Knecht or Tito. Defection and precipitate demise would suggest a loss of faith and fortitude and argue Knecht's inadequacy, and by implication question Castalia's own *raison d'être*. An institution's exemplary graduate and most celebrated Magister apparently fails his first test of practical experience, and an illustrious Order fails to justify its privileged existence. And all this would imply an old man's veiled acknowledgment of a lifetime's error: the futility and crumbling of Hessean dream. Such may be the immediate implications of the novel's enigmatic termination but is most certainly not its intended meaning and message, no more so than sex, jazz, drugs, and pathology are focal concern in *Der Steppenwolf*. To argue otherwise, in either instance, is to accord too much attention to surface events and to give too little heed to less obvious detail and to Hesse's undercurrents of argument, to forget the customary concluding upbeat of his tales and to ignore the characteristically positive connotation of death in his works, to gainsay Hesse's own unqualifiedly positive reading of the novel's abrupt and seemingly untoward ending, and to disregard the facts of his own life.

The emergence and politics of the Third Reich dismayed and angered Hesse, his brother's suicide and renewed public deprecation in Germany distressed him greatly, and the outbreak and events of the Second World War left him deeply depressed. But neither trying current events nor personal experience occasioned either the collapse of or the lapse in hope or belief that a negative interpretation of Knecht's defection and death would presuppose. Not despairing break but hopeful evolution characterizes Hesse's attitude to self and life following his brief Morgenlandean commitment to aestheticism. Nothing essential in belief or ideal was abandoned, all merely evolved. Hesse did not lose faith in the purposiveness of the independent course of life he had embarked upon in 1919, or in the ultimate efficacy of the spirit, and he continued to nurture his dreams of better possibility.[43] Self-realization, self-justification, and better pos-

43 See e.g.: *Briefe* (1964), pp. 53–54, 65, 80–81, 92–93, 170–171, 176–177, 196; *Materialien zu Hermann Hesses* Das Glasperlenspiel (1973), Vol. 1, pp. 91, 125, 135, 193, 232.

sibility, previously perceived primarily in terms of the self, art, and thought, now simply expanded to include fellow man and world. It is precisely this promising evolution in Hesse's life, and not failure and unavailing new beginning, that is depicted in the evolving course and termination of Knecht's life.

What biography would perhaps only question, Hesse himself roundly refuted. *Das Glasperlenspiel* was for him no more a story of decline and fall than was *Der Steppenwolf*, and in both cases he never ceased to argue the contrary. Although he readily acknowledged that an author was not necessarily the best judge of his own works, and was himself generally very tolerant of views divergent from his own, Hesse was distinctly irritated by this widespread and persistent "misunderstanding" of the most notorious, and the most ambitious, of his tales. From 1927 to 1942 and beyond he felt constrained to remind his readers in repeated protest and plea that Haller's story was not just a salacious depiction of shoddy actuality but also, and more significantly, a manifest argument for better possibility, that it did not just treat of sickness and despair, but ended in restored health and hope; and from 1943 almost to the end of his life, his swelling correspondence kept insisting, and in tones progressively more piqued, that Knecht's resignation and departure were not rank defection, but commendable response to conscience and concern, and that his icy plunge and death were not folly and failure, but sacrifice and success, commitment fulfilled for Knecht and admonition and inspiration for Tito.[44] That it was only in these two instances that Hesse ever took real issue with his readers, and that he continued in both cases to remonstrate as long as he did, was not coincidence and also not just stubborn whim. He had good cause for concern. To misunderstand either of these novels is to misunderstand their author.

The notion of folly and failure is just as untenable in the formal context of Hesse's art as a whole as it is in the context of biography and extra-textual assertion. Major tales preceding *Das Glasperlenspiel* are not only characteristically truncated, but also terminate with a veiled but unambiguous promise of better things to come. The abrupt and enigmatic termination of Knecht's story, like its nodal mode of

---

44 E.g., "Despite his illness, Knecht could sagaciously and artfully have avoided his leap into the mountain water. He leaps notwithstanding . . . because he cannot disappoint this youngster who cannot be won over very easily. And he leaves behind a Tito for whom this sacrifice of life on the part of a man far superior to him represents lifelong admonition and guidance, and will educate him more than all the sermons of the wise." *Materialien zu Hermann Hesses* Das Glasperlenspiel (1973), Vol. 1, p. 279.

narration and protracted exposition, its use of double self-projections, or its calculated choice of names, is clearly continuation and not innovation. The continuation of an unusual peculiarity in form would certainly argue for a continuation of its established implication. Such is no less true of Knecht's demise. That death, theretofore commonly associated with a tale's sudden termination and consistently representative of promising transition, should abruptly connote negative finality, is inconceivable. Knecht's death is obviously only a variation of and not a departure from Demian's, Vasudeva's, Hermine's, or even H.H.'s. Decease is in each case timely departure and auspicious absorption: Demian is absorbed by Sinclair, Hermine by Haller, H.H. by Leo, and Knecht by Tito. It was precisely because Knecht's death and the novel's ending were variation and not challenging change that Hesse was so ruffled by their misinterpretation.

Text itself convincingly corroborates what biography, author commentary, and literary precedent would insist upon. All is simply not what reflex response to unexpected departure and startling death would have it be. To assume that Knecht's departure is simple defection and that his plunge into the lake is nothing more than an impulsive act that leaves a man dead, a youngster stunned, and a world unaffected, is not to misinterpret, but virtually to bypass the text. Both the exposition and the informational asides of the body of the novel and its concluding observations explicitly gainsay this negative assumption. The text clearly argues the necessity and meaningfulness of Knecht's departure, plunge, and death, and in terms of both Knecht himself and Tito and of both Castalia and the world. Knecht's death and its circumstances do permit a wide but only positive sweep of symbolical meaning, and the novel's abrupt termination does leave to conjecture the particulars of Tito's future life and the details of history from 2200 to 2400, but not their promise and positive direction. The novel's framework of faith in the individual and life remains intact. All begins with hope, spirals its upward course, and peaks in fulfillment and with new promise of even better possibility: a grand finale, not a collapse.

Defection and death are of direct advantage to the two persons immediately involved and of delayed gain to the two worlds in the background. Knecht himself is the first to benefit. What is willful flight to Alexander is in fact but a necessary continuation of the upward and outward spiral of Knecht's self-realization, and death is not a premature termination of this evolutionary becoming of the self, but its paradoxical culmination. Having become all he can possibly become in the confines of Castalia, Knecht is left champing at the bit. He has had his fill of intellectuality but has starved his sensuality, his has been a life rich in abstraction, but wanting in action, and he has known enough responsibility but only to the self and to Castalia. Fuller self-realization is possible only in the greater world. Knecht's long-curbed libidinal urges find their needed greater expression in his close association with the Designoris, tutelage adds action to his world of thought, and his pressing ethical concern finds its satisfaction in unstinted commitment to a child of the world at large. Knecht does not realize the balanced expression of spirituality and sensuality he had envisaged as a student in Waldzell, his interplay of *vita contemplativa* and *vita activa* is of but short duration, and his belated commitment to man and society hardly balances his longtime dedication to Castalia, but all does represent yet another and higher stage in his self-realization. The Magister Musicae with his belief in the sanctity of the individual and his advocacy of self-fulfillment would have nodded approval, and Pater Jakobus with his disdain for aestheticism and his eye to history must have applauded. Knecht proves to be a true disciple of each and a combination of both. Commitment to the world, action, and sensuality do not replace but complement dedication to Castalia, thought, and spirituality. Knecht does not become a man of the world but a Castalian given to the world. As such, departure and death are certainly not the defection and failure they may appear to be. Not only Knecht the individual but even Knecht the Castalian is the better for this turn of events: the former becomes more of himself, a fuller human being; the latter becomes what his predecessors once were and his successors would again become, a more responsible Castalian.

The Magister Musicae and Pater Jakobus are Knecht's major models, teachers, and inspiration. One prepares him for Castalia and the other directs him to the world. In the characteristic manner of Hessean wards, he virtually absorbs both and becomes more than either. Knecht in turn becomes inspirational model and teacher, is himself similarly absorbed, and yet another ward promises to surpass his guardian. Tito's encounter with Knecht is an unmistakable repetition of Knecht's encounter with the Magister Musicae. A ward again stands in awe of a distinguished and equally gentle guardian, is again awakened to higher human possibility, again becomes solemnly aware of a pending critical turning point in his life, and again foresees an exciting and meaningful future. The concluding observations of the novel give ample reason to conclude that Knecht's example and death will not be lost on Tito, and the chronicler's better world of 2400 would confirm this implication.

Knecht's death leaves Tito stunned and frightened, conscious of a great loss, troubled by his conscience, and seized by an awesome premonition that both he and his life would now change drastically, and that far greater things would now be demanded of him than he had ever asked of himself. Guilt is obviously associated with responsibility, and radical change with atonement. The details of this atonement are left to surmise, but the world of 2400, the better tomorrow for which Knecht and Tito are by and large responsible, not only points to its success but suggests its very nature. How can Tito better atone for the consequence of his wanton challenge and at the same time help usher in the chronicler's era, with its renewed harmonious interplay of Castalia and the outside world, than by becoming something of the man whom he has learned to respect and to love and for whose death he feels responsible? Designori is perpetuated and Knecht is essentially reborn in Tito. The youngster is heir to his father's and falls heir to his guardian's legacy. In him two polar worlds converge: that of the body, material concerns, business, politics, and action, and that of the spirit, intellectual pursuits, and meditation. He promises the balanced interplay of spirituality and physicality to which Knecht and Designori can only aspire, and will enjoy the interplay of *vita contemplativa* and *vita activa* that eludes Designori and that Knecht only manages to begin. Tito will not only realize the personal synthesis of life's polarities that his actual and spiritual father can merely court, but will also help achieve something of that synthesis of Castalia and the world to which both Designori and Knecht can only look forward. Tito's atonement therefore serves both person and institution, just as does Knecht's defection: Knecht proceeds farther along his road of self-realization and Tito begins his in earnest; Knecht prepares Castalia and Tito prepares the world at large for the better tomorrow of 2400. Tito will clearly become the exemplary person and leader Knecht himself foreshadows. Knecht was Hesse's reality, Tito was his latest and last vision of better human possibility.

Knecht and Designori are absorbed by Tito in the same manner in which the Magister Musicae and Pater Jakobus are absorbed by Knecht, and in both cases the resultant synthesis is something more than either of its components. This absorption of the past by the present and of the present by the future, an upward spiraling spiritual

continuum, is both consonant with Hesse's abiding faith in the ultimate meaningfulness of life, and illustrative of his notion of reincarnation.

Thanks to Knecht's admonition and example, neither Order nor
province succumb to moral dry rot, and thanks to his impact on Tito
they do not collapse for want of further support from the outside
world. Castalia remains structurally intact and its *raison d'être* is restored. It again emerges a conscientious guardian of cultural heritage
and spiritual values, again becomes the socially responsible educational authority it formerly was, and again stocks the world's schools
with dedicated teachers as it once did. And in the year 2400, Castalia
is still a realm of the mind committed to the service of mankind, the
outside world is still committed to the province, and both tradition
and chronicler accord ultimate credit for this renewed bilateral commitment of life's polar worlds to the Order's rebel-hero of 2200.
Knecht's unprecedented doomsday exposure of Castalia's parasitic
aestheticism and his equally unprecedented defection, humble tutelage, and death must have jarred the Order as severely and to just as
good advantage as his demise unsettles young Tito. Institution, ward,
and world are awakened by Knecht's own awakening. Tito is reborn,
Order is rejuvenated, rift between Castalia and world is repaired, and
a defector rightly becomes a folkhero. Censure and defection are
therefore not a repudiation of that which Castalia represents but of
that which the province has become; plunge into icy water is not an
act of folly but unhesitant commitment pedagogically necessary for
the retention of Tito's confidence; death is not proof of personal failure and institutional bankruptcy but a necessary prelude to success;
and Knecht's defection and death are as responsible and as necessary
for the reconciliation of the province and the world as his friendship
with Pater Jakobus was responsible and necessary for the closer relationship that developed between the Order and the papacy.

The novel's conclusion is no less positive in its symbolism than in
its actuality. Belpunt was probably as deliberate a choice of name for
the Designori mountain retreat as Monteport was for the Magister
Musicae's mountain asylum or as Planvaste was for a school specializing in mathematics. The name is also just as clearly positive in its implications as a name such as Road's End would be ominously negative. Among high peaks and in rare atmosphere, Belpunt is both an
appropriately located and named point of departure from high to
even higher and more demanding possibility: Knecht is Tito's bridge
to Castalia and things spiritual, and Tito is Knecht's bridge to the

world and commitment to man, and together they are the first of the many bridges that help to restore the once closer and mutually more beneficial relationship between the Order and the world. Belpunt's immediate surroundings would confirm its name's and location's positive connotations. Soaring peaks and rocky terrain afford a cathedral-like setting, and rising sun adds its promise of new life. The tiny glacial lake cradled in rock is not just exuberant recreation for Tito and deadly challenge for Knecht, but also a baptismal font for both. Icy water swallows Knecht's body and Tito's is left numb and exhausted, but immersion also signals a spiritual break and a new beginning for both guardian and ward. Theirs is clearly a rewarding sacral experience located in a carefully chosen and appropriately transfigured natural setting, and narrated in the consonant fervent tone, figurative mode, and cultish vocabulary of religion.

To argue Knecht's folly and failure is clearly both to ignore the guiding context of Hesse's life and his art, and to accord the text itself less than the meticulous reading it demands. This is precisely what those who have argued the failure of Harry Haller have done. Like Haller's, Knecht's only failure, if it is to be so termed at all, lies in his failure fully to realize an ideal. Haller does not become a Mozart or a Goethe and Immortalia remains a goal, and Knecht does not achieve the full self-realization to which he aspires and does not live long enough to enjoy the better world he helps to usher in, but in both instances actuality moves an important step closer to ideality. And this is as tantamount to success for Hesse's protagonists as it was for him.

One might wish that Hesse had added the Tito-story to his continuum of tales: the concluding link in his narrative chain. Protagonist would have been a cross between Goldmund and Narziss, a Plinio Designori and a Josef Knecht as much at home in the province of the spirit as in the world of the body, in polar realms that have themselves become reconciled. Tito's tale would have been that contrapuntal rendition of life's two melodies envisaged in *Kurgast* and only approximated in *Narziss und Goldmund*. But just as Siddhartha's wisdom is beyond words and Goldmund's mother image eludes chisel, the Tito-ideal was not for the pen. All three are ultimates, final distillates of life's experiences, and each defied expression. The ultimate inadequacy or failure of art argued by H.H. and previously fictively illustrated by the ineffable wisdom of Siddhartha and the uncut statue of Mother-Eve is perhaps confirmed in actuality by the untold story of the last and potentially most exemplary of Hesse's protagonists, the Hessean hero in his final reincarnation. Art's limitations had long frustrated and depressed; abetted by declining creative energy and decreased psychological need, they now deterred. Hesse never again attempted the impossible, the narrative expression of the ideal possible. For the rest of his life he was to confine his craft to observation, reminiscence, and rumination.

THE WESTERN WORLD AND THE GLASS BEAD GAME

Das Glasperlenspiel is another and the last of Hesse's many reappraisals of the self and of life. Like all preceding novels, it revolves about the artist-intellectual's encounter with the self and the world, and this central theme continues to evolve originally and dynamically. Previous tales depict the bitter outer and inner struggle that contemporary self-becoming is, Knecht's biography illustrates the jubilant evolutionary process it could and should be. This progression from troublous actuality to relatively problemless ideality not only added a new dimension to an old drama but also accommodated Hesse's shift in focus of interest from self-becoming to social self-justification. Matters once acute, but which by the early thirties had lost much of their urgency, and about which Hesse had already said all he had or cared to say, could be given short shrift without slighting them, and Hesse's latest pressing concern could enjoy undivided attention. Accorded no parents and privileged to attend Castalia's exceptional schools, Knecht is spared the usual Hessean agonies of childhood and adolescence, and Hesse was spared their superfluous and detractive repetition. And Castalia itself—a world that has proscribed artistic creativity, ostracized women, banned marriage, and sublimates sexuality,[45] knows no politics, practises no religion, cultivates collegiality, nurtures anonymity, and frowns upon psychology, is unconcerned about history, untroubled by fate, and has become oblivious of time—spared Hesse any further and equally superfluous and detractive pursuit of most of his many long-time adult concerns. Of old themes, and except for self-realization and closely related mat-

---

45 For this virtual omission of women in his last novel, Hesse commonly pleaded ignorance. To have written about something that had again become a mystery to him, would have been both dishonest and presumptuous (see *Briefe* [1964], pp. 211–212). It was not that he disliked women, but that he knew too little about them: "That a novel deals only with men should not be looked upon by women as antifeminist. Any woman who has really learned how to read and possesses the requisites for a Castalian way of life . . . will actually share in the spiritual and the suprasexual in such a book without any resentment. And if she has the urge, she will write a book in which she will depict the same problem from a woman's point of view. Every sensible man will only be thankful to her for so doing." *Briefe* (1964), p. 339.

ters, only Hesse's continued preoccupation with the Western world and its middle-class matrix found a prominent place in his last novel. Hesse's antipathy to the twentieth century and its bourgeois-dominated society is manifest in most of his writings. His age was for him what it characteristically is for his protagonists: a world spoiled by technology and despoiled by nationalism, a cultural and spiritual void where money, machines, depravity, and violence prevail, and where all too much is glitter, sham, and hypocrisy. And Hesse was convinced, as most of his protagonists are, that this world was of and for a vacuous middle-class mass: the herd, child-adults, philistines, sedentary citizens. He was also persuaded that this world's time was fast running out. Impassioned excoriation extending over more than three decades culminated in a calm pseudohistorical summary statement: Knecht's dispassionate chronicler's protracted and facetiously studied characterization of a troubled era long past.

From his vantage point of 2400 and largely dependent upon the historian Plinius Ziegenhalss alias Hermann Hesse, the chronicler draws attention to the distinctive idiosyncracies of life in the twentieth century. It was an age when feuilletons were the prevailing rage. Unbelievable quantities of pap were churned out by journalists, literary hacks, and even professors of repute, published by skads of newspapers and magazines, and eagerly consumed by an undiscerning culture-hungry public. Anecdotal trivia such as "Friedrich Nietzsche and Women's Fashions of 1870" and "The Favorite Dishes of the Composer Rossini" were particularly popular reading fare. Scandal in high places, matters erotic, and interests psychological were equally attractive grist for the paper mill. The interviewing of celebrities was no less a passion than the mass production and consumption of feuilletons. Eminent chemists and piano virtuosos were queried about politics, and popular actors, dancers, aviators, and even poets were drawn out on the merits of bachelorhood or the presumptive causes of financial crisis. The twentieth century was also an age of the popular lecture, a cousin to the feuilleton. Experts and intellectual frauds provided a restive middle-class citizenry with a wild array of witty and charming or learned and incomprehensible discourses on every imaginable topic ranging from art and artists to world tours. And whatever leisure time was not absorbed by printed or spoken word, was devoted to crossword puzzles, intricate card games, the automobile, and tempestuous or sentimental music. Debasement of learning and art, debilitation of religion, and corrosion of morality were no less extensive than this proliferation of anxious and joyless diversion. It was a time when professors married wealthy women and cultivated brilliant salons, and students neither knew nor cared about intellectual discipline, when writers enjoyed vast royalties and attractive country homes, physicians were decorated and kept liveried servants, and philosophers were fêted publicly for their mass feuilletons and their charming lectures. It was also an age torn by political and economic ferment, and devastated by frightful wars. Values had lost their value, morality was no longer a guide, religion no longer a solace, and reason of little comfort. Doom lurked behind a glittering façade. A civilization had clearly passed its apex, and cultural disintegration was at hand. Some acknowledged and stoically endured this awful truth, many could not accept and argued strongly against its reality, and others dismissed it lightly or even celebrated it cynically. A very few, singly and in small groups, chose to withdraw from the fray, hopeful of preserving for posterity at least some of the best of their cultural heritage. Chief among these were musicologists, mathematicians, and members of the Order of Eastern Wayfarers. In their retreat and dedication, these scholars and dreamers helped to stem the rush of decline and to prepare the way for Castalia.

The bead game itself began in England and Germany toward the middle of the twentieth century, and only as a lowly memory-sharpening pastime for musicologists and musicians. It acquired its name and became an exercise both in memory and in improvisation when sometime later Bastian Perrot of the Academy of Music of Cologne substituted glass beads strung on wires for previously used letters of the alphabet, numbers, notes, and sundry symbols. Perrot's abacus-like invention became popular in Germany, found its way to England, and for two to three decades remained a fashionable game of musical exercises. It was then adopted by students of mathematics in France, England, and Germany, and subsequently spread to almost all the sciences, the humanities, and the visual arts. Each of the many fields of learning attracted to the new interest evolved its own intricate game language, mathematical processes were soon rendered symbolically, and study in such diverse disciplines as music, philology, logic, architecture, sculpture, and painting began to be expressed in mathematical formulae. Perrot's actual glass beads also gave way to an abstract game of symbols. What had emerged as a confined and relatively simple diversion gradually became a widespread and progressively more flexible, sophisticated, and demanding intellectual discipline. The elite among students took passionately to the bead game, renounced the worldly ambitions, practices, and pleasures of the several preceding generations of scholars, and found their satisfaction in a fanatical and penitent devotion to their disciplines. Universities again became places of dedicated study, staffed by competent and scrupulous professors, intellectuals regained community respect, twentieth-century feuilletonism was stemmed, and Western civilization won a reprieve. Fifty years of entrenchment followed. Each field of learning continued independently to cultivate and to refine its own game. This specialism did not begin to move in the direction of universality until a Swiss musicologist, known to posterity only as the Joculator Basiliensis, ascertained the principles of a language of symbols and formulae capable of reducing music and mathematics to a common denominator. The game's new medium quickly evolved into an international language able to embrace almost any discipline. A synthesis of all learning was now possible. The *Unio Mystica* of the separate branches of the *Universitas Litterarum*—an idea that had intrigued the thinkers of ancient China, of Greece, the Arabic world, the scholastics, humanists, mathematicians of the seventeenth and eighteenth centuries, and romantic philosophers of the nineteenth—had finally become a reality. Years passed before this sublime art and science underwent its last modification. When the game threatened, for want of adequate built-in restraints, to become primarily a dazzling display of intellectual virtuosity, contemplation gradually became an obligatory, and in time, an integral component of its practice. By the middle of the twenty-first century the game had become the supreme spiritual-intellectual exercise over which Knecht presides in 2200, and which is still practised in the chronicler's world of 2400. But even before this legacy of the Eastern Wayfarers was adopted to counterbalance pure thought, the game had become the nucleus of a rapidly spreading Order of intellectuals. Enclaves of initiates that had sprung up in country after country, and of which Castalia is but one, united to form a world-wide monastery-like hierarchy. A World Commission (*Weltkommission*) was established to supervise the game's language, regulations, and purview; a Directorate (*Ordensleitung*) assumed the general governance of the Order in each country; a National Commission (*Landeskommission*) was put in charge of each country's Archive of Idiograms (*Spielarchiv*); an Academy (*Akademie*) comprising a Game Commission (*Spielkommission*) from every country involved became responsible for the continued development and purity of the game's language; a Magister Ludi was to preside over each Game Commission, to conduct the public celebrations of the game, to further its players and schools, and to keep strict watch over its development; the direction of education in each country was assigned to a Board of Education (*Erziehungsbehörde*) consisting of twelve masters; and selection of a country's most talented students for the Order's elite schools became the task of a Council of Studies (*Studienrat*) numbering twenty members representing both the Order and the Board of Education. Thanks largely to Knecht's defection, this international cultural structure, like the game itself, is still intact in the year 2400. And so is the Western world, thanks to the Order and its educational provinces.

In the concluding chapter of *Demian* (1917) Hesse gave expression to a strong belief in the imminent dissolution of Western civilization, and in his *Blick ins Chaos* (1920) he argued a supportive psychology of history. His culminating appraisal of the Western world, and his glance into the future are less a retraction of this earlier conviction and theory than a modification of the time factor and a shift in focus of interest. By the early thirties, Hesse had become persuaded that our declining civilization was more likely to experience a prolonged and relatively tranquil reflective twilight than to disintegrate quickly and violently, and his earlier fascination with dissolution and rebirth had gradually receded and yielded to a growing interest in preservation. Sinclair is a Nietzschean iconoclast prepared to support a holocaust to hasten the impending demise of our Christian-bourgeois age and the advent of a new tomorrow; Knecht is a Burckhardtean conservator anxious to prolong the best of our culture long past its prime, and willing to defect to help repair a political rift that could lead to its demise. Our civilization had enjoyed its creative heyday from 1500 to 1800, its subsequent decline in art and thought was not likely to terminate before 2000, an extended twilight of reflective cultural guardianship would follow, and ultimate dissolution could hardly be expected until long after 2400. It had become Hesse's firm conviction that our culture's values and beliefs were not yet spent; its mathematics would long remain a tribute to human geniality; and classical music, its very quintessence, was still and would long continue to be a grand and inspirational gesture: both a reflection of keen awareness of the inherent tragedy of life, and an expression of joyful and brave affirmation of man's lot. The Western world was not yet about to return to its primordial morass, and Sinclair's new world with its new man, morality, God, and religion, was not yet about to follow. In the personally and politically difficult years after *Demian*, Hesse had learned that a civilization's self-realization, its rise and decline, like an individual's becoming and unbecoming (*Werden* and *Entwerden*), was a decidedly slower process than he had assumed. He had also learned to accept this reality.

THE AUTOBIOGRAPHIES

Like the novel proper, each of its satellite tales is essentially but one more of Hesse's repeated appraisals of the self and of life. Time and guise shift and change from one Knecht biography to another even more radically than they do from *Demian* to *Siddhartha*, *Der Steppenwolf*, *Narziss und Goldmund*, and *Die Morgenlandfahrt*, but substance remains as intrinsically personal as ever. Each of the four stories, like Sinclair's, Siddhartha's, Haller's, Goldmund's, and H.H.'s, is also but a variation of what Hesse believed to be the timeless predicament of the exceptional: the artistically, intellectually, or spiritually gifted. They differ from these preceding novels only in their common shift of focus from self-realization's necessary initial commitment to the self and to art, intellectuality or spirituality, to self-realization's necessary ultimate obligation to serve the community. Like these earlier novels, Hesse's concluding narrative composite also attests to a belief in the universality and timelessness of man's preoccupation with things spiritual and intellectual. With their kindred protagonists randomly located in widely dispersed times and places but similarly engrossed in thought and moved by ideals, the novels from *Demian* to *Die Morgenlandfahrt* were an unwitting expression of a growing interest and deepening belief in a universal spiritual-intellectual continuum. What is only intimated by this series of separate works, and symbolically expressed by the timeless and widespread membership of Haller's Immortalia and H.H.'s Order of Eastern Wayfarers, is clearly illustrated and deliberately argued by Hesse's organized cluster of concluding tales with their common protagonist, who in several reincarnations experiences some of the major epochs of human history from the stone age to a distant future far advanced in something akin to cybernetics, and who in each reincarnation partakes in an appropriately different but analogous spiritual-intellectual tradition. The ultimate implication of history's separate and dated but continuous expressions of culture had in the twenties become an important adjunct concern to Hesse's earlier and continued interest in the life cycle and particularly in the decline of Western civilization. Adjunct concern, like major interest before it, eventually spawned a theory, and a philosophy of history was added to a psychology of history. Previously intent primarily upon the behavioral dynamics of culture, Hesse now fixed his attention upon the generative thrust behind all culture: the

316 / Hermann Hesse

innate spiritual-intellectual impulse of man. Culture and cultural institutions were obviously transitory, but the universal impulse of
which these were temporal manifestations was a continuum that
guaranteed a constant flow of culture. This emerging belief of the
twenties became literary possibility when Hesse in 1927 first envisaged a multibiography involving many epochs of history to argue a
spiritual continuum behind life's flux. It became a literary certainty
when it subsequently found assuring confirmation in Burckhardt's related view of cultural history.[46]

In *Der Regenmacher, Der Beichtvater,* and *Indischer Lebenslauf,* just
as in the novel proper, Hesse not only fixes his narrative attention
upon the exceptional few and their spiritual-intellectual world, but
also casts his customary apprehensive glance at the ordinary many
and their world of matter and appetite. These polar camps are as similarly and sharply differentiated as ever. Each of the four biographies,
like all the tales from *Demian* to *Die Morgenlandfahrt,* is both a variation of Hesse's notion of the timeless story of the artist-intellectual or
kindred soul, and a variation of what he believed to be the timeless
story of the population at large. Both stories vary with time but
neither ever really changes. The common world of the many, of politics, action, raw urges, and material things has and will always be
dominant, just as the exclusive world of the few, of thought, spiritual
quest, renunciation, and ideals has and will always be subordinate,
and the native tension between these polar realities will never be fully
resolved. And all this is the timeless story of the human community.

The rainmaker, hermit-confessor, yogi-to-be, and Magister Ludi
are all kindred members of kindred orders. Each quester and order
are to their world at large what every other quester and order are to
theirs, and these worlds at large are as related as are questers and orders. Questers, orders, and worlds at large are no less but cultural
translations than Knecht's various names are but linguistic translations. In both cases there is a change in form but not in essence. The
rainmaker, astrologer, and herbalist, primitive society's dedicated
man of science, the hermit-confessor, early Christianity's most zealous man of God, and the yogi, Indian mysticism's most revered man
of the spirit, like the twentieth-century's Sinclairs, Hallers, or H.H.s,
the medieval world's Narzisses, and ancient India's Siddharthas, are

---

46 Burckhardt argues that the spirit is mutable but not transitory, and that a
spiritual continuum prevails behind life's perpetual flux. See *Weltgeschichtliche Betrachtungen* (Bern: Verlag Hallwag, 1941), pp. 46–50.

all clearly ancestral equivalents of the Magister Ludi, tomorrow's distinguished man of learning. These are the human community's marked few, its enclave of those who are given to the spirit and not the body, who are inspired by visions of meaningful wholeness and harmony behind splintered appearance and cacophony, and who are dedicated to better possibility rather than to actuality. Theirs is a common spiritual-intellectual office, and like the elect themselves, this office varies only in accordance with the age depicted. The institutions of pagan rainmaker, Christian confessor, Hindu yogi, and Knecht's Castalia, like H.H.'s Order of Eastern Wayfarers, Narziss's medieval monastery, and Haller's Immortalia are all related manifestations of the spiritual continuum of history. None of these cultural institutions is here to stay, and others will follow.

In each of the three satellite tales, and just as in the Castalia story, the world of the ordinary man only receives Hesse's customary background attention, and each depiction is but another of Hesse's habitual disparagements of that segment of the human community, another variation of what he believed to be the timeless predicament of the world at large. The irresponsible mass (*Menge der Unverantwortlichen*) of *Der Regenmacher* is the child world (*Kinderwelt*) of *Der Beichtvater*, the surface world (*Oberflächenwelt*) of *Indischer Lebenslauf*, the world of feuilletons (*Feuilleton-Welt*) of the twentieth century, and the great other world (*grosse andere Welt*) beyond the pale of Castalia. And this is also the world of Sinclair's herd, Siddhartha's child-adults, Haller's philistines, Goldmund's sedentary burghers, and H.H.'s blind many. In Knecht's pagan stone age this predominant segment of the human community consists primarily of those who are neither thoughtful nor informed, who are given to blind impulse and folklore rather than to reason, who are cowardly and grasping, who deceive and expect to be deceived, and who accord swindlers and quacks more respect than they do men of thought. In Josephus Famulus's fourth-century Palestine, the corresponding part of society consists for the most part of people who are troubled and angry, selfish and arrogant, who indulge in adultery, commit murder, and zealously ply their trades. And in Dasa's India of the early middle ages, the same social sector is given to an illusory world of the senses and of matter, to greed, conceit, and suspicion, and to intrigue, politics, and war. The worlds at large of the twentieth century and of tomorrow's Castalia differ little from their equivalents of the past, and all these worlds at large depicted in *Das Glasperlenspiel* differ just as little from their equivalents in Hesse's novels from *Demian* to

Die Morgenlandfahrt. Indeed, this conception of the world of the many is clearly anticipated in the earliest of Hesse's writings.

In their bipolar conception of the human community, their background deprecation of the many, and foreground embrace of the few, all four biographies of *Das Glasperlenspiel* are basically varied continuation. They are innovation in their shift from psychology to ethics, in their shift of emphasis from self-realization's becoming of the self to self-realization's ultimate justification of the self, and in their extension of responsibility from commitment to the self, art, and intellect to involvement with the community. Having by the end of the twenties exhausted his interest in the psychology of the artist-intellectual, Hesse became steadily more concerned about the exceptional individual's relationship with general society. From Goldmund to H.H. to Knecht, substance flitted from psychological to aesthetic to ethical concern, and narrative focus moved from inner to outer world. The major problem of Hesse's four Knechts is no longer the self in terms of the self, but the self in terms of the community at large. Theirs is an ethical burden and not a psychological quandary. Hesse ably accommodated this change in his own life by arguing a general Castalian disinterest in individuality and psychology. Thus, neither chronicler nor Knecht was obliged to heed what the author himself was no longer inclined to pursue.

Hesse's shift from psychology to ethics was not a disavowal of his long-time championing of self-realization but a predictable culmination: a climax virtually dictated by his religious background and bent, foreshadowed by his early extolment of Saint Francis of Assisi, and promised by Siddhartha the self-seeker become Siddhartha the servant-ferryman. Like Sinclair, Siddhartha, Haller, Goldmund, and H.H., the Magister Ludi and each of his companion protagonists are intent upon becoming that which destiny holds in store for them, but this realizing of the self now involves an ultimate self-justifying transcending of the self in a spiritual-intellectual *and* social commitment. To become rainmaker, confessor, and yogi is for stone-age Knecht, Famulus, and Dasa just as tantamount to self-becoming as Knecht's progression from novice to Magister Ludi, and each Knecht's conscientious conduct of his office is the self-transcending spiritual-intellectual and social commitment upon which ultimate self-justification is contingent.

From *Demian* to *Die Morgenlandfahrt* to *Das Glasperlenspiel* Hesse's sense of commitment and the service it entails had expanded from the self to the realm of art and thought to the community. This major thematic link with the past is also the major concern in each of the four biographies. Each of their protagonists serves the self, a spiritual-intellectual office, and the world at large, manner of service—like self, office, and world at large—differs from instance to instance only as history demands, and service in each of these three areas is necessary for complete self-realization. Each protagonist serves the self by becoming the self, that is, by becoming the rainmaker, confessor, yogi, or Magister Ludi destiny intends him to become, and each protagonist's self-becoming is decidedly more a matter of the mind and spirituality than of the body and sensuality. Stone-age Knecht grows personally as his elemental knowledge of nature expands; his physical self, wife, and child are incidental concerns with no bearing upon this self-growth. Self-becoming is for Famulus a progression from his physical to his spiritual self; flesh and matter are now the evil world from which man in self-quest must emancipate himself. Dasa's self-becoming is a path leading from involvement with temporal self and world to meditation's release from both; the world of appearance and the senses is now but seductive illusion. And the Magister Ludi's becoming of the self is a flowering of the mind that climaxes in pure intellectuality; neither love nor marriage, nor even sex has any place in his service of the self.

In each of the four biographies, dedication to a spiritual-intellectual office is the second of the protagonist's three major commitments. The three areas of commitment now converge. Service to an office is in each case also a continuation of service to the self, and the beginning of service to the community. The rainmaker reads the skies and studies nature; he also determines when the fields should be planted and when they should be harvested. His office is given to learning *and* to learning's practical application. He continues to grow, learning benefits, and society is served. The hermit-confessor scourges his body and devotes himself to endless prayer; he also listens to confessions and dispenses his blessings. His office is given to piety *and* to good works. He continues to grow, religion benefits, and society is again served. As a yogi, Dasa will eat sparingly, sit silent and immobile, and meditate; he will also be an inspirational example of human possibility. His office will be given to meditation *and* will be a consoling reminder of actuality's illusion. He will continue to grow, philosophy will benefit, and society will again be served. The Magister Ludi cultivates the realm of the intellect and seeks wisdom and harmony in meditation; he also serves Castalia as an administrator and educator, and Castalia in turn provides the outside world with teachers. His office is given to the mind *and* erudition's application in education. He continues to grow, intellectuality benefits, and society is served yet again. The situation in 2200 differs from the earlier situations only in so far as office has become a complex institution, and institution is no longer as responsive to the world as it once was and will again become. The Magister Ludi's parting letter and defection are his warning to Castalia for this remissness; his tutelage is his personal atonement for it.

The satellite tales are not only three of four biographies written by Hesse during the thirties, but also three of four conjectural autobiographies written by Knecht during his ten years of relative freedom preceding his acceptance into the Order. As biographies, they are reflections of the shift in Hesse's focus of interest from self-becoming to self-justification, and, as autobiographies, they are veiled recollections of Knecht's past, intimations of his future, and revealing exposures of his person. Indeed, had the conclave of officials responsible for the appointment of a successor to Magister Ludi Thomas von der Trave taken the trouble to read these autobiographies, it might never have settled upon Knecht, or only with serious reservations.

Much in the first half of the lives of Knecht's protagonists derives directly from his own experience. Knecht the foundling knows no family background; he accords little or none to his projected selves. His encounter with the Magister Musicae awakens him to the world of the mind and to his calling; each of his self-projections enjoys a similar inspiring human encounter and spiritual awakening. And Knecht's protracted education in Castalia becomes stone-age Knecht's drawn-out schooling under Turu the rainmaker, the years Famulus spends listening to presbyters, and the long road that the yogi expects Dasa will have to travel to master the art of yoga. In his recollection of fact, none of Knecht's autobiographies could have ruffled anyone, but in their fancy and its exposure of a personality, they, like some of his poems, would have given Castalia's appointment committee ample cause for real concern. Knecht the rainmaker would have met with general approval: he believes in the infinite powers of the mind, is a disciplined, responsible, and self-assured seeker of knowledge, has absolute and enduring faith in his calling, and remains loyal to his office to the extreme of self-sacrifice when the elements no longer respond to his art. He is by and large an exemplary stone-age bead-game player and Magister Ludi. On the other hand, as Famulus and Dasa, Knecht would have prompted decided disapproval. Like a good Castalian, Famulus renounces the world, sublimates his sensuality, and commits himself to his office. But he is not made of the consistent stuff of the rainmaker. He is a dedicated, gentle, and patient confessor, but also a man prone to vanity, scorn, and indifference, and subject to boredom and fatigue, and a man whose vulnerable faith in himself and his office leads to despair and confusion, and ends in flight. His is hardly the certainty and constancy expected of a model Castalian. Like Knecht the rainmaker, the yogi of *Indischer Lebenslauf* would have met with the selection committee's approval. He is a wise man, dedicated to the spirit and to meditation and is unwavering in his absolute commitment to his office: an Indian variant of the commendable bead-game player and Magister Ludi. However, *Indischer Lebenslauf* is not the yogi's but Dasa's story, and Dasa, a worldling who only expects to become a yogi, would have disturbed the committee even more than Famulus. Knecht's third projected self is the son of a rajah, marries, kills his wife's paramour, chooses to become a servant to a yogi, then hopes to find peace by becoming a yogi himself. He, as was Famulus once, is given to the life of the many: to the material world, the gratification of the senses, and despair. Famulus renounces this world of indulgence for the desert and sackcloth, and Dasa hopes to exchange it for the forest and meditation. This swinging back and forth between fascination with the world and sensuality and a bent for radical isolation and denial would scarcely have recommended either for office in Castalia. Nor would the extreme servility and timidity of Famulus, or Dasa's concluding choice of abject obedience and service in preference to authority and responsibility have sat well with the committee.

Stone-age Knecht is not just a rainmaker devoted to his high office, but also a married man living very much like every other member of his community. Famulus was long a man of the world before he became a man of God. And Dasa wearies of the flesh before he turns to the spirit. Collectively and basically, these protagonists represent a willful person drawn to the realm of the mind *and* to the world at large, given to spirituality *and* to sensuality, and not likely to be content with one possibility exclusive of the other. Knecht proves to be the person his protagonists reveal him to be. He is of Castalia and its intellectuality, yet leaves for the world and its breath of life, and neither attraction can separately satisfy his insistent desires or needs. His self-projections' polar tug-of-war is his, and their major decisions become his. Like his rainmaker, Knecht remains irreproachably loyal to his cause just as long as his faith in himself and his office persists. Like his hermit-confessor, he takes to flight when he becomes troubled about his person and upset about his office. And just as the rajah's son would in conclusion rather serve a yogi than rule a realm, the Magister Ludi chooses in the end to forego rank and recognition to become tutor to a youngster. Knecht's autobiographies are fact become fiction, and fiction that in time becomes fact. They are indeed the revealing self-studies these annual written assignments were intended to be. Fortunate for Knecht, and no less for Castalia and the world at large, the tales were taken only lightly by his teachers and never brought to the attention of his appointment committee. Their warning went unheeded, Knecht's self-realization went its unhampered course, and the chronicler's world is the better for it.

Since Knecht's period of independent study extended over ten years, he must have written more than just three of Castalia's annually required fictive autobiographies. The chronicler was not able to locate any of these other tales, but in Knecht's letters, he did come across detailed references to an attempted eighteenth-century autobiography. Following his *Indischer Lebenslauf*, and at the behest of Castalia's Board of Education, Knecht had apparently undertaken to locate himself in a setting and period less removed and historically more documented than his preceding choices of place and time. For his role as a Swabian theologian of the eighteenth century he had steeped himself in a study of church government, liturgy, and music, of Pietism and such of its leading figures as Albrecht Bengel and Friedrich Christoph Oetinger, and of Graf Nikolaus Ludwig von Zinzendorf and his Moravian Brethren. All, however, had been of little avail. Unable to fashion the accrued burden of historical detail into a personal experience, Knecht had ended his undertaking with his research. Hesse himself had been much more persistent than Knecht. He had actually not abandoned his eighteenth-century project until after two lengthy troublesome fragments had convinced him of the futility of his venture. Like his preoccupation with the eighteenth century and his intent, Knecht's failure and its reasons had also been Hesse's. An overabundance of historical fact simply left too little room for private fancy, and an actual age, its problems, and its personages threatened to overshadow a fictive protagonist and his lot. To counteract this possibility, Hesse shifted from the third person of his first fragment to the first person of his second. It was of no avail. History and story were in competition. History prevailed and story remained fragment. But even if Hesse had persisted and completed his eighteenth-century tale, he could not, nor would he have added it to Knecht's autobiographies. A historical novel, and this it was well on the way to becoming, would not only have been disproportionately long for an appended autobiography, but would also have seriously marred the otherwise basically legendary texture of both the Castalia story and its appendages.

Like the novel proper, the eighteenth-century tale is basically but another of Hesse's many instances of fictionalized autobiography. Except for its historical trappings, it is essentially Hesse's own story: what was and what might have been. Josef Knecht's Beutelsperg, a small town bisected by a river and surrounded by woods, with steep, twisted streets, gabled half-timbered and closely set houses, and an imposing marketplace flanked with a prominent city hall and a Gothic church damaged during the Thirty Years' War, was another of Hesse's repeated recollections of Calw. Knecht's parents are as pious as Hesse's had been, the Bible, hymns, prayer, and church service are as much a part of childhood for him as they had been for Hesse, he is also as drawn to music as Hesse had been to literature, and parental wish and circumstances mark him for the cloth just as they had Hesse. Preceptor Roos, Knecht's eccentric and irascible old teacher of Latin and Greek, was another of Hesse's memorials to Professor Schmid, his own and equally erratic and choleric teacher of Latin and Greek in Calw. Albrecht Bengel is for Knecht the inspiration and example in Denkendorf that Rector Otto Bauer had been for Hesse in Göppingen. Knecht then leaves for Maulbronn, just as had Hesse. But here actuality becomes conjecture, and paths part. Knecht's life now assumes a course that might have been Hesse's if he had not rebelled. As does Knecht, Hesse would have gone on from Maulbronn to study theology in Tübingen, could have become a pastor, and some years later would probably also have exchanged his alien profession for his real passion. Knecht becomes an organist, and Hesse would have become a writer.

Like the novel proper and each of Knecht's other stories, the eighteenth-century autobiography also reflects the shift in Hesse's focus of interest from the psychological to the ethical plane of self-realization. Again the process of self-becoming is no longer the ordeal it was in the twenties, again a life realized also involves becoming a useful part of the human community, and the second of these considerations is again Hesse's and his protagonist's critical concern. As usual, too, the protagonist moves and has his being in a spiritual-intellectual realm. The church is to Knecht of Beutelsperg what Castalia is to Knecht of Berolfingen. Each institution can make possible the tripartite commitment necessary for self-realization: service to the self, an office, and the world at large. However, the church is torn by theological dissension, Castalia has become decadent, neither serves its purpose adequately, and both protagonists defect. Defection and readjustment to life is in each case to general advantage: the Magister Ludi's apostasy and tutorship are of benefit to him, the Order, and the world, and Pastor Knecht is convinced that in defection and as an organist he can better serve himself, the church, and the community. Music is for the pastor the passion that pedagogy is for his bead-game counterpart, and to become an organist is as necessary a next step in his self-becoming as Tito's tutelage is in the Magister Ludi's. Twenty-second-century Knecht, inspired by the theory of history and the ethical example of Pater Jakobus, turns his back upon jaded intellectuality to teach; eighteenth-century Knecht, encouraged by Bach, abandons contentious theology and a disenchanting pulpit to make music; and each of these decisions is to the advantage of both the institution involved and the world. The Order is alerted to its decadence and the world at large is well-served by a Castalian teacher, and both church and community are spiritually revitalized by Christianity's magnificent new-found expression in music composed by Bach and propagated by such of his devotees as the organist Knecht. But commitment to music is not only as much an immediate service to the self and society as commitment to the education of a youngster, it is also as much a benefit to posterity. Except for the propagation of classical music over the centuries by such enthusiasts as ex-Pastor Knecht, the bead game would never have evolved, and except for the revival of the Order's responsible tradition of teaching by such pedagogues as the Magister Ludi, Castalia would soon have dissolved.

Like each of the novel's four stories, the eighteenth-century fragment is also another of Hesse's many variations of the timeless lot of the talented few and the ordinary many, and an extension of his attempt in the thirties to give narrative expression to his belief in a spiritual-intellectual continuum of history. The human community is its usual bipolar self: the estranged few, the pious and the learned who sublimate base appetite and cultivate spirit and mind, and who dream of better possibility, and the down-to-earth many, the naïve and instinctual, those given to the senses and to the world as it is. Hesse's protagonist belongs as usual to the featured and favored few, and the many are accorded even less background attention than usual. But for whatever reason, the profane world is not subjected to its customary disparagement. Singly, the eighteenth-century fragment and the novel's four stories depict variations of Hesse's notion of the human community, together, they demonstrate his belief in a continuum of history: man's timeless spiritual-intellectual quest. Knecht and the church are an eighteenth-century repetition of the rainmaker, confessor, yogi, and their institutions, and an eighteenth-century anticipation of the Magister Ludi and Castalia. And Hesse was convinced that these cultural equivalents would continue as long as man endured. This was for him history's consolation: a mutable but not transitory continuum.

Like each of the Magister Ludi's other projected lives, eighteenth-century Knecht's is in essence both veiled recollection and accurate anticipation. Except for Knecht's parents and for his childhood in Beutelsperg, the Magister Ludi's fourth autobiography, or the tale that but for its excessive historical ballast, would have become his fourth autobiography, derives primarily from personal fact. Eighteenth-century Knecht attends a Latin School in Beutelsperg, the Magister Ludi had done so in Berolfingen; he is spiritually awakened by Bengel at the same age and in the same inspirational manner as the Magister Ludi had been by the Magister Musicae; his two years in Denkendorf and two more in Maulbronn recall the Magister Ludi's four years in Eschholz, and his seven years of seminary study in Tübingen correspond to the Magister Ludi's same span of time in Waldzell, Knecht of Swabia becomes a theologian, then a pastor, and in his forties he elects to leave the pulpit for an organ, and Knecht of Castalia will become a member of the Order, then a Magister Ludi, and will in his forties choose to be a tutor. This eighteenth-century self-projection could only have given Knecht's selection committee even more cause for concern than either *Der Beichtvater* or *Indischer Lebenslauf*. A student's zealous spirituality and selfless dedication would have impressed the committee, but a young man's continued predilection for music, incipient doubts about theology, and reluctant acceptance of church office would have prompted second thought, and the frustration and defection of a mature man would probably have convinced Castalia's officials that Knecht was a person too troubled and unpredictable to be their next Magister Ludi.

Individually, the Knecht stories are traditional tales. Together, they are the experiment in biography that Hesse envisaged as early as 1927, and that was intent more upon a philosophical comment on life than upon narration. In its novel temporal variations, the chance story of *an* artist-intellectual and *his* age became a deliberate story of *the* artist-intellectual and *the* human community, and a direct expression of belief in the cultural continuum of history. Except for their focus upon the artist-intellectual's becoming rather than upon his ultimate justification of the self, *Demian, Siddhartha, Der Steppenwolf,* and *Narziss und Goldmund* are collectively much the study and expression of belief that the Knecht stories became. Indeed, analogously organized, these earlier works could have become an antecedent companion composite to *Das Glasperlenspiel*. Or with appropriate minor changes, Hesse might even have increased the number of Knecht's extant autobiographies by adding *Siddhartha, Narziss und Goldmund,* and either *Demian* or *Der Steppenwolf* to represent ancient India, the Western world of the Middle Ages, and the twentieth century respectively. These additions together with a completed eighteenth-century tale would perhaps have made Knecht's ten years of independent study fruitful beyond credibility, and would certainly have marred the novel's otherwise consistent legend-like quality. But with its more extensive representation of important historical epochs and its added emphasis upon the artist-intellectual's self-becoming, *Das Glasperlenspiel* might also have afforded a more richly textured depiction of the human community and a fuller study of its talented few. A monumental culmination and termination of a lifetime's work might have become the monumental work of a virtual lifetime.

NODAL NARRATIVE AND EXPOSITION

Demian was Hesse's farewell to traditional narration. Pioneer venture in storytelling now began, and this exploration of literary possibility continued to his last novel. A body of spasmodically evolving concerns basic to the individual found expression in boldly innovative form changing unpredictably from work to work. In quick succession, autobiography became an exercise in literary psychoanalysis on a mythical plane, realistic psychological drama, feverish fantasia, a stylized Oriental depiction of the human condition, surrealism, medieval romance, mystery and allegory, and finally chronicle and legend. Though unique works of art, these tales from *Demian* to *Das Glasperlenspiel* are essentially as alike as they are different. Each is as unmistakably Hessean in its manner as in its matter. The artistic whole changed regularly and radically as Hesse doggedly explored new literary possibility, but basic mode of narration remained relatively constant.

Just as Siddhartha's and Goldmund's stories could easily have burgeoned into expansive Oriental and medieval romances, Knecht's biography could readily have become a comprehensive utopian chronicle. But Hesse was too little interested in the many and man's outer world to be tempted by epic possibility. He was and remained more ruminator than storyteller, and *Das Glasperlenspiel*, like *Siddhartha* and *Narziss und Goldmund*, became another of his many inner dramas and personality portraits featuring the exceptional individual, a continuation of his discourse on self-realization and related concerns, and one more jaundiced exposure of the human community. Though more sweeping in spatial and temporal embrace than such more direct self-projections as *Demian* or *Der Steppenwolf*, none of these exotic and narratively more promising novels is essentially any more story-oriented. As usual, settings and stories are primarily changing backdrop and example for argument. As usual, too, plots are skeletal, mode of narration is nodal, narrative movement is slow and linear, descriptions are more evocative than depictive, double self-projection is featured, dialogue is as temperate as it is profuse, chapters are linked concatenatively, and all terminates abruptly with a suspensive upbeat flourish.

Though epic in length, *Das Glasperlenspiel* is almost as narrowly biographic as any of Hesse's tales. As is consistently the case from *Demian* on, narration is focused upon the self-realization of an exceptional individual: a gifted loner whose short life is rich in inner but meager in outer experience. As usual, too, society is only characterized and not portrayed. Hesse's customarily small supporting cast receives its usual minimally necessary attention, human relationships are limited to their function, and events are even fewer than ever. Narration, in fact, consists primarily of a series of significant stations in life, and a small number of formative human encounters: the nodal technique of storytelling that Hesse had adopted in *Demian* and had continued to explore in each of his major works that followed.

Berolfingen is the first of Knecht's stations, and the Magister Musicae the first of his critical encounters: a nondescript Latin school is a stepping-stone to exclusive Castalia, and one of the province's venerables becomes a thirteen-year old's sponsor and model. Four fruitful but uneventful years in Eschholz follow. Knecht's educational experience is only sparsely recounted, and little is known of whatever else he may have experienced during this period beyond the fact that he had been very troubled by the dismissal of those of his fellow students considered unfit for Castalia.

Narratively, Knecht's following seven years in Waldzell are just as threadbare as his four in Eschholz. Study and meditation are enlivened by little more than the continued patronage of the Magister

Musicae and two new friendships. For several years Knecht and Ferromonte do nothing together other than play and discuss music, a subsequent two- or three-year friendship with Designori is marked only by a running debate and serious conversations, and the seventh and last of these years is devoted to the bead game. Knecht's debate with Designori opens his eyes to the reality and validity of the profane world, but also convinces him of the Order's primacy and of his own place in Castalia, and leaves him with a wistful hope for a harmonious interplay of life's poles on both a personal and social plane.

During his subsequent ten years of independent study, Knecht is much more mobile but even less involved with others. Except for three new human encounters, his continuing intellectual growth takes place in splendid isolation. He long avoids familiar Waldzell, studies Chinese for more than a year in removed Sankt Urban, spends months of solitude with the Elder Brother, and becomes a confident to Tegularius. Yearly visits to Waldzell for advanced study, sessions of fasting and meditation in Hirsland, and frequent trips to Monteport are only alluded to. Toward the end of his ten years of freedom and withdrawal Knecht makes the acquaintance of Thomas von der Trave, becomes a member of the Order, and is immediately selected to give bead-game instruction in the monastery Mariafels. Knecht's encounters continue to be straightforward educational experience rather than actional narrative, significant milestones more than rich involvements. The Elder Brother is both an introduction to the Oriental world of thought and a warning against withdrawal into esoteric pursuit; Tegularius is both a loyal confidant and a warning against decadent geniality; and Thomas von der Trave's testing and selection of Knecht for Mariafels mark the beginning of his rapid rise in Castalia's hierarchy.

Mariafels is a change in setting but not in action. Knecht continues his solitary way, self-realization continues to be a primarily intellectual experience, and narration continues in low key. During these three to four years and apart from his regular meditation, usual pursuit of musical studies, and initiation of a few monks into the bead game, he does little other than write reports and correspond with his few friends. This tranquil routine is animated only by Knecht's encounter with Pater Jakobus. The old scholar awakens Knecht to the reality of history and alerts him to the shortcomings of the Order, and Knecht, in turn, acquaints his new mentor with Castalia's history, structure, and bead game. And when he finally succeeds in persuading Mariafels's celebrated historian to support Castalia's interest in establishing permanent diplomatic relations with the Vatican, Knecht returns to Waldzell to attend Thomas von der Trave's last bead game, to mourn his unexpected death, and to be appointed his successor.

This dramatic flurry is as brief as it is unexpected, and the eight years that follow are narratively anticlimactic. The novel resumes its slow and measured tread, and then virtually comes to a narrative standstill before it finally terminates with a brief exciting rush. During his first year in office Knecht quickly acquaints himself with his new duties, wins the respect of Castalia's elite, and celebrates his first public bead game. The next five years in Knecht's life are by and large an incubative interim, more reported than narrated. He becomes an. exemplary administrator, teacher, and bead-game player, but rank and authority soon lose their attraction. Administrative responsibilities become onerous, teaching all but younger students joyless, bead-game virtuosity questionable, and Knecht becomes progressively more disturbed by the province's unidimensionality and deteriorating relationship with the outside world, awakens to new possibility for himself beyond Castalia, and begins to court flight. Narration resumes when Knecht chances again to encounter Designori during his seventh year in office, and quickens with the renewal of their old friendship. The following year Knecht leaves Castalia several times for short visits with Designori and his family, informs his friend of his impending resignation, and agrees to become his son's tutor. Events now move rapidly. Knecht writes a circular letter warning his peers of the perils threatening Castalia and requesting that he be relieved of his office and assigned a teaching position in the outside world, is officially reprimanded for his views and denied his petition, argues his case in person and in vain with the president of Castalia's Directorate, submits his resignation of office and withdrawal from the Order, and promptly departs for the outside world.

The last of Knecht's stages of life is his briefest, and the last of his encounters his most critical. Narration continues to accelerate and ends in a flurry as dramatic and unexpected as that which swept Knecht into office. Following his departure from Castalia, Knecht spends less than twenty-four hours with the Designoris, joins Tito in his family's mountain retreat, and the very next morning plunges to his watery death in response to his ward's thoughtless challenge. Tito stands stunned and troubled, but also convinced that he will become the better for the tragedy.

Knecht's biography is not only the least narrative, but also the most fragmented of Hesse's stories. He was clearly more intent than ever upon argument in literary guise, and he managed adroitly to accommodate this intent with his recourse to a chronicler of 2400 who, like his fellow Castalians, is not particularly interested in such inconsequential considerations as his subject's family background, physical self, or psychology, and who is furthermore entirely dependent upon sparse archival materials and legend. Novel use of an old narrative device permitted Hesse to take almost whatever liberties with storytelling he desired. Story could easily and justifiably be abstracted and constantly interrupted by correspondingly augmented exposition. Hesse was thereby able to push his characteristic mode of narration to its extremes without loss of literary merit.

The chronicler's sources—notes, recollections, memoirs, and letters written by Knecht, his friend, and his students, and preserved in Castalia's archives—were meager in specifically biographical information, but replete with closely and loosely related material. The result was biography slight in story, heavy in supplemental ballast, and laced with extended comment and brief asides. For the benefit of those of his readers who may not be members of the Order, Hesse's chronicler chooses to provide a slight introduction to the bead game and its history. An explanatory preamble becomes a chapter-length exegesis which not only accounts for the character, function, and evolution of the game and the structure of the Order, but involves related observations on classical antiquity, the Middle Ages, and China, a survey of Western culture, an excoriating depiction of twentieth-century civilization, a paean to classical music, and asides on Castalia of 2400, and even includes quotations from Nikolaus of Cues, Novalis, Lü Bu We, and Knecht himself. This preparatory expansiveness is a good foretaste of things to come. For want of many of the usual bare facts of biography, the chronicler is compelled to narrate in the expository manner in which Hesse preferred to narrate. He lingers over Knecht's passion for music and Oriental thought, preoccupation with polarity, synthesis, and self-realization, skills as a bead-game player, sympathy for life's unfortunates, exposure to history and religion, pedagogical interests, cultural concerns, sense of mission, and commitment to his self and to his fellow man; comments on Knecht's poetry and autobiographies, expands upon his introduction to the *I Ging*'s oracle game, gives a detailed account of the first of his annual public bead games, characterizes his friends, and expounds upon the significance of all of his major human encounters; and reveals Knecht's evolving concerns, attitudes, expectations, beliefs, and aspirations by interlacing his halting narration with numerous of

Knecht's own protracted conversations, letters, lectures, reports, remarks, and reflections in part or even in their entirety. To this swell of exposition the chronicler adds a profuse scattering of remarks about the Order, Castalia, and the bead game, and comments on schools, education, and student life; allows himself to trace the political and cultural history of the monastery Mariafels, to dwell upon the Confucian pattern of building a Chinese house, to reflect upon the notion of luck in life, and to make much of a Ludwig Wassermaler who had but chanced to write a handbook for the beginning Magister Ludi some seventy years before Knecht's investiture; and even keeps interrupting himself with apologies for his scant biographical facts, and with his interjection of private sentiment, anticipations, and allusions to Castalia of his own day. He also permits his characters freely to interrupt his narrative and to add to his volume of exposition: the Magister Musicae discusses music, elaborates on the concept of freedom, focuses philosophically upon the individual and upon life, and recounts a crisis in his own past; Pater Jakobus, Knecht, and Tegularius hold forth at length on the subject of history; Knecht and Tegularius weigh the merits of a poem; Designori reviews his life; and Knecht recalls a memorable experience of his youth, lectures on music, gives a character analysis of Tegularius, delves into the intricacies and capacities of the bead game, describes the rise and argues the decline and possible fall of Castalia, and insists at length upon the justification of his decision to resign and to leave. Thoroughly fragmented by this vast mélange of exposition, a threadbare and quite simple story emerges a complex study. Outer biography thereby became inner biography, and that is precisely what Hesse was always intent upon.

Except that they are not burdened by this type of supplemental ballast, Knecht's autobiographies are as meager narratively as the chronicler's biography. Each of the three tales focuses upon an exceptional individual, cast is small, plot simple, narrative movement slow, and ending abrupt. And each, like the biography, is decidedly more inner than outer story. But the autobiographies are narratively also as different from as they are similar to the biography: a literary manner of storytelling lends drama to Knecht's meager tales, and the chronicler's prosaic presentation reduces his story to an informative but rather unexciting report.

EVOCATIVE DESCRIPTION AND DEFINITION BY ASSOCIATION

Exclusively dependent upon Castalia's archives and legend, the chronicler is not only compelled to carry Hesse's usual nodal and expository manner of narration to an extreme, but also by and large to depict in Hesse's customary enumerative and evocative manner, or to forego description entirely. Indeed, *Das Glasperlenspiel* is both the least narrative and the least descriptive of Hesse's major tales. Castalia is an enclave of indeterminate size and shape, located somewhere in a nameless country equally undefined in its dimensions and location. Geography consists only of mountains, chasms, passes, valleys, forests, and rivers, neither described nor located, and but for Zaberwald, without name. Except for the sunny terraced vineyards, brown walls, and chestnut groves of the approach to the Elder Brother's hermitage, and the peaks, twisting road, thinning forests, rushing streams, and bridges of the approach to Designori's mountain retreat in a dark valley with a small, motionless grey-green lake at the foot of a steep and jagged cliff, landscapes once irresistibly attractive for Hesse go unnoticed. Years pass vaguely and with only an occasional mention of season or month, and weather, sky, and clouds no longer attract any attention. With rare exception, cities, streets, parks, gardens, buildings, houses, and interiors are merely concepts. The country's capital is just a nameless big city, and Hirsland only the Order's administrative headquarters. Berolfingen, Monteport, Keuperheim, Porta, and Planvaste are but names with which educational institutions are associated. The school Eschholz, the town Waldzell, the Elder Brother's bamboo grove, and the monastery Mariafels alone are accorded Hesse's usual only enumerative and evocative detail.

With a paucity of information at his disposal, the chronicler is not compelled to abuse his Castalian disinterest in human physicality, and Hesse was left free to concentrate as usual upon man's being and not his body. The individual is more than ever his thoughts, feelings, and human relationships and not his appearance and daily activities, his words more than his meager actions, and his expressions rather than his features. Knecht himself is only blond and handsome, and not one of his three close friends (Ferromonte, Designori, and Tegularius) or the three youngsters (Petrus, Anton, and Tito) he befriends emerges even a faint silhouette. Knecht's three mentors fare only slightly better: the Elder Brother is frail, blue-eyed, and wears glasses; the Magister Musicae is not very tall and has white hair, light blue eyes, red cheeks, and white fingers, and Pater Jakobus has a hawk-like head, sinewy neck, boldly curved forehead, deep furrow above the bridge of his hooked nose, and a short chin. The Pater's profile is the most generous of the chronicler's meager descriptions. All other dignitaries and novices of Castalia and Mariafels and representatives of the profane world go undescribed. Clothing goes as un-noticed as physical characteristics, and food and drink are rarely even mentioned.

Settings and events, physical attributes, clothing, and food were for Hesse potentially both distractive and detractive trappings of the outer world. They could distract from the inner world he was intent upon and detract from the timelessness and universality of his depictions. He had begun as early as *Demian* to try to emancipate his major tales from the accoutrements of actuality enough to minimize this distraction from intent, and to permit real situations to become timeless, and individual concerns to become universal, but not enough to reduce all to only lifeless symbol. What Hesse had accomplished earlier in his *Märchen* he now achieved in his novels. Each of these hovers between place- and time-bound reality and the universally typical and timeless. *Demian, Der Steppenwolf,* and *Narziss und Goldmund* are perhaps closer to the former, and *Siddhartha, Die Morgenlandfahrt,* and *Das Glasperlenspiel* closer to the latter, but each is something of both, and all depict what Hesse believed to be the human community as it is, has always been, and will always be, and with Hesse's usual primary emphasis upon the exceptional few and background consideration of the ordinary many.

Even the bead game is accorded only minimal descriptive attention. However, it is not want of information that deters the chronicler, or literary consideration that dissuaded Hesse. The game itself is the determinant. Its history can be outlined, its language characterized, its potentialities enumerated, and its impact upon participants and spectators observed, but in its essence, the experience itself is beyond the capacity of direct verbal description: a highly intellectual and deeply mystical mental exercise upon which only simile and metaphor can shed light. In the course of fewer than one hundred years the game spread from music to the sciences, humanities, and fine arts, and evolved from a mere memory-sharpening practice with recourse first to notes, letters, and numbers, then to glass beads of various sizes, shapes and colors strung on dozens of wires, into a sophisticated intellectual exercise first involving as many special game languages as there were participating disciplines, then espousing a single international and interdisciplinary set of game symbols. The resultant universal language, a veritable *lingua sacra* which draws upon all sciences and arts for its plethora of symbols, ciphers, formulae and abbreviations, and which enables an adept to play with a culture in a manner that an organist might play with music on an instrument with innumerable manuals, pedals, and stops, is capable of giving expression to, interrelating, and reducing to their common denominators the contents, concepts, and values of all intellectual and artistic disciplines. But the game is not only a cultural, but also, and more significantly, a profound life experience: a miraculous step beyond the temporality, disharmony, imperfection, and meaninglessness of the world of appearance, a venture into the heart of reality, an exposure to cosmic mystery, a union with the divine. Participants and spectators alike are exhilarated by this wonder, spiritually rejuvenated, and left in fervent awe.

Except for this transcendent experience, all aspects of the game are directly accountable in words. To help express the virtually unaccountable, Hesse turned as usual to religion. In *Narziss und Goldmund* his realm of the spirit had found expression in a monastery, as H.H.'s Order of Eastern Wayfarers it had assumed the guise of a papal hierarchy, and as Knecht's Castalia it had become a secularized monastic order. A verbally elusive concept was characterized and rendered more intelligible by familiar associations. Castalia's renowned public bead game is an extension of this associative mode of definition from elusive concept to elusive experience. In its setting, ritual, trappings, and aura, this annual spectacle is not just an obvious association with Roman liturgy, but an intentional lay variation of the papal Easter-day Mass.

The *Ludus sollemnis* celebrated every spring by the Magister Ludi in the spacious festival hall of Waldzell's community of bead-game players (*Vicus Lusorum*) is clearly a secularized version of the Solemn Mass celebrated on Easter Sunday by the *Romanus pontifex* in St. Peter's of Rome's Vatican City. The solemn days or even weeks of prescribed self-denial and meditation associated with the game equate with Lent's forty days of penitence and prayer. The ten-day duration of Knecht's first public game is an equivalent of the liturgical drama of Holy Week. The meditation hour on the evening before the day of the game's commencement corresponds to the one to two-hour night vigil preceding Easter Sunday. The Magister Ludi, like the pope, is akin to a prince, and is almost a deity. Each dignitary, tranquil and august, celebrates a sacral mystery, garbed in the white and gold vestments of his office and assisted by a train of ready acolytes. The several acts and separate actions of Knecht's first game approximate the two stages and many steps of the Mass. His ritualized gestures at the outset of each act are a celebrant's opening and repeated reverences to the altar. He stands before a panel inscribing his wondrous idiograms like a priest before the altar incanting in Latin. His glittering golden stylus recalls the eucharistic chalice and paten, and may even have derived from the lance used in the Eastern Orthodox Church to cut particles from the loaves of altar bread. His assistants bow as reverentially as a priest's altar attendants. The game's devotees rise and sit down as responsively and repeatedly as the worshipers at Mass, and their whispered responses suggest the responsorial prayers and psalms of the faithful. Bells play as important a part in the procedure of the game as in the rites of the Mass. Each act of Knecht's game concludes with communal meditation just as the Liturgy of the Word ends with the prayer of the faithful, and the Liturgy of the Eucharist with postcommunion prayers. And like the pope's Easter service, this annual public celebration of the game is broadcast to the world.

The bead game's mystical-intellectual transcendence, like Klein's euphoric prelude to death, Klingsor's climactic creative frenzy, Siddhartha's culminating religio-philosophic ecstasy, and Haller's illuminating drug fantasy, is a glimpse of life's harmonious and meaningful oneness. Until *Das Glasperlenspiel*, Hesse customarily had recourse to an entrancing rush of highly emotive and suggestive images, thoughts, and sounds to give expression to such elusive and ineffable moments of grace. His association of the Order's game with Catholicism's Mass was a new device to describe indirectly experience otherwise indescribable: in this case, to define the game's unfamiliar miracle of transcendence by relating it to the Mass's familiar miracle of transsubstantiation. Analogy, like rush of evocative language, could at least give an intimation of the mysteries that lie beyond the pale of words in their common usage.

Description is given even less attention in Knecht's autobiographies than in the chronicler's biography. Landscapes, sky, communities, dwellings, gardens, fields, forests, swamps, deserts, mountains, birds, and animals are hardly more than mentioned, and human beings are almost only what they say, do, think, or feel. The rainmaker's stone-age village, Famulus's Gaza, Rajah Ravanna's capital, and the surrounding terrains are but conceptual settings or mere reference points. Dwellings are mud, bamboo, and fern huts, or desert grottos, and nothing more. Only the wizened face of an ancestress in *Der Regenmacher* and the beautiful body of Pravati in *Indischer Lebenslauf* are accorded slight enumerative detail. Physically, Knecht's three protagonists, their three mentors, and all others are virtually ignored. And food and drink are again left almost entirely to the imagination of the reader. Knecht was clearly interested primarily in the inner and not the outer world of his protagonists; more detail would have been extraneous if not distractive.

TIMELESS PORTRAITS

Like its expository nodal mode of narration, profuse dialogue, spare descriptions, double self-projections, slow narrative movement, and abrupt termination, the novel's structure is essentially more continuation and culmination than innovation. Its unique segmentation is basically a variation of the structural novelty of *Der Steppenwolf*. In each of these works, Hesse was not only intent as usual on portraiture more than storytelling, but also on portraits fuller than traditional narrative could afford without becoming tediously prolonged discourse, and moreover clearly representative of more than themselves: portraits both very actual and typical. To achieve this common intent he resorted to similar ruses: to an editor and an inserted tract and drug fantasy, on the one hand, and to a chronicler and appended poems and tales, on the other. A composite consisting of introduction, story proper, and appurtenances, and featuring a series of complementary pairs of portraits, emerged in both cases. The editor's introduction, Haller's autobiography, the tractate of an Immortal, and the Magic Theater furnish, respectively, physical, psychological, actional, and supplemental portraits of Haller and of the society that he abhors. Collectively, these four pairs of special studies constitute a culminating pair of multidimensional portraits that are both the actual portraits Hesse intended them to be, and the representative depictions of the artist-intellectual and bourgeois society in the Western world of the twentieth century that he was convinced they were. This technique of coupled portraits was employed even more extensively and no less effectively in *Das Glasperlenspiel*. The chronicler's obliging introduction for his inadequately informed readers was Hesse's opportunity for another of his scathing characterizations of his age, and for a preliminary sketch of an exceptional individual and an unusual spiritual-intellectual realm. In the twelve chapters of the story proper, focus shifts from the ordinary many to the gifted few: the introduction's detailed depiction of the twentieth-century world at large yields to a shadowy twenty-third-century counterpart, to Designori's background world of matter, appetite, politics, business, and strife, and Knecht and Castalia become foreground depiction. Knecht's appended writings continue these polar studies. His very personal poems lend more intimacy to the chronicler's portraits, and *Der Regenmacher*, *Der Beichtvater*, and *Indischer*

Lebenslauf add their paired supplemental studies: stone-age, early Christian, and Indian versions of Knecht and Castalia, and of the world at large. Combined, these many depictions, like those of *Der Steppenwolf*, furnish their intended full portraits of an actual person and a social situation. Aligned, they not only evidence the cultural continuum of history that Hesse had first been intent upon illustrating, but also argue a mundane continuum of history. Aligned, these paired depictions also mirror the universal and timeless condition of the exceptional individual and his world and of the ordinary many and their world, and individually, in turn and by obvious implication, they are not just something actual and timebound but temporal variants of the universally typical and timeless. The story of an individual, an intended multibiography, the whole of which would be both actual and archetypal and would demonstrate the cultural continuum of history, evolved into the story of the human community, into a composite of tales that are both collectively and individually actual and mythic, and that demonstrate both the cultural and mundane continuum of history.

SECULARIZED HIERATIC LANGUAGE

From *Demian* on, language, like structure, changed from tale to tale. Each work found what Hesse believed to be its necessary organization of parts, and for each, Hesse effected what he considered an appropriate mode of expression. The language of *Das Glasperlenspiel* had to be as Castalianized as *Siddhartha*'s had been Orientalized. Hesse had to accord his Castalian chronicler a language as convincingly institutional as Haller's is appropriately artful, his middle-class editor's properly prosaic, and his benefactor-Immortal's fittingly brilliant and witty. The language he fashioned was therefore not the gauche product of an aging writer's odd caprice or growing ineptness with words, as some critics have chosen to argue,[47] but a necessary response to a conception of art and another example of verbal virtuosity. The chronicler's officialese something between the involved, stilted, and impersonal mode of expression of the church and the court, is absolutely in accord with monastic Castalia's intellectuality, formality, and its ideal of anonymity. Hesse managed to affect this secularized hieratic language by adopting deferential modes of ad-

---

47 E.g.: Werner Kohlschmid, "Meditationen über Hermann Hesses *Glasperlenspiel*," *Zeitwende*, 19 (1947), 154–179, 217–226; Wolfgang von Schöfer, "Hermann Hesse, *Peter Camenzind* und *Das Glasperlenspiel*," *Die Sammlung*, 3 (1948), 597–609.

dress, resorting to meticulous elevated dialogue, and particularly with his liberal recourse to protracted convoluted sentences, burdened by an excess of principal clauses and subordinate clauses within subordinate clauses, strings of prepositional phrases, clusters of nouns, abundant adjectival and adverbial modifiers, frequent repetitions, parenthetical asides, and quotations, and heavily punctuated with semicolons, colons, and dashes. This is the staid and stiff language for which Castalia settled when it chose to ban literary writing and to reduce what had been a means of artistic creation to but a means of common communication. For Hesse to have continued to resort to his usual imagery, symbolism, and interior monologue, or to his characteristic harmonizing of inner state, outer situation, and flow and rhythm of language, would have been to ascribe the impossible to his chronicler, and therefore to mar rather than to enhance the art of his novel.

This same consideration, and not flagging artistic sensibility, required that all of Hesse's Castalians speak and write more or less like the chronicler. The Order's ideal of anonymity expresses itself as much in its communal language as in its communal lifestyle. One Castalian's politely impersonal involved monotone had therefore to be almost indistinguishable from another's. Hesse allowed himself to deviate from this imperative only when plausibility permitted. It did so in the legendary last chapter and in the appended tales. The first of these segments of the novel was authored by several of Knecht's students, and the second by Knecht when he himself was still a student. Both segments were therefore written, as the chronicler puts it, before youth's creative urge was channeled into the sciences or the bead game. Not yet fully institutionalized, youth was still able to give relatively personal expression to private sentiment.

Knecht's lengthy concluding conversations with Tegularius and Alexander are rendered, and correctly so, in typical Castalianese. But the sentences of the narrative and descriptive passages of the final chapter are generally shorter, syntactically less complicated, and flow more rapidly. And to this quickened pace, a liberal recourse to lively interior monologue added an urgency and intimacy that the chronicler's blander chapters never achieve. A long study recorded in Castalia's scholarly language ends as a story told in a decidedly literary manner, and this literary manner peaks appropriately with the story's climactic termination. The formidable mountains, glacial lake, dazzling sunrise, Tito's Panic dance, and Knecht's watery death are tableau and drama, gripping actuality and complex symbol. Continuing to resort to shorter sentences and interior monologue with even greater recourse to insistent anaphora, impatient parataxis, anxious repetition, and tense successions of nouns and verbs, Knecht's students were able to recreate and transfigure what the chronicler could only have reported.

Not bound by fact or hampered by any dearth of information, and with official permission to exercise his creative urge and to express himself as he chooses, Knecht waxes even more literary than his students were to. Touches of archaic word order, old-fashioned modes of addresses, bygone figures of speech, and occasional obsolete words, dated expressions, and old grammatical structures lend his language an enhancing patina of times past and places removed. Each of the three autobiographies is narratively as frail as the novel proper, but whereas the chronicler's reported story is almost smothered by interruptive formal exposition, Knecht's fictive tales are accorded body and atmosphere by their copious dynamic commentary and brought alive by extended dramatic interior monologue. Though Knecht shares the chronicler's proclivity for protracted sentences, his are simply additive rather than syntactically involved, flow strongly rather than lumber along, and are clearly more intent upon emotional effect than meticulous explanation. Like his students, Knecht achieves his gripping effect with liberal recourse to anaphora, parataxis, repetition, clusters of nouns, verbs, adjectives, and adverbs, and to series of clauses and prepositional phrases. And just as in the final chapter of the Knecht biography, this decided literary manner peaks at climactic junctures: when the elements become adverse, the rainmaker's art ineffectual, and his sacrifice imperative; when Famulus loses faith in himself and his calling and flees his desert grotto; and when Dasa awakens from his dream of worldly power, wealth, pleasures, and violence, aghast, with his fill of Maya, and ready to follow in the footsteps of his yogi-mentor. At these critical junctures Knecht also manages to add to both his verbal and human drama by resorting to a typical Hessean harmonizing of language with inner state and outer situation: his sentences assume a rapid flow and frantic rhythm, and the inner agitation of his protagonists and the turmoil and tension of the outer circumstances become dramatically immediate. Of course, this skillfully used language, like Knecht's able story telling and unlike the chronicler's Castalianese and reportage, was Hesse's very own. Paradoxically the very artfulness of the autobiographies is perhaps *Das Glasperlenspiel*'s only major blemish. These tales are obviously less the fumbling verbal exercises of a novice bead-game player than the literary gems of a master writer. Hesse admitted as much.[48]

Hesse's scrupulous attention to language goes beyond just affecting appropriately different styles for the chronicler's introduction and biography, the students' concluding chapter, and Knecht's autobiographies. Knecht is not only accorded his personal idiom when in order, but all his reports, notes, letters, conversations, and lectures are properly written, conducted, and delivered in a Castalianese virtually indistinguishable from the chronicler's, the Magister Musicae's, Ferromonte's, Tegularius's, Ludwig Wassermaller's, Thomas von der Trave's, or Alexander's. The language of non-Castalians, few though they are, is given just as careful attention. Pater Jakobus's formal and complex mode of expression approximates that of any non-Castalian, as well it might and should, for he is not only a kindred intellectual but also a member of a brother institution. Designori's language, like his person, is appropriately both of Castalia and the outside world: Castalianese somewhat simplified and personalized, or mundane idiom considerably sophisticated. And Designori's wife and his son Tito speak in the casual everyday manner one might expect of a cultured and concerned mother and a precocious and headstrong teenager in the world at large.

Das Glasperlenspiel is clearly a monumental culmination of a brilliant career and not an anticlimatic last effort of an aging author. A thinker and writer in full control of substance and form produced his masterpiece: a classic that will age well, a memorial to Western culture, and a prognostication that may well materialize.

OTHER PROSE WORKS, POETRY, AND REVIEWS

The abundance and variety of prose and poetry that Hesse wrote from 1919 to 1931 was followed by *Das Glasperlenspiel*, together with but one short fairy tale (*Vogel*, 1932), a halting flow of diverse essays, a trickle of poetry, and a brief surge of reviews. The first of his scant fifty new prefaces, epilogues, recollections, birthday congratulations, memorial articles, and literary studies were published as freely and widely as similar works had been in the past. This changed quickly with Vesper's vilification of 1935 and 1936. Newspapers and periodicals throughout Germany abruptly lost interest in Hesse. Individual

---

48 See *Materialien zu Hermann Hesses* Das Glasperlenspiel (1973), Vol. 1, pp. 297–299.

tales, poems, and articles, both new and old, soon ceased to be published. From 1937 to 1942, only the *Neue Rundschau* continued to pay attention to Hesse, and even it chose merely to print five segments of *Das Glasperlenspiel* and a few scattered poems. After 1942 and until the end of the Second World War, Swiss periodicals and newspapers remained the only real outlet for casual publications. Less than half of the fifty items written from 1931 to 1945 were included in Hesse's collections of miscellany; the rest have not yet appeared in book form. Of the dozen fragments written during these years, only the two versions of the eighteenth-century Knecht tale have since been published.[49]

As usual, change in lifestyle affected Hesse's poetry as much as it did his prose. Dramatic free verse, consonant with the turbulence of the twenties, now yielded to the calmer descriptive, to the more purely reflective, and to the longer narrative poems of the still tense but less discordant thirties and forties. Protracted agitation with its shrill protest and anxious fervor became growing tranquillity, contained lament, and the acceptance of faith. Hesse wrote only a bare eighty-five poems during his first fourteen years in the Casa Bodmer; only five of them have never been published.[50]

Hesse's interest in editing both culminated and virtually terminated in the twenties. He continued occasionally to preface publications during the thirties and the war, but his own editorial work was limited to a single small volume of poems commemorating the hundredth anniversary of Goethe's death.[51] This was also the last of the fifty-eight books that Hesse edited.

With ample time in the early thirties for his reviews, Hesse increased his serial contributions to *Der Bücherwurm*, *Die Propyläen*, and to *Der Schwabenspiegel*. When, with the ascendance of National Socialism, German publishers began to lose interest in his literary opinions, he simply stepped up his reviews for the *Neue Zürcher Zeitung* and particularly for the *National-Zeitung* of Basel. During the restive lull in creation that followed the completion of *Der Regen-*

---

49 Unpublished: an untitled five-page beginning of a recollection or a tale (see Manuscripts X:252), three snippets of diary (see Manuscripts X:426t–426v), two remnants of autobiography (see Manuscripts X:427d, 427e), a six-page series of dreams (see Manuscripts X-B:11a/9), a one-page reflection on China (see Manuscripts X-A:7/22), and brief notes about his friends Josef Feinhals and Will Eisenmann, and about two of his grandchildren (see Manuscripts X-A:7/23, X:269, 274a).

50 Some of these eighty-five poems became part of *Vom Baum des Lebens* (1934) and *Neue Gedichte* (1937), and sixty-five were included in *Die Gedichte* (1942).

51 *Dreissig Gedichte* (Zürich: Lesezirkel Hottingen, 1932), 65 pp.

macher and the introduction and eighteenth-century fragments of *Das Glasperlenspiel*, reading and reviewing almost became Hesse's sole preoccupation. In the autumn of 1934, he began a new series of essay-reviews for the *Neue Rundschau*, later that year he became a staff reviewer for the *Schweizer Journal*, and the first of his surveys of contemporary German literature for *Bonniers Litterära Magasin* appeared in the spring of 1935. A breach of contract persuaded Hesse to discontinue his contributions to the *Schweizer Journal* after the publication of but two of his articles at the beginning of 1935, and his harassment by both Nazis and Jews induced him to terminate his assignments with the *Neue Rundschau* and *Bonniers Litterära Magasin* in mid-1936. He continued to contribute reviews only to the *Neue Zürcher Zeitung* and the *National-Zeitung* (Basel), and these only until the spring of 1938. He also persisted, in spite of his émigré Jewish detractors, to feature Jewish authors. When, as now happened, Josef Knecht's actual story began to absorb Hesse, he ceased to have any further interest in or time for reviews. His prolific reading and reviewing had been, among other things, a manner of escape from the new challenge of his writing proper. Knecht's world, in turn, became a necessary mental retreat from Europe's troubled times.

8

Reminiscence and
Rumination

MONTAGNOLA 1945–1962

REUNIONS AND FAREWELLS

The last period of Hesse's life and career began with the end of the Second World War. Except for the progressively slower flow and more even rhythm of these final seventeen years, all continued to revolve ritually about his writing, reading, painting, gardening, correspondence, and music. He treasured the seclusion of Montagnola and the privacy of his home, had little hankering for the world at large or for further involvement in its affairs, and traveled even less than during the thirties and early forties. A weakened heart compelled him in 1952 to discontinue his annual autumn cures in Baden. His customary sporadic visits with the Bodmers in Zürich and Wassmers in Bremgarten continued only until 1955. In the following years, but for four-week summer vacations spent regularly in upper Engadin after 1950, frequent appointments with his physician Dr. Clemente Molo of nearby Bellinzona, and occasional short holiday and birthday jaunts into the mountains, Hesse rarely left Montagnola and vicinity.

However, just as during the period preceding 1945, withdrawal never became ivory-tower isolation and uninvolvement. Again the world would not let him be. It sought him out to satisfy its curiosity, make its demands, and extend him its honors. In the immediate postwar years and on into the mid-fifties, relatives, friends, devotees, and political refugees, young and old, again converged upon Montagnola. Among those who came frequently and for longer stays were

Hermann Hesse, 1947.

Hermann Hesse, 1950.

Hesse's sons and their families, his sisters Adele and Marulla, cousins, nieces, and nephews from Germany, and members of his wife's family from Rumania. Close friends, longtime acquaintances, many new and old enthusiasts from Germany, and frequent callers from abroad came for shorter visits.[1] The postwar years brought with them an equally unprecedented flow of mail. Hesse left few serious letters unacknowledged and seldom rebuffed callers.

But these were for Hesse years not only of happy family reunions, sentimental renewals of long-interrupted friendships, and interesting new associations, they were also years of painful final farewells, highly unwelcome invasions of privacy, and of more public sociopolitical involvement and added calumny, distress, and disillusionment. Life's repaired bonds proved to be provisional. Hesse's younger brother Hans had committed suicide in 1935, and his older half brothers Karl and Theodor had died in 1937 and 1941. Adele's death in late 1949 and Marulla's in early 1952 left him a sole surviving sibling. Another important link with childhood and youth was severed when Otto Hartmann, the closest of Hesse's remaining few friends of Maulbronn, died in the autumn of 1952, only five days after a visit to Montagnola. More intimate ties with earlier years were broken with the postwar passing of most of the writers, painters, and composers with whom Hesse had struck up lasting friendships during his years in Gaienhofen.[2] Hesse's links with the twenties became just as frail with the demise of Fritz Leuthold, Georg Reinhart, H. C. Bodmer, and Josef Englert in successive years from 1954 to 1957, and with the resultant dissolution of the close-knit circle of Swiss patrons he had attracted after the First World War. Later but no less cherished friendships fared no better. Ernst Wiechert died in 1950, André Gide in 1951, Theophil Wurm in 1953, followed by Ernst Penzoldt and Thomas Mann in 1955, Hans Carossa in 1956, and Peter Suhrkamp in 1959.

1 The Bodmers, Leutholds, and Wassmers were always welcome guests, as were Hesse's old schoolmates Otto Hartmann, Hans Völter, and Edmund Natter, such writers as Thomas Mann, André Gide, Hans Carossa, Ernst Wiechert, R. J. Humm, Friedrich Schnack, Ernst Penzoldt, and Ludwig Finckh; the painters Ernst Morgenthaler and Gunter Böhmer; his publisher Peter Suhrkamp; the mythologist Károly Kerényi; the philosopher Martin Buber; and such dignitaries as Theophil Wurm the protestant bishop of Württemberg, and Theodor Heuss the president of West Germany.

2 Among them Emanuel von Bodman, Wilhelm Schäfer, Martin Lang, Gustav Gamper, Olaf Gulbransson, Ernst Kreidolf, Alfred Schlenker, Othmar Schoeck, and Fritz Brun.

For Hesse, renewed contact with the past and the growing actuality of death primed recollection well and to good advantage. The world of memory gradually became for septuagenarian Hesse the fascination and consolation that the beautiful world of imagination had been for a young Lauscher, and the Platonic realm of life's Immortals had been for a middle-aged Haller. Another treasured reality beyond the reach and crush of time again became the very substance of life and another antidote to its untoward actuality. Remembrance of things past quickly filled the painful vacuum left by death, and life remained tolerable. Hesse's art, in turn, now recollection more than anything else, continued as always to lend both purpose and meaning to his existence.

RENEWED POLITICAL AND SOCIAL INVOLVEMENT

Politically, the last period of Hesse's life began most inauspiciously. Hostilities had hardly ended and he and his German publisher had scarcely begun to make their postwar printing plans before yet another altercation with authority again threatened to silence him. Incensed by the unauthorized publication of one of his poems by the *Weser Bote* in the summer of 1945, Hesse berated the officer who was in charge of the restoration of the German press in the American sector and who was personally responsible for the indiscretion. Captain Hans Habe's rejoinder of October 8 was as incontinent as the rebuke of September 20 had been sharp. Hesse was snidely reminded of his silence during the Nazi years, chastized for his mean monetary concern, and bluntly informed that his works were not likely to be printed again without or even with permission. Hesse had with luck escaped the Nazi blacklist only to be unceremoniously proscribed by a piqued and impetuous officer of the American occupation forces.[3] Though infuriated by this effrontery, he carefully avoided public embroilment with Habe. After another and somewhat more contained exchange of letters in January 1946, the affair petered out.[4] Habe's authority never extended to the many newly licensed German newspapers, nor to book publication, and by the summer of 1946 even the

3 "Hermann Hesse auf der amerikanischen Proskriptions-Liste," *Basler Nachrichten*, November 16, 1945, No. 489.

4 Hesse's letters to Habe (September 20, 1945; end of January 1946) and Habe's responses (October 8, 1945; January 3, 1946) are in the Hesse-Nachlass, Marbach a.N. Hesse also wrote but never mailed two other undated letters to Habe and an appeal to an American Embassy (January 25, 1946); these too are in the Hesse-Nachlass.

network of German newspapers published under the auspices of the American army ceased to heed his proscription of Hesse.

Although Habe's bark proved to be worse than his bite, the protracted tangle took its toll on Hesse. His nerves, already taxed by the war, became dangerously frayed, his long-standing frail faith in America became even feebler, and his hesitant hope for a more enlightened and humane postwar world was all but dashed. Nor did the virtual flood of letters from his former countrymen in the summer and autumn of 1945 help to bolster his sagging spirits. Insistent profession of innocence, loud complaint, and brazen accusation characterized their content. Most German prisoners of war were primarily intent upon protesting their undeserved lot and requesting impossible aid; some aired self-righteous hatred, and a few already looked forward to the day Germany would avenge her defeat. Many former readers and even acquaintances who had seen fit to join the Nazis now loudly affirmed their unbroken friendship and good will. Some had become members of the party merely to help temper its policies, threat had forced others into its ranks, not a few preferred discreetly to avoid all mention of the Nazi interlude, and none had actually ever been a true Nazi or even a real sympathizer. While Hitler was freely denounced, expressions of personal guilt were conspicuously rare, and private hardship and the blunders of the occupation forces were favorite themes. Even fellow-writers all too commonly argued for the innocence of ignorance.

Hesse was appalled by this prevailing sentiment. There was little reason to believe that Germany would be any more inclined to bear its cross after the Second World War than it had been after the First World War. Nevertheless, he felt impelled to break his silence, once more to admonish and to exhort. With little faith in the efficacy of his pleas, and with much less spirit than some twenty-five years previously, he again reminded the Germans that defeat could be a new beginning, an opportune historical moment for a moral regeneration, and an intellectual awakening (*Schluss des Rigi-Tagebuches*, August 1945). Again he pleaded for patient and brave acceptance of life and argued the brotherhood of man (*Ansprache in der ersten Stunde des Jahres 1946*, November 1945). Again he took Germany to task for its continued nurturing of militarism, again berated the many intellectuals who once more proved to be only fair-weather friends of humanity, and again argued the merits of individual self-scrutiny (*Ein Brief nach Deutschland*, April 1946). Nor was Germany alone his concern. Addressing himself to the world at large, Hesse again cautioned against the two scourges of the twentieth century: the megalomania of technology and that of nationalism (*Danksagung und moralisierende Betrachtung*, September 1946).

Each of these four essays first appeared in Swiss newspapers and periodicals, and none was ever widely reprinted in Germany. Theirs was anything but an enthusiastic reception. In 1949 all four items were added to the German edition of *Krieg und Frieden*. The general silence that greeted this collection of sociopolitical essays extending over more than three decades did little to disabuse Hesse of his persistent suspicion that Germany had learned virtually nothing from experience. Nor did his postwar reinstatement in popular favor persuade him to think otherwise.

CELEBRITY AND NOTORIETY

With the termination of the Second World War, history began to repeat itself in an uncanny manner. Twice officially denied in Germany, Hesse now found himself as abruptly reacclaimed as he had been immediately after the First World War. Books that had been all but banned could suddenly not be published in numbers adequate to meet popular demand. Critics who had maligned or had long ignored him seemed frantically eager to atone for their deprecation and neglect; in 1947 alone, as many pamphlets and books about Hesse were published as had appeared in the preceding twenty-five years. Literary academies eagerly extended their invitations. Intellectuals who had branded him an alien and dangerous element in German society now looked forward to his participation in Germany's restoration. And German youth seemed once more to have found a spiritual guide. A notoriety was again a celebrity, and when Hesse was awarded the Goethe Prize in August 1946, his rehabilitation received its official recognition.

Hesse accepted the renewed plaudits of his former countrymen with considerable reservation, and acknowledged his latest literary prize with the gravest of misgivings. Bitter experience had left him far more skeptical than he had been in the years immediately following 1918. Hate letters, too, had again begun to pour into Montagnola following the first German publication of *Ein Brief nach Deutschland* on August 2, 1946.[5] Hesse's assessment of Germany was no more palat-

5 *Die Neue Zeitung* (München-Berlin), August 2, 1946, No. 61. See Hesse's "Antwort auf Schmähbriefe aus Deutschland," *Neue Zürcher Zeitung*, August 23, 1946, No. 1489.

Hermann Hesse, 1951.

Ninon and Hermann Hesse, 1951.

Hermann Hesse and his youngest son Martin, 1952.

able to her nationalists than it had ever been, and their rejoinders were no less irate and denigrating than in the past. He was still a defector pontificating from his comfortable refuge in arcadian Switzerland, and his admonitions and exhortations were still the presumptuous blathering of naïveté and ill will.[6] The Habe-affair, the inauspicious moral climate in postwar Germany, policy tiffs with his German publisher, frustrating lags in the republication of his books, a marriage become temporarily strained, together with these hate letters, gradually undermined Hesse's health. To ward off a general collapse, he literally went into hiding. Casa Bodmer was locked up at the end of October 1946, Ninon moved to Zürich, and he retired for an indefinite spell of rest to an out-of-the-way sanatorium in Marin près Neuchâtel. The Goethe Prize of August had not helped to counter his growing depression, and the Nobel Prize, awarded just fourteen days after Hesse's departure from Montagnola, only retarded his recovery. Both acknowledgments were more burden than honor, more intrusion when seclusion was most needed. Withdrawal proved beneficial. By the end of February 1947, Hesse had recovered sufficiently from his psychic malaise to leave for Baden and another rheumatic cure. He and Ninon then returned to Montagnola in the middle of March and life resumed its old and more even course.

Hesse was never quite German enough for nationalists. He was also never quite activist enough for youth. His reception by the young in Germany following the Second World War was very much what it had been after the First World War. Youth of the late forties was no more taken with patient reflection and trying self-realization than its counterpart in the twenties had been. Initial enthusiastic acclaim again yielded quickly to vociferous disclaim. For the many intent upon answers to life's immediate sociopolitical problems, Josef Knecht's utopian Castalia was as removed from the realities of a postwar Germany as Siddhartha's Eastern world had been. Hesse again became a dangerous seduction, an impractical aesthete, a spineless dreamer too estranged from the German world to be of any consequence in its physical and intellectual resurgence.[7] This recurrent sentiment, quite common again by the end of the forties in the swelling ranks of Germany's young activists, pained but did not surprise Hesse any more than his persistent maligning by arch patriots. The

---

6 E.g., Dr. Gnamm, "Offener Brief an Hermann Hesse," *Universitas* (Stuttgart), 1 (November 1946), 1048–1050.

7 See Wolfgang von Schöfer, "Hermann Hesse: *Peter Camenzind* und *Das Glasperlenspiel*," *Die Sammlung*, 3 (1948), 597–609.

antipathy of these factions was inevitable. Hesse's uncompromising emphasis upon the individual and his inner reality was too alien to their institutional concerns. His continued attempts to humanize simply ran counter to their determination to socialize and to politicize. For activist youth in quest of a dynamic leader with a pragmatic ideology, Hesse again proved to be a disappointment. As in the twenties, he now also continued to be extolled only by a shrinking band of sensitive young outsiders appreciative of the solace afforded by an older and wiser kindred sufferer. And this, rather than actual leadership, was precisely the role to which Hesse had always aspired: "I am a man of premonitions . . . a fellow sufferer . . . an older brother . . . a sufferer in the stress of our times, but not a leader out of them. . . ."[8]

Unlike his friend Romain Rolland, a militant humanitarian ever ready to organize his fellow liberals against war, social injustice, and political corruption, Hesse had never felt drawn to the public arena and its collective causes and programs. He had always preferred moral challenges for the few to rectifying ideologies for the many. It was not that the world was no longer in need of or capable of improvement, but that any meaningful social reform was actually contingent upon the more fundamental reform of the individual, and this, in turn, might better be encouraged by example than by mandate or even persuasion. Experience had taught Hesse that public involvement in sociopolitical causes was both an unavailing misapplication of an artist's talents and a violation of his office. He had carefully shunned the public scene during the Nazi years, and but for his expostulations of 1945 and 1946, he was to continue to do so for the rest of his life. For his silent withdrawal in the thirties he had been branded a Nazi sympathizer, and for his refusal to become a party to organized causes after 1945 he became for many an ivory tower elitist unwilling to grapple with reality lest he sully his hands. Opprobrium notwithstanding, Hesse remained fixed in his resolve to keep aloof. When the editors of the periodical *Aufbau* of East Berlin attempted in March 1948 to draw him into a discussion of a peace settlement for Germany, his response was curt and unmistakably clear: "I consider literary discussions of politics worthless."[9] His reply to Max Brod's urgent plea of May 1948 that he help bring international opposition to bear upon the pending invasion of Israel by the Arab world was decidedly longer and more sympathetic but equally uncompromising:

8 *Briefe* (1964), pp. 78–84.
9 *Briefwechsel: Peter Suhrkamp-Hermann Hesse* (1969), p. 86.

I consider every would-be intellectual action . . . on the part of intellectuals vis-à-vis the masters of this earth to be wrong, a further damaging and degrading of the intellect. . . . It is not for us either to preach or to command or to beg, but to stand steadfast in the thick of hell . . . and not to expect the least either of our personal fame or of an alliance of as many as possible of our kind. . . . Since the First World War opened my eyes inexorably to actuality I have raised my voice many times. . . . As a writer and man of letters I have always tried to keep reminding my readers of the sacred fundamental commandments of humane behavior, but I myself have never attempted to influence politics, as has happened and happens solemnly ever and again in the hundreds of summons, protests, and admonitions of intellectuals, but all to no avail and to the detriment of respect for humaneness. And I intend to continue to do as I have done.[10]

Anna Seghers' request of the autumn of 1952 that Hesse lend his support to a Communist-sponsored congress for peace to be held in Vienna, went unanswered. The editorial staff of *Aufbau* reiterated Segher's appeal, only to be politely but firmly informed that international associations of writers were not likely to improve the world situation, would quickly be politicized, and could only further undermine the credibility of artists.[11] The many similar appeals of the remaining fifties met similar responses.

Hesse's refusal to become publicly engaged in causes other than art and related fields was no more tantamount to a withdrawal from the sociopolitical scene than it had been before 1945. He maintained his usual informed contact with world affairs and European politics, and there were few if any major issues in which he was not interested and about which he did not have his own decided opinions. He also gave his usual frank expression to these views in his continued extensive correspondence. While Germany afforded little cause for rejoicing, the international political scene afforded even less. What could be expected of world powers bent upon pursuing traditional power politics and intent upon stock-piling atom bombs for peace? Power-conscious government leaders continued blithely to declare their wars, eager generals to wage them, irresponsible scientists to lend them their genius, money-minded industrialists to profit from them, and society at large to condone or endure them. The Korean War, the occupation of Tibet, the militarizing of China, the Americanizing of

10 "Versuch einer Rechtfertigung," *Gesammelte Schriften* (1957), Vol. 7, pp. 465–467.

11 *Briefe* (1964), p. 402.

Hermann Hesse in his study, 1952.

Hermann Hesse and Theodor Heuss in Sils Maria, 1957.

Japan, and the worldwide increased collectivizing of man did not augur well. Force and violence had not yielded to persuasion and tolerance, ends still justified dubious means, causes and institutions continued to overshadow the individual, and common sense remained a rare commodity. Political leaders had again learned nothing from experience, and the future was likely to be a repetition of the past. Germans were as politically immature, irresponsible, and unpredictable as ever, still too sentimentally attached to their heroic past, and still dangerously authoritarian.[12] Germany offered no hope, and the United States and Russia posed new threats. America was still the paradoxical colossus it had always been: enviably youthful, vigorous, and free, but also appallingly technologized and culturally naïve, an exponent of democracy, yet not loath to support dictatorships, and a stronghold of capitalism, but also a collectivized world.

Hesse had been afraid even before the First World War that the United States would one day Americanize Europe.[13] He lived long enough to deplore the beginnings of what he had once only feared. American capitalism would seduce Europe, and Russian Communism would reduce Europe. Neither possibility appealed to Hesse. Both camps were far too militant, not patient enough, uncreative, and essentially indifferent to the individual. Neither could benefit man materially without normalizing him spiritually. America's democracy and capitalism had gone awry, and Russia's Communism was a social experiment whose time had come and which had promised much, only to degenerate into an inane and inhumane dictatorship of the proletariat. Capitalism was no longer viable and Communism was not yet viable.[14] Hesse found comfort in neither. Indeed, a man such as Gandhi had been a greater blessing to the world than all the American presidents of the twentieth century, together with all the leaders of Communism from Marx to Stalin. The sociopolitical history of man

12 See "Briefmosaik 2: 1945–1961," *Politische Betrachtungen* (Frankfurt a.M.: Suhrkamp, 1970), pp. 142–163.

13 "The Americans are a people by whom we will be devoured in the future; it is therefore good to become acquainted with the enemy beforehand. The book in question [Harry Franck, *Als Vagabund um die Erde*] can be useful for this purpose; it reveals the American in his very imposing smartness just as in his spiritual-cultural inferiority." *Der Bücherwurm*, 2 (1912), 250.

14 For Hesse's attitude to the United States and Russia see: *Briefe* (1964), pp. 220, 264, 268, 276–277, 298–299, 322, 344–345, 347–348, 411, 485, 498; "Das Veto der Mütter gegen die Bedrohung des Lebens," *Zeitdienst* (Zürich), April 30, 1955; Brief an einen Kommunisten (November 1931), unpublished letter in the Hesse-Nachlass, Marbach a.N.

was a hopeless horror. His spiritual story, on the other hand, was replete with magnificent intellectual and artistic achievements. This
alone was enough to justify life.

ELDER LITERARY STATESMAN

Although Hesse had become one of the most widely read of contemporary German authors very early in his career, he was not accorded the recognition of any of Germany's many literary awards
until after the Second World War. The official literary world had preferred to honor less controversial figures. The Bauernfeld Prize of 1904
and the Gottfried Keller Prize of 1936 had been Austrian and Swiss
tributes, and the Theodor Fontane Prize of 1919 had been awarded not
to Hesse but to his Emil Sinclair. Long ignored or damned and already approaching his seventies, Hesse suddenly found himself fêted
by government and academia, press and radio, and by literary associations and society. A maverick became an elder literary statesman,
the very dean of German letters. It was all too much and too late. The
Goethe Prize accorded him long overdue official national acclaim and
the Nobel Prize lent him its international recognition. Hesse was
more astounded and amused than flattered or honored. He accepted
each award but attended neither of the formal ceremonies.

And all this was only the beginning of the most improbable of
grand finales. More honors followed: in November 1950 the city of
Brunswick selected Hesse for its Wilhelm Raabe Prize; in January 1955
he was appointed a member of the Peace Class of the Order *Pour le
mérite* (*Friedensklasse des Ordens pour le mérite*); and in October of that
same year he was awarded the coveted Peace Prize of the German
Book Trade (*Friedenspreis des deutschen Buchhandels*). In each of these
cases and as usual, Hesse chose to avoid publicity by remaining in
Montagnola. Every fifth birthday anniversary after the Nobel Prize
and beginning with 1947 also became an occasion for renewed national applause. Hesse's seventieth birthday was warmly acknowledged in newspapers and periodicals throughout Germany, radio
added its felicitations, Maulbronn celebrated its truant student, and
Calw named its native son an honorary citizen. Switzerland added its
congratulations and accolades in press and radio, the University of
Bern conferred an honorary doctorate, and the Association of University Students (*Freistudentenschaft*) elected its latest honorary member.
Hesse's seventy-fifth anniversary occasioned a veritable carnival of

Hermann Hesse, 1955.

eulogy. A celebration in Stuttgart's opera house, dignified by government officials, notables of academia, leaders of the business world, and artists of repute, and addressed by Theodor Heuss, president of West Germany, attracted an overflowing and enthusiastic crowd. The *Schauspielhaus* in Zürich hosted a somewhat less ostentatious but equally laudatory celebration. Similar programs were sponsored in major cities throughout Germany, public lectures were given everywhere, bookshops featured Hesse's works in their display windows, and he was again touted magnanimously by press and radio.

Hesse was removed from but was not left untouched by the fray. Increased correspondence taxed his time and waning strength, and the curious began to invade his privacy. Enterprising German travel agencies actually took financial advantage of his newfound popularity by adding to their Swiss itineraries a bonus excursion to Montagnola. Hesse's wooded hillside and garden were at times almost overrun by meddlesome strangers, all anxious to catch a glimpse of their celebrity, and not at all averse to absconding with some memento or other. Neither trash pails nor compost heaps were left untouched. A placard at the entrance of his property requesting politely that his privacy be respected went unheeded by and large. In fact, the sign itself disappeared regularly.

This belated swell of official and popular acclaim crested upon the occasion of Hesse's eightieth birthday. Man and artist were now virtually venerated throughout both Germany and Switzerland. Universities, schools, literary societies, student organizations, libraries, and museums sponsored numerous literary-musical celebrations, lectures, radio programs, and exhibitions. Press coverage was generous and reverential. Swabia was again the center of these festivities: Martin Buber addressed an overflowing crowd of celebrants in Stuttgart's huge concert hall (*Liederhalle*); the Schiller-Nationalmuseum in Marbach am Neckar housed an extremely popular major Hesse exhibition from May to October; Baden-Baden awarded its newly established Hermann Hesse Prize to Martin Walser; and celebrations took place in Ludwigsburg and Calw. Switzerland paid its respects at similar festive gatherings in Zürich, Bern, Winterthur, St. Gallen, and Olten. And behind the public scene, more than two thousand congratulatory letters poured into Montagnola.

In the following years, public interest in Hesse waned steadily. His eighty-fifth birthday anniversary was still widely acknowledged, but with more deference than enthusiasm. Newspaper and periodical articles were less numerous, briefer, and decidedly more subdued in

Hermann Hesse, upon the occasion of his 85th birthday, July 2, 1962.

tone than five years before. Public celebrations were few and inconspicuous, radio accorded the occasion only passing notice, a couple of minor exhibitions attracted little attention, the second awarding of the Hermann Hesse Prize caused much less stir than the first had, and Hesse himself was burdened by less than half the previous volume of congratulatory letters and telegrams. Montagnola, on the other hand, finally saw fit to fête its German writer. Local musicians serenaded him. and the council appointed him an honorary citizen. The small community's simple but genuine display of esteem touched Hesse more deeply than most official literary adulations ever had. He acknowledged both honors with warm thanks spoken in Italian.

ILLNESS AND DEATH

Until 1945, Hesse had been chronically troubled by his eyes, rheumatic ailments, and intense headaches, and had constantly complained of poor health. He had been treated by many doctors and had taken regular cures but had actually never suffered from any serious illness and had never been hospitalized for more than a few days. His medical history would suggest hypochrondria more than just a frail constitution. From 1945 until 1950, his health continued its characteristic pattern: periods of comparative well-being followed by spells of exhaustion or depression, or both. After 1950, it deteriorated slowly but progressively. A heart condition compelled him in 1952 to discontinue his exhausting cures in Baden, and after 1955 general infirmity prevented him from leaving the area of Montagnola except for short summer vacations in the Engadin and his numerous medical visits to Bellinzona. Hesse was never informed that he was suffering from leukemia and assumed that his debilitation was just a matter of old age. The disease progressed slowly for a few years, then became virulent in December 1961. Frequent injections and blood transfusions kept him comfortable, physically active, and mentally alert. He continued to write, to paint his watercolors, to enjoy music, and to tend to his garden until the end. He wrote the third version of his last poem (*Knarren eines geknickten Astes*) on August 8, 1962, listened to a Mozart sonata that evening, retired in good spirits, and died in his sleep the next morning. He was buried on August 11 in the nearby old cemetery of Sant' Abbondio. The funeral was attended by immediate family, old friends, a few dignitaries from Germany, and a cluster of curious tourists. The ceremony was as simple and the parting words as brief as Hesse himself had wanted them to be. The occasion was acknowledged by newspapers throughout the world.

LAST WORKS AND LATEST PUBLICATIONS

With *Das Glasperlenspiel*, Hesse exhausted his interest in storytelling. During the seventeen years following the Second World War, he increased his previous flow of memorials, congratulatory articles, reminiscences, essayistic ruminations, landscape descriptions, circu-

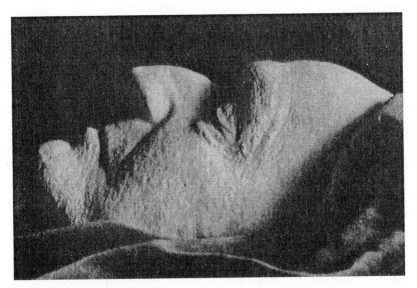

Hermann Hesse's death mask.

The cemetery Sant' Abbondio.

The grave of Hermann Hesse
and Ninon Hesse.

lar letters, prefaces, epilogues, and literary studies, added an ever-decreasing trickle of poetry, but wrote no novels or short stories. Only his very imaginative and personal *Bericht aus Normalien* (1948) might have evolved into fiction of sorts had it not bogged down in sociocultural satire and remained a fragment. Although Hesse was now rehabilitated in Germany, his loyalties remained with Switzerland. Almost all of his new writings were first published by Swiss newspapers and periodicals, and only thereafter reprinted by the German press. Of the some 110 prose items written during this period, almost half were eventually brought together in Hesse's collections of miscellany, and only five have yet to be published.[15]

Hesse wrote but a meager fifty poems from 1945 to 1962.[16] Like his postwar prose, his last poems did not mark a thrust in new directions as much as a continuation of and a return to old themes and past modes of expression. Except for its greater economy of language and its more subdued emotionality, some of this poetry is reminiscent of his earliest three-quatrain musical utterances of vague uneasiness and romantic yearning. Other poems recall the more contained of Hesse's free-verse laments of the twenties. And just as in the thirties, quiet contemplation and detached observation again found their accordant expression in purely descriptive and reflective lyrics. Autumn, winter, night, and nature continued to be favorite backdrops, and aloneness, transitoriness, and death remained characteristic leitmotifs. Lament, however, now became gentle, all quarrel with life ceased, and lingering toleration gave way to grateful affirmation.

Hesse had lost interest in the editing of books in the mid-twenties, and had stopped writing reviews in the late thirties. Neither activity ever again became a serious literary pastime. Although he himself edited no books during the last years of his life, he did continue to write his sporadic prefaces for others. His postwar return to book reviewing was equally half-hearted. Between 1945 and 1960 he only contributed some thirty-two reviews to a scattering of primarily Swiss newspapers.

Though Hesse was an avid correspondent even as a child, only

15 A two-page fragment of autobiography, a one-page foreword, a one-page memorial to Conrad Haussmann, and two remnants of diary (see Manuscripts X:294, 363, 371, 426/w, 426/x).

16 Most of these poems were first widely published in newspapers and periodicals, twenty-nine became part of *Die Späten Gedichte* (Frankfurt a.M.: Insel-Verlag, 1963, 54 pp.), and seventeen have not yet appeared in print.

some 130 of his numerous letters had appeared in various newspapers, periodicals, and books before the publication of his *Briefe* in 1951.[17] This collection of 200 letters was augmented by 94 others in 1959, and then by another 137 in 1964. From 1951 to 1962, about 130 more letters not included in any of the editions of *Briefe* were published in a wide scattering of newspapers, periodicals, and books; and almost 100 other previously unpublished letters have appeared in sundry publications since 1962.[18] *Kindheit und Jugend vor Neuenzehnhundert* (1966) included 159 of Hesse's letters written from 1881 to 1895; and 392 written from 1895 to 1921 were published in *Gesammelte Briefe* (1973).[19] Extensive letter exchanges between Hesse and six of his friends have already appeared in print and three other collections of correspondence and two volumes of letters to Hesse are scheduled for publication.[20] And all this represents but a tiny segment of the 25,000 or more letters and postcards that Hesse wrote, and most of which are still extant.

The last period of Hesse's life was primarily one of literary entrenchment. A lifetime's work was sifted and made readily available in numerous reprints, new editions, and particularly in collections. From 1945 to 1961, the Suhrkamp Verlag added fifteen new or expanded volumes to its collected works, and Fretz & Wasmuth of Zürich increased its series by nineteen volumes. Selected prose written from the beginning of the century to the end of the Second World War appeared in a succession of separate book publications.[21] The

17 (Berlin: S. Fischer, 1951), 431 pp.

18 See Briefe VIII-B.

19 (Frankfurt a.M.: Suhrkamp, 1966), 599 pp.; (Frankfurt a.M.: Suhrkamp, 1973), 627 pp.

20 *Briefe: Hermann Hesse–Romain Rolland* (Zürich: Fretz & Wasmuth, 1945), 118 pp.; *Briefwechsel: Hermann Hesse–Thomas Mann* (Frankfurt a.M.: Suhrkamp, S. Fischer, 1968), 239 pp.; *Briefwechsel: Peter Suhrkamp–Hermann Hesse* (Frankfurt a.M.: Suhrkamp, 1969), 509 pp.; *Zwei Autorenporträts in Briefen 1897 bis 1900: Hermann Hesse–Helene Voigt-Diederichs* (Düsseldorf-Köln: Diederichs, 1971), 184 pp.; *Briefwechsel aus der Nähe: Hermann Hesse–Karl Kerényi* (München-Wien: Langen-Müller, 1972), 204 pp.; *Briefwechsel: Hermann Hesse–R. J. Humm* (Frankfurt a.M.: Suhrkamp, 1977), 345 pp. Scheduled for publication by Suhrkamp: Hesse's correspondence with Heinrich Wiegand and Alfred Kubin, volumes 2 and 3 of *Gesammelte Briefe* (1973); and *Briefe an Hermann Hesse*.

21 Such miscellanies as *Der Pfirsichbaum und andere Erzählungen* (Zürich: Büchergilde Gutenberg, 1945), 51 pp.; *Traumfährte: Neue Erzählungen und Märchen* (Zürich: Fretz & Wasmuth, 1945), 244 pp.; *Dank an Goethe* (Zürich: W. Classen, 1946), 95 pp.; *Der Europäer* (Berlin: Suhrkamp, 1946), 73 pp.; *Krieg und Frieden: Betrachtungen zu Krieg und Politik seit dem Jahr 1914* (Zürich: Fretz & Wasmuth, 1946), 266 pp.; *Frühe Prosa* (Zürich:

Gesammelte Dichtungen (1952) in six volumes were published upon the occasion of Hesse's seventy-fifth birthday, and the *Gesammelte Schriften* (1957), a one-volume expansion of the *Gesammelte Dichtungen,* marked his eightieth anniversary.[22] This brisk publication continued even after Hesse's death and in spite of his sharply declining popularity. New prose miscellanies followed each other in rapid succession,[23] sagging sales of major works were bolstered by a stream of paperback editions,[24] and even Hesse's collected writings were packaged for more popular consumption. *Gesammelte Werke,* published by Suhrkamp in 1970 and comprising twelve soft-cover volumes, were essentially the *Gesammelte Dichtungen* of 1952 supplemented a second time, and Suhrkamp's *Die Romane und die Grossen Erzahlungen* of 1977 is an eight-volume edition of major prose works. Each of these editions of collected works is far from complete, and all are deficient in information, careless in text, and rather unreliable in dates.

Fretz & Wasmuth, 1948), 303 pp.; *Gerbersau* (Tübingen und Stuttgart, 1949), Vol. I, 409 pp.; Vol. II, 430 pp.; *Glück* (Wien: Amandus Verlag, 1952), 145 pp.; *Magie des Buches: Betrachtungen und Gedichte* (Stuttgart: Höhere Fachshule für das graphische Gewerbe, 1956), 94 pp.; and *Tessin* (Zürich: Verlag der Arche, 1957), 86 pp.

22 (Frankfurt a.M.: Suhrkamp, 1952); (Frankfurt a.M.: Suhrkamp, 1957).

23 *Geheimnisse: Letzte Erzählungen* (Frankfurt a.M.: Suhrkamp, 1964), 77 pp.; *Neue Deutsche Bücher: Literaturberichte für Bonniers Litterära Magasin, 1935–1936* (Marbach a.N.: Turmhahn Bücherei, 1965), 160 pp.; *Prosa aus dem Nachlass* (Frankfurt a.M.: Suhrkamp, 1965), 605 pp.; *Aus Kinderzeiten und andere Erzählungen* (Frankfurt a.M.: Suhrkamp, 1968), 96 pp.; *Erzählungen* (Berlin: Aufbau Verlag, 1970), Vol. I, 474 pp.; Vol. II, 462 pp.; *Politische Betrachtungen* (Frankfurt a.M.: Suhrkamp, 1970), 168 pp.; *Beschreibung einer Landschaft* (Pfullingen: Günther Neske, 1971), 72 pp.; *Der Steppenwolf und unbekannte Texte aus dem Umkreis des* Steppenwolf (Frankfurt a.M., Wien, Zürich: Büchergilde Gutenberg, 1972), 343 pp.; *Eigensinn: Autobiographische Schriften* (Frankfurt a.M.: Suhrkamp, 1972), 248 pp.; *Materialien zu Hermann Hesses Der Steppenwolf* (Frankfurt a.M.: Suhrkamp, 1972), 418 pp.; *Materialien zu Hermann Hesses Das Glasperlspiel* (Frankfurt a.M.: Suhrkamp, 1973), Vol. I, 389 pp.; *Die Erzählungen* (Frankfurt a.M.: Suhrkamp, 1973), Vol. I, 512 pp.; Vol. II, 509 pp.; *Die Kunst des Müssiggangs: Kurze Prosa aus dem Nachlass* (Frankfurt a.M.: Suhrkamp, 1973), 377 pp.; *Glück: Späte Prosa, Betrachtungen* (Frankfurt a.M.: Suhrkamp, 1973), 143 pp.; *Meistererzählungen* (Stuttgart: Europäische Bildungsgemeinschaft, 1973),478 pp.; *Siddhartha: Hermann Hesse und der ferne Osten* (Frankfurt a.M.: Suhrkamp, 1973), 378 pp.; *Dank an Goethe: Betrachtungen, Rezensionen, Briefe* (Frankfurt a.M.: Insel Verlag, 1975), 217 pp.; *Die Fremdenstadt im Süden* (Frankfurt a.M.,Wien, Zürich: Büchergilde Gutenberg, 1975), 476 pp.; *Legenden* (Frankfurt a.M.: Suhrkamp, 1975), 183 pp.; *Musik* (Frankfurt a.M. Suhrkamp, 1976, 273 pp.; *Das Nachtpfauenauge: Ausgewählte Erzählungen* (Stuttgart: Reclam, 1976), 175 pp.; *Kleine Freuden: Kurze Prosa aus dem Nachlass* (Frankfurt a.M.: Suhrkamp, 1977), 401 pp.

24 Fischer Bücherei, Deutscher Taschenbuch Verlag, Knaur Taschenbuch Verlag, Reclam, and Suhrkamp Taschenbuch.

FORTUNE'S EBB AND FLOW

Hesse's popularity in the German-speaking world increased steadily during the postwar years until it finally peaked upon the occasion of his eightieth birthday. After 1957 official literary interest declined sharply and literally expired in 1965. Hesse became passé, an innocuous romantic of little relevance to modern man. Literary critics almost ceased to review his latest publications, established scholars and doctoral candidates no longer found him or his works to be a matter of serious concern, and the press relegated him to the level of occasional filler material. Despite this official literary ostracism, prewar generations of Germans continued to read Hesse in respectable, albeit declining numbers. The postwar generation, on the other hand, has remained unresponsive to his world of private concerns, preferring such more sociopolitically committed authors as Bertolt Brecht, Günter Grass, and Peter Weiss. Declining interest at home has, however, been more than offset by increased popularity abroad. Many of Hesse's major works have now been translated into more than thirty languages. They have been best sellers in Japan since the thirties, and promise to remain attractions indefinitely. After the Second World War, Hesse gradually became and still is a favorite among foreign writers in the Spanish- and Portuguese-speaking worlds. He has also come to the fore in Italy since the fifties, and interest has more recently begun to spread in Poland, Rumania, and even to Russia. Translations have also begun to appear in such unexpected places as Burma, Vietnam, Korea, Taiwan, and Hong Kong.

While Hesse's popularity waned progressively in Germany, it waxed strong in the United States. The writer whose *Demian* and *Der Steppenwolf* had first been maligned by the critics and had then gathered dust for three decades in warehouses and bookshops suddenly became a luminary. With the exception of *Siddhartha*, none of the nine novels available in English translation by 1961 fared particularly well until the mid-sixties. Most then quickly became best sellers. The fourteen volumes of fiction, essays, poetry, and letters that appeared from 1970 to 1976 are likely to do as well. In the course of a decade, Hesse became a veritable byword on the American scene: a subject of avid discussion in the classroom, the home, and on the streets; a spiritual guide and self-confirmation for estranged young seekers, disenchanted dissidents, mystics, and drug cultists from the East Village of New York to the Haight-Ashbury district of San Francisco; the most widely read of all foreign authors, a topical concern in many of the country's most prominent magazines, and a popular subject for serious literary scholarship. This unprecedented swell of reverential popularity will pass just as surely as German youth's enthusiastic acclaim after the First and then again after the Second World War. But there is also as much reason to believe that such discoveries by youth will repeat themselves in the future. It is this rhythmic ebb and flow of Hesse's fortunes that is likely to secure his place in both German and world literature.

Selected Bibliography

WORKS BY HESSE

1. COLLECTED WORKS

Gesammelte Werke in Zwölf Bänden: Werkausgabe edition suhrkamp. Frankfurt a.M.: Suhrkamp, 1970. These twelve volumes are a supplemented version of the seven-volume *Gesammelte Schriften* (Suhrkamp, 1957), which are in turn the *Gesammelte Dichtungen* (Suhrkamp, 1952) supplemented by one volume.

Die Romane und die Grossen Erzählungen: Jubiläumsausgabe. Frankfurt a.M.: Suhrkamp, 1977, 8 vols.

2. MAJOR PUBLICATIONS NOT INCLUDED IN THE COLLECTED WORKS

Neue Deutsche Bücher: Literaturberichte für Bonniers Litterära Magasin, 1935–1936. Schiller-Nationalmuseum, Marbach a.N., 1965, 160 pp.

Prosa aus dem Nachlass. Frankfurt a.M.: Suhrkamp, 1965, 605 pp.

Die Kunst des Müssiggangs: Kurze Prosa aus dem Nachlass. Frankfurt a.M.: Suhrkamp, 1973, 377 pp.

Kleine Freuden: Kurze Prosa aus dem Nachlass. Frankfurt a.M.: Suhrkamp, 1977, 401 pp.

Briefe: Hermann Hesse–Romain Rolland. Zürich: Fretz & Wasmuth, 1954, 118 pp.

Kindheit und Jugend vor Neunzehnhundert: Hermann Hesse in Briefen und Lebenszeugnissen 1877–1895. Frankfurt a.M.: Suhrkamp, 1966, 599 pp.

Briefwechsel: Hermann Hesse–Thomas Mann. Frankfurt a.M.: Suhrkamp, S. Fischer, 1968, 239 pp.

Briefwechsel: Peter Suhrkamp–Hermann Hesse. Frankfurt a.M.: Suhrkamp, 1969, 509 pp.

Zwei Autorenporträts in Briefen 1897 bis 1900: Hermann Hesse–Helene Voigt-Diederichs. Düsseldorf-Köln: Diederichs, 1971, 184 pp.

Briefwechsel aus der Nähe: Hermann Hesse–Karl Kerényi. München-Wien: Langen-Müller, 1972, 204 pp.

Gesammelte Briefe: Erster Band 1895–1921. Frankfurt a.M.: Suhrkamp, 1973, 627 pp.

Briefwechsel: Hermann Hesse–R. J. Humm. Frankfurt a.M.: Suhrkamp, 1977, 345 pp.

3. IN ENGLISH TRANSLATION

Demian. Trans. N. H. Priday. New York: Boni & Liveright, 1923, 215 pp. New York: Henry Holt, 1948. Trans. W. J. Strachan. London: Owen; Vision Press, 1958, 184 pp.; London: Panther, 1969. Trans. Michael Roloff and Michael Lebeck. New York: Harper & Row, 1965, 174 pp.; New York: Bantam Books, 1966. (*Demian*, 1919).

In Sight of Chaos. The Brothers Karamasov. Thoughts on Dostoevsky's Idiot. Trans. Stephen Hudson. Zürich: Verl. Seldwyla, 1923, 64 pp. (*Blick ins Chaos*, 1920).

Steppenwolf. Trans. Basil Creighton. London: Secker, 1929, 322 pp. New York: Henry Holt, 1929; Toronto: Oxford University Press, 1947; New York: Frederick Ungar, 1957; New York: Holt, Rinehart and Winston, 1970. Revised by Joseph Mileck and Horst Frenz. New York: Holt, Rinehart and Winston, 1963; New York: Bantam Books, 1969. Revised by Walter Sorrell. London: The Modern Library, 1963; London: Penguin Books, 1964. (*Der Steppenwolf*, 1927).

Death and the Lover. Trans. Geoffrey Dunlop. London: Jarrold, 1932, 287 pp. New York: Dodd, Mead & Co., 1932; New York: Frederick Ungar, 1959; *Goldmund*. London: Owen; Vision Press, 1959; *Narziss and Goldmund*. London: Penguin Books, 1971. *Narcissus and Goldmund*. Trans. Ursule Molinaro. New York: Farrar, Straus & Giroux, 1968; New York: Bantam Books, 1971. (*Narziss und Goldmund*, 1930).

Magister Ludi. Trans. Mervyn Savill. London: Aldus, 1949, 502 pp. New York: Henry Holt, 1949; New York: Frederick Ungar, 1957. *The Glass Bead Game*. Trans. Richard and Clara Winston. New York: Holt, Rinehart and Winston, 1969; New York: Bantam Books, 1970; London: Cape, 1970; London: Penguin Books, 1972. (*Das Glasperlenspiel*, 1943).

Siddhartha. Trans. Hilda Rosner. New York: New Directions, 1951, 153 pp. London: Owen; Vision Press, 1954; New York: Frederick Ungar, 1957; Calcutta: Rupa, 1958; New York: Bantam Books, 1971; London: Pan Books, 1974. (*Siddhartha*, 1922).

Gertrude. Trans. Hilda Rosner. London: Owen; Vision Press, 1955, 208 pp. New York: Farrar, Straus & Giroux, 1969; London: Penguin Books, 1973; New York: Bantam Books, 1974. (*Gertrud*, 1910).

The Journey to the East. Trans. Hilda Rosner. London: Owen; Vision Press, 1956, 93 pp. New York: Noonday Press, 1957; New York: Farrar, Straus & Giroux, 1968; New York: Bantam Books, 1972; St. Albans: Panther Books, 1973; London: Pan Books, 1974. (*Die Morgenlandfahrt*, 1932).

The Prodigy. Trans. W. J. Strachan. London: Owen; Vision Press, 1957, 188 pp. Calcutta: Rupa, 1961; London: Penguin Books, 1973. *Beneath the Wheel*. Trans. Michael Roloff. New York: Farrar, Straus & Giroux, 1968; New York: Bantam Books, 1970. (*Unterm Rad*, 1906).

Peter Camenzind. Trans. W. J. Strachan. London: Owen; Vision Press, 1961, 201 pp. London: Penguin Books, 1973. Trans. Michael Roloff. New York: Farrar, Straus & Giroux, 1969. (*Peter Camenzind*, 1904).

Klingsors Last Summer. Trans. Richard and Clara Winston. New York: Farrar, Straus & Giroux, 1970, 217 pp. London: Cape, 1971; London: Pan Books, 1973; New York: Bantam Books, 1974. (*Klingsors letzter Sommer*, 1920).

Poems by Hermann Hesse. Trans. James Wright. New York: Farrar, Straus & Giroux, 1970, 79 pp. London: Cape, 1971.

Rosshalde. Trans. Ralph Manheim. New York: Farrar, Straus & Giroux, 1970, 213 pp. New York: Bantam Books, 1971; London: Cape, 1971; London: Pan Books, 1972. (*Rosshalde*, 1914).

If the War Goes on . . . Reflections on War and Politics. Trans. Ralph Manheim. New York: Farrar, Straus & Giroux, 1971, 186 pp. Toronto: Doubleday Canada Ltd., 1971; London: Cape, 1972; London: Pan Books, 1974. (*Krieg und Frieden*, Berlin edition of 1949).

Knulp: Three Tales from the Life of Knulp. Trans. Ralph Manheim. New York: Farrar, Straus & Giroux, 1971, 114 pp. Toronto: Doubleday Canada Ltd., 1971; London: Cape, 1972. (*Knulp*, 1915).

Autobiographical Writings. Trans. Denver Lindley, New York: Farrar, Straus & Giroux, 1972, 291 pp. London: Cape, 1973.

Strange News from Another Star and Other Tales. Trans. Denver Lindley. New York: Farrar, Straus & Giroux, 1972, 145 pp. Toronto: Doubleday Canada Ltd., 1972; London: Cape, 1973. (*Märchen*, Zürich edition of 1946).

Wandering: Notes and Sketches by Hermann Hesse. Trans. James Wright. New York: Farrar, Straus & Giroux, 1972, 109 pp. London: Cape, 1972; Toronto: Doubleday Canada Ltd., 1972. (*Wanderung*, 1920).

Stories of Five Decades. Trans. Ralph Manheim and Denver Lindley. New York: Farrar, Straus & Giroux, 1972, 328 pp. Toronto: Doubleday Canada Ltd., 1972; London: Cape, 1974.

My Belief: Essays on Life and Art. Trans. Denver Lindley and Ralph Manheim. New York: Farrar, Straus & Giroux, 1974, 393 pp. Toronto: Doubleday Canada Ltd., 1974.

Reflections. Trans. Ralph Manheim. New York: Farrar, Straus & Giroux, 1974, 197 pp. Toronto: Doubleday Canada Ltd., 1974. (*Lektüre für Minuten*, 1971).

Crisis: Pages from a Diary by Hermann Hesse. A bilingual edition. Trans. Ralph Manheim. New York: Farrar, Straus & Giroux, 1975, 121 pp. Toronto: Doubleday Canada Ltd., 1975. (*Krisis*, 1928).

The Hesse-Mann Letters: The Correspondence of Hermann Hesse and Thomas Mann. Trans. Ralph Manheim. New York: Harper & Row, 1975, 196 pp. (*Briefwechsel*, 1968).

Tales of Student Life. Trans. Ralph Manheim. New York: Farrar, Straus & Giroux, 1976, 233 pp. Toronto: McGraw-Hill Ryerson Ltd., 1976.

WORKS ABOUT HESSE

1. MAJOR BIBLIOGRAPHIES

Bareiss, Otto. *Hermann Hesse: Eine Bibliographie der Werke über Hermann Hesse*. Teil I. Basel: Karl Maier-Bader & Co., 1962, 118 pp. Teil II: Zeitschriften- und Zeitungsaufsätze, 1964, 228 pp.

Koester, Rudolf. *Hermann Hesse*. Stuttgart: J. B. Metzlersche Verlagsbuchhandlung, 1975, 79 pp. Realien zur Literatur. Sammlung Metzler, Band 136. Works by and about Hesse.

Mileck, Joseph. *Hermann Hesse: Biography and Bibliography*. Berkeley and Los Angeles: University of California Press, 1977, 1402 pp. Works by and about Hesse.

Pfeifer, Martin. *Hermann-Hesse-Bibliographie: Primär- und Sekundärschrifttum in Auswahl*. Berlin, Bielefeld, München: Erich Schmidt Verlag, 1973, 104 pp.

Waibler, Helmut. *Hermann Hesse: Eine Bibliographie*. Bern/München: Francke, 1962, 350 pp. Works by and about Hesse.

2. OTHER AIDS IN RESEARCH

Materialien zu Hermann Hesses Der Steppenwolf. Ed. Volker Michels. Frankfurt a.M.: Suhrkamp, 1972, 420 pp.

Materialien zu Hermann Hesses Das Glasperlenspiel. Ed. Volker Michels. Frankfurt a.M.: Suhrkamp, 1973. Vol. I, 389 pp.

Materialien zu Hermann Hesses Siddhartha. Ed. Volker Michels. Frankfurt a.M.: Suhrkamp, 1975, Vol. I, 353 pp.

Materialien are in preparation for *Demian* and *Narziss und Goldmund*.

Mileck, Joseph. *Hermann Hesse and His Critics: The Criticism and Bibliography of Half a Century*. Chapel Hill: The University of North Carolina Press, 1958, 329 pp. (University of North Carolina Studies in the Germanic Languages and Literatures, 21).

Unseld, Siegfried. *Hermann Hesse: Eine Werkgeschichte*. Frankfurt a.M.: Suhrkamp, 1973, 321 pp.

3. MAJOR BOOKS

In German

Ball, Hugo. *Hermann Hesse: Sein Leben und sein Werk*. Berlin: S. Fischer, 1927, 243 pp. Zürich: Fretz & Wasmuth, 1947, 351 pp. (supplemented by Anni Carlsson and Otto Basler).

Böttger, Fritz. *Hermann Hesse: Leben Werk Zeit*. Berlin: Verlag der Nation, 1974, 550 pp.

Hermann Hesses weltweite Wirkung. Ed. Martin Pfeifer. Frankfurt a.M.: Suhrkamp, 1977, 364 pp.

Hsia, Adrian. *Hermann Hesse und China: Darstellung, Materialien und Interpretationen*. Frankfurt a.M.: Suhrkamp, 1974, 339 pp.

Lüthi, Hans Jürg. *Hermann Hesse—Natur und Geist*. Stuttgart, Berlin: Kohlhammer, 1970, 158 pp. (Sprache und Literatur, Ed. 61).

Materialien zu Hermann Hesses Das Glasperlenspiel. Ed. Volker Michels. Frankfurt a.M.: Suhrkamp, 1974. Vol. 2, 378 pp.

Materialien zu Hermann Hesses Siddhartha. Ed. Volker Michels. Frankfurt a.M.: Suhrkamp, 1976. Vol. 2, 390 pp.

Matzig, Richard B. *Hermann Hesse in Montagnola: Studien zu Werk und Innenwelt des Dichters*. Basel: Amerbach, 1947, 119 pp. Stuttgart: Reclam-Verlag, 1949, 147 pp.

Middell, Eike. *Hermann Hesse: Die Bilderwelt seines Lebens*. Leipzig: Reclam, 1972, 376 pp. (Reclams Universal-Bibliothek, 169).

Stolte, Heinz. *Hermann Hesse: Weltschau und Lebensliebe*. Hamburg: Hansa, 1971, 287 pp.

Über Hermann Hesse: Erster Band 1904–1962. Ed. Volker Michels. Frankfurt a.M.: Suhrkamp, 1976, 481 pp. *Zweiter Band* 1963–1977 (1977), 533 pp.
Zeller, Bernhard. *Hermann Hesse in Selbstzeugnissen und Bilddokumenten.* Reinbek bei Hamburg: Rowohlt, 1963, 179 pp. (rowohlts monographien, 85).

In English
Boulby, Mark. *Hermann Hesse: His Mind and Art.* Ithaca: Cornell University Press, 1967, 352 pp.
Casebeer, Edwin F. *Hermann Hesse.* New York: Warner Paperback Library, 1972, 206 pp.
Field, George W. *Hermann Hesse.* New York: Twayne Publishers, Inc., 1970, 198 pp. New York: Hippocrene Books, Inc., 1972.
Hesse: A Collection of Critical Essays. Ed. Theodore Ziolkowski. Englewood Cliffs: Prentice Hall, 1973, 184 pp. (Twentieth Century Views).
Rose, Ernst. *Faith from the Abyss: Hermann Hesse's Way from Romanticism to Modernity.* New York: New York University Press, 1965, 175 pp. London: Owen, 1966.
Sorell, Walter. *Hermann Hesse: A Man Who Sought and Found Himself.* London: O. Wolff, 1974, 144 pp. (Modern German Authors).
Ziolkowski, Theodore. *The Novels of Hermann Hesse: A Study in Theme and Structure.* Princeton: Princeton University Press, 1965, 375 pp.

In Japanese
Ide, Ayao. *A Study of Hermann Hesse up to the End of the First World War.* Tōkyō: Sanshu-Sha, 1972, 638 pp.
The Road to Hermann Hesse. Festschrift for Kenji Takahashi. Tōkyō: Shinchosha, 1973, 368 pp.
Takahashi, Kenji. *Hesse-Studies.* Tōkyō: Shinchosha, 1957, 296 pp.

In French
Beaujon, Edmond. *Le Métier d'Homme et son Image mythique chez Hermann Hesse.* Génève: Editions du Mont-Blanc, 1971, 240 pp.
Schwarz, Armand. *Création littéraire et Psychologie des Profondeurs.* Paris: Ed. du Scorpion, 1960, 189 pp. (Hesse and C. G. Jung).

Index of Hesse's Works

Both German and English titles and first lines of untitled works (in quotation marks) are listed alphabetically according to **first** word.

General Index

Abel, 95
Abélard, Peter, 276
Abraxas, 91, 97, 98, 100
Adler, Alfred, 101
Aestheticism, xii, 15, 19, 27, 28, 29, 30–31, 33, 42, 50, 53, 55, 67, 82, 84, 110, 112, 138, 172, 173, 207, 208, 215, 226, 231, 234, 235, 237, 238, 264, 270, 272, 273, 276, 284, 286, 291, 295, 296, 300, 303, 306, 308
Albertus Magnus, 219, 222, 225, 226, 278
Alter ego, 94, 123, 231
America, xi, 13, 177, 180, 346–347, 353, 355, 365
Amiet, Cuno, 42, 82
Andreä, Volkmar, 42, 44n
Aquinas, Thomas, 276
Aram, Kurt, 64
Ariosto, Ludovico, 53, 222, 226, 229
Arnim, Ludwig Achim von, 223, 228
Arp, Hans, 236
Art: and disease, xi, 106, 107–109; creative process, x, xii, 36–37, 57, 58, 59, 60, 61, 68, 93–99, 110, 121, 140, 154, 158, 207, 208, 236, 254, 255–263, 283, 310; and life, x, xi, xii, xiii, 29–30, 84, 88, 110, 111, 120, 140, 143, 149, 153, 154, 155, 157, 172–174, 199, 202, 204, 206–208, 214, 234, 235, 236, 284, 288; and religion, 55, 226, 231; theories of art, xi, 26, 58, 107–109, 110, 206, 207–208, 210, 236; ultimate failure of art, 236–237, 309–310, 333, 335
Artist-burgher, xii, 58, 82, 173, 203, 207, 208, 284
Artist-intellectual, 30, 133, 174, 185, 199, 215, 234, 269, 286, 290, 310, 316, 318, 336, 353
Asceticism, 29, 56, 160, 161, 162, 164, 169, 170, 172, 173, 183, 184, 203, 205, 292, 321
Aus der Heimat, 70, 126. See also Editorial work

Ausländer, Ninon, 222. See also Hesse, Ninon
Autobiographical matrix of Hesse's art, xi, xii, 21, 29–30, 32–33, 34, 35–36, 47, 58–59, 61, 83–85, 88, 89–92, 93, 110, 111, 112, 113, 114, 115, 116, 117, 118, 119, 120, 121, 122, 140–141, 142–143, 148–153, 158, 159, 174–181, 191, 199–200, 218, 221–223, 226, 229–230, 231, 233, 238, 239, 264–283, 284, 293, 315, 322, 323
Autobiography, xi–xii, 61, 91, 125, 144, 194, 240, 241n, 341n, 362n
Awakening, 77–78, 93, 114, 155, 167–168, 233, 306, 307, 308. See also Self-realization

Bab, Julius, 71n
Bach, Johann Sebastian, 42, 147, 177, 182, 256n, 276, 278, 279, 324
Bad Boll, 10, 12, 35, 133
Baden, 130, 140, 173, 245, 270, 343, 360
Ball, Hugo, 124, 124n
Bandello, Matteo, 53, 53n, 56, 62
Barbarossa. See Friedrich I von Hohenstaufen
Basel, 3, 5, 7, 12, 21, 22, 23, 24, 26, 27, 29, 31, 33, 37, 42, 55, 58, 60, 110, 117, 131, 179, 219, 222, 230
Basler, Otto, 279
Basler Missionsanstalt, 3
Baudelaire, Charles, 222
Bauer, Rektor Otto, 7, 323
Bäumer, Gertrud, 138n
Beethoven, Ludwig van, 177
Bengel, Johann Albrecht, 259, 322
Beringer, Professor Kurt, 181
Bermann-Fischer, Gottfried, 257
Bern, 42, 44, 47, 48, 61, 63, 66, 67, 68, 70, 73, 75, 77, 82, 83, 110, 111, 120, 126, 127, 130, 131, 139, 147, 218, 222, 242, 245, 254, 356, 358

Printed in the United States
44251LVS00002B/32